Discoveries of a Music Critic

BY THE SAME AUTHOR

THE BOY IN THE SUN: *a novel*
MUSICAL PORTRAITS
MUSICAL CHRONICLE
PORT OF NEW YORK
MEN SEEN
BY WAY OF ART
AN HOUR WITH AMERICAN MUSIC

DISCOVERIES

OF A
MUSIC CRITIC

Paul Rosenfeld

HARCOURT, BRACE AND COMPANY

NEW YORK

COPYRIGHT, 1936, BY
HARCOURT, BRACE AND COMPANY, INC.

All rights reserved, including the right to reproduce this book or portions thereof in any form.

first edition

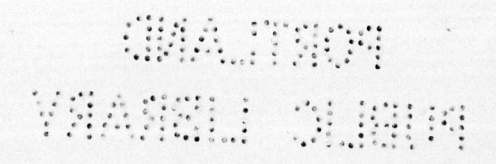

PRINTED IN THE UNITED STATES OF AMERICA
BY QUINN & BODEN COMPANY, INC., RAHWAY, N. J.
Typography by Robert Josephy

TO EDMUND WILSON

Acknowledgments

A NUMBER of the chapters of this book are expansions of pieces published by me in *Disques, Modern Music, The Musical Review* and *The New Republic:* a very few of them, almost integral reprints; and I wish to thank the editors of these periodicals for the courteous permission to republish material contributed to their pages.

I wish also publicly to thank Mr. Israel Citkowitz for his most friendly assistance in the preparation of this volume.

Books and articles which I have found illuminative of my subjects and which have not been cited in the text, have been mentioned by me in the bibliographies appended to it.

All of my chapters excepting those on American music have been arranged in accordance with the chronological order of their subjects: if I have bunched the American chapters somewhat arbitrarily, it is for the sake of a special effect.

P. R.

Contents

The World of the Phonograph	3
The Court Masque	13
Monteverde	20
J. S. Bach: Three Glimpses	28
i. Bach the Colorist	28
ii. Bach the Physician	32
iii. *Die Kunst der Fuge*	36
Mozart the Romantic	44
Cimarosa	61
Beethoven	67
Glinka at Last	82
The Nazis and *Die Meistersinger*	89
Cosima Wagner's Story	100
Khovanstchina	124
The *Elektra* of Richard Strauss	130
D'Indy	143
The Place of Ravel	152
Scriabin Again	158
Bloch and His *Sacred Service*	164
The Evolution of Strawinsky	170
Bartók	197
Gurrelieder	204

CONTENTS

Wozzeck	211
Neoclassicism and Hindemith	217
Milhaud	230
Auric	234
Shostakovich	237
Weill and *Gebrauchsmusik*	250
Ionization	256
Gershwin	264
Cowell	273
Recent American Operas	281
1. *Peter Ibbetson*	282
2. *Jack and the Beanstalk*	286
3. *The Emperor Jones*	293
4. *Four Saints in Three Acts*	297
5. *Merry Mount*	302
6. *Helen Retires*	306
7. *Maria Malibran*	308
Ives	315
Harris	324
Copland	332
Chavez	337
Riegger: A Note	344
Union Pacific	346
Epilogue: The Land Awaits	349
Biographical Appendix	361
Index	391

Discoveries of a Music Critic

The World of the Phonograph

IT was a metaphysical world, very like the physical. It was particolored, of many substances, on high a region of cloud and light, and below a mass that was dense, gritty, and resistant to light. Between the roof that was all ethereality and luminosity and the substratum that was all granite and material weight there lay a belt of mixed and clashing elements, partaking in various degrees of the substance of both the higher and the lower regions—storms, mountains, rainbows, sky-attaining trees. Here human forms passed, wandering, searching, seeing. Momentarily, there were harmonies of the whole, of the heaven, the bedrock, and the blue air and green mountains in between them: a complete interfusion; an afternoon Olympus.

At my friends' on the hill overlooking the lake, the Orthophonic stands between a screen door and a window both of which afford ever-changing views of the lakeward slope, the low-lying water, the surmounting mountain wall with its undulant southward-streaming line, and over it the sky. Almost regularly, while the machine was active, that grave summer of 1931, bits of the landscape suddenly curiously significant attracted my eye through the vine leaves festooning the door and window and the eaves of the old porch outside. The curious visual experience began the evening we arrived in the old farmhouse, weary with the trip and feeling our personal defeat in the defeat of the times. Someone had placed a record of one of the Gregorian chants made by the friars of the Abbey of Solesmes in France on the machine, and while the monkish voices intoned the unfamiliar, subtly rhythmical monody with its amazing, expressive intervals, I promptly perceived through the window, almost as if for a first time, faint opalescent light traveling in streaks across the gray evening clouds. Delicate silvers and golds I had never previously appreciated cheered my feelings, and the gray cloud-masses over the darkening earth seemed actually warm with the pale treasure afloat in them. They were remote, inaccessible, on high, these treasures. Human hands could never reach them. And still their presence made the world endurable once more, habitable and beautiful. Dimly a capacity to find life in objects so inaccessible announced its existence within. Simultaneously the intuition that these streaks of delicate, softly aureate light in some way represented the content of the chant revolving on the Orthophonic, actually were the content, began to define itself.

A few nights afterward another record stimulated a very similar experience. As the Gregorian chant had made me conscious of the lights in the gray sky, so the second act of *Tristan und Isolde* made me conscious of the earth below the house and facing me across the narrow lake. The smoking, high-pressure music, with its wild fanfares, suspensions, brusque surges and eddies of sound, had scarcely begun before I forgot it and the action of the drama in which it participates, in the perception of a dark, deep-lying region of earth, the hearth of somber flames. I would have called it the night, had not some density and viscousness in the sinuous phrases of the reeds and the brass, some feeling of nerves and blood and the source of instinct in the precipitate rhythms, persuaded me that what I was suddenly seeing and feeling was the material night of earth herself, as it were the inwardness of the ground the senses knew. The many little flames starting from it twisted into two tall brands, the one with masculine, the other with a femi-

THE WORLD OF THE PHONOGRAPH

nine quality and color. Dark flames themselves were vocal; and within them, sensible for all its invisibility, rich and fecund, lay the great deep that sent them towering in song. There was a passage where a voice other than the two lovers' was heard: then, the glamorous abyss beneath the level of the flames itself rose into view, like Kundry at the commencement of the second act of *Parsifal*. In the music drama, we know this passage as the fabulously scintillant aubade of the watchful Brangäne, with its division of strings in sixteen parts. But on the Orthophonic, on the hill, it was a revelation of the womb of life itself, lying close and rumorous and bestarred. There was a stirring in its soft mysterious depths, a sighing, a whispering as of myriads of unborn creatures. Luminous atoms like the ringing notes of vibrant harp strings traversed the pregnant gloom. Dusky waves slowly mounted, subsided, making way for others with ever higher crests, till the night itself seemed bearing upward to some birth. Slowly at last the sparkling fathomless abyss faded from view; and the music had the voice of exile from the source of life, and of yearning backward toward its enveloping tides.

Again, a few afternoons later, the music of the machine made me similarly conscious of still another segment of the world outside the door and window, even more deep-lying than the darksome one I had seen through *Tristan* and inferred its content and its meaning. The disk of the entr'acte from *Khovanstchina* by Moussorgsky was revolving at that time. While the funereal bell tones and the moody depressed notes of the horns and the brooding drum beats rang, and the melancholy melody, broad as the very base of the mountains, slowly evolved, I seemed to perceive a region of life far below the surface of the earth itself, but a different region from that revealed by Wagner. This bore the colossal tonnage of the mountains, the globe's entire weight, and with it the entire world's tragedy: continuous funeral marches endless as the mountains' lines; the vital progress from darkness into gray and into darkness again; the overwhelming sum of human pain and human defeat. I took this region to be the grave's, or one as close to it as consciousness can attain. That of *Tristan* was near it, perhaps, and resembled it in earthiness and darkness; but, nevertheless, was charged with electric sparkle and with flames. Possibilities existed in it. Creation was in process there. But in the strata revealed by Moussorgsy there was no possibility, no gestation, no light. It was all burial; prisoned force; a death in life; a grave.

And still other records made me similarly conscious, as of something indicative of their own content and in some way their own meaning, of still other fragments of the constant and still continuously various scene before the vine-hung porch. Bach's D Minor organ Toccata and Fugue, in Stokowski's successful orchestral version, had something to do with the angular lightning and the slanting rain that seemed to wreck the world and cleared the air. And Beethoven's quartets made me feel the variegated surface of the earth, a human motion as of a man who strode among the liquid trees, amid fresh winds, dampness, and mingled sun and rain, searching under the rainbow's prismatic arch. Brahms' piano Quintet had reference to the smoldering clouds of a regal, low, dark sunset. Mozart's E Flat Symphony referred to certain exquisite conditions of light, temperature, and air enchanting the scene, till one doesn't know which is the more heavenly, which more earthy—the shimmering cool green below, the warm and smiling blue above.

So it went that summer. What was most curious was the circumstance that the individual records, and the individual

THE WORLD OF THE PHONOGRAPH

portions of the landscape impressed upon me while the records revolved, proved very rigidly paired. No matter how frequent the performances, the particular disks invariably recalled their particular partners in the visual sphere. Even when I did not happen to glance out of doors, or when a dark night and the electric lamps blinded the doors and windows, the appearances of the regions specially associated with the different disks quite spontaneously rose to mind at the sound of their associates and remained, with a significant obstinacy, full of some meaning and indicative of the meanings of the pieces in process of performance. Nor were they ever confused. Certain of them overlapped and included identical fragments of the great scene from which they were abstracted. Yet each was distinct and contrasted with its neighbor, and gradually the lot of them began forming an independent whole, visible to the mind whether there was music or not. One was reminded of it when the sensual eye raked the landscape, for now each bit of the macrocosm, intenser in beauty and interest than before, was infused as it were with some of the reality of the machine's repertoire. To see the clouds and skies was to feel both them and the thing signified by the Gregorian chants. To see the sloping earth, the lake and its long banks, was to feel both the ground and the meaning of the second act of *Tristan* and of the plangent page from *Khovanstchina*. To find the mountain wall rearing stark and gray through the sweeping rain and the dithering lightning of a summer storm was to get a new sense of its beauty and that of the stormy precipitous expression of Bach. The earth between the trees and under the rainbow made one feel Beethoven's spirit; the splendor of the low dark sunset, that of Brahms; the perfections of the cool miraculous sunny summer afternoons, Mozart's. At last it became visible in its entirety, to the mind's eye itself, small but distinct, like a chart or sphere, a microcosm, somehow indicative and even inclusive of the meanings and the forces of the great world: particolored like it, on high a region of cloud and light, and below a mass that was dense, black, and resistant to light, containing, between the roof that was all ether and the base that was all rock, mixed and clashing elements partaking of the nature both of the higher and of the lower regions, and capable as a whole of perfect harmonies and interfusions. I called it the world of the phonograph.

At the end, its features dimmed. It had become a mere scheme of relative values, representative of the particular meanings of the music and the forces of the world. This final transformation took place after I had absorbed the music sufficiently to attain a thorough grasp of its content and of the world-forces and their contrasts and relationships it expressed.

An idle creation, this little sphere? The dream of a vagrant mind? I believe not: I believe it was the almost inevitable consequence of the nature of the music recorded upon the disks in the possession of my friends the artists on the hill and of the position of the Orthophonic, between the door and the window giving on the noble landscape, in their home. Music conveys a feeling of the world. Music has a consciousness of life, presenting the forces of the cosmocreation and their relationships to the mind, revealing both the will of things and its object. This is no new truth: it is at least as old as E. T. A. Hoffmann and the essay on Beethoven he published in 1807. There he declared that music, in particular Beethoven's and Mozart's, could make a man a *Geisterseher,* a percipient of the realm of the inner truth of life, the metaphysical realm of essences and ideas. This conception was one of the lights of the whole romantic movement. Several of the romantics, Schopenhauer, Wagner, and Nietzsche in particular, repeated and ex-

THE WORLD OF THE PHONOGRAPH

tended it. Wagner, in fact, declared that the complete comprehension of Beethoven's music entailed a complete comprehension of the world. Indeed, the various musical revelations but complement each other, summing up to a universe—at least to the extent to which the mind it instructs is capable of receiving the picture: their differences and contrasts flowing from the differences of the degrees to which certain essences and ideas are affinitive to men of different sorts and conditions in different ages, and to individuals at different times; and from the circumstances that the evolution of the race has from time to time brought into being musical expressions ever more comprehensive and representative of the elements of the universe. All, in fact, express something of what each expresses.—And the circumstance that the Orthophonic permitted music to make its revelation that summer flowed first of all from the broadness and contrastiveness, the selectness and representativity, of the instrument's repertoire, and from the circumstance that its position, close to the open, the "inanimate" nature, provided it with a puissant ally. The presence of the natural embodiments of the essences expressed by the music reinforced the expression with the provision of points of contact and symbols that clarified the revelations. Thus the phenomenon that during the performance of the Gregorian chants the eyes of their audience had involuntarily taken in the aspect of the clouds and that the cloudlands had in some way represented to them the content of the music was the almost inevitable consequence of the fact that these chants contemplate a Power man has always situated in the ethereal regions his feet cannot tread nor his lungs inhale, and express the human force that, mysteriously related to and the child of this ethereal and solar and stellar region, is magnetized by its parent, and seeks to find and approximate him and grow in his likeness.

DISCOVERIES OF A MUSIC CRITIC

The first is the medieval godhead, throning in the invisible outside creation, mildly shining into a world that would be dark but for his radiance, and a treasure as beautiful and gentle and as remote from those of the flesh and earthly desires as the silver and violet and golden streaks in the gray evening clouds. The second, the force that seeks him, is the ascetic will that yearns to free itself from all that binds man to this darksome planet and separates him from the serene one remote from creation and from the spiritual realm that is his final home. Both are forces in this world: both, curiously enough, help man to survive in it.

If, for its part, the second act of *Tristan* evoked the parturient earth, the womb of material creation, it is for the good reason that the music, in particular Brangäne's call, reveals another aspect of the cosmocreator. Here it is the Great Mother and the force born of and directed toward her. She is the divinity of romantic and of pantheistic ages, a Frau Venus, an Erda close to the dark Will of Schopenhauer, the biological urgency of the orthodox Freudians, and situated in the substance man treads and plows; an imperious goddess avid of generation, doing her indomitable will in utter disregard of the individual, proliferating untold millions of lives out of her fathomless night, proliferating unknown worlds and superpeople, grandly, abundantly, with godlike abundance and inventiveness.

If Moussorgsky's plangent page with its power and its inertia and chained force evoked the bedrock and the mountain bases, it was because the music was familiar with another Mother, the dark one, and expressed man's secret yearning for death, its attraction and hold on him, the secret suicidal direction of his energies. And if the play of the elements stood for Bach's D Minor organ Toccata and Fugue, it was for the reason that

THE WORLD OF THE PHONOGRAPH

the music knows a still other male aspect of the cosmocreator, the god of storm, of volcanic upheaval, roaring landslides, deadly lightning and the elemental, mechanical, almost Cartesian play of the force—man's too—that annihilates worlds with its outbursts and builds them up again with it. And if the surface of the earth, midway between the superior and inferior extremes and partaking of them both, was Beethoven's, it was because of all music, that of his quartets, especially the quartets of his second period, is the most human. It is a decidedly subjective expression, but one which has immensely increased man's consciousness of himself. Impelled by a confessional-autoportraitive impulse, Beethoven was among the foremost of those artists who in revealing their personal selves express the general one. All is Man in this music: Man's internal struggles and conflicts, exultations and valleys of despair: Man in his limitless capacity for suffering and for purity and innocence; and all is the specifically human urge that seeks Man—father, wife, brother, child—to be united with him, and on the highest plane of love and ideal and endeavor. Havelock Ellis has wisely called Beethoven the titan as distinguished from the god. Certainly in these middle quartets he is the bound Prometheus of the world, and the force that, rising from the human breast, strives to set him free.

Again, if the regal color of the low sunset, gorgeous and still soft after the sting, turbulence, and heat of the day, was the sign of the content of the Brahms piano Quintet, it was such largely for the reason that this composition, like so much of Brahms, and despite its ruggedness and power, projects a tension that has the quality of the late light, the glow of the already sunken sun. There is great richness and great passion here. There are struggles and triumphs. As in some canto of the Eddas, one hears a clash of shields and battle-axes; and the beauty and the fervor of lovers flare against the dark. But the struggles and the triumphs are bare of possibilities of consequences and overhung with inevitable tragedy. For all its glow and magnificence, life is already encompassed by night and wrapped in its passionless calm. Was it the force of the musical artist that for Brahms seemed to have come to an end with Beethoven? Was it the life of Clara Schumann that possibly had come to an end with Robert and her relationship to the sick man? Or was it somewhat always on the point of departure in this world—love, beauty? The music merely says, "It was," that something which once was grand is passing away, already is remote and legendary, like a dream.

As for the Olympian afternoons, they were symbolic of Mozart's idea for the reason that Mozart in all his melancholy persistently felt a heaven somewhere in this earth, a potentiality of harmony and recurrent actualization of it, and expressed those rare but recurrent conditions, and man's consequent divinity upon the planet, with music that is like mellow light. In works like the E Flat Symphony, "earth's full of heaven." All its forces seem to have come into a concord, and if there is desire here, it is light and joyous; and if there is longing, it is that of the gods themselves among their stars and on their deathless roses, with fulfillment and perfection hovering close. Man treads on airy luminous mountain tops, strong and harmonious of body and of spirit, seeing before him in his kind the grace of the children of Zeus, the arms lifted in beauty, the garments that flow ethereally light, the bodies that pulse with divine energy and have a deathless bloom, and move in music, and are music.

Thus the world, incompletely articulated but still a whole, reached me through the phonograph; and I learned to appreciate the mechanism and its peculiar force. The tone of the instrument, I recognized, is far less accurate and rich than the vibrations of instruments that are directly sounded. The adventitious drone-bass ground from the plates by the needles always is distinct. For all the wonderful recent improvements in the science of recording, the Orthophonic's tones still whiffle and snort and cough, particularly during the performances of orchestral works. While making one conscious of many beauties and intricacies and monumentalities of structure and line, it does not invariably distinguish all the strands and timbres in its foggy roar. But it has a unique power. It can let you perform all kinds of music: it permits you to juxtapose absolute and programmatic, instrumental, vocal, and pianistic, polyphonic and homophonic, symphonic and chamber and operatic works, of every style and period, and juxtapose them in conformity with the mood of the moment. And it lets you juxtapose them in the best of conditions, out close to the natural world that can interpret the experiences they express. That is to say, it can give you the world in the sole way in which it can really pass into your possession.

The Court Masque

ITS name flowed from the circumstance that in England, its species developed simultaneously out of pageants enacted in the palaces of Henry VIII and his peers by minstrels, ladies, and pages, gorgeously and fantastically costumed in the carnival fashion of Italy, and out of torch-lit court dances of the equally gorgeously and fantastically disguised king and lords.

DISCOVERIES OF A MUSIC CRITIC

Like its French equivalent, the *ballet de cour,* it actually was precursive of opéra comique and of grand opera itself. The form of the masque regularly admitted of dramatic dialogue, poetry, scenic effects, pagan allegory, satire, comedy, concerted and solo singing, instrumental music, fancy dress and dancing—combining them in the framework of a fable. In some instances, doubtless influenced by the operatic experiments of the Florentine *camerata,* the dramatic dialogues and speeches, set to monodies, were chanted or sung. While its essential spectacularity and sumptuousness confined the masque largely to princely courts which infused it with their spirit of pomp and glory and affirmed its original ceremonial functions—homage to the sovereign, and the chivalric dance parade—the form possessed a general interest. Masquelike episodes figured frequently in the Elizabethan theater, most notably in plays by Shakespeare and by Beaumont and Fletcher; and masques proper continued to hold the stage until well into the middle of the eighteenth century.

The genius that brought the elastic little form to perfection was Jonson's. Campion's masques and Milton's both follow in the wake of his. From the time of the coronation of James I well into the reign of his successor, rare Ben wrote, first under the patronage of various noblemen, then under that of the elegant queen consort Anne of Denmark, and last under that of her equally elegant son Charles, twenty-nine masques proper and six of the smaller sort of masques called "entertainments," in each of his splendid little shows beautifully equilibrating and merging the heterogeneous elements of the form in definite units. The masque heretofore had been made up of two independent parts, a serious one and a comic or parodistic one called the antimasque. These Jonson fused into artistic wholes in direct collaboration with the scenic architect Inigo Jones,

THE COURT MASQUE

with eminent writers of dance music like Thomas Giles and Jerome Herne and song writers like the English-born Alfonso Ferrabosco. Jonson's own literary-dramatic contributions to these masques were prime: one need not specially be "sealed of the tribe of Ben" to find them little jewels of the English Renaissance. They endowed what had hitherto been a pastime with "dramatic life and deeper meaning." The intense thought spent on their conceptions gives the allegorical and mythological personages freshness and force. Of course the expressions are erudite: Jonson could not help being learned. But in these occasional pieces, he is happily off his buskin and wears his erudition with charm. Masculine as ever, he is fanciful, ingenious, delightfully witty; and the lyrics, which he provides with a greater generosity than in his plays, have his characteristic hard brilliance, and are finely accorded with the movements of dance and vocal music.

One cannot doubt the legitimacy of his immense satisfaction with the production of these magnificent little inventions of his. Inigo Jones was the most genial and imaginative architect of the day, and "movable scenery of the most splendid and costly kind" was notoriously lavished on the performances. The younger Ferrabosco was a gifted melodist, one of the first of the serious English composers to discard successfully the complex form of the madrigalists in favor of a light monodic style. A musician who, though "never rising to great intensity, again and again achieved an emotional utterance by very simple means," he had a dramatic sense, to boot. Besides, the best professional singers and instrumentalists were engaged for the performances. And the orchestras, which were divided in the fashion of the day into several choirs, were large. Accounts of a masque given in 1610 mention the fact of the participation of sixty-nine professional instrumentalists in the production.

DISCOVERIES OF A MUSIC CRITIC

The Stuart court doubtless shone in the dances. Various passages of Jonson's verse express his delight with its grace.

This form, today, is by no means old-world.

During the February of 1933, in the hall of the MacDowell Club of New York, a company of fertile amateurs treated several audiences to a revival of the masque *Oberon* which Jonson wrote for Henry Prince of Wales and which was given for the first time on New Year's Day, 1611. The revival was bare of elaborate mechanical and other external effects; passable in respect to the singing and dancing in the masque proper, the recitation of the dialogue and poetry, and the sets and costumes based on the original designs of Inigo Jones; expert in respect to the instrumental music, under Sandor Harmati, and the dances of the antimasque, undertaken by the local English folkdance society. The spirit of the piece was nonetheless thoroughly transmitted, to the point of the amusing re-creation of the very atmosphere of the court masque. Before the curtain, six of the feminine members of the cast, representing ladies of the court, decorously seated themselves in the front row of the spectators; and during the portions of the play designed for execution by the court itself, the actors impersonating the prince and lords "disguised" as Oberon and his knights descended to them from the stage, deferentially escorted them on to the boards, and ceremoniously led them through the mazes of pavannes, galliards, and correntos there. Again, during the first performance, the central places of honor were occupied by the British Consul General and his lady; and to these regal representatives were cleverly addressed the splendid compliments intended for James I and "his great empress"—compliments which the first of the original recipients is said to have had the grace occasionally to interrupt with gruff admonitions to the performers to "get on with

THE COURT MASQUE

the dancing." And the total effect of the revival was the surprising demonstration of the present pertinency of the old form, a demonstration actually emphasized by the production's bareness of those spectacular effects which had been supposed to constitute the masque's chief means of interest and by the unavoidable bald competence of certain of the participants.

One had been treated to no snobbishly exhumed antique, but to a piece which despite its slightness was the consummation of a living type of entertainment! *Oberon* was a tiny idealized musical comedy! Dance passages preponderated in it to a degree certainly unusual in the current musical shows. For all the predominance of the dancing, the form still had the characteristics of the conventional musical entertainment: the easy pace, the loose structure, the formal musical, dramatic, saltatory numbers that make the genus so pleasant and relaxing. Only, instead of a string of gaudy beads interspersed here and there with brilliants, one had been given a string of evenly matched little pearls. The versification was delicious, the songs and choruses fresh, exquisite, gay, the dances robust and noble. The elements had been idealized, subjected to aesthetic processes, and made in all their lightness to convey a fine and decorous feeling of life. The lightly sensuous forms of the verse, the music, the dancing, the symbols of the relationship of the sexes down to the wannest parade of the male participants, had a fine dignity that was essentially neither the conventional manner and the ritual of a ruling military caste nor a matter of taste, but the tone with which all self-respecting, vigorous life naturally expresses itself.

Thus, prompt revivals of specimens of the court masque by institutions which, like the Metropolitan, dispose of superior musical, theatrical, and choreographic resources, would appear to be very much in order: for various valid reasons. The first of these is the form's intrinsic beauty and suitability to the lyric stage. Perhaps the loveliest of all theatric molds and one of the ancestors of the opera—the step from the pieces of Jonson and Ferrabosco to the ballet opera of Lulli and Rameau is very brief—it remains the perfection of a living type of musical entertainment, and one which, because of its healthy decorum and noble formalities, would prove immensely refreshing and civilizing, if not actually "hygienic." The revivals would also bring to light again, under very favorable circumstances, the treasure of Elizabethan and Jacobean dance and song literature. The individually colored little compositions contained in it are still very stupidly neglected. They have the very "freshness of an earlier world." The expressions of a time which preceded that which regulated and cut and dried musical forms and methods of structure, they have a kind of freedom which subsequently tended to disappear; and they are curiously simultaneously sweet and firm: subtle and vigorous in their rhythms, amusingly abrupt in their modulations, pungent in their frequent melodic minor tonalities. Among the songs, one finds apparently blithe and simple melodies infused by skillful artists with the meanings of gravely poetic lyrics: from out their musical phrases the feeling of Being reaches one as poignantly as out of some of Shakespeare's lines. With tact, a choice of these little expressions of pre-Puritan England could felicitously be interpolated into the choreographic sections of the selected masque. Such interpolations, indeed, were in the spirit of the period. For their part, the revivers of *Oberon* added dances, songs, and choruses by Hilton, Holborne, Giles, and other Jacobean composers to the music they found in the original manuscript of the piece; and with happy effect.

Again, the masque would afford the Opera excellent oppor-

THE COURT MASQUE

tunities for the pompous, ceremonious spectacles whose occasional provision is the duty of the lyric theatre, particularly in democratic countries that see too few such spectacles under ordinary conditions. Nor might the masque prove impractical. The form is a short one, and masques might effectively serve as curtain raisers in place of the perennial, brutal *Cavalleria Rusticana* and the perennial, cheap *Pagliacci*.

As for the second more important of the reasons that make the old English pieces call for prompt revival on the part of theaters disposing of superior musical, theatrical, and choreographic resources: it lies in the fact that, as an idealized musical comedy, the Jonsonian masque might very readily give creative American composers the feeling of a theatrical genus likely to prove responsive to their approaches. American composers have not as yet shown themselves highly gifted for dramatic music. They have indeed written operas. But it is the choral and lyrical parts of *Mona* that contain the work's best music. In *The Emperor Jones* the music is mainly atmospheric. And the dances in the first act of *Peter Ibbetson* stand out from the rest of the score. The intuition that the dramatic vein, so common among Italian, French, and to a smaller degree among German and Russian composers, is actually as foreign to Americans as to English musicians, and that our forte, as far as the theater is concerned, is lyrical and formal dance music, is not to be dismissed. Now the form of the idealized musical comedy, as it is illustrated by the masque, requires no dramatic music, either vocal or pantomimic. The dialogue is spoken; the drama is negligible; and the composer is left free to devote himself to the composition of songs, choruses, and formal dances: the very sorts of expression for which Americans have shown decided talent.

It might, at a first glance, appear that anyone encouraging

an American composer, as we suggest the Opera might very well do by reviving the court masque, to get a poet to provide him with the frame and literary components of a modern masque, and then to sit down and compose the music for it, were encouraging that composer to devote himself to a genus predestined to neglect. There are few theatrical institutions able to provide the instrumentalists, the speakers, the singers, and the dancers the form requires. We nonetheless believe the impression deceptive, the encouragement advisable. The very heterogeneity of the faculties which these pieces would demand of their performers might make them particularly attractive to communities, colleges, and other bodies able to marshal the talents of semi-amateur musical and dance associations and thus provide the American composer with a new order of impresario, performer, and audience. We are convinced that American cities and colleges will, in the near future, come more and more to look for the focal point of their social life in collective aesthetic expressions. And how better could they find that focal point than in applying the musical, dance, scenic, and declamatory talent they could readily develop in their midst to the realization of living expressions provided them in the form of the masque by creative American poets and composers?

Monteverde

THE masterworks resemble the gods of eld. Their beauties shine through heavy disguises, revealing their identities, imparting intuitions of the grandeur of their parents.

MONTEVERDE

During the winter of 1932-3, the operatic pupils of the Juilliard School gave the first New York performance of the five scenes from *L'Incoronazione di Poppea* of Monteverde, restored by D'Indy. It was clumsy. But the excerpts from the two-hundred-and-ninety-odd-years-old vigorous and melancholy music drama, the initial historical one, upon the subject of Nero's repudiation of Octavia and enthronement of the ambitious Poppea in her stead, had indeed not been concluded before I was, happily, prepared by them to agree with André Suarès' judgment of the old Cremonese composer in *Voyage du Condottiere*. From a name directly connected with the gorgeous and pathetic lament of the deserted Ariadne, and more vaguely with the origination of the harmonic style of composition, the first use of the instrumental tremolo, the suspension of the dominant seventh, and the authorship of sundry madrigals and an embryonic sort of *drama per musica,* Monteverde had become for me, too, "the greatest of Italian musicians, Pier Luigi alone excepted, and the least superficial Italian subsequent to Michelangelo."

What had been presented to us was plainly anything save the fragments of an embryonic and archaic music drama. Discreet, austere, the little scenes nonetheless indicated a whole not as much the rudimentary forerunner of the dramatic works of Wagner, Moussorgsky, and Debussy as their leaner, older, nobler brother. The expressions composing these excerpts were extremely realistic. Rarely approaching formally textured song, mostly recitativelike in style, they conformed exactly to the strong drama not only of the words but of the situations—often breath-takingly, especially in Octavia's scene, with its violently disjointed line marvelously embodying the agitation of the hapless woman. Nor was this realism an illustrative one. The expressions were complete musical forms, like those of all the great composers of opera, who, refusing to arrest the action of their drama for the sake of formally textured expressions, achieved broad forms modulated in accordance with every change in the situations and the psychology of the characters. Neither were these forms in any way cheaply veristic, conventionally and rhetorically expressive. They were profoundly so: deeply articulative of the human heart and its passions in all their nobility and misery, their incandescence in moments of intense desire, ambition, moral elevation, despair, cruelty, and endurance of anguish. Each expressed a human essence and communicated the actual forces of the human creature, almost the force of nature in him, and, for all the brevity of the pattern of the five scenes, with a variety, a broad representativity well-nigh Shakespearean. It was the libido itself one felt, in all its fire and power, its capacity for the infliction and endurance of pain: sublime, philosophical, spiritualized in the scene of the dying Seneca: warm, martyred in that of the rejected, humiliated, banished Octavia, whom even a word of love would recall to her spouse's side: roguish and animal in that of the insinuatingly amorous little page and his damsel: low and ambitious in the imperial lovers', and still tending to mount and purify itself under favorable conditions. Rarely had one felt it either so grand, or found it so truthfully given. Noble or light, earthy or sublime, its expressions had a complete truthfulness, a profound relevancy to the dramatic symbols and situations with which the composer had connected them. There was no striving for effect. One felt nothing but a stark faithfulness to inner life. Thus, somber and magnificent in the aristocratic black of the early seventeenth century, the composer seemed to hover there in the depths of the proscenium arch, one of the superior genus of men and of men of art: an uncoverer of god-nature with the means of music; the seeker and the finder of the truth.

Whereupon, books were opened, books on music by Monteverde, books about that music and Monteverde. Notes were tried on the piano. And they fortified the revelation, the gift of the little performance on Claremont Avenue—the revelation of the figure of a great artistic representative of the spirit of the naturalistic Renaissance added to humanity's rank of heroic, inspiriting ones. He seemed ahead, not behind: the projector of exalted standards and values. The picture had merely been intensified. . . . Monteverde's expressions all proved realistic: possibly not all as extremely so as those of *L'Incoronazione,* the work of his high old age—the exquisite *Orfeo,* its junior by thirty-five years, was somewhat more classical and florid—but distinctly in the realistic category. Most of the vocal music in the operas and in madrigals of the type of *Il Combattimento di Tancredi e Clorinda*—a sort of chamber cantata on an episode from Tasso for solo voices, clavichord, and strings—is indeed a mezzo recitativo, oftentimes scarcely more than an intonation of the spoken sounds. It resembles that used by Debussy in *Pelléas*—which is the reason for D'Indy's salutation of his contemporary with the epithet "Notre Monteverde à nous." The climaxes of all the musical forms correspond with the climaxes of the dramatic action: in the madrigals, with the ideal action. Many of them are even distinctly imitative of external nature. In *Il Combattimento*—incidentally, the piece in which Monteverde first exhibited the new musical style he called *stilo concitato,* an heroic, aggressive, turbulent style which effectively added a new mode of expression to the armory of music, furbished hitherto only with modes capable of expressing passive states—one discovers a rhythm, andantino mosso, literally representative of the tramping of war horses. The chivalric madrigal also includes an instrumental tremolo—the first example of its sort, and at its time a seven-day wonder—which represents the tragic combat between the knight and his visored warrior-mistress. Other, purely vocal madrigals display equally imitative details, representing in "Ecco mormorar l'onde" the purling of the wave and the sweetness of the auroral light upon the summits; in "Ohime! Se tanto amate" the sighs of the sly lover; in "Sovra tenere herbette," with the repetition of the musical phrase of the words "Bacciam mi," the suspense of the amorous girl. *Orfeo* brought to light an instance of what might be taken for instrumental scene painting, at the beginning of the third, the Stygian, act, in the lugubrious music for five trombones, which is repeated at the end of the act by strings, after the slumber of Charon lets Orpheus pass; and another in the horrid glissandi for harps that follow the gloomy music for the brass.

Yet this realism again proved itself neither illustrative nor cheaply veristic. As in *L'Incoronazione,* all the pictorial and dramatic characteristics showed themselves part and parcel of musical shapes born of the whole melody and rhythm of the pieces in which they figured. Even the simple imitations and tremolos of *Il Combattimento* were organic. The mezzo recitativos of *Orfeo* were entire musical forms, like those of Debussy; and the sighs of "Ohime" and the warblings in "Ecco mormorar" composed vocal symphonies which, divorced from the words whose sense they conveyed, and instrumented, would constitute perfect, perfectly satisfactory little pieces of music; possibly quite as specifically expressive as their originals. Certainly, they were singularly beautiful and fresh, full of phrases as poignant and haunting as the pieces of Wagner, Debussy, Moussorgsky, and Latin in their delicacy and grace and suavity. These realistic expressions were evidently those in which Monteverde's experience naturally took form and which conveyed it as a whole: a consequence of the naturalistic spirit of his epoch, directed toward the "imitation of Nature," the approximation of her life through exact reproductions of her manifestations and the exact reproduction of her moods. Monteverde's manner of expression, indeed his very form, were given him. His *stilo rappresentativo* and mezzo recitativo indeed were not his own inventions, but those of the Florentine reformers of the late sixteenth century. Extremely realistic madrigals, dramas with ideal protagonists—those of Orazio Vecchio in particular—had also anteceded his own; and his shared their excessive chromaticism, their dissonances, and other harmonic audacities with those of certain of his contemporaries, the Prince of Venosa's particularly. His method of composition, which "made the poetic expression the mistress of the harmony instead of her slave," the "one most productive of beauty and satisfactory to the reason" was—as he had his brother Julio Cesare say in his reply to the violent attacks of Canon Artusi of Bologna—also the invention of another, Cipriano de Rore. And certainly, Monteverde's desire that that expression be a fine one was also shared by him with most of the madrigalists of the later Renaissance, since Willaert the setters of poems by Petrarch, Ariosto, Sannazaro, Guarini, Tasso, and other literary artists. Even his moods were in line with theirs. All the madrigalists had striven to express erotic experience, and he followed in their train. What, however, distinguished his realistic expressions from those of the composers contemporary with himself, even the best of them, those of Gesualdo, securing him during his very lifetime the fame of the greatest composer in Europe, and now assigning him a place beside that of Wagner, Moussorgsky, Debussy, and the other great exploiters of the musico-dramatic forms, was their profundity, their full articulation of the passions and the forces of the human heart. It was some essence in the human breast, and even at times outside it too . . . that of the stamping charger . . . of Nature herself in the heroic furore of her conflicts . . . those of the dawn . . . they almost invariably conveyed; and many of the striking idiosyncrasies of the forms are but manipulations of the medium in conformity with the character of these inner forces and their directions. One of these striking idiosyncrasies is the audacity of the harmony, its abrupt succession of minor chords with major and equally abrupt transitions from the major to the minor again; just as another is the freedom of its rhythms; and another the frequency of the mezzo recitativo; and still another a daring use of appoggiaturas which anticipates—precisely as the poet's triumphant hymn to his lyre in the fourth act of *Orfeo* forestalls the pompous music of Monteverde's younger contemporary Lulli, and of Purcell and Händel, and the delicious scene of the page and the damsel in *L'Incoronazione* the style of the rococo —the stunning appoggiaturas of Debussy and Strawinsky, his juniors by three centuries. Well, any number of the abrupt and daring modulations in the recitatives in *Orfeo,* particularly those of the affecting scene between the poet, the messenger, and the shepherd in the second act, convey the leap, the direction, of these profound forces under the impacts of circumstance. So too do numbers of the modulations in the ritornellos or sinfonias, particularly those of the poignant little ritornello for viols and clavichords—itself merely an exquisite harmonization of a descending and ascending, part major and part minor scale—which is played at the close of the second act, after the poet's inception of his journey down to Hades. It is precisely the luminosity of the unexpected major chords that ultimately gives this flowing postlude the whole movement of love drawn through space, down to Hades, in an enduring search for its high object.

Thus the resemblance of the old Cremonese to Wagner, Moussorgsky, Debussy, and all the rest of the great composers who have expressed essences in the realistic forms of the music drama grew ever plainer. One found that even the madrigals composed patterns of erotic experience not unlike Wagner's and Debussy's; that like one of Monteverde's editors, one could easily arrange the separate numbers serially and find in them, developing expressions of the force of love with something of the depth, the variety, and subtlety of those of his great latter kinsmen. And again one saw Monteverde in some ways more the prince of these relatives of his than their elder brother. Perhaps it was possible to match the feeling of human death, rendered with such desolatingly poignant accents in the last words of Tancred and Clorinda, with that most affecting of all death scenes in music drama, the end of *Boris*. Possibly the passionate intensity and depth of expression of such pages as the lament of the deserted Ariadne, the farewell of the rejected Octavia, the whole of the latter half of the second act of *Orfeo* ending with the departure of the sorrowing poet, the recognition scene and the scene of the death in *Il Combattimento,* are equaled by those of portions of such music dramas as *Die Walküre* and *Tristan, Pelléas,* and *Boris* and among the more formally textured operas by portions of Gluck's *Alceste,* particularly the heroine's delirious air at the close of Act II. But what is matchless is the thoroughly severe, unaffected truth of all Monteverde's various, beautifully consummately musical communication of human forces, the light and roguish as well as the profound and tragic; and the truthfulness of their relevance to the dramatic situations with which they are connected. Wagner, complete in musical form most of the time, is truthful half the time. He had his rhetoric, and his attention to theatric effect. Debussy, musically more complete, is still more completely truthful. Moussorgsky is always truthful, as uniformly as Monteverde, and as nobly indifferent as he to any mere theatrical effectiveness and virtuosic display. But Moussorgsky is sometimes a hampered technician, Monteverde never, for all the circumscription of his means. Thus in his patrician raiment the old Cremonese—least superficial of all the Italians subsequent to Michelangelo—seemed ever to loom potently ahead as in the proscenium arch of the theater, the prince of all those who have held the mirror of realistic music up to god-nature as it burns in man: such by virtue of what I at last had to recognize as one of the freest, broadest, noblest contacts with it ever achieved by a composer—a deep, mature, entirely certain and undeluded feeling of Creative Nature, and a proud glory in her actuality.

J. S. Bach: Three Glimpses

I. *Bach the Colorist.* Belatedly enough, the discovery of the present writer that Bach was a colorist took place, in the April of 1934, in the rooms of the New Music School in Fifty-ninth Street in New York, tense with the presence of a deeply, studiously interested, eagerly receptive crowd of musicianly people. The medium of it was a young man looking like somebody grinding for a Ph.D. in English in the Yale Graduate School: Ralph Leonard Kirkpatrick, who is a Yankee from Massachusetts, and a magnificent artist. Equipped with a fine

J. S. BACH: THREE GLIMPSES

sense of style, a strong grasp of the form of the complex music he plays, and a reverence for that music's quality and meaning as well as a fine technical control of the clavichord and the harpsichord on which he performs it, he executed, on two memorable evenings, several of the preludes and fugues from the *Well-Tempered Clavichord,* a couple of the French Suites, a *Partita,* the *Chromatic Fantasy and Fugue,* and all the *Goldberg Variations,* magnificently upon the instruments for which Bach originally cast them. And while he played, he gave the writer, who isn't very highly educated but who on these occasions probably shared his experience with many of his fellow hearers, a glimpse into the immortal cantor's imagination in a way completer than any previously afforded him.

The experience a bit resembled that of some hypothetical, untraveled art-lover in the New England of a hundred years since who knew Tintoretto's paintings only through prints of them and found himself, magically transported, in the *antecollegio* of the palace of the Doges in Venice. Like the art-lover before the original Tintorettos, the writer was confronted by unexpectedly spacious, tridimensional objects. With voices and volumes surprisingly discrete and round, and strongly antithetical for all their delicacy, the polyphonic structures stood astoundingly up and out, the effect, here too, flowing from the actuality of the color. The melodic lines resembled fine gilt or lizard-green threads and wires; the individual notes were tiny sparks; while the sustained volumes hung in the air, so many golden clouds or colored shadows. Like the greatest Venetian, and his great Cretan pupil, and *his* nineteenth-century rediscoverer Cézanne, Bach had modeled, it was plain, in color itself, with antitheses not only of tones but of qualities of tones: playing timbre against timbre as well as note against note and distinguishing the various voices by means of color as well as pitch, a feat made possible by the fact that both the clavichord and the harpsichord are capable of producing great varieties of quality of tone. And like the amazed traveler in the famous anteroom, the writer had to recognize that he had hitherto incompletely conceived the medium in which his beloved artist had worked; that his conception of it had embraced merely one of its elements, that of design. In his case, the mistake had resulted from the circumstance that he had hitherto heard Bach's clavier works performed only upon the piano, an instrument valuable for its force of tone, but dull of timbre, and therefore able to give what to all effects amounts only to a black-and-white version of the work of a supreme colorist.

Since the writer preserves a nineteenth-century affection for the piano, he was relieved, later while reading up on the subject of J. S. Bach and his congruous instruments, to learn that the modern instrument is by no means so unserviceable in the performance of Bach as, during the excitement of the Kirkpatrickan revelation, he had momentarily thought it might be. Schweitzer, for example, called to his mind the comparative limitations of both the older keyboard instruments: that of the clavichord flowing from the fact that its tones are too weak to be distinguishable at a distance greater than twenty-five feet; and that of the harpsichord, which for the reason of its abruptness of attack and its incapacity to sustain single notes, remains incapable of doing justice to pieces requiring singing tones. Nonetheless, he cannot but feel that never to have heard Bach played on an old instrument by scholarly artists like Mme. Landowska and Mr. Kirkpatrick is to remain ignorant alike of the sensuosity of his imagination and of the exquisiteness of his power of definition; of the delicacy of the values, the oppositions and relationships of tones his representations of his world involved; and hence, not at all to know the wonder-

J. S. BACH: THREE GLIMPSES

fully prismatic nature of those powerful forms of his which the piano must, to the best of its ability, somehow be made to body forth.

Another consequence of the discovery of this particular amateur was the creation of a respect, greater than he had previously had, for the Bach transcriptions of musicians like Schönberg and Adolph Weiss: in especial for Schönberg's transcription of the E Flat Organ Prelude and Fugue for grand orchestra and Weiss' transcription of certain of the preludes and fugues of the *Well-Tempered Clavichord* for woodwind quartet. None of these arrangements seemed any more successful now than they had seemed to him when he had originally heard them. Still, he saw their rationale plainly, saw that they represented attempts to solve the actual problem confronting the musician attempting to give works of as great a colorist as Bach to instruments other than those for which he composed them. This actual problem was generated by the necessity of the complete reconception of the piece in the new medium; the creation, in the terms of the new instruments, of polyphonies of timbres corresponding to the polyphonies of tones. Schönberg, for his part, had decidedly overshot the mark. Dividing his orchestra into various sonorous groups in the style of the concerto grosso, he had played these units too systematically, too formally, off against each other, substituting for Bach's subtle color clashes and color harmonies extreme and even obvious ones that were true to his theory, true even to his own feeling, but not to Bach's fine material sense. And Weiss had erred in attempting to recouch delicate clavichord preludes and fugues in the relatively hard medium of English horn, oboe, clarinet, and bassoon. But the interests of music demanded the attempt. And these musicians at least had understood their problem, and taken steps in the direction where the solution lies.

DISCOVERIES OF A MUSIC CRITIC

II. *Bach the Physician.* Johann Gottlieb Goldberg was a harpsichordist, a pupil of Bach's, and house musician to Count Kayserling, Saxon ambassador to the court of Russia. The Count was an insomniac. During nights when sleeplessness tortured him, he used to have Goldberg, who lodged in a room close to his master's, called, so that the musician might quiet his feverish mind by playing for him. Through Goldberg, Kayserling commissioned Bach to write him a harpsichord work of a quiet and cheerful character to brighten these dolorous nights, and in gratitude for the *Aria with Thirty Variations* which Bach composed for him, sent the composer a golden cup containing two hundred ducats.

According to Busoni, these variations, the *Goldberg Variations* to the musical world, constitute one of Bach's three great achievements in the form, the others being the organ Passacaglia and the Chaconne for violin. He felt the Passacaglia the most perfect, the *Goldberg Variations* the most ingenious and comprehensive of the three, and saw the latter piece rightfully eminent among the master's clavier works. Lacking the rich multivariety of the *Well-Tempered Clavichord* and the poetic freedom of the *Chromatic Fantasy and Fugue,* it nevertheless seemed to him to stand with these gigantic things.

Busoni's view may well be sound: what specially concerns us here is the *Aria with Thirty Variations'* reintroduction to our minds of the fact that among the Greeks and perhaps the other classic peoples, the god of music also was the god of medicine. Again we find or seem to find the priest of the one divinity quite naturally taking upon himself the function of the priest of the other.

The reintroduction of this conception by the *Goldberg Variations* would seem almost ineluctible. Even if one were unacquainted with the circumstances of their origin, one could

J. S. BACH: THREE GLIMPSES

scarcely help feeling something of a healing intention in the composition. Based on a particularly blithe, lyrical theme, with a quality like that of clear cool water, which Bach extracted from his *Grosses Klavierbüchlein,* the thirty enchanting variations—pianistic and imitative clavier and contrapuntal studies, canons, fughettas, fugatos, including a gigue, an andante, a French overture, an adagio, and a quodlibet on two cheerful little folk songs—are, with three exceptions, all in major keys, and with only one exception, blithe in humor, bright, high-spirited, and, what is most important, objective in spirit. By objective one means impersonal: here, Bach as usual is letting essences as it were declare their natures through the medium of music. But there is one exception to this string of objective movements, the adagio: it is a complete contrast to the rest, and very effectively so. The richest and most deeply moving of them all, it is extremely chromatic, and plaintive, and above all subjective, as music by Bach sometimes, and music by Beethoven and the other romanticists very frequently, is. For some reason we feel that in this adagio the composer is calling our attention to himself, perhaps the reason that the acute leaps of the melodic line resemble those of the human voice under the stress of intense experience. Whatever the cause, this adagio is one of those pieces by Bach—the prelude of the E Flat Minor Fugue in the first book of the *Well-Tempered Clavichord* is another—which makes us feel the prince of composers exquisitely expressing in the firm form that is always his, and with all the tenderness and fine warmth of his great magnanimous soul, his personal sense of the sufferings of the world. The sorrowfulness of things themselves is vocal nonetheless; and still, along with its plaint, we hear him gently speaking, too, quietly saying he knows: as if he were addressing someone almost physically present to him.

DISCOVERIES OF A MUSIC CRITIC

Now this adagio is the climax of the entire composition: by reason of its intrinsic beauty, its contrast with all the rest of the variations, its anticipation by the two preceding imitations in minor keys amid the series of ascensively significant canons, and its own climactic position in the work: it actually constitutes the twenty-fifth variation. And, their climax, the adagio is responsible for the dramatic effect of the variations and our conviction that their order is not only a formal but a dramatic one; that something more than a pure musical intention underlies the work. As we have said, the adagio expresses an indubitable compassionate sense of the sorrow that inheres in the world, expresses it almost personally, with a peculiar emphasis enlarged by its climactic position in the scheme, and as to a present listener. The consequent movements, too, derive a dramatic quality from it. The quodlibet seems to bring humanity itself in its warmth and gayety and trustworthiness before the mind, and the recapitulation of the basic aria to make the world simple and peaceful about us again and quiet us like the touch of a healing hand. And, apprized of the circumstances of the entire composition's origin, we cannot help recognizing the work of a great musician who was temporarily taking upon himself the rôle of the physician.

From the very beginning of the piece we feel Bach standing facing the cheering, quieting aspects of the world to which the request of his patron has referred him, with a purpose relative to the poor insomniac. In expressing in all their robustness and sweetness the friendly, humorous, fresh, and trustworthy spirit of things in the form of canons and fugues, he is "ministering to a mind diseased," bringing life to it and at the same time getting it out once more, atop these affirmative pieces' wings, into objective reality. At length he turns toward the sick man, intimately personal with telling effect, revealing to

J. S. BACH: THREE GLIMPSES

him his suffering's origin and participation in the inevitable suffering of the entire world, indicating his own understanding of what the man is enduring, taking the sickness as it were on to himself. (Who should better understand it than himself, whose art displays an imaginative comprehension of every nuance of spiritual experience? And who should better be able to take it on to himself than he who always had the capacity to project and objectify his own states of soul?)

This personal address, too, seems to us a way of projecting the listener's interest, bringing him into imaginative relationship with things again, weaning his interest from his own person. Then once more we see Bach turn away from the ailing subject to the cheerful truths of the world and humanity, as if both to bring them close to the sickbed, and the sick interest into them: redintegrating the sufferer with the race through his participation in the affirmative spirit of the quodlibet. And at last, in the recapitulation of the basic aria, he seems to be making the world about the bed very still and small again and, with this peaceful simplification, addressing the invalid to sleep.

There is no reason for entirely doubting the realism of this picture. The criticism that sees in Bach an exclusively pure musician is an extremely erratic one. Bach's music is not only frequently dramatic and descriptive, but plainly informed by a feeling which is not only connected with thought, but at times appears to be generated by it. Witness the breath of mystery and tragedy that steals over the music of the "Incarnatus" in the *High Mass* in connection with the words "homo factus est." Indeed Bach, as has so frequently been said, not only harmonized the melodies of the Protestant chorales he treated, as his predecessors had done: he harmonized the words as well. And precisely as a poetic, an "extramusical" idea, if one will, would plainly seem to be included in the root of many of his compositions, so too what might be called a poetic and extra-musical effect would plainly seem to be one of the aims of numerous compositions of his, the cantatas in particular. They are *Gebrauchsmusik* not only in the sense of compositions serving ritualistic purposes but in the sense of compositions serving to teach, to communicate, a high ethic. They are sermons, those of an artist who, because he was a great artist, found himself spontaneously in the rôle of the priest, the religious teacher, for the reason that the artist nature embraces that, too. What alone one doubts is that the purpose was at any time his music's raison d'être. One sees that music coming to be without clearly conscious end or purpose, born through the circumstance that his experience spontaneously excited a feeling of form, and then, during the process of realization, spontaneously shaping itself to some particular use. But since that use was frequently a religious one, we cannot shrink from supposing that in one instance its use was a medical one. As we have said, functions of the religious teacher, the guru, and of the physician and the artist were all once exercised by one individual; and in the personalities of the greatest priests, healers, artists, we invariably discover traces of the primitive unity of their only latterly specialized functions. They cannot indeed be teachers, doctors, artists, even now, without simultaneously being something of all three.

III. *"Die Kunst der Fuge."* This, J. S. Bach's last great work —wonderfully enough, one virtually new to the world and a novelty in New York last season—begins with a simple fugue in four voices on a melancholy little theme in D minor, terminating in a D major chord. This fugue is severe, entirely unornamented, built with extremely independent voices that in all their extreme independence nonetheless

J. S. BACH: THREE GLIMPSES

create rich harmonies. And eighteen times subsequently, the germinal theme expands anew in equally severe contrapuntal forms terminant in D major, with equally independently conducted voices and ever more magnificent harmonies: forms, all of them less melancholy than sober and aristocratically dark of color, like Ruysdaels; and singularly gentle, strong, warm, passionate, intense: rich in prodigiously long, minutely inflected, clearly modeled lines and majestic cadences, and sustained and full to perfection. To the original simple fugue there succeed three more simple, four-voiced fugues, sharply differentiated in their rhythms. They in turn are followed, in ever different rhythms, by three four-voiced fugues, the first with inversion, the second with inversion and diminution, the third with inversion, diminution, and augmentation. These again are succeeded by a triple fugue in three voices and two double fugues and a triple fugue in four voices, all of them naturally using additional thematic material, and by four canons, the first in the octave, the second in the twelfth, the third in the tenth, and the fourth in augmentation and contrary motion. Then come two pairs of mirror fugues—the second of each pair being the exact inversion of the first—and following that, an exact repetition of the first pair, with the addition of a fourth free voice; and, in conclusion, an unfinished triple or quadruple fugue abruptly terminating during the third section, which is on the notes B–A–C–H (B–A–C–B). And eighteen times we follow independent incarnations of the germinal theme, each deeply infused with some powerful, distinct essence—they may be portraits, for all we can tell; each time feeling something filling the void like life moving in freest accord with the stern immutable law of things, prepared to understand Goethe's words that in the *Well-Tempered Clavichord* of J. S. Bach he sometimes "seemed to hear the eternal harmony conversing with itself, as it might have done in God's bosom shortly before the cosmocreation." Then, in the nineteenth counterpoint, on a choralelike form of the theme, we recognize the accents of a suddenly, mysteriously renewed and heightened faith. A brightness would seem to have pervaded the warm but somber skies. Ecstatic cries resound in the major, cries that resemble the tones of the "In remissio" of the B Minor Mass, and here seem to convey some new vision of identity, perhaps vision of eternal union with the highest good. Significantly the notes B–A–C–H stand out in the tonal web, the little sonorous universe. And we understand the old cantor, quietly, firmly anticipating with his symbols Walt Whitman's joyous

> My foothold is tenon'd and mortis'd in granite,
> I laugh at what you call dissolution,
> And I know the amplitude of time.

It is, this *Art of the Fugue,* a musical *summa* comparable with the great philosophic and poetic ones, a culmination of the polyphonic thought and style in the expression of a tremendously largely, subtly, intricately, and warmly world-embracing Idea; and the misconception and neglect of it remains extraordinary even in a world chronically unappreciative of things of the highest order. The fact that such a "sum and summit," not only of Bach's own life and art but of the whole polyphonic period which reached its fullest development in him, should until very recent years have remained practically unknown to the musical world, and only in 1935 have attained complete performance in New York, characterizes the state of musical culture of the last two centuries. To be sure, the mighty work originally reached the world under unfortunate circumstances. Already during Bach's final years, the time of its composition, the trend of music was definitely averse

J. S. BACH: THREE GLIMPSES

to polyphony and contrapuntal forms, even to absolute music itself, and directed toward homophonic forms, toward the sonata, the galant, light, sweet, rococo style, and under the influence of the French encyclopedists, toward exclusively programmatic and literary expression.

Always more famous for his virtuosic organ-playing than for his creative power, Bach, who had begun life as a "modern," a champion of the new diatonic system and a censor of "the old music, which no longer sounds good to the ears," ended it with the reputation of a crabbed, pedantic, distinctly old-fashioned composer. In the second place, blindness and death prevented his completion of the work. The last counterpoint, as we have said, remained unfinished, and save for an arrangement of the pair of four-voiced fugues for two pianos there remained no indication of the instruments for which the whole was intended. On his deathbed Bach dictated the chorale prelude "Vor deinem Thron tret 'ich hiermit" to his son-in-law Altnikol; and this piece was conceived by the family to be the conclusion of the great work. Two years after Bach's death, the whole was published in an open score with the title *Die Kunst der Fuge*—a title very doubtfully Bach's own—and with the little chorale prelude by way of conclusion; and while it was offered for sale at the Leipzig Fair and was greeted with a favorable review by Matthieson, the circumstances that no one save a few professors was longer interested in fugues, and that the title and the openness of the score proclaimed it a theoretical work, to be read rather more than heard, helped militate against its reception. In six years less than thirty copies were sold, and at the end of the six, Philip Emmanuel Bach disposed of the plates for the value of the metal in them. A few defective copies of these copies persisted into the nineteenth century, and as the result of the dawning recognition of the almost incomparable greatness of the whole of the old cantor's creation, new editions of *Die Kunst der Fuge* slowly began to appear. And still, for almost another hundred years, during the gradual re-ascent of the polyphonic and contrapuntal forms, the work continued to be ignored and at best misprized. Beethoven's pupil, Karl Czerny, arranged it for piano solo. Still, the musical world insisted on considering it a theoretical piece, and a dry one at that, full of exhibitionistic solutions of exhibitionistically posed problems, and abhorrently austere and even barbarous in sonority. Musicologists here and there gradually began allowing sublimity to this one of the nineteen counterpoints or that; but even those very rare individuals who allowed musical beauty to the work as a whole held it to be fundamentally esoteric and always destined for a place among works like Beethoven's *Hammerklavier* Sonata, *Diabelli Variations, Grand Fugue,* and others that could never to any advantage be offered the general public. Early in the new century, Busoni, who, as has been said, "knew his Bach," * composed his *Fantasia Contrapuntistica* on material derived from it and also sought to complete the unfinished fugue. So, too, did the Englishman Tovey. The experiment of a public performance of the work in its entirety, either in Czerny's version or another, was, however, never attempted, till at length in 1927, precisely a hundred and seventy-five years after its publication, *Die Kunst der Fuge* was tried out for the first time in Leipzig. A German musician named Gräser had arranged it for orchestra, assigning different fugues and canons to different choirs and aggregations of instruments; and to its astonishment, the musical world—prepared for the perception, it is true, by a hundred years of more and more fully poly-

---

* I am obliged for some of this history to an article by M. D. Herter Norton and Roy Harris in *The Musical Quarterly.*

J. S. BACH: THREE GLIMPSES

phonizing and contrapuntalizing music, from that of the last Beethoven and the last Wagner, to that of Strauss, Reger, and Hindemith—discovered its possession of a new superlatively great piece of instrumental music by J. S. Bach! The Gräser version was subsequently played in various cities, including Paris, with each performance filling whole theaters and

> with dancing and with delight
> The maenad and the bassarid.

In 1930, a performance of it under Stokowski was the feature of the Coolidge Festival in Washington; a short while later, the orchestra of the Juilliard School presented it to New York. Yet it cannot be said that these performances of the colossal work were more than adumbrations or *Die Kunst der Fuge* yet fully known. Brilliant as it is, the Gräser orchestral version essentially remains a masquerade, since the music does not really lie in the variously colored instrumental style of the orchestra. Nor can the more recent version for string quartet by M. D. Herter Norton and Roy Harris, which has been recorded by the Roth Quartet, be regarded as the definitive ... simpler and purer than the Gräser version although it is; and not alone because of its omission of the four canons. Czerny was right, whether or not he took his hint from Bach's own arrangement of the pair of four-voiced fugues for two pianos. The music of *Die Kunst der Fuge*—exceptionally among Bach's creations—is percussive. Only a piano version can represent it with the requisite character and majesty of sound. And only the impotence of ten fingers confronted with the problems of fully bringing out the intricately interweaving voices finally places his version, too, among the merely approximative ones. The veritable version we believe to be the magnificent one of Richard Buhlig for two pianos. It supplies the instrument required by the style, the majesty of sound, and the twenty fingers necessary to the polyphony—quite as Bach's own partial arrangement does. Besides, the Buhlig version is complete, including the four canons, and, by way of an effective finale, the chorale prelude *Vor deinem Thron*. As the genial transcriber has written, "It is right that the chorale prelude be included—even though it does not really belong to the work; not only because it is the very last thing Bach wrote and therefore appeared in the first edition of the work prepared by Bach's sons, but because in itself it is an *Art of the Fugue* in miniature." The New York performance of this arrangement by Buhlig and Wesley Kuhnle in celebration of the two hundred and fiftieth anniversary of Bach's birth, at the New School last March 22—incidentally flanked by the complete silence of the New York press—thus constitutes the first true public performance of the mighty piece, and its thorough revelation!

Repetitions of this memorable event are safely to be prophesied. In the meanwhile let us hasten to remark that this performance of *Die Kunst der Fuge* provided a view of the progress of Bach's art clearer than any previously enjoyed by us. That Bach the artist developed in power during his career has, of course, been the common knowledge of the musical public for many years. Even though the monumental C Minor Organ Passacaglia, the product of his twenty-fifth year, evidently set him among the major artists, the freedom of his later work from the idly repetitive passages that blemish some of his early pieces, the toccatas for example, and the superiority of the second book of the *Well-Tempered Clavichord* over the first in point of richness and intricacy, had plainly indicated his steady growth. Yet by the side of the prodigious evolution of Beethoven's genius that brought him from the high level of his first style to the highest of his third, and from essentially

J. S. BACH: THREE GLIMPSES

homophonic to distinctly polyphonic and contrapuntal forms, that of Bach has appeared small. The host of a creative energy massive and steady and strong to a very rare degree, and the inheritor of the major style and forms of music, Bach, it seemed, had merely maintained himself by a slow progress upon the high level which he had reached in early manhood. This conception, the revelation of the uniqueness of his last great work now stamps as wrong. It proves Bach's development in plastic power to have been as great as Beethoven's, merely less saltatory, more gradual, finally enabling him completely to relate and unify in the grasp of a single material, a single theme, and with the conservatively variational form with which he had begun, a prodigiously powerful and inclusive idea. His work now displays its course to us. At first, his plastic power is such a one that can grasp in their fullness simpler ideas, simpler at least in comparison to those Bach ultimately mastered; the *Chromatic Fantasy and Fugue* exhibits this stage of its growth. Then, we see it able to comprehend extremely intricate ones, as in the first book of the *Well-Tempered Clavichord*. But it is not yet fully mature: the grasp is relatively loose; the ideas not yet comprehended within single materials and single forms. Colossal structures like the High Mass and the second book of the *Well-Tempered* reveal a growing power of organization and an enrichment of feeling and workmanship. At length, it impends, the ability to seize and express, within strictest limits, immensely comprehensive ideas in all their intricate coherency. The *Goldberg Variations* and *Das Musikalisches Opfer,* the piece written for performance before Frederick the Great, announce its arrival: still, both these pieces are intimate, in a style not uniformly sublime. But during the creation of the long-misjudged nineteen counterpoints, it was in fullest play; and then, one whose like may have been at the disposal of individuals a few times during the life of the race, but whose distinct superior probably never has existed.

Mozart the Romantic

OF course it's funny to find an article in one of the littler magazines concluded with the phrases, "the charm that music had before Beethoven, the charm of Mozart, *who is as heartless as the birds.*" What price the form of the statement, with its flourish peculiar to haberdashery displays! And what price the idea! Mozart heartless, and "as heartless as the birds"! Regarding the heartlessness of birds, one has necessarily to remain agnostical, even though it is a trifle difficult to conceive which of their manners the superb writer had in mind when he denied the feathery ones' capacity and disposition for love and hate, scorn and pity, fear, courage, and faith. But regarding the incapacity of the composer of the G Minor Symphony, the G Minor Quintet, *The Magic Flute,* the *Requiem,* the D Minor and the E Flat piano Concertos, for feelings of hate, love, pity, scorn, courage, and faith——! Mozart without the spirit of a man?

We can nevertheless not afford to laugh. Exposed as the smartest thing in intellectual neckwear, the strange idea is little other than a garish replica of an article long in circulation in the musical world. Very serious musicians, possibly with an eye on *Così Fan Tutte* and possibly with an eye on nothing at all, have continued to give it currency—the weird conception of a

MOZART THE ROMANTIC

Mozart very much the elegant fribble, the *petit-maître* of music, the composer typical of the rococo period for which, in the famous phrase of the Goncourts, "the ideal of love was desire, and love itself a pleasure." While they have not perhaps found the coldness and the frivolity, the "heartlessness," the source of "charm," these serious representatives of their sphere nonetheless have continued to posit it there: they have found his product full of the incomplete images of life which weak, ambivalent or unsustained feeling invariably generates. You will hear them declare the outlines of these images matchlessly pellucid; their delicacy, marvelously exquisite; and single movements, arias, pages, Greek in their perfection. Nor will the passionateness of such compositions as the D Minor piano Concerto and the F Major piano Sonata, remain unacknowledged; or the sublimity of the choruses in the second act of *The Magic Flute,* or that of the stone-guest scene in *Don Giovanni,* or of the *Jupiter* Symphony. And still, in the eyes of these good musicians, Mozart's figure appears slight besides those of Bach and Beethoven; without the light irradiating the great revealer of life; without the beauty of the perfect lover. "He was not strong or serious; he cracked too many little jokes; he was a child" one everlastingly hears. And wholehearted sustentations of such judgments of Mozart and his work like the one pronounced by Haydn when he told old Leopold, "I swear to you your son is the greatest composer I know either personally or by reputation: he has the most consummate knowledge of the art of composition"; or the one Wagner made when he called Wolfgang *ein Genie aus Licht und Liebe,* are most infrequent.

Take the unusually comprehensive piece on Mozart included in *The Heritage of Music* by the very sympathetic English music critic Mr. W. J. Turner and reprinted in the recent

DISCOVERIES OF A MUSIC CRITIC

musical anthology *From Bach to Strawinsky*. The essay rejects both the time-worn conceptions of the "childlike" Mozart and of the excessive conventionality of his music, true. Yet it argues that Mozart cannot be regarded as the world's greatest composer since he did not "adequately conclude" so "profound and pathetic" a composition as the G Minor Quintet: one in which he rises to heights not surpassed by Beethoven himself. For, it pretends, after the poignant, heartbreaking intensity of the slow movement, some "affirmation of the soul" is inexorably demanded; and that affirmation Mozart did not, could not, make. "He had no faith, he could not lift up his heart and sing from the bottom of the abyss—he could only shrug his shoulders and blow us another bubble." "His personal life was a failure. In the last years he abandoned himself to frivolous gayety. Bach and Beethoven 'walked with God.' Without being dissipated, Mozart danced with the masked daughters of Vienna and wasted his spirit, not in passion or in sudden excesses of lust—which might not have harmed him—but in the aimless dissipation of the man without faith. . . . Light, sparkling and gay, the finale [of the G Minor Quintet in particular, but of all Mozart's symphonic music by inference] masks an abyss of black melancholy."

And what, indeed, is that but another version of the idea of Mozart's spiritlessness or heartlessness, and the consequent imperfection of his images of life, seen through the blue spectacles of British puritanism rather more than the pink ones of its inverted American equivalent; and another proof that our musical culture, which fledged it, is at this late date not entirely incomparable with that of Joseph II who remarked "always so *many* notes, my dear Mozart!" Item: "He could not lift up his heart and sing from the bottom of the abyss—he could only shrug his shoulders—Bach and Beethoven 'walked with

MOZART THE ROMANTIC

God'—Mozart danced with the masked daughters of Vienna and wasted his spirit"—Mozart, whose creative tension must have been matchlessly fierce, who wrote his three chief symphonies within the space of six weeks, and must have labored sixteen hours a day merely to set down the notes! Item: "He blew us another bubble." The "light-hearted, gossamer allegros" are bubbles; and Mozart, with his technique equaling Beethoven's, "declined the gambit, showed fatigue." The *petit-maître*. The rococo.

Certainly, Mozart gave away his money whenever he had any and danced with the daughters of Vienna, the masked as well as the unmasked, and indulged in other dreadful extravagances. Certainly, the finales of many of his works besides the G Minor Quintet, are in comparison with those of Beethoven, uniformly "light." Exceptions may be cited to this rule—that of the *Jupiter* Symphony, for example. They but prove it. Mozart's symphonic form, like that of Haydn and in instances that of Brahms, is differently balanced from Beethoven's. The latter has its center of equilibrium in the finale; that of the former three had its center in the second movement and assigns to the two last movements an essentially postludial function. And it is also true that we find Mozart, like Haydn in this respect, passing from expressions of the sublime, and deeply pathetic and tragic passages, with a relative abruptness to light and jovial ones. The declination of the exalted, almost prophetic passage of steadily mounting fourths and fifths near the close of the great piano Sonata, No. 17, into music of the playful mood of the commencement of the movement is a good instance of this idiosyncrasy so very puzzling and disconcerting to modern sensibilities. Even though Mozart transforms the stuff of the exalted expression logically into that of the smiling, the transition, and those it typifies, are surprising

DISCOVERIES OF A MUSIC CRITIC

to a degree that momentarily tempts one to doubt the composer's seriousness. Nonetheless, that Viennese gayety and light-hearted gossamer finales and rapid changes of mood necessarily betoken the absence of deep, strong, sustained feeling, above all the spontaneously expansive feeling which simultaneously apprehends the universal and fully concretizes it in the terms and within the limits of an esthetic medium, this—under the high authority of Haydn and of Wagner—we categorically deny.

Open a volume of Mozart: your eye will fall upon swelling unbroken forms that sing rapturously. They have the *petite bouche* of good society; their minor forms and their details are exceedingly delicate. But the moods are enchanted, ecstatically joyful: those of skylarks rising from the marshes and pouring forth delight; those of thrushes singing and swinging in summer treetops. The music jubilates like light; wellnigh is light itself, and leaps and overflows scintillantly. Then, next these jubilant allegros, your eye will find music of an exceeding tenderness and sweetness. Its enchanted song is ardent, at instants expressive of purest passion, at others of a profound sympathy, at still others of a seraphically sweet affection. At moments it swells like the heart when it passes utterly beyond itself; and all in all it communicates the bedazzlement of a young breast with some beloved object. But it expresses not only subjective feelings. With them it conveys the feeling of the object itself; one suffused with the softness and loveliness of woman. This music somehow is "she." Like the waking violin in Rilke's poem, the medium says *ganz langsam: Eine Blonde;* and appears to comprehend a feminine way of being and the forces that make a gentle woman what she is. Did not Mozart himself say of certain of these poignant movements "this is She"? He meant "das Bäsle"; but the shadows of

MOZART THE ROMANTIC

breathing Dresden shepherdesses, very radiant, sweet and good, haunt all these images: we see the graceful tension of skirts athwart slim laps in the measures of a minuet: and feel a world containing paradises and perfections. Then, once more the music jubilates; and a great expansive feeling seems to embrace Life that holds the loveliness and the love of woman.

It is the music of a great romantic. Has it not often been remarked that, more fully than Haydn, Beethoven, or any other composer of the great Viennese period, Mozart foreshadowed nineteenth-century romantic music? Guido Adler for example has stressed his romantic love of color, his predilection for irregular rhythms, increased exploitation of minor keys; the complexity of the modulations in his later works; his cantabile style, his propensity to use unusual instruments, basset horns, harmonicas, unusual percussion (including whips); his favoritism of operatic texts permitting expressions of the fantastic, the macabre, the supernatural; his invention of themes which, like the first in the G Minor Symphony, and the second in the clarinet quintet, are veritable heraldic calls of the new movement. But Mozart anticipated more than the technique of the romantics. He anticipated their feeling with matchless tenderness and strength. . . . The intense musical expression of the feeling of woman and her identity with Life itself as it leaps in the breast of the composer, indeed is but another name for romantic music.

Chopin, Schumann, Wagner, Debussy, Schoenberg, and many of their lesser kinsmen, all are eloquent of nothing so much as this experience: the torment and rapture of its moods, the worldful of new lights and colors and shadows connected with it, the profound effects of their lovers on themselves, the inner stir and ache, the intuition of woman's power and what she really is. One can recognize the fact from the very literary symbols with which these composers connected their music. To a preponderant degree, and one not matched by the literary symbols with which the composers of the centuries previous to theirs connected their scores, they are images of intense erotic relationships, including very complex, fascinating and sympathetically felt feminine essences. While music by Händel is to be found in conjunction with erotic literary subjects, these subjects, like all those of the operas of the period, are conventional, expressive of feminine essences that are fixed and unindividualized. But with the operas of Gluck and Mozart, the feminine forces of the dramas begin to grow complex and the ideas to symbolize complex, tremendously significant relationships. The *Don Giovanni* of Mozart and Da Ponte is distinguished by the fine characterization of the three "victims" of the volatile gentleman and by the evident sympathy of the authors for his gay expansiveness. The *Marriage of Figaro* is distinguished by its marvelous depiction of the enchantment of the adolescent Cherubino—conscious for the first time of the climate of sex—and of the wounded love of the noble Countess. Beethoven's *Fidelio* contains at its center a glowing portrait of a powerful and loyal woman. The reader probably needs no special reminder of the power and complexity of the feminine figures in the Wagnerian music dramas, from *The Flying Dutchman* to *Parsifal,* and the degree to which these essences figure in the ideas of the works. Here their rôles are almost the dominant ones, a circumstance which inspired James Huneker to declare that the name of one of these dramas had better have been *Isolde und Tristan*. Women and their self-sacrificial love are the saviors in *The Flying Dutchman, Tannhäuser,* and *Der Ring der Niebelungen*. It is Isolde and Brünhilde who "know all" over the corpses of the tragic heroes.

MOZART THE ROMANTIC

Equally indicative of the connection between the feeling of woman and the archromantic musical expressions are the programs and other literary symbols attached by the romantic symphonic composers to what are, frequently, the most distinctive of their works and pages. The musically finest portions of Liszt's greatest work, his *Faust* Symphony, are the second movement and the final page: the one is named for Marguerite; the other is a hymn on the "Chorus Mysticus" with which the poem concludes:

> Das Ewig-Weibliche
> Zieht uns hinan.

The musically most exquisite portions of Liszt's *Dante* Symphony are connected with the canto of Paolo and Francesca. One of Schumann's very characteristic song cycles is *Frauenliebe und Leben;* another is a setting of poems drawn from the bitter and passionate *Dichterliebe* of Heine. The *Symphonie Fantastique* of Berlioz—memorable for its superb and feverish first movement—is the confession of an obsessive passion, that of the composer for the Englishwoman whom he eventually married: and the best of his symphonies is the *Romeo and Juliet*. And the work of the minor and of the late romanticists furnishes numerous other instances of the association of literary symbols, expressing the interest of the sex and the feminine principle, with characteristically romantic music. The two most brilliant operas of the nineteenth century are the *Faust* of Gounod and the *Carmen* of Bizet: the one is based on the amorous episode of the first part of Goethe's cosmic poem and contains a ballet in which the feeling of woman degenerates into a feeling of women; the other is the freshest and most direct of all expressions of the power of woman and the primitive sexual struggle. The most popular French opera of the early twentieth century, *Louise,* glowingly portrays the sentimental French midinette and identifies her with the atmosphere of Paris itself. The Russian Rimsky-Korsakoff calls the very delicate third movement of his *Scheherazade* "The Tale of the Young Prince and the Young Princess"; and his operatic masterpiece, *Le Coq d'Or,* is a half-burlesque expression of the sex's diabolic side. Debussy's, the sensuous Frenchman's, choice of literary symbols indicates a great and constant feeling for the feminine subject: almost as great and constant a one as that of Johann Strauss, and much subtler too. His first little masterpiece is a choral setting of Rossetti's dreamy, curiously half-spiritual, half-sensual *The Blessed Damozel.* His next, the *Prelude to the Afternoon of a Faun,* evokes the sensuous, pagan, arcadian world of the nymphs and their swains. *Pelléas et Mélisande* of course is the expression of a tragic erotic idea; then, among Debussy's *Images* for orchestra, we find *Sirènes,* identifying the naiads with the spirit of the ocean: and *Danseuses de Delphes* and *Ondine* among his little piano pieces. The work of Richard Strauss too includes numerous literary symbols indicative of conceptions of the nature of woman and the erotic experience in the now comic, now tragic spirit of a disappointed idealism: *Don Juan, Don Quixote, Ein Heldenleben, Sinfonia Domestica, Feuersnot, Salomé, Elektra, Der Rosenkavalier, Josephs Legende,* etc., etc. The most moving passages of Mahler's very romantic *Das Lied von der Erde* are associated with a despairing summons to an absent "friend": the whole work may easily be the expression of an incomplete relation. And so forth down to Schönberg, the composer of the loveliest of contemporary romantic music: the majority of his texts represent experiences of the more subtle, complex feminine forces.

But not alone the literary symbols of the romantic composers are indicative of what they felt. One recognizes the reality from the character of their music's moods, ardent and troubled, tender and passionate; indeed, from the very quality of their sonorities. It is as though the essences these composers apprehended and embraced in their hours of unity with their beloved objects had modified and shaped and tempered the expressive medium in accordance with themselves. Beginning with the Gluck of the fourth act of *Armide,* and in Mozart, in Chopin and in Schumann, Wagner and Debussy, certainly we find, to a degree to which we do not in the music of the preceding masters, pages with a quality of floweriness, of loveliness, of sensuous warmth and tenderness. Passionate, music had always been: but these men provided a music that doubles passionateness with sensuousness. It has a bloom, a shimmer, a *sfumato:* wellnigh a tactility—that of down in Mozart's case, of ivory in Chopin's, of petals in that of Schumann, of silks and satins in those of Wagner and of Debussy. There is ice here, too; and softly curvate outlines, and melted colors, and cloudy and mysterious sonorities. A feeling of the germinal, the latent, the arcane prevails. In instances, as in the Schumann A Minor Concerto, the music moves tidewise, and appears like water on a brilliant night to hold the lunar fire in its mirror. The shadows of very ladies haunt these pieces: most plainly, the graceful Valses and Mazourkas of Chopin. The very forms reflect the sex: the finite severe, closed forms have made way for indefinite, infinite ones: long before Wagner spoke of unending melody, the fugue, the canon, the chorale, the *da capo* aria had steadily been giving way before the open dynamic forms steadily developing their material and including unpredictable evolutions of themes and melodies. Possibly we are overbold in entirely connecting this evolution with the erotic experience. Still, we find a certain corroboration in the intuitions of the man in the street concerning this very wonderful kind of music. The man in the street may not have the vision beyond vision, the poet's. He nonetheless possesses a keen capacity for detecting the presence of the feeling and the interest for and the sympathy with the sex; and he has continually detected reflections of this feeling and interest and sympathy in the specifically romantic music. He has called it "love music"; intuitively associating it with his own erotic experience. And he has consistently inferred the pervasion of the world of the characteristically romantic composer with the figure and the face of woman: he has shown a considerable and not altogether incomprehensible interest in books discussing this artist's intimate relations.

To be sure, the romantic feeling is not only a personal one. It is a feeling of life itself, possibly of life through, about and beyond the being of the woman: certainly a feeling of the feminine quality of nature, the feminine smile gleaming upon its million surfaces; ultimately, an intuition of the feminine aspect of life and its unknown form-giver. Imaginative deep sympathy with the feminine essences undoubtedly attuned these composers to an equally deep sympathy with nature, particularly with those of its forces which are symbolized by feminine characteristics—progenitivity, tenderness, inscrutability, bountifulness, mysteriousness—and with the entire feminine side of the creation. Had it perhaps recurred, the chivalrous spirit that had risen particularly among the romance-speaking peoples of Europe in the twelfth and thirteenth centuries, after the crusades: the epoch in which there appeared the gentleman and the refined and emancipated chatelaine? Then, as in the nineteenth century, a half-musical, half-poetic art, that of the troubadours, had expressed an imaginative sympathy with the being of woman, and the feminine in nature, and represented the high erotic relations; and the whole of society had had an intuition of the feminine side of the cosmocreator: in the twelfth and thirteenth centuries the worship of the Virgin reached its pitch in western Europe, threatening even to overshadow that of the Trinity. To that chivalrous spirit we owe the great poem of love, the *Divine Comedy,* a world-embracing idea with the eternally unfolding, radiant, and compelling Mystic Rose at its apex, and inclusive of a magnetic feminine essence, possibly that of the evolving human race, but with the figure as well as the name of the little Florentine girl adored by the youthful Dante, and "known to every drop of his blood."—Herself an emissary of the Queen of Heaven, this force first sends Virgil to guide the poet through Hell and Purgatory, and at last personally accompanies him through Heaven up to the face of its archetype.—It also gave us the architecture of the French cathedrals—called by Huysmans the architecture of the Virgin Mother and her Child, in contradistinction to the Romanesque, the male, architecture of God the Father; it is so charged with the feeling of her grace—and the sculptured images of which Henry Adams says: "They are full of feeling and saturated with worship; but what is most to our purpose is the feminine side which they proclaim and insist upon. . . . So at the entrance the Virgin declares herself divinely Queen in her own right, divinely born, divinely resurrected from death on the third day . . . seated by divine right on the throne of Heaven, at the right hand of God the Son, with whom she is one." And the nineteenth century, called by Victor Hugo the "century of the woman," in many ways recalls that early "romantic" epoch. At its commencement there stands a poetic world-embracing idea very comparable to Dante's. It is the *Faust* of Goethe, capped like his with an intuition of a feminine principle in creation, *Das Ewig-*

DISCOVERIES OF A MUSIC CRITIC

Weibliche; and containing a dynamic feminine essence, which, figured first as a bourgeois maiden, then as Helen of Troy, and last as the divine penitent, draws her lover upward and on into ever higher realms of experience. During the century, the church declared the conception of the Virgin immaculate, thus directly associating her with the Trinity; and as typical a Calvinist as Henry Adams felt her power enormously, half abstract although his expression of it was.

Goethe meanwhile has asserted that Mozart might perfectly have written the music for the final scene of *Faust* Part II, thus indicating his conviction of the relation between the feeling expressed in Mozart's music—and by extension, in that of the entire company of composers successive to him—and the deeply chivalrous one triumphantly eloquent in the poem's mystical conclusion: thus corroborating our own hunch of the relationship. Certainly, the body of music commonly considered the apex and sum of the entire movement initiated by Mozart, that of Wagner, is powerfully pervaded by this feeling: it was probably Wagner's own constant suffusion with it that persistently fascinated him with certain of the myths produced by this spirit during the Middle Ages, notably those of Tannhäuser, Lohengrin, Tristan, Siegfried, and Parsifal. His music-dramas are magically representative of the feeling about woman and of woman and of a large, detailed and noble erotic experience, including experiences of the utter discovery of the desired flesh matchless because of their burning intensity, and for all the broadness and the ardency with which both Chopin and Debussy reflect their like: the prelude to *Tristan* for example conveying it with piping reeds, blazing 'celli and winding horns so fully and so ecstatically that the sounds grow almost as concretely definitive of gorgeous and utterly known contours and masses as the flesh-tones of Giorgione, Renoir, and

MOZART THE ROMANTIC

Rubens. And Wagner's music magnificently expresses a large, inclusive and deeply sympathetic feeling of nature's moods: the fresh morning of the world in *Das Rheingold;* and her wildness and animality, her gods, giants, and pixies in the entire *Ring*. And like the cathedrals at Rheims and Amiens, it utters an intuition of the feminine aspect of life itself. Life in Wagner is not only divine. It is a crowned queen, a goddess. One feels Her in the very movement of the musical images that body her forth. Wagner is full of slow, gradual passages for strings, and slowly mounting rhythms; and more frequently opulent, fluid, cloudy, surgent, than severe and agile and rapid. Again and again, his music has a kind of attentiveness, a quality as of a state of suspension, like that of Brünhilde with Siegfried's ring; and oftentimes an oceanic heave, a forestal shudder, a slow fiery lambency. We feel Life now as Frau Minne, the blind and glamorous biological force, with its intoxicating potions; now as Erda, the Mother from out whose sleep the motion of existence with its gods and heroes emerges for its brief day. She is glorious in unbridledness, in her thunderstorms, her fires, her moon-bright spring nights; oftentimes possessive and daemonic, a Frau Venus, a Kundry, a *Kali;* and full of longing and suffering, and desire for redemption and release in death. And powerful and splendid in innumerable manifestations, she bears no long-joyous masculinity. Gods and heroes, the men all have wounds, and in their desire there is a yearning for extinction; and they but temporarily ride the whirlwind and attain Valhalla and the Rock. They wake their partners and free them; they make *das wissend wurde ein Weib*. But from their day of struggle and brief triumph, heroes and gods sink into Her with broken swords and spears. Only rarely, as in the prelude of Act III of *Die Meistersinger,* is She an Abundantia, benign and nourishing like the earth, out-

DISCOVERIES OF A MUSIC CRITIC

stretched with her lark-betrilled breast of rippling rye, under the grisaille of the German heavens. And only once in a rare moon does the unvanquishable innocent, the male with the disinterested force of "pure" folly, emerge from Her side. Then, benign at last, Life shines redeemed, with the warm ray of blood and wine and the dazzling whiteness of the dove.

Still, it is only in Mozart of all composers that one finds this chivalrous feeling utterly strong and pure. The head of the romantic movement in music, he was also its loftiest representative. Search the entire field of the lyric opera including the music-dramas of Wagner himself: you will discover in it no finer, rounder, more convincing expression of the feeling about women than Cherubino's arias, of youthful love than Tamino's, of utterly high and selfless devotion than Octavio's; no feelings of sweeter and nobler feminine essences than those conveyed by the arias of the Countess, Donna Anna and Elvira, Pamina. These last are the creations of types that permit us to comprehend and approach the Lady. So too in the realm of instrumental music, you will find no music, not even Schumann's, more deeply charged with expressions that make you recognize the utter love and honor of women, woman, a woman, than Mozart's compositions. In Wagner's, there is passion, longing, desire. But in Mozart's, there is what Wagner personally most of his life seemed to have lacked, tenderness, humility, and love. And if these images also make us feel the feminine aspect of life itself, they make us feel it preponderantly sunny and lovely and warm. There are Ortruds and Kundries in Mozart's world-principle, too: the contemporaries shuddered at the "daemoniacal clangor" of portions of his work, and we still hear it in the cruel and icy arias of the Queen of the Night. And still, when as in portions of his cosmic poem the *Jupiter* Symphony, the music has the veiled trill and thrill of earth and woman, we feel something dancing as does a delighted girl, and smiling as smile meridional blue skies and the flowering earth. Nor are Mozart's images of life revelatory of a world-principle wanting the contrasts and oppositions we sometimes miss in the one known to Wagner. Mozart's music has a severity which Wagner's pretty constantly lacks; and it is full of forms with the distinctly masculine characteristics of rapidity and starkness and alertness that, nimble and martial, appear to spring nakedly and luminously from the earth; and all in all it gives us the feeling of a masculinity as well as a femininity in life itself. There is a positive male tread in this cosmos, sometimes a gay Don Juanesque one, sometimes that of the man who leads on the dance with alacrity; and above all, something majestic and jovial: whether the title *Jupiter* was or was not given by himself to his great C Major Symphony, we feel its utter relevance to Mozart's feeling of life. The music innumerable times utters this empyrean containing both a mysterious feminine sweetness and gentleness and an emphatic virility: affirmatively, as in a full embrace of the antithetical and complementary forces. There is an acute feeling of tension and tragedy, to be sure; of the struggle and the sorrow of life, and conflict, injustice, mortification; and of relationships not only between man and man, but between man and woman, in which tenderness has too small a part, or none at all. Full and generous hearts can misunderstand and wound each other, the music says; and it knows as much of yearning and unrequited love as it does of desire for high, spirit-permeated planes. Still, the tension, the struggle, the grief, are not limitless. The music knows life's tendency to perfection; and its inclusion of the possibilities of perfect relationships and the responses awaiting generous passion, of steady growth in wisdom and understanding, and of consummations in beauty upon spiritualized planes contained in it. Somewhere within it, it knows a region of light and of love where man and woman are seraphic antiphonies and partners in a flowing dance; and sings man's recurrent achievement of that realm: man the inheritor of tension and sorrow, but potentially a god on earth. The music finds the heaven at the heart of life in a final cadence.

And, fully given in these images, the feeling and the world eternally the lover's, laugh down all conceptions of a Mozart less than the composer most capable—more capable than Schubert and Schumann, even—of utter unity with the object of his love.

But, it will be demanded, are the luminous, bubbling finales in which these images almost regularly terminate, merely to be understood as expressions of his sense of the ultimate leap, goodness, and glee of life? The answer is a partly affirmative one: there can be no doubt that to an extent they must be so understood; but only to a certain degree. They also, without question, reflect a reality even deeper than the joyous vital dance; possibly the deepest it is given man to know. They reflect the eternal stillness and peace as it were beyond and above the dancing adventurer in the universe. They reflect it as do the smiles upon the lips of the most spiritual people; as do the clear, straight, remote looks in the eyes of some of the women one sees standing in the doorways of cabins in the Appalachians. Gay and light and distant, they say that all this here, all this we are and feel and that surrounds us, the nameless delight as well as the sorrow and the misery of existence, has no eternal importance. They say it as those creatures of profoundest vision, the Shakespearean fools, say it; and as the final comedies of the poet; and the essential lines of the last of those conclusive plays. Ultimate reality is not here below:

MOZART THE ROMANTIC

The cloud-capp'd towers, the gorgeous palaces,
The solemn temples, the great globe itself,
Yea, all which it inherit, shall dissolve,
And like this insubstantial pageant faded,
Leave not a rack behind. We are such stuff
As dreams are made on; and our little life
Is rounded with a sleep.

Cimarosa

IT was Henri Beyle-Stendhal as well as Cimarosa, the musicality of the first and the reason for his musical preferences, no less than the geniality of the second, that the operatic pupils of the Juilliard School revealed with their revival of the enchanting *Matrimonio Segreto* in the spring of 1933.

Both the musicality of the glorious egoist and the geniality of the foremost Neapolitan composer of opéra bouffe had previously been doubted by at least one ill-informed member of the audience, and Stendhal's lifelong adoration of Cimarosa's masterpiece ascribed to either a pose or lack of musical culture. *The Clandestine Marriage* had been ignored in New York during a hundred years, and the opinion of the musical world, always fairly reliable over long stretches, had assigned to its composer a rank far inferior to Mozart's. And Stendhal had written in his autobiographical *La Vie de Henri Brulard,* "I find perfectly beautiful only the airs of two composers, Cimarosa and Mozart, and you'd have to hang me before you could make me sincerely say which of the two I prefer," and "I often drove all the way from Saint-Cloud to Paris merely to hear an act of *Il Matrimonio*," while his Italian epitaph for his own tombstone ran:

HARRY BEYLE

MILANESE

HE LIVED. HE WROTE. HE LOVED.

THIS SOUL

ADORED

CIMAROSA, MOZART, AND SHAKESPEARE

And, a "literary man who loved music," he had notoriously begun his career of letters with the reckless publication of a volume on Haydn made up of anecdotes cribbed from a German work and of remarks on compositions he himself had evidently never heard. Thus one had a basis for believing that he either knew little of Mozart's music or had no ear for beauty and in coupling Mozart's (to say nothing of Shakespeare's) name with Cimarosa's had outdone the Germans. You remember: "What is acutely irresponsible in the Germans is their use of the conjunction 'and,'" Nietzsche declared. "The Germans say, 'Goethe and Schiller.'"

The performance of *Il Matrimonio* hadn't, however, advanced far before Stendhal seemed to be standing with his "whiskered, big-nosed, low-browed, oval face and small but piercing eyes, and his stocky form in its three-fold cravat, moiré waistcoat and skin-tight trousers," somewhere close to the present writer; all-vindicated, accredited, shining, understood. Despite the hundred-per-cent Americanism of the beat of Albert Stoessel, the conductor, and of the voices of the singers, they were unrolling a delicious little opera down there on the stage. True, the exhibition was one by no means entirely discreditable of the musical world's judgment. Cimarosa plainly showed a man distinctly smaller than Mozart, a musical Power by the side of a musical Domination, and his music lesser in every respect than the great Salzburger's. It was almost unrelievedly light and comic where Mozart blent comedy with pathos and gravity and tragedy too—and even within the comic limits less varied, inclusive, significant, ardent, and deeply sentient than that of his greater contemporary: a thing of shorter lines and less capacious forms; and more largely blemished by operatic formalities and conventional cadences, too; and because of the poverty of its harmonies, entirely vocal in interest. And still, the difference was not of kind—entirely of degree. Stendhal had heard truly. Cimarosa and Mozart are comparable, even if, in the style of another generation, they compare as Guido Reni to Raphael. The little Neapolitan was free like Mozart, a genial composer. From out his music as out of Mozart's a wholeness addresses us: something that has the quality of life itself; and light radiates from it as from a tiny hidden Sol; and it gives us back our own balance and wholeness and capacity for enjoying life. Those little arias and duets, trios and quartets, sung ever so artlessly by the voices of the Juilliard scholars, contain each of them a whole musical breath, in every instance effortless; and in many instances, like Mozart's, exceedingly fresh and pure as well as sprightly and charming. Again, like Mozart's pieces, they combined dignity with grace, simplicity with elegance. They too were of their time—the whole Cimarosan buffo style has a fineness, a freedom from exaggeration, a relevance to the dramatic situations, which that of Cimarosa's successor and successful rival, Rossini, has not.

And the feeling of the music of *Il Matrimonio* was very close to Mozart's. It too was the feeling of human forces in the erotic relationship, and the work itself a sort of idea of love. In Cimarosa as in Mozart, the experience of sex must have been a highly conscious one, well known in the self and in the objective world—perhaps a trifle more cynically, less spiritually than in Mozart, but found and expressed in the characters and situations of a comedy with equal truthfulness and delight. But in Cimarosa the forces and the situations are distinctly Italian. The passions related and brought to expression by his opéra bouffe are thoroughly direct, warm, simple, sunny, infused with a laughter like that of insolated water, and with a levity and an irony that belong to very sentimental dispositions. Later, moved by the discovery of this sly and rident little opera to read in Stendhal's music criticism, we found that he had been perfectly conscious of the eroticism of the score. The style he called *le style comique et passionné*. The score painted for him *l'amour supérieurement et dans toutes ses nuances:* while Mozart, for Stendhal, *le génie de la douce mélancolie,* made one *songer aux malheurs de la plus aimable et la plus tendre des passions.*

But long before that reading, even during the performance up on Claremont Avenue, the meaning the little opera had always possessed for Stendhal, impelling him even late in life to "drive from Saint-Cloud to Paris" merely to hear an act of it, had grown clear.

One seemed to see what the music made the shadowy figure beside one see and feel. And that was a plain, with sun and poplars and canals: Lombardy, the Milanese, Italy; and vaguely but certainly there, its pervasive glamour and aeriality, the ways of the Italians in love, the softness and sunniness of the Italian woman; and all that had taught an impressionable young French "ideologist" that life could be a feast and his own self an endless wonder and a joy to him.

Il Matrimonio Segreto was Italy! It was his "favorable environment." The little opéra bouffe was actually one of Stendhal's pristine revelations of this happy clime. He heard it for the first

CIMAROSA

time as early as 1800, in Ivrea, during his initial fling in Italy in Napoleon's train during the Marengo campaign. He had ridden across the Alps; endured the gunfire from the Fort du Bard; and then, in the theater at Ivrea, as one of his recent biographers says, "he was out of this world and in heaven; completely swept off his feet by Caroline's story—poor Caroline, who had secretly wed her beloved Paolino when her father would have had her marry Count Robinson, the stupid noble. The music wept and murmured, but gracefully and lightly. Ten and twenty times the same theme came back without ever growing tiresome: a winged phrase whose coming was awaited; sweet passionate strains lending tremulous emotion to banal words; violins thrilling to the finger tips. Beyle was in transports, in ecstasies!" In another crucial hour he heard it again. It was in Dresden, in 1812, on the eve of the invasion of Russia. All during the last years, while wearying of the army and the emperor's everlasting wars, he had had hanging on the walls of his rooms a portrait after Raphael, a *Cena* after Leonardo, a luminous Claude Lorrain. They "symbolized the *Midi*." His German lady-love "sang songs by Paisiello" (like Cimarosa, a member of the Neapolitan group of composers of comic operas). Then, long before Waterloo, long before Elba, even, he returned to Milan. "France was a trivial, pallid country, a country without virility, a country of eunuchs.... How could such anaemic people understand Michelangelo?" He was back at last with Angela Pietragrua; for the sake of Angela Pietragrua; and for something that happened in him in her vicinity; something whose event Angelo almost favored, and Italian manners and landscapes, and Italian art and music, and finally all art, no less. It was a kind of inner incandescence, we presume, an intoxication with life, connected with his ability to feel love and enjoy the experience, that

DISCOVERIES OF A MUSIC CRITIC

turned his own inner man into the awake and self-conscious and glittering medium of sensations and ideas. To be, here, was a joy. During the day he visited art galleries; in the evening he visited the theaters, principally the lyric, carefully preparing himself for the operatic performances by reading the librettos, carefully selecting his seat, and, if possible, sitting alone. After the theater there were receptions, society.

Later he wrote that he frequently had sought out, "with an exquisite sensibility, the view of beautiful landscapes. Landscapes were like bows which played upon his soul." And again, "Music, too, when it is perfect, places the heart in exactly the same situation in which it finds itself when it enjoys the presence of that which it loves"; and "The sight of everything that is extremely fair recalls the memory of that which one loves— the love of the beautiful and love mutually giving each other life."

That must have been after some audition of *Il Matrimonio* in Paris, after his soul had leaped on the waves of Cimarosa's music as it leaped among the Italian trees, and as it seemed to rise that afternoon up on Claremont Avenue—like a balloon— floating lightly and luminously; and the magnificent egoist had grasped the relation of the essences and ideas of the music with those of the Milanese people who first had revealed to him the miraculousness of the ebullient inner companion which life had given him to be his constant one.

BEETHOVEN

Beethoven

THE most important chapter of Romain Rolland's superb *Beethoven the Creator* is the one which throws the searchlights of science upon the subject of the composer's deafness and its causes. It affords us a glimpse of the source of the gigantic edifice the music of Beethoven; thus revealing the structure's thorough living unity more clearly and completely to our eyes than ever; letting it now stand before them distinct and tall, shapely and upspringing as a column, aglow with inner informing fire: the fire itself taken solid form.

The surface and bulk of the presented pile do not differ considerably from those revealed to us by the century-long loving labor of musicians and critics. Their outline is that of a tree, an elm's, perhaps; while the substance comprised within the spreading contours is not arboriform but solid, composed of a basal columnar mass surmounted by another broader, higher, cubical one, itself topped by still another mass of even greater width and depth and height. The three homogeneous but distinct forms are the three sections into which the prodigious work falls. They are separated by differences of style, of quality, of content, though possibly not quite to the degree presumed by Wilhelm von Lenz and the other early discoverers of the nature, the individuality, and the greatness of Beethoven's work. In the lowest section, the music of the first period, which comprises most of the compositions anterior to the three piano Sonatas, Op. 31, we discern, for instance, the presence of forms and feelings which Lenz and other early

DISCOVERIES OF A MUSIC CRITIC

Beethoven critics ascribed almost completely to the music of the second. We detect forms containing unpredictable, independent, and original episodes much like the grand ones that appear in the first movements of the *Eroica* and of the F Major Rasoumowsky Quartet. We furthermore find symphonic molds with some of the new proportions, remarkable in the second period: distentions of whole sections in sympathy with new kinds of experience. The lengthy coda of the last movement of the D Major Symphony is an instance. Rudimentary species of the highly individual scherzos of the second period also crop out. And the dionysiac, the almost daemonic, feeling of the latter is represented in some of the very earliest of the pianoforte sonatas. Again, the second section obviously contains forms once ascribed almost completely to the third, which starts with the A Major piano Sonata, Op. 101: the contrapuntal ones, to begin with. The finale of the C Major Rasoumowsky Quartet is a fugue, and fugatos plainly figure in the funeral march and the finale of the *Eroica* and in the allegretto of the Seventh Symphony. An example of the new variational form distinguishing the works of the last period is also exhibited by the *Eroica* in its fourth movement. The *Choral Fantasy* offers an example of still another late Beethoven form, one coherently succeeding purely instrumental sections with a finale inclusive of the song of human voices. The closing scene of *Fidelio* prefigures the experience calling for expression through the human voice and consummately conveyed in the Credo of the *Missa Solemnis* and the last movement of the Ninth Symphony: the experience of freedom, the one ecstatically tasted by the aging Faust when he beheld himself *auf freiem Grund mit freiem Volke stehn*. With instrumental means, the last movements of the C Major Rasoumowsky Quartet and the Seventh Symphony likewise foreshadow it. The first movement of the violin Concerto adumbrates the serenity we meet with so frequently in the works of the last period. And the last movement of the *Waldstein* Sonata reflects an experience dimly anticipatory of the one so powerfully expressed by the last Beethoven. It is the experience of a complete transcendence of the intense conflicts of nature in the state called "cosmic consciousness" by Maurice Boucke, the state of beyond-good-and-evil, beyond-struggle-and-will, of recaptured pristine unity with the whole of things.

By and large, the three sections composing the lofty pile and representing the three styles nonetheless present themselves as discretely and as contrastively to our eyes as they did to those of their first discoverers. We still perceive a distinct basal first one, inclusive of work cast more or less in the predominantly homophonic forms developed by Beethoven's predecessors P. E. Bach, Haydn, and Mozart, containing, as has been said, "melodies and passages that might be mistaken for theirs, and whole sections apparently molded in intention on their patterns." But the traditionalism is superficial. A personality glitters fiercely through these adopted forms, in themselves exceedingly various, individual in movements and in whole pieces; also, an exceedingly meticulous and subtle craftsmanship. A new century is heralded in the deep, invariably spiritually passionate moods of this predominantly rugged, occasionally, in Romain Rolland's words, squarely "Empire" work: a century of individualism and romanticism. The feeling is new, restless, occasionally unhappy, and also subjective in cast, projecting the personality of the composer; and it is broodingly melancholic, traversed by romantic yearning, even in instances verging upon a theatrical Wertherism. Still, for all its drama, it is predominantly robust and masculine; and it is pure—clear, decided, profound. We recognize the activity of a brusque, dolent, but strong personal energy. And atop the section of this early work we still perceive a relatively mightier second, distinguished from the inferior one by the stupendous originality and puissance of the forms contained in it: among them the Third, Fifth, Sixth, Seventh, and Eighth Symphonies; the string Quartets, Op. 59 and 95; the G Minor piano Concerto; the Trio, Op. 97; the violin Sonata, Op. 96; the *Leonore Overture No. 3,* etc. Here everything is starkly individual, revealing the play of energies rising from profound levels of the personality. The sonata form of P. E. Bach, Haydn, and Mozart has been replaced by a much more highly integrated, complex, and inclusive symphonic binary one, apparently constituted not by any conscious development of given ideas and themes, but emergent whole from the unconscious like a volcanic island from the ocean, and animated by the opposition and combination of two complementary principles: one more dramatic, the other more lyrical, which Beethoven in several instances identified as the masculine and feminine principles of things. The Beethovenesque scherzo has developed in its full individuality, and an entirely new type of musical piece, the Beethovenesque allegretto, has appeared. They are indeed so powerful in impulse, direction, and line, some of these forms, that it seems to us as if, like rocks, they had existed since the beginning of things: we find it difficult to imagine a world without, say, the opening movement of the Fifth Symphony. The feelings connected with these forms, and apparently their motives as well as their burdens, are equally profound and new and often triumphant. The personal-subjective consciousness has evidently given way to one so deep-seated that it communicates what seems to be racial experience, the feelings of the tragedy, the struggle, the humor, and the glory of life accumulated by innumerable anterior generations and inhering profoundly in the human psyche: in the face of the funeral march of the *Eroica,* or the adagio of the E Minor Rasoumowsky Quartet, at the very least we find it difficult not to assume the existence of faculties such as that of race-memory. A number of these feelings are actually unprecedented, at least in music. Such is that communicated and named by one of the first and grandest pieces in this section and one of those most thoroughly typical of it, the *Eroica,* and also by the fugue in the C Major Quartet. It is the feeling of the heroic will, the interior power through which the embattled individual stands up to the world. Possibly some of Händel communicated it before Beethoven; certainly not to the degree to which the music of the latter's middle period did. Here we recognize it as the composer himself recognized it, as the power not, as has been said, of the mere revolutionary or the rising middle classes, but that of all men in all times who have known themselves ultimately the match for their circumstances. Equally unprecedented is the feeling of Dionysiac expansivity communicated by the Seventh. And the forces of life whose existence, as it were, out in the universe these forms make us feel, seem really present in the expressive revelatory heroic forms. The will of the embattled individual is actually in the tones of the *Eroica!* Limited, defined, it moves and leaps and languishes and renews itself there, a creative duration ceaselessly productive of beginnings of new things out of the decline of old, falling into patterns of defeat and mortality, and still triumphantly attaining sublime regions "where the eternal are." The Seventh is well called the Dionysiac symphony. Its serried tones contain the spiritual force of the grape. The exuberant god of life is really present.

And the section topping the huge pile before us, that of the works in the third style, bulks as previously largest of all, including as it does the most powerful of Beethoven's forms. The giant molds figure among them, the Herculean *Hammerklavier* Sonata, the *Thirty-Three Variations on a Theme of Diabelli's;* the gigantic exploitations of large sonorous aggregations in the *Missa Solemnis* and the Ninth Symphony; the titanic fugues in the finale of the *Hammerklavier* Sonata, the Credo of the Mass, the finale of the original version of the B Flat Quartet. But these forms do not represent a grandeur merely physical. They and the entire last works, from the piano Sonata, Op. 101, to the Quartet, Op. 135, plainly embody the freest play of ponderous energies. All is mass movement, unity. The contrapuntal forms which put in frequent appearances strictly conserve the material. A new kind of variation form which puts in full appearance deploys it unbrokenly while essentially maintaining it in sustained, unbroken, rhythmical, melodic, and harmonic transformations. The arabesque is completely free, evincing a disencumberment from all theories, formulae, preconceptions and everything inhibiting ideas from expanding in accordance with their proper laws; and the irregularity, in point of size as well as of number, of the minor forms making up the greater, bears out its testimony. The prevalent refinement spreads even to the instrumental color and effects, now frequently luminous and exquisite. The compositions in details and as wholes are marvelously worked together. They grow like trees, one in root, bole, and branch: it is as though the composed material had been presented by some power to Beethoven and then subjected by him to a secondary, even more severely integrating, process of composition. And, intense, concentrated, weighty, refined, delicious, in instances piercingly sweet, the forms flow, slowly or dancingly or lightly or aerially, ever dynamically ahead. The feeling is equally free: miraculously pure and even more sustained and connected and unified than it was during the second section, serene even in its desolation, and in the *Diabelli Variations* and portions of the quartets as impersonal, as detached and objective, as that of Bach. The defiance, the self-assertion, the whole sense of struggle, indeed, disappears precipitately with the first movement of Op. III. The seraphic song of the Sonata's second movement conveys the feeling of a will completely sublimated and transformed in sympathy with that of the One which is "our peace." Feelings of the profoundest tenderness attain expression. But they are those of a superhuman love asking absolutely nothing for itself. It is as if Beethoven had become wholly conscious, wholly receptive, wholly worshipful of a One including and abolishing his own self and those of all other beings; that his feelings had affirmed an All containing patterns of sorrow and tragedy and death, and through the existence of these as well as the brighter patterns, inclusive of a humanity evolving in power and wisdom and destined for the state of fraternity and consciousness of the all-pervading Divinity. Certainly the feeling of an external and inimical Fate, which haunts or seems to haunt the Fifth Symphony, is entirely absent from the Ninth. The storm, the ravening of forces rocking and destroying man which the first movement of this work seems to symbolize, appear to us whirlwinds within man as well as without and facets of the whole of things themselves; and one also senses that the composer's feeling of the forces which his mood betokens was suffused with some sense of their goodness, their friendliness to man's strength. The adagio of the *Hammerklavier,* the fugue of the C Sharp Minor Quartet, certainly communicate both an experience of eternal nights of sorrow, a whole world's, and with it a sense of the consecration of sorrow. And in composition upon composition, by no means only in the solemn Mass, the composer seems to be celebrating with priestly ritual the unfathomable beauty and goodness of life. The music prays; indeed, if any music can be said to be prayer itself, it is the brief *adagio molto espressivo* in the Quartet, Op. 127, and the movement in the Lydian mode in Op. 132, as well as the prelude of the Benedictus and the Dona in the *Missa*. States of transcendent peace, too, communicate themselves throughout the last quartets, the B Flat, C Sharp Minor, Op. 135; and the grand fugue seems definitely to reflect an experience of the conciliation of freedom and necessity, even in its title (*tantôt libre, tantôt recherché*). And as in the works in the second section, those in the third seem to be really informed by the ponderous basic, cosmodynamic energies their attitudes appear to indicate. In instances, particularly in the *Hammerklavier* fugue, they show their animality, stamping like stallions or bulls, recalling to mind winged Assyrian effigies. In others, the *adagio ma non troppo e simplice* of the C Sharp Minor, they spread roselike, irradiating warmest, sweetest love. In the grand fugue, they seem to course out and out unfailingly into futurity and infinite veiled depths and distances. At times they are dolorous, at others triumphant. It is because at times they are passive, and active at others.

And still, we see Beethoven differently from the earlier critics. Within the tremendous monument that, translucent now like alabaster, his whole work presents to our gaze, we can perceive and recognize what former observers could not.

For those former observers, the monument, relatively opaque, was without signs of having, as it were, been projected by inner force. The causes of its erection, at least the causes of its character, were conceived as more external than internal. While such opinions as that Beethoven wrote the *Eroica* for the reason that he admired Bonaparte; that because he was deaf he withdrew into himself; that because his epoch was a revolutionary one he expressed revolutionism in music; that because his time saw the rise to power of the middle classes, he sang their power; finally that, for the reason that he was solitary, sick, and hopeless, he intoned the "Ode to Joy," but grotesquely parody these pioneers': the truth that the early critics all had the tendency to ascribe, if not the entire structure, at least its modifications and extensions to the effect of external circumstances upon the composer, is not to be denied. Even the recent volume of the most penetrating of them all, J. E. D. Sullivan, still suggests that Beethoven's feeling and thus his style underwent its final change for the reason that during the period immediately preceding the composition of the *Hammerklavier* Sonata he had to give up all hope of the wedlock he so earnestly desired. But for us, an informing fire, an inner motive, and the evidences of a motive fundamental even to itself, are plain; and the credit for the clairvoyance is due to Romain Rolland.

A student of the world of some of the greatest of contemporary Indian minds who have practiced yoga, "notably the extraordinary Ramakrishna and his great disciple Vivekananda," he is familiar with "their strangely precise descriptions of all the degrees of this yogist concentration, and of the physiological and moral effects of what they call the rising in the canals of the body of the Kundalini Sakti, the essence of energy"; and he has recognized in Beethoven's deafness a phenomenon extremely similar to those produced in the persons of yogis by "exercises in passionate and boundless concentration." Those consequences, besides deafness, include the brink of apoplexy and mental alienation, and eyes red and bleeding "as though eaten by ants"; and he has been fortified in his diagnosis by the independent diagnosis of the causes of Beethoven's deafness by Dr. Marage of Paris, communicated

DISCOVERIES OF A MUSIC CRITIC

by the physician to the French Academy of Sciences. This medical interpretation set aside as unreasonable not only the confused diagnoses of the causes of his malady made at various times by the composer himself and also those which declared it to be catarrh of the ear, typhus, chills, and acute influenza, the heavy fall on the back suffered by Beethoven in 1801, and finally syphilis; and found the causes to be, first, a pseudo-membranous enteritis and, second, a congestion of the inner ear and auditory centers due to intensive subjection to labor and overwrought states. Now Beethoven all his life was given to "furious concentration"; as Rolland says, it is the characteristic mark of his genius. "In no other musician has this grapple with thought been more violent, more continuous, more invincible than in Beethoven. . . . All his music bears the imprint of an extraordinary passion for unity. . . . The whole of his work is stamped with the seal of a will of iron; we feel the man's glance sunk in the idea with a terrific fixity. And it is not merely a case, as might be thought, of the solitary immured in himself by deafness, who is untroubled by any sound from the outer world. Long before the deafness, the same characteristic is observable. . . . Nothing will distract him from the pursuit of an idea. He describes this frantic chase to Bettina in the language of hallucination: 'I pursue it, I grasp it, I see it fly from me and lose itself in the seething mass. I seize it again with renewed passion; I can no longer separate myself from it: I have to multiply it in a spasm of ecstasy, in all its modulations.'" Now, whether or not it is true that Beethoven's deafness, itself so influential upon his development, was entirely the consequence of fierce and continuous cerebral concentration, and whether or not those are right who claim that it was actually *willed* by his genius, or whatever we choose to call that which ultimately had him in its power, to act as blinders interposed between his creative energy and dissipating influences, this diagnosis has succeeded in directing X-rays upon an animating, shaping, creative motive entirely immanent in Beethoven himself; freely definitive of his life, his human relations, their beauty and tragedy; and generative of his work and its increasing weightiness. It has thrown light upon an internal process anterior, as it were, to the external circumstances once considered influential upon the form and character of Beethoven's work; and responsible for the greater weight and significance of the later as compared to the earlier work; a process certainly in cahoots with these apparently external circumstances and very possibly generative of them. We now perceive, there in the interior regions, the flame of a prodigiously large, prodigiously free, concentrated, organized libido, subjecting its mortal tenement to its own interests, working itself out half imperiously, half with the assistance of Beethoven's own will, materializing itself prodigiously through the sonorous medium; and feel within that leaping, emanating, materializing fire, the invisible but all-suffusing, freely impulsive Agent of this concentration and subjection and ideal expression.

The free, concentrated, organized libido we see is the vitalistic energy of the individual who disengages himself from personal objects. In the words of the ancient Brahmins (profoundly conscious of all this process of disengagement and its consequences) which are quoted in Jung's wonderful *Psychological Types,* it is the energy of one gradually but in the end completely "indifferent to all objects," who "overcomes greed and anger, attachment to the world and lust of the senses," "surrenders wish and hope," "grows indifferent to blame as to praise, thus to himself, to life and death, fortune and misfortune, love and hate," whose "soul is pacified, whose bodily element has disappeared, who has lost the feeling of self" and grown "free of supererogation and illusion, of the tendency to ascribe the Fault to things, and utterly true to the Light, the Atman." As the concentrated libido swells within, it produces an increased enchantment in the subject, an increased elevation of the feeling of life, its essences and ideas. And about these essences and ideas it materializes itself with ever greater freedom and orderliness in ever more powerful, inclusive, and divinely significant forms—for the libido itself is orderly and sublimated and its expressions representative and inclusive of the enduring force of things in proportion to its concentration and mass. The ancient Brahmins cited by Jung called this concentrated and plastically expressed libido Brahma, recognizing in it a seed of "the swelling," the basic force of the universe, the creator of all organs and their appropriate propensities, of the law of things, of the forces of "prayer, magic, incantation, holy speech, holy knowledge, holy transformation and of the human will to strive upwards toward the holy and the divine." They also recognized that this "swelling" in the human being and its plastic issue also creates Brahma himself conceived not only as the creator but as the continually created, the continually becoming. The human tenement of this libido, named by them "the Brahma-scholar," they said, "made Brahma to grow, through prayer, through self-creation, through teaching." The Brahma-scholar "carries Brahma, and all the gods are contained in him, and he nourishes and satisfies them." That He may "spin out the race's thread, [the scholar] plants a seed in Him, heaping spiritual power on Him, giving Him a voice and gestures."

And no superhuman stretch of imagination is required for the recognition, in the work of Beethoven, of precisely the sort of effects attributed by the ancient wisdom to the concentration of vitalistic energy and its plastic expression; and in the relative greatness of effect and weight and significance of the later works as compared with the earlier, and the whole shape of the monument, its augmenting bulk and value and meaning, the inevitable consequence of that concentrated vitalistic energy's gradual increase in mass. Steadily augmenting in tension, piece upon piece imparts ever greater, deeper feelings and meanings, and has acted and still acts upon life in the manner of the work of the "Brahma-Scholar." Beethoven has obviously hallowed the sonorous medium, consecrating it even more than Bach did, and Mozart and Schubert, to the highest service of the human being. Music and musical interpretation have somehow grown more valuable and admirable and important forces of life because Beethoven composed. The whole sense of "the goodness, the kindness, of music" we have is due him most of all. It is that Beethoven in his music seconded the forces of life, in a sense even helped "create the Creator," the continual Becomer. He gave the forces, if not a name, a gesture, many gestures; he "lent a myth to God." Through his music we have become aware of an Heroic Will in life itself, of a Dionysiac Dancer, of an All containing the evolutionary urge and impulse to a fraternity of humankind pervaded with a sense of the divine fatherhood. This music is as divinely prophetic as Isaiah's words. What is even more important: Beethoven has supported the whole evolutionary process of the last century, the growth of man's sense of life and man, and the process of inner organization. The musical revealers who have succeeded him, from Schumann and Wagner, Liszt and Brahms, through Franck and D'Indy and Mahler to our own Ives have all derived an immeasurable amount of strength from him. They have not only been able to derive science from him; he has also stood above them, as it were a perpetual challenge, example, demonstrator of the highest values of sincerity and passion and craftsmanship. But his work has created a climate favorable not only to the noble composers and interpretative musicians, but to every musical being who stands up to the world because he has the seed of some new order in him, from Lenin to the least conspicuous of the soldiers of life. To them, his music has been the shadow of the mighty rock within the weary land. In a thousand ways it has refreshed, restored, reinspirited them, consoling them in their moments of weakness, revealing the essential goodness of nature and the human heart, redintegrating them with nature and humanity, bringing them into the rhythm of things again, freeing them, delivering, as Dannreuther long since wrote, "in unison with all genuine mystics and ethical teachers, a message of religious love and submission, of identification with the sufferings of all living creatures, deprecation of self, negation of personality, release from the world," and supporting the heroic will and the inner ordering and organizing principle by a companionship amid human solitude to which that will and that organization leads the individual.

Beethoven of course is by no means the only one who has "created the Creator" and supported the force of life. Indeed every great artist, and for that matter every human being who has lived and lives in a way making it possible for others to live, has to some degree done so. We are merely, at present, referring to Beethoven, certainly one of the most generous of these life-givers, and one more directly generous than most to great masses of men.

Thus we recognize the source of Beethoven's music, the ultimate source. Certainly a hierarchy of values, and intelligence and will, discipline and study, contributed mightily to the projection of that music. The world into which Beethoven was born placed or pretended to place an exalted value upon work done on the highest level of endeavor: and Beethoven forced himself to labor at his art, and disciplined himself, and studied his means and their treatment in the works of the great past masters, to the very close of his life. It is even possible that the continual tension of energies within himself was partly engineered by the existence of values in his world, and of the great work of the older masters, which provided him as it were with a star, a measure, and an incentive to the production of his best and utmost. Yet wanting the tendency to the immense concentration of vital energies and the perfectly natural and involuntary surrender to it—one could almost say the profound and superindividual will to the reservation itself —the values and intelligence and discipline and study would have been without the substance with which they could work. That had to be supplied them from within the man; for values, intelligence, discipline, and study cannot unassisted engender it. They are as it were secondary. Even where values are absent, and will and intelligence are weak, the conserved libido can as it were engender and fortify them; and in the last analysis they are always dependent upon that inner swell which gives them their power over itself and their ability to play the rôle of accoucheurs. What the principle, the center of the prodigious concentration of basic energy we perceive amid the flame that Beethoven's music is; who is the director of the process by which the libido becomes concentrated, organized, and free, and projects and enacts the Divinity through material, we do not know. We call him Genius, Divine Possession, Daemon, and many other names. He is some Will stronger than the individual's, some Will that has the individual in his power. We can also call him the Artist. He appears to be the original and untiring Creator of this universe: at least a part of Him. To some degree, He is in every freeman, continuing the creative act by which this universe originally was called out of chaos. But in the artist's case He works through form. And in Beethoven's, he created with a force almost uniquely stark among the world's musicians.

Glinka at Last

A LARGELY Russian-speaking audience, inclusive of persons on whom the shadows of terrible experience still visibly lingered, half filled the auditorium of the Pythian Temple that evening in the winter of 1932. It had assembled to hear the Russian Artists' Mutual Aid Society give a concert version of twelve excerpts, mostly arias, but comprehensive of the overture, the oriental dances, and the finales of the first and the last acts, from Glinka's fairy opera *Ruslan and Lyudmila*. And by the time the musicians on the platform—their numbers included a band of instrumentalists under Eugene Plotnikov and the singers Nina Koshetz, Max Panteliev, and Michael Shwetz —concluded the performance, their delightful art had given at the very least the Americans among their listeners the benefit of an important, deeply warming disclosure.

It was, foremost, that of the genius of a single musician, hitherto pretty thoroughly hidden from New York. Whatever sense of the power of Glinka New York till now had been able to gather, had been garnered from the infrequent performances of a couple of his overtures: the *Kamarinskaia* and the overture of *Ruslan and Lyudmila*. And to know an operatic achievement merely through an instrumental prelude and a

GLINKA AT LAST

concert piece is to know it scarcely at all. True, the representation at the Pythian Temple was also a partial one, revealing as it did the composer's genius within the limits of a single one of its important expressions—the other being Glinka's patriotic opera *A Life for the Czar*—and without the instances constituted by the highly vigorous, superbly written choruses, like their predecessors in the patriotic opera, some of the glories of his art. Any presentation outside the frame of the opera house indeed could hardly, at best, have been otherwise than partial. Glinka requires the stage, particularly in *Ruslan,* his masterpiece for the reason that it is freer of the conventional than its predecessor is. To be sure, this ninety-odd-year-old fairy opera is based on a libretto in some ways a model of incoherency, and makes poor drama. Derived from episodes in the fruit of Pushkin's youthful enthusiasm for Ariosto—a poem which, through the subject of a chivalric conflict between fair, candid Russians and dark, mysterious, sinister Asiatics, expresses the cleft in the national psyche—but furnished the composer by four of his literary friends, all of them amateurs, who set to work simultaneously, and it is said in perfect independence of each other, it is idiotic. It is also long. Yet since the piece is spectacular, more spectacular indeed than dramatic—very much like the *Sadko* of Rimsky-Korsakoff—it belongs in the theater.

Still, while perfectly characteristic of the dramatis personae, its vocal solos verge on pure music: thus it was possible for an excellently musical concert performance like the one of the Russian Artists' Mutual to afford an audience a good if not a complete feeling of the composer's fire. Indeed, since the culture of the managers of the Metropolitan Opera is not of the sort that encourages us to hope for productions of either of Glinka's operas inside its walls, prompt and frequent repetitions of the performance at the Pythian Temple are consummations devoutly to be wished. To miss even the half-loaf is in this circumstance to miss a feast.

For, no longer the composer of a couple of light overtures, Glinka loomed there in space that evening, a force realizing itself in music that resembled decoctions of sparkling spirits. The forefront of the evening's great disclosure, his genius bulked, one of the most spontaneous and exuberant and one of the freshest of the musical creators of the nineteenth century. It sang out with a will, a warmth, a *joie de vivre,* that made one happy and intoxicated. It gave itself generously in an abundance of juicy, naïvely and healthily vigorous music that justifies Calvocoressi's dictum that the opera "speaks in a powerful and new idiom—it is a work born not of a fashion but of creative necessity." The business of uncertainly feeling out the true expression of a dawning young power, so evident in *A Life for the Czar* amid the testimonies of a considerable métier, was absent here. One heard simple and characteristic melodies, with intervals sometimes extraordinarily modern, richly and appropriately harmonized; amazingly free and expressive recitatives; and an orchestration that, crystalline and brilliant, had perfect point. One heard a plethora of new ideas, many of them forecasting the forms which give the music of the nationalistic Russian school its peculiar character and color. Much of the music had the archaic tone reviving the old chivalric Russia, so magnificently deployed by Borodin in his Second Symphony and in *Prince Igor*. The score incorporated Slavonic and oriental folk songs of the sort which became a touchstone for Moussorgsky and the rest of the Five. Our famous friend, the Greek liturgical whole-tone scale, which triumphed in Moussorgsky and was grafted from him by Debussy on to post-Wagnerian music, put in a conspicuous appearance: actually if not the virgin appearance in European instrumental music, at least the

GLINKA AT LAST

first important one. So likewise did the 5/4 measure, one of the favorites of the entire Russian school. Again, passages such as the dreamy introduction to Ratmir's aria were well-nigh Rimskyan in their orientalism. Movements of the oriental dances proved themselves capable of figuring among the members of Tschaikowsky's *Nutcracker Suite,* while others anticipated the gorgeous savagery of the *Polovtsian Dances* from *Prince Igor.* And one heard the characteristically Russian harmonic devices the musicologists have detected in the score: the Rimskyan device of opposing to each other dominant sevenths in distant keys, at the commencement of Farlav's aria: and heard harmonies built on fourths and fifths; and besides, a polyrhythm or two. These innovations were actually but a part of those contained in the whole of Glinka's music, full not only of anticipations of the music of the Five, but of the very stark Strawinskian, and even of some German music. One of Glinka's powerful warrior choruses, for instance, amazingly foreshadows the rough Viking chorus that is one of the gems not only of the second act of *Götterdämmerung* but of the whole music-drama.

Indeed it was impossible not to recognize the reason why Glinka has been called the father of the Five. He not only was the bannerman of their movement. His expression anticipated theirs. A representation of the national idea in music as individually colored as the music of Balakirev or Moussorgsky, *Ruslan and Lyudmila* cannot, of course, be said to be. It has its root in the western classical tradition as well as in the tradition of the folk and liturgical music of old Muscovy. In form, the piece is an old music opera composed of separate, finished numbers; and the arias regularly follow the traditional pattern of introductory recitative, slow movement, and final fast allegro. Lyudmila's first song is even definitely coloratura music of the sort at which the French and Italian operatic composers of his epoch aimed. Weber is recalled by other numbers: one cannot help feeling the kinship between Ruslan's heroic and long-limbed aria and that of Adolar in *Euryanthe* and the relationship between the eerie music of Ruslan's scene with the giant head and the forest gorge music in *Der Freischütz*. It has even been suggested that both the romantic faërie and the orientalism of his master score represent developments of the similar elements in Weber's *Oberon*. This is certain, that in concluding his opera with a chorus based on one of the themes of his overture, Glinka was, whether consciously or no, treading close on the heels of the German nationalist. The case undoubtedly was that even while aiming at a music whose very tone would give him the feeling of "home"—that is, express the essences dominating the Russian people—Glinka remained expressive of the forces of the Russia that faces westward and feels itself part of Europe and not isolated from it, and finds itself no less in the classical forms of that west than in the more traditionally Russian and autochthonous ones: in this way paralleling his contemporary Gogol and his junior Turgenev, and as De Schloezer has said in his book on Strawinsky, the Russian architects of the reigns of Catherine the Great and Alexander I. Indeed, *Ruslan and Lyudmila* parallels most of all such representative works of the later, classicizing, westernizing Strawinsky as the *Symphony of the Psalms* and *Perséphone:* though in the inverse sense; for Glinka's work represents a bridge thrown from classicism toward Russian nationalism, while Strawinsky's represents one thrown back from nationalism toward what we still hope may prove to be the new catholic music, that of the all-folk. Possibly political events might have made Glinka more "barbarous" than he was. His career antedated by several decades the Russian nationalism and the Pan-Slavism of the later 1860's and '70's: and it probably was under the influence of this religion that the "Liszt-born barbarians," the Five, went the limit in swinging toward the east, and that Moussorgsky deliberately set out to found an aesthetic on the expressions of the Great-Russian *moujik,* and Rimsky to emulate Ukrainian, and Balakirew and Borodin Caucasian peasant art and peasant song.

Still, even when his rhythms do not kick out like Russian peasant dancers and flow with a more classic kind of grace, Glinka is the typical Russian composer as the Russian nationalist movement produced him. One felt it distinctly that evening at the Pythian Temple. One of the hallmarks of the art presented then was concision, so definitely indeed that Bülow's famous exclamation that the *Corsair* overture by Berlioz sped like a bullet from the pistol's mouth seemed to have deprived Glinka of a praise that was his due even more than the Frenchman's. Another of these traits was a vigorous physicality, a happy animality and sensuality as distinguished from the more metaphysical, intellectual, and sublime. *Ruslan and Lyudmila* proved full of the joyous earthiness that caused elegant St. Petersburg society of the 1840's to dub it and its predecessor "music for coachmen"—to which Glinka is said to have answered by remarkably dryly, "What matter, since the lacqueys are plainly superior to their masters?" And the ballet music was exuberantly motory. Again, the music conveyed a kind of virile warmth and magnanimity, like that of some patriarchal, kingly primitive nature. And these hallmarks of his art are those of his whole group's and have correctly been related to it. The Russian nationalists are extremely concise in their expressions, Balakirew, Moussorgsky, and their offspring Strawinsky in particular, and many of the non-nationalistic Russian composers as well: Scriabin, for example, at least in his aristocratic salon piano music. Intellectuality, metaphysicality, too, is not their forte. They are not great symphonists—apparently incapacitated for the erection of great intricate sonorous objects. Their symphonies, Tchaikowsky's, Borodin's, at best are lyrical, extended, frequently over-extended songs. They themselves probably are incapable of the concentrations and suspensions of energy of which the Germans were capable, the concentrations and suspensions whose fruits were Bach's and Beethoven's and Brahms' tremendously intricate forms and communications of complex ideas and forces of nature. Their music constitutes a much more simple expression of experience. It is the lyrical music of singers and of dancers. But it is deeply and truthfully lyrical, without the sentimentality which dogs the heels of so much German delivery of sentiment: infrequently subjective—the songs of the later Moussorgsky, after all, are an anomaly among those of his compatriots—and articulate with a natural power and grandeur like that of a rich, full bass voice. And it has a physical, almost animal, uninhibited and even undisciplined vitality, the wildness of spirits that blaze up and sometimes prematurely exhaust themselves, and a richness of color that indicates a revelry in touch and smell and taste. It is extremely pantomimic, too, reflective of the gestures and the movements of vigorously mobile and saltatory bodies, and includes some of the most exciting ballet music ever penned. This music, too, as a whole, has the simple, virile warmth and magnanimity, the expression, the essences of big males and broad fields that, joyous in Glinka's music, make one conceive of him as kingly, and makes one figure them all, Balakirew, Borodin, and Moussorgsky in particular, in all their joyousness and sorrow, as patriarchal individuals, old Tartar chieftains in sober nineteenth-century clothes, and, following Gorki's picture of Tolstoy, as "old Russian gods under their linden trees."

Thus the disclosure of the evening, primarily that of Glinka's genius, actually was a double one. In and through and behind this genius revealed to New York for a first time, there was evident the power and gorgeous spirit of the group. Essential in that genius and typified by it, the whole generic power seemed to hover about Glinka's music, restoring to one the warming sense of a matchlessly vigorous and warm, strongly animal, sensitive human feeling, the gift to the world of the emergent, musically genial Russian individuals of the nineteenth century. Again the world contained among its immensely various treasures that individually colored, lovely distillation, the music of the Russian nationalists; and, it is to be hoped, not only for the newly instructed New Yorker among the audience. It is to be hoped the joyous fact of its existence was equally evident to the Russian-speaking members of the gathering, especially those on whom the shadows of a certain experience still lingered. On these it would have had a surpassingly vital influence. It would once more have given them the sense of the living greatness of their national past and reaffirmed the magnanimity, native to the Russian, that once imbursed the world.

The Nazis and "Die Meistersinger"

DIRECTLY after the news that the Nazis had captured the government of Germany reached us, we learned that on the day of their coup d'état they had commanded the Berlin opera to perform *Die Meistersinger von Nürnberg*. To those of us eager to see American artists, by musical or poetic means, project a symbol of the national idea as magnificent as the symbol of the German superindividual entity constituted by Wagner's comic masterpiece, this latter revelation brought an additional shock.

Various phenomena indicate that such an American expression is within the bounds of possibility and may actually appear during the next few years. And the image of an audience of Nazi porkers self-righteously taking in the concluding scene of the music drama, identifying their sinister Fascist state with the bright democratic order figured there, adopting the composer as their prophet and justifying their ways to men with his vision, made us wonder whether the comparable American expression would be the boon to civilization we had hoped it might prove, and might not turn out as susceptible of brutal perversion as this fragrant German work.

That the Nazis' identification of their national idea with the one *Die Meistersinger* symbolizes is false and perversive, is not to be doubted. Of course, the music drama is definitely German in idea and in expression, the most traditionally German of all Wagner's compositions. And still where the gods are, there surely is merriment today over Hitler and his followers' attempt to gild their Fascist order by identifying it with the relationship, the bond, the inner coherence and order among the German forces which Wagner felt and expressed, and which, after hovering coronally over the work, seems actually to descend into the matter at the close and display itself through the massed exultant figures on the stage, and in the music. And it meant no tyranny, no dictatorship whether of a monarch, a class, a faction, or the collectivity. *Die Meister-*

THE NAZIS AND "DIE MEISTERSINGER"

singer, true, is a nationalistic work, like its predecessor, Weber's *Der Freischütz,* and its Russian coeval, Moussorgsky's *Boris Goudonow*—certainly the greatest of the pieces that express the sheerly German life. But the social bond and order it embodies and displays is a spontaneous one, that of a free society of men with their soil sacred in their midst, in this instance the order latent among and adumbrated by Germans at their perihelion of freedom and power in the 1860's. The prelude outlines the idea. Stiff, ponderous, bourgeois, militaristic, pedantic, idealistic, the essences are full of malice and sentiment and strength. They conflict with each other, they quarrel and snarl: suddenly, at the signal of some marshaling power that seems to rise from among them out the depths, their conflict ends, and they unite in an orderly, mighty, aspiring, polyphonic progress. The drama but expands that idea, augmenting and extending the expression of the chivalric, bourgeois, plebeian, massive, pedantic, and idealistic Germany and its potential concordance in a free fellowship of spirited and aspiring knights and burghers, artists and people, against the background of the Free City of Nuremberg at its highest.

All nationalistic art, that of other musicians and poets as well as that of Wagner, is the product of individualizing, democratic times and movements and of individuals. All nationalistic art is expressive of the national superindividual entity at the moment that entity offers to form itself freely in the union of individuals—a formation inevitably flowing from the inner liberty of the individual. In itself this sort of art constitutes an emergent individual's fraternal embrace of those free men, present and future, a circumstance that in part accounts for the peculiarity of the form of nationalistic pieces of music. This is frequently a variation or an expansion of some traditional musical form or musical forms of the folk it expresses, or one inclusive of variations and expansions and even citations of such a form or forms; and a result of the sometimes unconscious, sometimes deliberate, but natural tendency of the composer to express his national essences, sometimes humorously, sometimes ironically, always affectionately, through molds related to the musical ones that have helped reveal these forces to himself, and which he has unconsciously absorbed. Thus, while the libretto of *Die Meistersinger* contains the figure of the old German poet Hans Sachs and echoes the rules of the Guild of Mastersingers and includes a poem of the historical Sachs, the score reflects "three hundred years of German music," from the chorales of the Reformation through the polyphony of Bach, the shakes of Händel, and Beethoven—the first of the *Diabelli Variations*—and Weberesque flourishes for the violins, up to Wagner's own *Tristan*.

And just as every nationalistic work of art constitutes an emergent individual's fraternal embrace of the past and present and future freemen of his nation, so too it constitutes his embrace of the superindividual entity emergent among them all. Spengler indicates as much. At least, he assures us that nationalistic ideas appear among a people at the period of its life when, in consequence of a growing individualism, it is removing its allegiance from the person of the monarch and transferring it to an idea which symbolizes the relationships of its members, and to the superindividual entity born of and inclusive of them all; nationalistic art but expressing that national idea and unity through form. Thus it is republican art: and various instances of it, instances other than Wagner's, too, lend substance to this thesis of the historian. A great literary nationalistic expression, the chronicle plays of Shakespeare, with their apotheosis of the "island set in silver," significantly date from a period of English life where, after the defeat of the great Armada, only

THE NAZIS AND "DIE MEISTERSINGER"

the personal popularity of the reigning monarch, Elizabeth, checked the arrogation on the part of the Commons of the supreme rule to itself. With her death, the struggle with the Crown began; and not forty years after the composition of *Richard II* and the rest of the chronicles, the English had decapitated their king and proclaimed a commonwealth. If thereafter they returned to constitutional monarchical rule, the doctrine of the "divine right of kings" was nonetheless dead among them forever, and by 1688 with it the last vestiges of absolute monarchy. Toward this English republicanism—at least that of the Commonwealth, elder brother of the American with its general principle of the equality of all men—the chronicles may even be thought contributory, since the playwright who brings the figures of kings on to the stage, letting them confess their inmost thoughts to the audience and making one of them declare, "Uneasy lies the head that wears a crown," puts every one of his spectators in the way of conceiving, and thus potentially becoming, a king, and feeling himself in some respects superior to him. Wyndham Lewis has called Shakespeare probably most justly, "the king-killer." —The date of another great nationalistic drama, *Wilhelm Tell* by Schiller, coincides for its part with the collapse of feudalism in western Germany during the revolutionary years. Its author, incidentally, was an honorary citizen of the first French republic. Still another great literary expression of nationalistic ideas, the writings of Maurice Barrès, dates mainly from the 1880's and '90's, the decades during which the French as a whole were definitely withdrawing their allegiance from the houses both of Bourbon and of Bonaparte and affirming their republic for the third and final time.

This connection is indicated also by the circumstances surrounding the production of nationalistic music from Weber to

DISCOVERIES OF A MUSIC CRITIC

De Falla. The first nationalistic opera, by virtue of its definitely German feeling, its German forest feeling, and its expression of this experience in a form inclusive of German-Bohemian folk songs and arias and choruses in the folk-song style, was Weber's *Der Freischütz*: the whole nationalistic movement in music being originally German and impelled to a degree by Herder's critical work. Now *Der Freischütz* dates from the years when, disappointed by their sovereigns' repudiation of the liberal pledges made them during the wars of liberation against Napoleon, the German peoples were traversed by republican tendencies. The work's first performance took place on the fifth anniversary of the battle of Waterloo, probably by no means fortuitously, and the coincidence was remarked. The piece in itself was an expression of the dawning feeling of self-reliance: it is significant that the *deus ex machina* of the finale is not the prince but a venerable anchorite "who dwells in the woods." A subsequent body of nationalistic art, in this instance Polish, the work of Chopin, was also synchronous with a liberal and republican movement, that of Polish intolerance of Russian despotism: and its idealized national dance rhythms have conveyed revolutionary-republican ideas to many of its audiences. The nationalistic music of the Russian Five also dates from the liberal decades of Russian life when, in consequence of the reforms of Alexander II—themselves to a degree inspired by the broad human revelations of such Russian artists as Gogol and Turgenev—the Russian people for the first time began to feel its fatherland its own. It is significant that while originally patronized by the court, the music of the Five fell from grace as the reaction triumphed: Rimsky complains that *Mlada,* the first of his operas produced during the extremely reactionary reign of Alexander III, was snubbed by the powers, the Czarina and her children alone assisting at one of

THE NAZIS AND "DIE MEISTERSINGER"

the matinee performances of the new piece. And De Falla's nationalistic Spanish music but anticipated by a few years the proclamation of the second Spanish republic and the initiation of democracy.

Wagner himself, at least the Wagner of the first three parts of the *Ring*, with their recapitulations of the old Teutonic pantheism, and of *Tristan* and the consciously Germanic *Meistersinger*, was, of course, a liberal, a revolutionary, and an anarchist. All five of these works of his date from the period before the patronage of Ludwig II of Bavaria, the successes of Bismarck in unifying most of the German peoples under their thirty-odd monarchs, and the influence of Cosima had reconciled him with monarchism. It is well known that the tetralogy was conceived by him during his revolutionary days in Dresden prior to 1848, that the figure of Siegfried was partially inspired by his friend the anarchist Bakunin, that the Brünhilde of the "second day" was the New Woman, and thus, since Woman was always somewhat the Race for Wagner, and the race feminine—*das menschlich-weibliche*—the free new people. The idea of *Die Meistersinger* had come to him in its first vague form while he was reading Gervinus' extremely nationalistic-democratic *History of German Literature* in 1845. As late as 1859, while he was completing *Tristan* and when the idea of the *Meistersinger* must have been in process of final clarification, he wrote to Mathilde Wesendonck that he was for France and Sardinia in the current war (Napoleon III's for the liberation of Italy), since Austria and Germany were the contemporaneously regressive and reactionary powers. It is noteworthy also that while he was composing the prelude of the *Meistersinger* at Biebrich on the Rhine, his eyes were drawn continually to the distant prospect of Mayence. He does not tell us what he felt as he gazed out, and perhaps he did not clearly know; but for us the reference is significant: like Nuremberg, *das goldene Mainz* had been a free city.

And evidence internal to his musical comedy, the action itself, impresses on us the relation of its idea not only to that of the liberal and democratic state but to a state the very opposite of the Nazis' totalitarian one and its brutal tyranny of a class, a faction, and its domination of the individual by the collectivity. Let us briefly glance at the action. It exhibits a knight, Walther, who comes to Nuremberg of his own will to become the citizen of the free city. It repudiates the authority of the past, the "rules" of the mastersingers' guild, and glorifies experiment; if there is any authority, it says, it resides in the spirit, alike in the poet and in the people. An individual emergent from the people, Hans Sachs, represents that spirit, indeed "includes the whole" within himself; and, generously enacting it, induces the final union of all its representatives in the light of the great day before the walls. The grand chorus in the third act is set to the words in which the historical Sachs hailed Martin Luther, the asserter of the inviolacy of the private conscience and the personality, the prophet of symbiosis. At the conclusion of the drama, Sachs bids the people look for a unity, no longer recoverable in a royalty deluded by false and foreign ideas of majesty, but in the honor of the German masters, the German artists, and German art—we have said that the work of art is one of the great potential agents of relationship among a democratic people. The Holy Roman Empire, symbol of autocratic rule and authority external to the human being, might, if it would, fall to dust. The good spirits would nonetheless favor the nation. The curtain falls on a scene of triumphant concord among spirited individuals and a people that situates the national idea at the inevitably single goal of the aspirations of free Germans.

THE NAZIS AND "DIE MEISTERSINGER"

Indeed, if any national idea is different from the Nazis', it is this: and with it all the national ideas that are the content of nationalistic art. If when rightly seen they make for the establishment of any political state, it is ultimately toward (dreadful name) the "anarchist commune," the commune of individuals who neither rule others nor are ruled by them, and, freely active—aware of their embodiments of the whole in which they live and move and have their being—are the state and enact it. Intrinsic symbols of the superindividual entity which exists among and over individuals, like Wagner's Sachs they bring other individuals into harmony with that entity and thus give life to all. And the individual ultimately is the man who wants neither to rule nor to be ruled, and for whom work and workmanlike quality and the perfect function of the whole of which he is an organic part are ends in themselves; and who, no matter what mental and physical distinctions nature has raised between him and other individuals and whatever his job, freely enacts the whole in continual consciousness of the whole within and without himself. His city, his land, alone are free.

For all artists are fundamentally "anarchists." Their intuitions reveal to them a continually changing order, and their embodiment of the symbols of this continually changing order adjusts them spontaneously to it. They touch material selflessly and shape it in accordance with its own nature and the idea to which it conforms; and work is a joy to them, an end in itself. And the social order to which they are natively directed could easily be an order based on the private ownership of the means of production, and the operation of those means for profit, in which labor got its just reward, and social, political, and intellectual advantages were shared by all.

Such, then, is the social order adumbrated by *Die Meister-*

singer and other great nationalistic pieces. And into our faces there stares the truth that these liberating symbols of the free community can be misunderstood and made, like *Die Meistersinger,* to appear to gild a state the very contrary of the one related to the idea they body forth. There is the incident of the Nazis and that very piece—a sinister one, for what was involved was not only the attempt to make a great and representative German composer appear the prophet of a state which, the tyranny of a faction, of the collectivity over the individual, seeks to turn society into a mass of mechanical parts moved by a superior power—in Fascism, the rule, the organization, is all, the individual nothing; there is "regimentation in the place of initiative, authority in place of self-government, dogma in the place of experiments, obedience in the place of responsibility, submission in the place of conscience." (This is the sort of state which Wagner could not but have scorned, for both in art and life he was one of the most self-reliant, experimental of men: and nicknamed himself Freidank.) What was also involved was an attempt to turn Wagner into an academy, to make of his work a sort of musical dogma, a new set of rules and prescriptions which would serve to forbid musical experiment and in this way, too, suppress the self-regulating individual by depriving him of his power to express himself. Thus those of us in America who had been cheered by the signs that great American nationalistic works of art, projecting the national idea through musical or poetic means or both, and providing us with the basis for a superior unity, were within the bounds of possibility and might actually prove the event of the next few years, have been compelled to ask ourselves whether the possibility that these expressions might not serve even viler perversions of their ideas than that contrived by the Nazis with Wagner's comic opera, does not provide a good reason for

THE NAZIS AND "DIE MEISTERSINGER"

urging the artists to desist from their attempts. But the reply has always been negative. In the first place, the motive making for nationalistic art is a good and an irrepressible one. In the second, it seems possible that intelligence and perspicuity might make the ideas and symbols of this kind of art unpervertible. What has been the trouble with many of the nationalistic works produced in the past has been the carelessness and trustfulness with which they have been given to the world by their authors. In expressing the national idea, the authors have failed to envisage the chances for misunderstanding lying in their paths, and thus failed to guard against such misunderstanding by making their ideas so plain, so definite, that none can mistake them and use their works as weapons against their own objectives. They were thus a little less than highly intelligent: Wagner himself, for all his genius, was a very naïve man: one of the greatest of musical poets, chock-full of powerful and delicate musical feeling, but relatively simple-minded. One has but to read his writings and to compare the prolixity and slowness and looseness of his form with the far terser, quicker forms of such moderns as Debussy, Schönberg, Berg, and for that matter the later Beethoven, to become aware of it. Hence, like his fellows, he doubtless imagined that the ideas he was communicating in his music, and the symbols with which he communicated them, were intelligible to the least of men: and that blind confidence has proved, at least from the viewpoint of the present hour, to have been fatal.

Precisely how the new poets and dramatists and musicians, those of present America in particular, are to go about making their expressions of the national idea unmistakable, we unfortunately cannot say. They alone can discover how, if a way is indeed discoverable. We can merely fervently warn them that, in engaging in conveying to the nation the national idea as moments of energy and freedom constitute it, they must be with caution bold and speak with greatest clearness—in consciousness of the immensity of the profit to life that might flow from utmost clarity, and the immensity of the mischief to it that failure of the strongest lucidity might potentiate.

Cosima Wagner's Story

WHEN Cosima Liszt definitely left his house and took herself and her daughters to Wagner's villa at Triebschen on the Lake of Lucerne, Hans von Bülow first engaged in pistol practice and then declared to Klindworth that "if Wagner ever wrote another note, it would be due to Cosima." Thus this greatly injured husband, while consenting to the loss of his wife and jealously depreciating the creative independence of his rival, unwittingly set a snare for coming generations, and one into which they have periodically fallen. The world has seen the unpredictably triumphant conclusion of Wagner's work during the years of his life with Cosima: the completion of *Die Meistersinger* and of *Siegfried,* the creation of *Götterdämmerung* and of *Parsifal*. From an apparently hunted, homeless, unhonored man, an individual whom "nobody could help" and the author of a few fine romantic operas and of several untheatrical music dramas, it saw the composer, his ideas realized with a completeness rare in the annals of art, become a kind of monarch of music, acknowledged by the million, and master of a festival theater consecrated in the middle of Germany to performances of his "impossible" works. And comparing his estate during the years subsequent to his union with Liszt's extraordinary daughter with what it was previous to the time in which he found peace with her, the world again and again has come to the conclusion so flattering to the less genial run of men. It has paraphrased Bülow's words, ascribing the whole triumph to the influence of the woman.

One finds the old sentiment again in Mr. Ernest Newman's introduction to the English translation of Richard Graf du Moulin-Eckart's recent book about Cosima. There, it runs, "No one can doubt that—had she [Cosima] not taken the decisive step she did—i.e., thrown in her lot with Wagner—the world would never have had the completed Ring, or Parsifal, or Bayreuth." We are to believe that if not the actual author of Wagner's later work, Cosima nonetheless supplied the conditions indispensable to its achievement. If she did not actually place the pen in Wagner's hand, she alone could and she alone did manage to provide the energy and the faith that drove it and that brought the work it completed safely to port. Wagner, thus, was absolutely dependent on her.

This of course is an absurd idea, though not at all for the reason that Cosima was not a very great and illustrious personality, worthy of deepest admiration both for what she intrinsically was and for what she did for Wagner and his art. It is absurd for the reason that it entirely misrepresents the marvelous and fruitful relationship between the man and the woman: one which, as Wagner boasted, "will live in the memory of humanity," and which for all its blemishes was nothing if not a relationship between a man and a woman. Wagner may at times have thought Cosima was absolutely necessary to him and undoubtedly told her so. Certainly it was a statement of this sort that ultimately brought her for good to Triebschen. But Wagner was either deceiving himself or did not mean what Bülow meant, that without Cosima he could never write another note. Wagner was the most independent of men, utterly confident of his own senses and unswervingly faithful to his own lights and feelings. Of course he required money. Of course he required the deep communion of love. Of course, like many other extremely brave men, he was subject to profound periodic fits of discouragement. But at heart he never doubted his own power and the eventual realization of his ideas. From the beginning he stood up to the world quite alone, winning people to his side in the face of tremendous opposition: it infuriated him to hear that it was said "he was not to be helped." By the time of the fall of 1863, when, five years before the final break with Bülow, he and Cosima swore "with sobs and tears" to "belong to each other alone," his fortunes were definitely on the mend. He had an eccentric but faithful patron in Ludwig of Bavaria: and though he subsequently had to leave Munich because of the hostility of a political cabal resentful of his ascendancy over the mind of the young monarch, he retained the sovereign's loyalty—indeed, if Hohenlohe was eventually able to "gain Ludwig's confidence" and form a stable ministry, it was largely because he showed himself favorable to Wagner, enduring the dreamy king's interruptions of the business of the state councils with inquiries as to the progress of the plans for the production of *Die Meistersinger*. And certainly by 1868 Wagner had already completed the better part of his work: most of the *Ring,* and *Tristan und Isolde.* He was working on his most brilliant score, *Die Meistersinger von Nürnberg,* while in the recesses of his mind *Parsifal* was already taking shape, in consequence of certain experiences met on the Green Hill near Zurich—the Wesendoncks' place—and in Venice in 1859. Nor did his ideas subsequently change, as they must have done had he lost his initiative and become totally dependent upon Cosima for the energy and the faith requisite to their realization. True, the processes in *Götterdämmerung* are speedier, more concentrated than are those in the other members of the tetralogy; and *Parsifal* is more advanced in style than any other one of Wagner's works. But it is impossible to see in these maturities anything but portions of the evolution that Wagner's work as a whole embodies. The truth would appear to be that Cosima provided Wagner with the largest and deepest of companionships, that she helped give him energy and faith abundantly, that blood of hers ran as it were in his music, and that she became the most selfless and effective of his allies; but not that, had she not been there, another could not, and Wagner would have been unable to complete his mighty work.

Indeed, it would seem that it was not so much Cosima who evolved Wagner, as Wagner Cosima; and that the grand relationship between the two in the last analysis was that of pitcher and cup. Certainly she personally never claimed any of the credit for Wagner's achievement; and in her life, and in her letters and the portions of her diaries included in Graf du Moulin-Eckart's tome, she reveals herself a very feminine woman. The daughter of Liszt and Marie d'Agoult, she undoubtedly was more sentient, more spiritual, more idealistic than either of her parents; certainly she looked it. Only work upon the very highest levels of endeavor and expression of the deepest feeling had worth for her; and it had the capacity to become the lodestone of a marvelous devotion and utterly generative and perfective of her life. She was probably one of those very rare creatures who, given the choice between bearing the world's greatest musical genius and bearing her own child, would unhesitatingly have taken the former. At the same time, it was her nature's condition that this profoundly compelling deed, this highest type of art, and the will to it and the vision, be the man's, and her nature's fatality that the man endowed with the capacity for the psychic tension necessary to the creation of work gratifying the highest levels of mind could easily become in part the object of the passionate and grateful devotion which the emerging work of art excited. That probably is what George Moore intended to say when in his droll, typically irresponsible, and penetrating way he declared that from the hour she heard *Tristan und Isolde,* Cosima knew she had to live with the man who had written it. In Triebschen, certainly, when Wagner played her the Prelude on the piano, she could scarcely—the language is her own—"preserve her self-command. All she knew at such moments, was that, in Elsa's words, 'fur Dich möchte Ich zu Tode gehen,' and that she was powerless to express her feelings." Still, her realization of the power that the work and the personality of such a man as Wagner had over her, and her sense that only through life in common with such a creator could she attain her own life, was not quite as prompt and automatic an event as our Dublin gossip would pretend. Even this was dependent on Wagner's gesture. She had met this new Vanderdecken while she was still a girl under the guardianship of her grandmother in Paris. Liszt had brought Wagner and Berlioz to his mother's house one evening, and Wagner had read his lately completed poem of *Siegfried's Death* to the company. Then he had disappeared, and the man in Liszt's entourage who had interested her most was the young Hans von Bülow. It is possible that this interest was fed by Bülow's creative ambition. The gifted, nervous young musician then still hoped that his life would prove one more genial than an interpreter's. After the wedding, Cosima strove to help him realize his ambition to write an orchestral trilogy on the Oresteia by making a detailed abstract of the dramas for him.

But the piece simply wouldn't come forth. Bülow then decided to write an opera on the subject of Merlin, and with the help of a littérateur named Dohm, Cosima provided him with the libretto. But it was only by interpreting the greatest music to perfection that Bülow could add to musical art. And, one of the talented young men, like Ludwig II and Nietzsche, whom Wagner attracted, nurtured, and also exploited—and whose own little household in Berlin was tyrannized over by his mother—Bülow was continually running to Wagner, now that Liszt's pitiful decline had begun, and taking Cosima along with him. The pair were at the Green Hill at the time of the catastrophe involving Wagner and his wife and the Wesendoncks, and they were with Wagner at Biebrich on the Rhine while the unhappy composer was at work on the joyous *Meistersinger*. At such periods, for some reason or another, Bülow was inclined to break out hysterically in lamentations over his own incapacity to create. Cosima, meanwhile, had founded a little salon in Berlin, which was frequented by Lassalle and Varnhagen von Ense, and had become interested in the work and the personality of an author named Alfred Meissner and started translating one of his novels into French for the *Revue Germanique*. Her marriage with Bülow, as Newman writes, had imparted to her "an early sense of life as a struggle of idealism against harsh and ugly reality"; and to Meissner she sometimes wrote of the greatness of Wagner and his work. She made no protest when, at the urgent invitation of Wagner and of Liszt that he work for the new music in Munich while the new sun-king Ludwig shone, Bülow decided to transfer their residence to the Bavarian capital. The relationship between her and the composer would appear to have become intimate during the fall of 1863. In any case Cosima, who had named her first two daughters Daniela and Blandina, after her brother who had died of tuberculosis in very early manhood and her sister who had married Emile Ollivier, later the minister of Napoleon III, now began calling the children she bore by the names of characters in Wagner's dramas: Isolde, Eva, and Siegfried. From that time on, too, the young Frau von Bülow began to play the managerial rôle in Wagner's affairs that later in Bayreuth got her the nickname of "the property man." She became the medium of the communications between the exacting Bavarian monarch and the busy composer. When Ludwig expressed an urgent desire to own the original of all Wagner's manuscripts, it was Cosima who went to the great trouble of collecting them, even writing to her detested "stepmother," the Princess Sayn-Wittgenstein, to persuade her to give up those in her possession. She got up a biography from notes Wagner dictated to her. She personally forced the stubborn officials to honor the drafts the king drew upon the treasury in Wagner's favor. She even embroidered a cushion which delighted the receptive monarch for the reason that "it reminded him of all Wagner's compositions." Just how this cushion, silken though it probably was, quite managed to do so, has never been revealed to the world; and we are merely left to speculate, in view of the fact that in Bayreuth in after years, shirts embroidered with Wagnerian leitmotivs were offered for sale, whether this pillow might not possibly have been the archetype of those later confections. Whether it was or not, it certainly must have shown the individual's power to acquire perfectly the spirit of a race not his own. For in it Cosima, who had not a drop of German blood in her veins— her father being a Magyar and her mother the fruit of a union between an émigré of the French Revolution, the Comte de Flavigny, and a young woman with a background of Jewish banking, Fräulein Bethmann of Frankfurt—Cosima, despite her possession of that bugbear of the Nazis, a Jewish grandmother, in this creation consummately displayed a taste that, whatever else it may be, is very German.

Whether she could permanently have tolerated the division in her interest, we do not know. It is certain that she was attached to poor Bülow. Her diaries display a concern for his welfare that is not to be questioned, and Bülow himself did not permanently question it. He may have come to doubt Wagner. After the final break he played "nothing but Rubinstein, in Hanover." Later, he discovered that "in music there are only the three B's—Bach, Beethoven, and Brahms—all the rest are cretins." Last, he loudly acclaimed a promising young composer from Munich named Strauss whom he insisted on calling Richard III ("Richard II giebt es ja nicht!" he said, oblivious of the fact that the Richard Plantagenets do not correspond entirely to the Napoleon Bonapartes). But when Wagner died, he telegraphed Cosima: "Sœur, il ne faut pas désespérer"—so much more the gentleman than Nietzsche, who when he was going mad wired her, "Bacchus to Ariadne —greetings!" But for all her attachment to Bülow, "the call of destiny" summoned her elsewhere. Since 1866 she had paid several lengthy visits to the house on the Lake of Lucerne which Wagner called his Asyl. On the Palm Sunday of 1867, she and Wagner had taken a little trip on the lake, and while they gazed into the springs at the foot of the Grütli "where bloom the Parzival flowers," Wagner spoke, "It is at such moments as these that we create and live." At last, Bülow having carried *Die Meistersinger* to the baptismal font and Cosima having met Wagner in Genoa, she returned to Germany to arrange the permanent separation from her husband, and brought her daughters to Triebschen. And knowing well that the eyes of Europe were upon the house, and that there were aspects of her story that it would never judge softly or teach her children to judge softly, and, womanlike, caring intensely for respectability, she began keeping a diary "for her children": it is the one that serves as the basis of the Moulin-Eckart *Life*. At its beginning, she wrote that 1868 was the turning-point in her life: "In this year, it was vouchsafed me to carry into action what had been the inspiration of my life for five years past.— My life had been a desolate, unlovely dream. Outward appearances were calm and remained so, but inwardly, all was waste and desolation, when there revealed himself to me the Being through whom it was soon made clear to me that as yet I had never lived at all. My love was a new birth, a redemption, the death of all that was worthless and bad within me." Again: "Whoever is used to [Wagner's] company, whoever has had his mind penetrated by his, is indifferent to everything else. The cleverest people seem to me in comparison with him flat as the fields, since I have given myself to this pure and glacier-high being." "There is such a thing as happiness, but we do not know it. I know it and know how to value it. All the suffering and misery in the world has a happiness deep hidden in its heart, like the pearl in its shell. No pain can touch it; and in the most grievous hours the pearl of ecstasy was resting tranquilly in my heart." "My blessings upon you then, my children.—Never misjudge your mother, though you may never act as she has done. For fate has here ordained a thing which does not happen twice." And between the romantic lines, we can read the truth of what had actually happened to her. Wagner had made this clever, but really deeply sentient, spiritual, and idealistic woman, grandiose creature that she was —there was something about both him and her that was like a regal sundown among the high mountains—to "talk with the gods." He played her what he had been composing; and what he was composing was an expression of the divine forces underlying life; and she seemed to hear her own feelings articulated by these forms, and the eternal ideas she dimly felt, and "fate and metaphysical aid." In the evenings, he read and revealed Shakespeare, Schiller, Calderón, and Homer to her: she had ever been starved for such expressions of such intuitions. Once she went out into the upper garden, and then, she wrote: "As I stood on the hillside, I was enraptured at the circle of snow-covered mountains which represent to me the mysterious phenomenon of a motionless dance. As I gazed long upon the scene, my spirit became aware of the music through which exalted natures reflect themselves for us in sound. I felt the transience of all personal existence; and the eternal essence of all greatness arose, a radiant message, from the pale mirror of the lake."

Their common life, at the same time, was that of any little bourgeois German family. No anniversary was ever forgotten or solemnized without the recitation of verses. When Nietzsche came over from Basel to celebrate the Christmas of '69 at Triebschen, he brought with him, at Wagner's urgent request, costumes for the devil and the Christ child. The children were duly frightened by the person wearing the one and enchanted by the person wearing the other: and later, while Wagner and Nietzsche retired into the dining-room to smoke and converse, Cosima knelt with the young generation before the tree and sang carols. Their life had its levities, too. Have we not a letter from Nietzsche to Rée in which he announces, "Richard, Cosima and I are going to Paris to see them dance the cancan?" What it all meant to Wagner himself, two of his expressions unequivocally inform us. One is that tender reflection of interior peace and happiness, the *Siegfried Idyl,* which he composed in Cosima's honor for the celebration of the first anniversary of the birth of their son. The other is the verse which he had inscribed over the door of the house he built for them in Bayreuth:

> Hier, wo mein Wähnen Friede fand,
> Wahnfried sei dieses Haus genannt.

That their relations weren't invariably all roses other circumstances attest. Wagner, who had a propensity for flying into rages, from time to time was impelled to commit assaults upon the image of Cosima's father. She had to hear that all that Liszt was good for any longer was the composition of paraphrases, and that only two of his original pieces, the *Faust* Symphony and *Mazeppa*, were first-rate music. Wagner's autobiography, the product of his years with Cosima, also indicates certain dissatisfactions: it is full of unjust recriminations—very much at variance with the expressions in his letters to them—against his friends of former years, especially the Wesendoncks. If anyone had been magnificent, it was Otto Wesendonck. It was with the assistance of money that came from him, or through him from America, for he was the European representative of a firm of New York cotton brokers, that *Tristan* had been given the world, in the years subsequent to the crisis on the Green Hill. Wagner, indeed, had formerly felt and acknowledged the magnificence. And if Wagner had been entirely happy with Cosima, he would have seen the past fairly, perhaps even with a glow upon it. Memory lights the past with gold in proportion to our present satisfaction. And the bitterness against the Wesendoncks which spots the autobiography looks dangerously like an expression of the anger against others which conceals a deal of self-reproach: in this case, a self-reproach quite possible in view of a certain solitary flight to Venice. That Cosima also was not always happy may be gathered from the fact that her diaries, too, include numerous barbs directed against Mathilde Wesendonck. Certainly she saw the man's craving for luxury increase rather more than diminish with the years.

But in a letter written in after years by Nietzsche to Georg Brandes, the philologist declared that through the pair at Triebschen, during the time of his intimate association with them, he had met "everything even halfway alive between Paris and St. Petersburg"; and to read these words is to be put once more on the track of the real story of Cosima Liszt. In those years the personality of Wagner was attaining its final power, his art beginning to exercise its eventually almost world-wide influence, Cosima's being to attain its natural measure, too, and the world commencing to recognize that in this extraordinary couple it had something with the effect of mountains. Catulle Mendès, Judith Gautier, and the aristocratic Villiers de l'Isle Adam were simply the first to visit them. Their relation was legitimated by a marriage in 1870, and Cosima now found herself free to meet the whole world in the interests of the art and the artist to whom she had given her life and who had given her herself. She had influential social connections, and it is certain that her charm and tact helped the aristocratic German world, especially the aristocratic Viennese one, over the difficulties it still had in reconciling itself to Wagner and his revolutionary music. But that Wagner even then consulted her in matters pertaining to his art is doubtful; she herself relates only one incident that shows him doing so. It seems that sometime in 1875 he played her some new music and asked her how she liked it—it was the music of the Flower Maidens—but it appears that his main purpose in exhibiting this, as Huneker called it, "valse-caresse" to her was to show her how much he desired to go to work on

DISCOVERIES OF A MUSIC CRITIC

Parsifal and drop the pot-boiler for Theodore Thomas and the Philadelphia Centennial Exercises on which he was momentarily engaged. It is certain that she was not permitted to attend the musical rehearsals for the first Bayreuth Festival. Her contribution to the success of this festival was enormous, of course. She had supervised innumerable practical details during the construction of the theater, and she now supervised many practical details relative to the production of the *Ring*—the first entire one—on its boards. She superintended the creation of the costumes—in view of their atrocious quality it probably was a pretty humiliating task. She was ready to offer up the 40,000 francs she had inherited from her mother at the moment the exhaustion of the coffers threatened to jeopardize the festivals. With her unfailing tact she prevented many a rebellious collaborator from "taking the next train" and "brushing the dust of Bayreuth forever from his feet." At the Villa Wahnfried, she had to give and superintend constant ceremonious receptions. Imperial and royal visitors attended the performances: Kaiser Wilhelm I, King Ludwig II, Dom Pedro of Brazil, the Grand Duchess of Baden, and others. Symbolists arrived from Paris to assist at the splendid wake of poetry under the pall of music. Young Germany came on a pilgrimage to a spiritual director. The triumph of Wagner's art had assumed a social significance, following as it did upon the German political triumph whose imminence it had revealed. As Cosima herself said, in reference to that festival of 1876, adopting Kundry's words, "Da diente ich!" But the rôle she played, with all the joy and the loyalty of which her great and idealistic nature was capable, was, in the words of her collaborators, that of the "property man."

And in the meantime, Cosima's very way of feeling was being modified by Wagner's. She had always been a Wagnérienne; so it is not particularly remarkable to find her, for whom religiosity of spirit and solemnity of form were the conditions of gratification, rejecting practically all other contemporory expressions in favor of Wagner's and finding *Carmen* and its "brown" music repellent and *A Doll's House* intolerable. What is, is the fact that she too was beginning to "suffer" in the Wagnerian manner and find life itself an agony —her diary is full of *Weltschmerz,* that suffering born of the imperfection of the world. She was beginning to see and feel as her own what he felt, and not merely in the way of women who unconsciously tend to grow into their lovers' ideals.—Nonetheless, it was a fairly joyous informal group that the young D'Annunzio saw on the *vaporetto* coming from the Lido on an afternoon in the early '80's, and later described in a memorable passage in *Il Fuoco:* Wagner, bareheaded at the prow of the vessel, savoring the breeze and the sea view of Venice; Liszt, benevolent, in his long soutane; and between them, tall, consummate, and serene, the wife and daughter, Cosima.

The years following Wagner's death but emphasized the nature of the relation between the heroic pair. After the death in Venice, even after the majority of their son Siegfried, she enacted the dominant rôle at Bayreuth, but to a great degree always in the interests of what she unquestionably continued to hold one of the purest consequences of spirit and a religious revelation: not only the triumphant outcome of a life of unflagging high endeavor and of struggle, but the triumphant sign that the struggle of all life itself was capable of resolution in defication and unity. Wagner had intended the Festspielhaus—possibly in the interests of the family—to retain the exclusive rights to the performances of *Parsifal* and to secure the rest of his works the correct and entire performances which other opera houses were incapable of giving them at the time; he had even seriously considered the project of rewriting *The Flying Dutchman* for Bayreuth. And Cosima cherished his intentions in the way in which Nature is said to cherish the products of spirit: as her very own; but also, alas, in a way that indicated her personal bareness of any actual capacity for initiative and experiment. Not that one could have expected anyone in her position to do other than seek a realization of Wagner's intentions—especially in view of the circumstance that he continued to the end of her days to represent loftiest genius to her. But a free spirit could not have continued to hold that these intentions had already been perfectly realized, or perfectly indicated, and that in any case it was the business of the present to conform to the letter of the past. And yet that was what the Bayreuth idea came a little to do under her sway. The performances breathed a rigid traditionalism and consecrated the frequently languid readings which Wagner had given his works during his declining years, and the costumes and the scenery—though in this matter it is possible that a solid German economy precluded innovations—remained ridiculous. In this sense, unfortunately, we owe Bayreuth to her. The somewhat hieratic ceremonial introduced by her at Wahnfried also breathes a conservatism slightly degenerating into ritual. Of course it was the ceremonial of a salon. One had to dress specially for an audience. One wasn't received unless one had been granted an appointment. One had to remain standing until bidden by the hostess to be seated. And one had to defer, infinitely, to "first-hand" knowledge; and as musicians are a very democratic lot, especially in Germany, all this proved extremely irritating to them; and the title of one of the sisters of Frederick the Great, the Margravine of Bayreuth, was surreptitiously revived for the majestic chatelaine. The semi-regal ceremonial was also observed in the drawing-rooms in Berlin and other cities which Cosima visited, generally in the intention of considering, and encouraging, candidacies for participation in the next festival. When she arrived, the company would be brought as a whole to its feet, the doors would be thrown wide, and through them Cosima, in a dress with a long train to it, would sweep in and graciously reproach someone for having played the accompaniment to *"Elsas Traum"* in a way unconformable with the true Wagnerian tradition. All this was of course very largely a consequence of her feeling of personal responsibility for a spiritual treasure and of a Bayreuth that was nothing if not a Capital of the Ideal and a refuge and an elixir for all persons with a religious feeling about life at war with the materialism of the day. And still it is impossible not to see that at more than single moments Cosima represented not so much the spirit of Wagner as that pathetic bore, "la veuve célèbre." It was not only that her "heart was in the coffin there with Caesar" and that she felt herself the relict of a god. It was that she was resting somewhat complacently upon her oars. One shudders at the report of her greeting of the young Richard Strauss at Wahnfried with "Ei, so jung und schon so *moderne!*" No German bluestocking could have trumped the bromide.

Yet simultaneously she gave people the feeling of personal grandeur, and not only as a woman for whom the highest values had an unchallengeable and ever-living virtue and a supreme magnetism, or as the extraordinary daughter of Liszt and the spouse of the magician. The impression flowed very largely from the dignity with which she met the frequently bitter attacks which came her way. Many of these were not personal: they were attacks on Wagnerism, harvest of seeds Bayreuth itself had sown. Even in Wagner's day it had become the seat

DISCOVERIES OF A MUSIC CRITIC

of a deificatory cult whose pronouncements, in the *Bayreuther Blätter* under the editorship of the harlequin Ernst von Wolzogen, the future co-founder of the artistic cabaret Das Überbrettl, had helped antagonize Nietzsche. It had known no better way of proclaiming the greatness of *Altmeister* Liszt and *Grossmeister* Wagner than by throwing off on all other contemporary musicians, especially Schumann and Brahms, and such antis as Hanslick and Joachim and Clara Schumann and Nietzsche. And the old hatreds continued to pullulate there long after the artistic battle which had called them forth was won. Everyone who came under the Bayreuth influence continues to proliferate them, from Chamberlain and Heinrich von Stein to Graf du Moulin-Eckart; and Cosima's diaries are little nests of them. Of course, the enemies replied from time to time, and not unvociferously *Das Judentum in der Musik*. This bête-noire, for example, pointed to the fact that Wagner's apparently impersonal prejudice against musicians of Jewish race was not entirely free of personal ingredients: that Wagner had periods of uncertainty when his feelings of rivalry threatened to become delusions of persecution; that he was ready to believe letters which informed him that seven thousand Jews of Breslau had sworn to have his blood; that an unacknowledged debt to Meyerbeer for generous assistance and to Heine for the whole plot of *The Flying Dutchman* rankled in his mind; and that whenever the interests of his own art impelled, he was quite prepared to modify his anti-Semitism to the point of Semitophilism. There was the incident of Hermann Levi, the son and grandson of rabbis. Levi had rapidly developed into a great conductor and was more than favorably inclined toward Wagner's music, and Wagner had declared, "I like that man: he calls himself Levi the way they did in the Bible." When, during the first rehearsals of *Parsifal*, Levi received an anonymous letter expressing regrets that a Jew should consent to conduct this piece and promptly threw down the baton, Wagner recalled him with a letter which disclaimed an exclusive connection between the piece and the Christian idea and related it to Buddhism. Thereupon Bayreuth would reply—it is possible that Cosima as well as Wagner had certain personal reasons for her anti-Semitism, for she attributed the decline of Liszt, which was so frequently brought to her attention, to her father's long association with the Princess Sayn-Wittgenstein, a woman, as the diaries and Moulin-Eckart frequently remind us, "of Jewish race"—Bayreuth, then, would declare that Cosima would have preferred that Levi should have been baptized before he conducted *Parsifal*.

But in instances, these counterattacks from the outer world, and by no means only those of *Das Judentum,* called Cosima's personal integrity savagely into question: she had somehow acquired a reputation of cleverness. The most severe of them concerned the autobiography of Wagner which was published in 1911. Nietzsche, who had seen an autobiography of Wagner's in 1869—Wagner in fact had intrusted it to him in order that he should have six copies of it privately printed in Basel—had claimed that it contained an acknowledgment of Wagner's filiation to Ludwig Geyer, the young actor who had married Wagner's mother shortly after the demise of her first husband, Wilhelm Wagner, and the posthumous birth of Richard, and with whom Richard had physically as well as spiritually identified himself all of his life. But not only did the published autobiography fail to contain this acknowledgment, but it appeared materially to differ from an earlier edition, privately circulated in 1892; and as it expressed sentiments about the Wesendoncks that varied considerably from those in Wagner's letters to them and appeared to be written in a "German that was not that of a German," the suspicion that Cosima had not only edited the original, but very largely rewritten and falsified it, was not at all gingerly aired by the press. To this imputation of fraud, Cosima made no reply: perhaps, as Newman says, "She had gone through too much in the years between 1864 and 1883 to be surprised at any baseness on the part of average humanity, or to care in the least about combating it." Not until after her death, in 1930, did the Wagner family place at the disposal of the critic of the Berlin *Lokal-Anzeiger,* Dr. Julius Kapp, a copy of the privately printed edition and permit him to compare it with the public edition and absolve Cosima of the imputed dishonesty. Only fourteen small discrepancies between the two editions came to light, the most important of those being the suppression of the lines in which Wagner relates how in November, 1863, he and Cosima "swore with sobs and tears to belong to each other alone," a suppression that might have been forgiven Cosima, in view of the fact that it threw the paternity of two of her daughters in question. At the same time, while acquitting her of having published anything materially different from what Wagner appears to have dictated to her or what she got up from Wagner's notes with Wagner's permission, the examination did not entirely convict Nietzsche of prevarication. The hypothesis that the autobiography which the honest Nietzsche saw and whose six copies have mysteriously disappeared, was a different one from the official, and that Wagner, who had once gloried in being a revolutionary and having been born in defiance of man's little laws, had later in life recast his ideas about other things than the Wesendoncks' friendship, was not entirely discredited by it, even though left the merest of hypotheses.

But we anticipate: once more, before the ugly business about the autobiography and long before her death, Cosima had the experience of becoming involved in momentous and influential work produced by someone intimately related to her, and as it were under her own wing. This was not the music of her son, Siegfried. Siegfried, like his sisters, had been given the best of educations by their mother. She had striven to open all their minds upon the great achievements of the human race. Few who ever met the son did not grasp the fact that the greatest of efforts had been expended on him to the end of developing his very mediocre gifts: he had actually for a time had the young poet-philosopher Heinrich von Stein as a private tutor. But the Wagnerian music dramas of this apprentice-sorcerer were anything but momentous and important, a fact that can indicate to those who still doubt it the truth that, inspiring as it must have been, Cosima's influence was dependent for its effect upon the existence of something creative outside herself. The work to which we refer and which played a historical rôle was the critical work of the husband of Cosima's daughter Eva, Houston Stewart Chamberlain. Chamberlain was a passionate admirer of Wagner's music and Wagner's thought. He regarded his own work as a sort of wing of his father-in-law's, and so, it appears, did Cosima. She adored this brilliant, handsome, enormously cultured, semi-invalid Englishman of French education; and Chamberlain, who came to live in Bayreuth, enjoyed the informal sanction of Bayreuth and the Wagnerian tradition. And through him Bayreuth became identified with a certain German political idea. Chamberlain believed in the existence of distinctly demarked entities which he called races, and believed that one of these races was destined to conquer the others. It was the Germanic race, the central Aryan one: the idea had come to him while he watched the German battalions advance to the invasion of France in 1870. Another member of the Wagnerian circle, the Frenchman

DISCOVERIES OF A MUSIC CRITIC

Comte Arthur de Gobineau, had had a similar idea of the superiority of the Germanic race, but he had not seen it predestined to a conquering rôle; on the contrary, he had seen in history the story of its ultimate tragic defeat. But Chamberlain also believed that the world was the progressive embodiment of God—he was a sort of evolutionary Christian and a neo-Hegelian—and thus believing that the Germanic people were predestined to conquer, he had to believe that its flesh in some way specially and messianically embodied spirit and mind and culture and everything that was good and superior. This convinction was made easy for him by his tremendous admiration for Goethe and Kant and Wagner, each of whom gave him concrete reasons for presuming that the expression of light and truth was intimately related to German blood. In fact, they seemed to him heaven-inspired prophets. In the remote distances of history he perceived a blond magnificent figure, a young Siegfried who was nothing but the original form of the luminous Germanic race, and who gradually advanced, though continually threatened by the two lateral branches of his stem, the western Celtic race and the eastern Semitic. Intermarriage with either, in particular, offered to compromise this hero's future, since it was likely to contaminate the source of his special destiny, his pure blood. But of late, his triumph seemed imminent. This appeared to Chamberlain an idea corresponding both to Wagner's *Siegfried* and to Gobineau's theory of the superiority of the Germanic race, and having written a book about Wagner, he now embodied his theory in the dazzling *Grundlagen*. He was at some pains to explain how everything that was superior, from the words of Jesus to the *Commedia* of Dante, was of Germanic origin; nonetheless, he succeeded, feeling as he did the blessings of Wagner on his efforts. That they were there is somewhat to be doubted. If we peer closely at Chamberlain's theory we shall see that it is little besides the expression of the worship of brute force and comes to an identification of God not so much with courage, magnanimity, and vitality as with the brawny six feet of the average Pomeranian grenadier. And whatever Wagner might have been, he was not a young berserker who because of his inability to project his aggressive components idealized men who could; and found himself believing that whatever wins in this world does so because of its possession of a divine essence, and erected theories of a mystical primordial race superiority. Nor would the doctors place him in quite the pathological category which the gallant Houston might seem to merit. Indeed it is quite credible that, had Wagner been able to do so, he might long since—in view of the influence that these theories, given out as the fulfillment of his own, have had upon events—have repeated the words of Nietzsche's savage telegram, "Bayreuth bereits bereut!" For after the appearance of the *Grundlagen,* Chamberlain discovered in somewhat close proximity one he felt might be destined to be the instrument of manifest German destiny.* This was Kaiser Wilhelm II. The author addressed a copy of his book to Potsdam and received appreciative words in reply from the *Allerhöchst.* The book had been a revelation: it had showed how greatly the imperial education had been neglected: they had failed to indicate (*they* were evidently the English Empress Frederick and her somewhat uxorious spouse) the Aryan source of truth. Chamberlain then wrote the Emperor that his own room was hung with the portraits of Goethe, Kant, Schopenhauer, and Wagner—he was writing about Kant and Goethe —while on the piano where the rising sun could strike it there reposed the imperial likeness in the form of a photograph

---

* See E. A. A. L., baron, Seillièrs, *Le néoromantisme en Allemagne.*

that had been sent to him bearing the imperial signature; and every evening he moved the photograph so the rays of the setting sun could illuminate it. An invitation now proceeded from the Neues Palais, and Chamberlain, sometime in 1905, traveled to Potsdam and was asked to explain his ideas to the supreme circle. After his departure, the Kaiser was delighted to be able to inform him of the progress his ideas were making. His book was being read by all the generals. It was being read by all the lieutenants. The Kaiserin was deep in it, etc. The correspondence kept up for several years. At the time of the war, it temporarily ceased; afterward it resumed with Doorn. Little was said about manifest German destiny, but much about the necessity of expunging all Semitic elements from the New Testament in order to make it represent the German people. Chamberlain was very feeble at the time; his health had been poor for several years; he was writing only about God. But before he died he had made a contact with another powerful instrument of German destiny. In 1923 a dashing young house-painter named Adolf Hitler paid a lengthy visit to Bayreuth and drank there from the source that had illumined the Kaiser.

And everything that was averse to the German Republic, from the monarchists to the race-fanatics, from the representatives of a degenerate aristocracy to those who conceived of national unity on the basis of the lowest level of intelligence; everything, in fact, that perverted the Wagnerian religion into a mad tribal idea now flocked to a Bayreuth that had become the symbol of the blackest reaction. But that this contemporary Bayreuth had any more relation to Cosima's idea than it had to Richard Wagner's is much to be doubted. Of course we do not know; the entries in Cosima's diaries of a date later than Wagner's death have not yet been published. Her mind was beclouded during her last years, but we feel—she was no fool—that long before it grew so, she realized her connection with something very different from what the cult centered in the old Guelph city had now come to represent. Wagner had intended a religion of love.—We see her once more through Cocteau's eyes. He recounts that during a revival of *La Belle Hélène,* in Munich just previous to the war, people caught sight of a stately old lady in one of the boxes, weeping. It was Cosima. As Cocteau says, it was not the *Götterdämmerung* that melted her spirits. It was the spry old music of the Second Empire that had brought the tears, and we feel that it must suddenly have called up about her days during which something wonderful that now was gone had existed; the days of Munich and Triebschen, Sorrento and Venice, carried on the flimsy wings of the "March of the Kings"; and that what she was weeping over was life, that goes and seems to take with it the gold of everything. Was it some faith, some hope, that had once been, and then been lost? We cannot say. Then, for a very last time, we see her through the eyes of an American journalist who visited her at Wahnfried toward the end, when she was very blind. He addressed her as "Mother"—he was a Middle Westerner—and we see this old lady who had assisted at the creation of *Parsifal* taking him out into the garden of the villa and there calling a bird which she had tamed. We see the bird fly to her and light on her hand. It pipes a few notes of a motiv from *Siegfried* which she has taught it. Then it flies off into the sundown; she stares after it and gently nods at the American correspondent. And we see her nodding and smiling at us, too, and read in that little dumb-show her ultimate feeling. Something it seems had once been, some idea, and had gone back into the All from which it came, and became part of it again. But there it lived, as much a portion of the cosmos as the mountains and the pines and the skies from which it was forever inextricable, and which inevitably must recall it to mankind: a musical idea the revelation of a universe that, divine throughout, sends power and suffering and light to those who represent it, and is at heart of love.

"Khovanstchina"

SINCE Strawinsky, with authority, has called Rimsky-Korsakoff's edition of *Boris Goudonow* a "Meyerbeerization" of the original, we cannot but presume that the Russian Opera Foundation's performance of Rimsky's version of *Khovanstchina*—the initial New York performance, during the winter of 1931-2—at best presented us with a Moussorgsky excessively "translated." From the words of the editor and his pupils alone we know that the orchestral version of this second of Moussorgsky's great folk music dramas—the only available one, since the composer's own score, for voices and pianoforte, still reposes unpublished in the vaults of the Public Library in Leningrad—represents a much more drastic piece of reconstruction than does that of its predecessor. In the name of a facile correctness, Rimsky had well-meaningly merely "improved" the harmony and the rhythm in *Boris* and rearranged the order of the scenes in conformity with grand-operatic traditions. But with equally good intentions he gave us in his *Khovanstchina* a stage version wanting not only a thousand-odd bars of the music in the manuscript but whole scenes, and unconformable to the tonality of the original, devoid of the

"KHOVANSTCHINA"

modulations which the editor considered "unnecessary," containing extra bars in certain choruses and new harmonies; also, fanfares extended for theatrical purposes, a re-written last act including a chorus embellished with realistic fire music and succeeded by a theatrical restatement of the steely march of the Preobrajensky guards: and, finally, orchestrated with an entire disregard of the original counterpoint and part-writing. It is even possible that some of the material which Rimsky contended he found amid Moussorgsky's sketches and worked into the uncompleted final chorus—in especial Martha's magnificent cry through the devouring flames, "Remember our ancient love!"—is not Moussorgsky's own. Strawinsky is said to have declared the beautiful phrase his master's invention. But both the actuality and the truth of this statement appear open to doubt, since the cry has a noble contour and accent entirely characteristic of Moussorgsky's music.

That to an extent Rimsky was acting merely as the composer's agent is more than probable. Moussorgsky, had he lived, might easily have cut and tightened the score, for it is incomplete, and his friends report statements indicating his intention to operate on it. And Moussorgsky did express his satisfaction with the effulgent orchestration of the ballet scene, the Persian dances, accomplished by Rimsky during his very lifetime. In any case, the question of the value of the editorial work cannot be decided before the Soviets publish and thus render generally accessible the original manuscript. Let us for our part meanwhile confess that together with the internal evidences of its bowdlerization, the score faithfully if not brilliantly performed by the Russian Opera Foundation as *Khovanstchina*, like *Boris* moves us as something magnificent and unique and utterly beyond the power of Rimsky-Korsakoff.

Like *Boris,* this folk music drama is a glowing portrait of the collective entity, the Russian people; one not only steeped in the deep colors of its subject, but executed with a feeling and a truthfulness and a power matched by no other of its musical portraitists and by only a few of the composers who have enriched the world. Like that of *Boris,* the music of *Khovanstchina* is vocal of the very essences of the people, its forces, its sense of the starkness of life, and of the inevitability of suffering, its Asiatic fatalism; and it, too, makes Moussorgsky himself appear the mere medium. The author as well as the subject seems to be the collective entity itself. The score appears to us a gigantic folk song uttering through the instrumental technique of the West a great people's semiconscious sense of its own nature: immense and childlike in its power; warm and sensitive; humorous and brutal, violent and realistic; humble as no other people of the earth, without the egocentricity of the German, the narcissism of the Latin, the cant and snobbery of the Anglo-Saxon; and predestined to endless sorrow and tragedy. One thinks of the passage in Jacques Rivière's eloquent study of *Boris* beginning: "The music of Moussorgsky is the very Russian voice. Russia, little mother—you speak to God for us.—You speak to him in your words ending in *ia* and *schka,* with your long humble phrases." In this piece too the composer's own labor appears to us the mere ordination of music pregnant with the forces of his own people in all its variety and its contrasts: music placed as it were in his hands by his own musicianly nature's comprehensive love of and utter union with his own people; sometimes in the form of traditional chants and oftener in the form of original ideas, and merely lovingly modified and adjusted and welded together by him to the end of the purer, nuder, more powerful self-expression of his people.

Some may prefer *Boris,* indubitably a more integrated work

"KHOVANSTCHINA"

of art than *Khovanstchina*. Stassov's libretto about the conspiracy of the princes Khovansky against the youthful Peter the Great, the consequent destruction of the old feudal nobility and feudal soldiery, the self-immolation of the fanatical sect of Old Believers, and the general end of the ancient Muscovy, is a much looser, duller affair than the play of Pushkin's basing *Boris*. And Moussorgsky did not, perhaps could not, pull his music together about it as in the case of the former work. None of the scenes, not even the highly effective assassination scene, is as cumulative and round as, say, the coronation and the palace interior scenes, and the scenes in the hostelry, Marina's garden, and the Forest of Kromy, in *Boris*. The various styles of music the piece embraces, original and folkloristic, liturgical, operatic and popular, are less completely fused here: certainly the voluptuous, oriental-chromatic Persian dances clash with the somewhat humbler, chaster quality of the rest of the score. Still, a preference for *Boris* appears to us much more a predilection for a particular sort of work as opposed to another sort than a predilection for a better as opposed to one on the whole inferior. *Khovanstchina* actually is a more classical work than its predecessor. Its vocal line, to begin with, is less thoroughly recitativelike, far more songlike, than that of the earlier piece. Its realism also is less extreme; the expressions of the various personages, while still very characteristic, are more generalized, more "typical," possibly because Stassov's somewhat wooden figures did not permit of highly individualized expression. While retaining all Moussorgsky's proper royalty and amplitude and its Russian inflection, the invention, too, approaches a catholic style more closely than does that of the highly individual, highly national *Boris;* the revolutionarily harmonic clashes of the bell music and the trumpets in the coronation scene or those of the hallucination scene, and the irregular time signatures of its folk scene and dances, are infrequently paralleled in *Khovanstchina*. And the beauties in this piece are scarcely less immense than those in its forerunner, or less frequent. They are possibly less stark. With the exception of the rude martial music of the Khovanskys, the music of the banishment and execution scene and some of the austere songs of Dosifei and his following of Old Believers, and the comic scene of the drunken scrivener, most of *Khovanstchina* is soft and mellow. An autumnal ripeness suffuses the deeply sweet melodies. Some of them glow like wines. And they have a grace and an elegance infrequent in Moussorgsky, something that makes one remember that he was a guardsman and a gentleman with fine manners. Melodies as light, as polished, as that of Galitzin's scene with the Tsarevna's letter, Martha's nostalgic song in Act III, those of the peasant girls in the assassination scene, and Andrei Khovansky's sorrowful lament in the last act, are without their counterpart. Russian, male, deep of mood and accent, they are closer to the common experience than Rimsky's soft and often lovely Russian music, and far more significant.

The feeling of the work, while distinct from that of *Boris,* is equally interesting. Both pieces are songs by the Russian people, of the Russian people, and both are something besides. If the first expresses the Russians' sense of their own nature, it also utters their unenthusiastic sense of Man in general. Old Vaarlam in his stews mutters grimly, ironically: "That's Man! That's lovely Man!" And the whole score seems to repeat his sorrowful phrase, at times cynically, at others tragically, at others reverently, and to exhibit the human being in his passions, in all his complexity and equivocality, his evil, suffering, ambition, cruelty, helplessness, loneliness. In *Khovanstchina* the secondary feeling is that of impending doom, world-surrender and departure. The mood and attitude were most certainly in part necessitated by the subject of the opera, as we have said a picture of the infliction by one of its forcibly westernizing rulers of many of the severe psychic traumas suffered by the people of Russia. But it is also a very personal mood of Moussorgsky's, one that haunted him in the closing years of his sad existence and which his last song cycles piercingly echo. It is the mood of a man who, left to waste his strength earning a living at a clerk's desk in a government office, feels himself unloved and rejected by life; and Moussorgsky at the end was rejected not only by his lady but by his friends, who saw in his drunkenness a betrayal of their hopes, but who themselves were thoroughly unfaithful to the artistic spirit in which the whole group of the Five had set out. The mood of a farewell haunts every bar of *Khovanstchina,* the sweet no less than the bitter ones, farewell to the passionately loved old Russia, to love and to life themselves. Sometimes the music seems to weep for births into pain and nothingness, for what might have been but never has, as well as for what has been and gone. Once, in the Persian dances, it seems to draw the veils of woman's flesh convulsively against the coming night. Oftenest, it voices the almost unutterable emotion of one who turns in going, and in a moment sees the ghastliness and the beauty of existence, and strangles with inexpressible wonder at the unfathomable thing. Other artists than Moussorgsky may have attained a similar expression *tout chargé d'adieux,* but none more consummately and more simply than himself.

DISCOVERIES OF A MUSIC CRITIC

The "Elektra" of Richard Strauss

TO hear Strauss' *Elektra* these days is to recognize the necessity of the late World War. It is to visit in full awareness the source of the slaughter: to find an intoxicated world charged with dynamite and without the inner energy to throw light on its condition and the causes of that condition and to create order.

The forces revealed by this feverish music drama are those "savage beasts," the "unbridled dynamics of the animal and the divine nature" whose co-agency in the birth of all tragic drama Nietzsche has pointed out to us: the "frenzy which dissolves the individual into his collective instincts," the "intoxication which makes him delight in the annihilation of the principle of individuation," the very most "disgusting alloy of lust and cruelty." Throughout its course, again and again we are made conscious of the dangerous existence of an energy ready at the flare of a match to dilate dionysiacally in an intoxication of the mind like that produced by the most potent alcohol, and issue in an orgy of death and deadly triumph. It smolders, spits, and darts tongues of flame almost incessantly in the verbal and the mimetic and musical expressions of its personages, repeatedly prefiguring its desired goal. The characters dwell on carnage, and the pantomime no less than the words frequently paints the way of slaughter, till we almost see the color of blood, and smell it too.

Hofmannsthal's compact, powerful drama, "freely after Sophocles," presents us with an Electra deliriously anticipating,

THE "ELEKTRA" OF RICHARD STRAUSS

amid feelings and conditions of intolerable degradation, the funeral rites of the murdered Agamemnon and the funereal slaughter of stallions and slaves. With the noise of dragged burdens, cracking lashes, smothered outcries, servants are seen lugging animals across the rear of the stage toward the propitiatory holocaust commanded by Clytemnestra. We find Electra craftily telling the drugged, depraved, decaying queen that only the sacrifice of a woman can appease the gods weighing heavily upon her being, and then, when the hate between mother and daughter shows its face, crying out to her that the woman to be offered is Clytemnestra herself. At the false report of Orestes' death, we observe Electra throw herself upon Chrysothemis, promising to enslave herself to this younger sister if Chrysothemis will but help kill their mother and her paramour; then, when Chrysothemis escapes into the house, dig in the earth with her own claws to recover the ax with which their father was slain. Following the appearance of the noble but sinisterly vengeful Orestes, we hear the hideous outcries of the stricken Clytemnestra and see Electra light the doomed Aegisthus to his end with poisonous irony, and at the moment his terrified face appears at the window screaming for help, triumphantly scream back at him, "Agamemnon hears thee!" Chrysothemis, beside herself, reports "courtyards filled with the heaped bodies of the slain, and survivors spattered with blood and full of wounds, and radiant, and embracing each other, and jubilating." Electra cries:

> Die Tausende, die Fackeln tragen
> und deren Tritte, deren uferlose
> Myriaden Tritte überall die Erde
> dumpf dröhnen machen, alle warten sie
> auf mich: ich weiss doch, das sie alle warten,

DISCOVERIES OF A MUSIC CRITIC

> weil ich den Reigen führen muss, und ich
> kann nicht, der Ozean, der ungeheure,
> der zwanzigfache Ozean begräbt
> mir jedes Glied mit seiner Wucht, ich kann mich
> nicht heben!

In unendurable excess of joy, she dances a "nameless dance" and falls dead.

And gloomy and lurid of hue, violent in movement and domineering in accent and gesture, the score simultaneously articulates hateful energy with a power and to a degree that prompt one to call the work the music of fatal exasperation and hysteria. There too the intoxication advances relentlessly to its release in a deadly expansion, meanwhile giving forth, as in the drama, symbols of its aim. Out of a sinister silence, the music mutters up, filling the scene with ominous tension. Whips and chains figure amid the immense aggregation of instruments called for by the score, and time and time again the whole musical organism lashes and thunders malevolently, or shrieks, or wails, or howls, morbidly laments or foams dangerously upward. The blows upon the timpani seem each to strike a man dead. The very shape of the theme of the passage in which Electra exults in prophetic visions of Agamemnon's holocaust conveys the spirit of the deadly blow: its short ascent precipitates a dynamic declension, like that of a viciously trampling hoof. The syncopes of the music accompanying the heavy train of animals to the sacrifice are equally brute, guttural, unendurable. Then, at the moment when the dazed Electra recognizes the brother whom she had believed dead, the orchestra bursts forth ferociously screaming. And the corybantic finale conveys the insurgence of energy flooding

THE "ELEKTRA" OF RICHARD STRAUSS

uncontrollably aloft and shattering the walls of the human tenement that had contained it.

These deadly forces are not the inhabitants exclusively of opera houses or of the private worlds of two artists. They are the essences which actualized themselves in the World War. This, before us, already is the World War, the machine guns, the T.N.T., the mass-murder. This is its crater. Red and black, the stage with its plethora of shrieks, screams, groans, and the sounds of dragged bodies and laboring whips, epitomizes a period, the one immediately preceding the inception of the catastrophe, around 1907, permitting us to revisit it in thorough awareness. It is an overloaded, hysterical one, immense in technical prowess, but luxurious, crass, fat, materialistic, satiated, incapable of sublimation, stewing with explosives that wear the steel caps of projectiles. (How inevitable that it should have discovered for itself African art and its fearful, death-signifying masks!) And, crater of this crater of the festering energies of the civilized man craving release in deadly expansion, we recognize, alas, the home. Greek décor notwithstanding, the red and black stage and the masterless woman-ménage it contains is an interior in Berlin or Charlottenburg or any large city of the period; and the whole explosive visibly cooks and seethes in the family circumstance. We know these steel-capped energies, "the frenzy which dissolves the individual into his collective instincts," the very most "disgusting alloy of lust and cruelty," to a tremendous degree the transformations of the prisoned creative energy; and its prisoner and poisoner the unhappy relationships conditioned by the institution of the family: particularly the incestuous attraction that is itself a consequence of the struggle for personal supremacy in the house and over the children—the struggle between father and mother. Passed augmentedly on from generation to generation, it breeds ever new prisonerships, ever new deadly entaglements between parents and children, sons and daughters. And, mangled by these terrible internal wars, directed toward forbidden objects and threatened by incest and homosexuality, the creative force streams nakedly before us toward the generation of death, its sole possible outlet. Electra herself is conscious of the poisoner: mournfully she informs Orestes that her virginity,

> diese süssen Schauder
> hab' ich dem Vater opfern müssen. Meinst du,
> wenn ich an meinem Leib mich freute, drangen
> nicht seine Seufzer, drang sein Stöhnen nicht
> bis an mein Bette? Eifersüchtig sind
> die Toten: und er schickte mir den Hass,
> den hohläugigen Hass als Bräutigam.
> Da musste ich den Grässlichen, der atmet
> wie eine Viper, über mich in mein
> schlafloses Bette lassen, der mich zwang
> alles zu wissen, wie es zwischen Mann
> und Weib zugeht.

Nonetheless, it is not only *Elektra's* revelation of the existence of these terrible forces in the period immediately prior to the outbreak of the war and their hotbed in the institution of the family that sends us from performances of the music drama convinced of the ineluctable necessity of the explosion and the carnage. Simultaneous with the direct revelation of the swell of dionysiac forces in that world, the work indirectly reveals to us the insufficiency, there, of power able to control them.

That which is able to control, regulate, and order the dio-

THE "ELEKTRA" OF RICHARD STRAUSS

nysiacally dilating forces in the individual and in society is intuition, itself a function of the concentrated and suspended libido. Intuition not only places itself in the inner realm of life itself, the realm of the forces, but illuminates that realm brilliantly and clearly identifies its components, unveiling them in all of their complexity and in all their subtle articulations and relations. Intuition apprehends the ideas, themselves symbols of the nature and reality of these warring forces in the interior of life, and with the clearest representation of these ideas, either in the medium of art or in other media, indicates and prophesies the trend of events and establishes a basis for intelligent action, for liberation, above all, from "the unbridled dynamics of the animal and divine nature," and for freedom and control in general. "Wherever thought is wholly wanting, or the power to act and forbear according to the direction of thought, there necessity takes place," Locke said. This brilliantly enlightening and controlling principle Nietzsche called Apollo —Apollo indeed being the god of light in the form of sun, of prophecy, of art and medicine; and by internal evidence *Elektra* shows that precisely the dionysiac forces, those of the "grape," of earth, and of instinctive life, were overpowerful in the immediate pre-war world—positivistic, scientific, and filled with ignorance of the boundless importance of the intuitive, the metaphysical illumination as it was. For *Elektra* is not a supremely clear and organic work of art. If it does with considerable power lay hold on and represent the forces of the world and in part define their interdependence and relationship, its illumination and definition is neither the clearest or the completest. There is a certain dimness here, as of fear: that we fully identify and measure these forces and recognize their source and their direction is due to a certain extent to lights other than those cast by the two authors; among them the luminosity most expensively purchased through experience of the actual catastrophe.

True, these forces and their idea are presented with a degree of clarity sufficient to indicate the existence, at least in the decade anterior to the outbreak of the conflict, of some intensity of insight, and with it of some power to control the wild forces of inner and of outer nature. We have said that Hofmannsthal's drama identified the "savage beasts," as baleful transformations of a tangled libido and related them to the erotic fixations in the parental circle more definitely than ever any of the Greeks did. This illumination probably was relayed by him from its source in the cabinet of Dr. Freud. This is certain, that in 1900, in his *Traumdeutung*, Freud had named one form of the fixated libido the Oedipus complex; that shortly after, one of his followers, Jung perhaps, had called another of these complexes the Electra; and that the discoveries of these psychologists had awakened enormous interest in the intellectual Viennese circles in which Hofmannsthal moved. One can see the effect of these discoveries in the stories of Schnitzler, and it seems certain that Hofmannsthal's subsequent orientation toward Greek drama—so irritating to some of his contemporaries—and his reconception and reconstitution of some of these tragedies with Freudian intuitions—first the *Electra* of Sophocles, then an *Oedipus und die Sphinx*, and last the *Alcestis* of Euripides—was equally consequent on them. We have already quoted from the passage in which his *Electra* confesses the connection of her hatred of her mother with her obsession by an image of her dead father almost amorously possessive and jealous of her love; and in his *Oedipus und die Sphinx*, Jocasta exclaims to the hero:

THE "ELEKTRA" OF RICHARD STRAUSS

> Selig
> die dich getragen hat. Sag' mir den Namen
> der Mutter, die dich trug! Ich will sie ehren
> wie keine Göttin,

and he replies:
> Nichts von der Mutter!
> Dies alles hängt nicht mehr an mir. Ich hab' mich
> mit Schwerteshieben losgelöst. Der Oedipus,
> der vor dir steht, ist seiner Taten Kind
> und diese Nacht geboren,

and again:
> Um dich,
> die mir kein Traum gezeigt, hab' ich die Jungfraun
> verschmäht in meiner Jugend Land;

and then with all the force of her most secret longing in her eyes, Jocasta answers softly, tenderly:

> O Knabe,
> bist du's, um den ich sterben wollte, wenn's mich
> hinunter zog zu meinem Kind?

It seems doubtful whether any of these speeches, tragic in their irony but ironical through a wisdom different from the Greeks', could have been written had Freud's intuitions not previously gained currency.

And still we see that neither could Freud project his light brilliantly into Hofmannsthal nor Hofmannsthal throw it brilliantly upon his ideas. We find Hofmannsthal expressing the forces and ideas to which Freud's intuitions had directed him in forms not truly or completely representative of them. What Freud had indicated to Hofmannsthal was the baleful energies of the modern man, the consequences of his familiar fixations and blind repressions, not those of Mycenaean or Boeotian Greeks; and Hofmannsthal's insertion of the symbols of these essences into the framework of the antique tragedies and expression of them through hybrid figures, part Greek and part modern, and through a form which jumbled primitive forms with others preciously expressive of a purely modern nervousness, constituted something of a miscarriage and compromised his vision. The German critics who affirmed that his reversion toward the Greeks was a mistake were instinctively right. It is also doubtful that he entirely understood the relation between the instability of European society felt by everyone about him, in particular the infirmity of the Austrian Empire—itself very largely contributory to the morbidity of the whole Viennese circle and the poison generated by the domestic imbroglio. No doubt he partly felt it: in his next drama, a free re-creation of Otway's *Venice Preserved* (*Das gerettete Venedig*), he significantly associates the sickness of a state with the Beardsleyesque erotic mess of fin-de-siècle Europe. But the very form of *Elektra* shows that, at the time of its creation, his understanding of the connection was still vague.

For its part, the score—by the musician most in sympathy with the time, most representative of it—powerfully reinforces the lesson of Hofmannsthal's drama. It has qualities of greatness; certainly it is Strauss' strongest piece and incidentally his most prophetic, prefiguring much of the music of the generation of composers immediately successive to his own: in such violent and lurid passages as the laboring, stammering one that accompanies the heavy train of animals to the sacrifice, the brutal, cubistic music of the early Strawinsky and of Ornstein, and in so nervously jittering a page as that in which Clytemnestra questions Electra a deal of the "middle" Schönberg. Always the supreme dramatist, here in his appointed realm, the the-

THE "ELEKTRA" OF RICHARD STRAUSS

ater, Strauss' natural bent has evolved a piece in some respects a summit of dramatic expression. It articulates many of the oftentimes horrible essences of the drama with an audacious realism and frequently tersely, compactly, and with a force, a virtuosic orchestration, a contrapuntal art equaled neither by its predecessor, the relatively sleepy *Salomé,* or its successor, the gay and hybrid *Rosenkavalier.* In spots, notably during Electra's funeral incantation, during Clytemnestra's horrid triumph over her daughter after her reception of the false news of the death of Orestes, and at the moment of Electra's recognition of her brother in the male whose mere presence has brought a momentary calm into the seething cauldron of hates, it seems to have a forcefulness greater even than that of Wagner at his strongest. And it is built up on large lines, and in square blocks contrastingly dissonant and consonant, chromatic and diatonic, now realistic and now formal. And yet its expression is sometimes cheap and weak, its force inconstant, and its apparent orderliness superficial, indicating thus the infrequency of a concentration of really creative energy in the composer. We have acknowledged that the score has considerable musical worth, certainly more of it than any other opera by Strauss and perhaps more of it even than the best of his tone poems, *Don Quixote.* The ominous opening, the quiet beginning of Electra's invocation of the murdered Agamemnon, the puissant music of Clytemnestra's hateful triumph and departure, even the somewhat Tchaikowskianly plangent music of the beginning of the scene between the brother and sister or the slightly childish melody that sounds while the pair embrace, have a certain fullness and majesty. But even at its best, in Electra's invocation, their quality is never a fine and distinguished one; the music wants both the purity and the arabesque of the best music. And these pages, of a quality that is scarcely prime, are offset, to begin with, by others that are conventional. Not only is the ironic music of the scene between Electra and Aegisthus fairly reminiscent of that of Siegfried's final parley with Mime, but some of the descriptive and mimetic elements of the score resemble less developments or expansions of Wagnerian ideas than conventional reproductions of them: for example, the trumpet calls symbolic of royal personality or descent. But this is not serious in comparison to the fact that the rare beautiful pages are also combined with coarse and vulgar ones, abject and corrupt in their banality. With its 6/4 measure the final cantilena verges, as is so often the case with Strauss' dithyrambic pages, dangerously upon a common waltz. And the music of the two scenes between the sisters does not verge upon the *walzerisch:* it *is walzerisch,* or rather, *ländlerisch,* and cheaply so to boot. We are not far, during Chrysothemis' declaration of her desire for the experience of maternity or Electra's embrace of the young woman, from the slow waltzes of *Der Rosenkavalier.* True, these pages are justified to a degree by their diatonicism, which contrasts with the dissonant chromaticism of the flanking sections, the whole score being built up on this scheme of contrasts. But they are unjustified in their vulgarity, and they are just as untruthful as they are banal, failing as they do to express with any quality the essence of the situations to which they are coupled, and constituting a kind of brutal glancing-off, at best a cruel and corrupt ironization of the motives of the two pitiable characters. All in all, the score is a half-expression.

Thus we recognize the imperfect operation of the regulative principle in the world of the late 1900's: for had it been perfect, we would have had an *Elektra* a far greater work of art than the one we have. (For Hofmannsthal and Strauss were artists

THE "ELEKTRA" OF RICHARD STRAUSS

deeply and acknowledgedly, sensitive and representative of their epoch.) And the reception the work received but bears out our idea. *Elektra* excited great interest. Even though Strauss had ceased constituting the subject of the kind of critical battles his chief tone poems had excited, he was still the contemporary composer most highly visible to the musical world, the author of sensations and wonders; and the scandal of his performance of the *Sinfonia Domestica* in the Wanamaker Auditorium in New York, and the sadistic subject of *Salomé* had thoroughly spread his fame. The Strauss week in Dresden in January, 1909, which featured the lately completed *Elektra,* actually constituted an international event, Germans being by no means the only people attracted to it. "All Europe is here!" the *portier* of Hermann Bahr's hotel proudly informed the visiting Viennese critic. And "all Europe"—critics and public alike—was without understanding of the work's significance and portent even while revealing, through the disturbance it engendered, an unconscious sense of it. There was a great flutter concerning the "horrors" exposed in it and the "unbridledness" of something, probably the expressivity; and everyone remarked on the unendurable "dissonateness" of the style and the shocking vulgarity of some of the tunes. But here, too, fear and intoxication prevailed: here, too, there was inner complicity. The omens were unseen, or ignored. One perceives it in the case of Hermann Bahr. Bahr was perfectly familiar with Nietzsche's theories of the womb and the components of tragic art and aware that tragedy itself is a "metaphysical miracle," the child of the control of the "savage beasts of nature" through the expressive power of the energy of light and beauty. He was the author of a *Dialog vom Tragischen* embodying a wisdom developed in part from Nietzsche's *Die Geburt der Tragödie:* and in Dresden in January, 1909, he connected the "horrors" in *Elektra* with something out in the world and permeating his Europe itself. His charming journalistic account of the week and the performance, later republished by him in his volume of *Essays,* conveys this hunch and at the same time reveals the superficiality of this earnest critic's vision and understanding, indeed making us feel as if his ratiocination had, at the bidding of a secret devil, muddled and miscarried his intuitive findings. Bahr was troubled by what he saw in Dresden, to the point of calling the atmosphere of the comfortable old city *wunderlich*. Observing the nervous swarming of the cosmopolitan throng about Herr Generalmusikdirektor Strauss of Berlin, he recognized a hellish dance. He studied the composer's face and described the mouth as "weak, feminine, secretive—and darkly haunted by all manner of chicanery, tenderness, weariness, sadness, dangerous cunning and malignant wishes." What he heard in the opera house the night of *Elektra* called to his mind the whole "questionableness" of this epoch: reminding him of its hybris born of a limitless feeling of power, that tempted it to play with all sorts of dangers; its barbaric defiance leading it to break all laws and luring it back into chaos; its bitter contempt of itself and mad self-love; its utter confidence in the omnipotence of technics and its immedicable, poverty-stricken yearning for some sort of simple, tranquil, unbroken feeling. But he returned happy to Vienna. The performance had filled him with joy: "Mir war's ein herrlicher abend!" He had felt a nameless spiritual blitheness, a continuous inner ebullition, a radiancy in all senses and nerves like that of one who, having attained a summit, sees about him abysses which he no longer has to fear and lifts his feet in Dionysiac dance. This was "what Nietzsche had prescribed for himself, and merely been unable to find." The music had filled him with pride "in the human power to bring

THE "ELEKTRA" OF RICHARD STRAUSS

the horrors of the poem to expression." Expression itself has beauty! And Strauss' blue eyes were wonderfully childlike, and his accent was ever his native Bavarian. And it was merely snobbery that talked about the cheapness of the composer's tunes. As for the hellish stew of the cosmopolitan throng about Strauss, it was purely symptomatic of the poverty of the rich, who never had any experiences of their own and turned to music to gain them. Only one wish remained: that folk in Vienna might some day enjoy an experience of the sort he had just enjoyed.

We perceive that the concierge of Bahr's hotel was right. All Europe was there: the handful of it that came and the myriad heaps that remained at home in their chancelleries, countinghouses, newspaper offices, places of business, schoolrooms, homes. They were all there. But where they all were, the cruel Huns and the rest, was not so much Dresden as the edge of the trenches.

D'Indy

ONE cannot resist the conviction that, were the Germans a truly musical people, long before 1914 they would have known that the French were not decadent. D'Indy's pungent *Symphony on the Song of a French Mountaineer* would, almost unassisted, have been able to apprise them of it.

The crisp, brilliant, and racy little cyclic symphony has the healthiest of contents. Like its immediate successor among D'Indy's compositions, *Le Chant de la Cloche,* it is a little

DISCOVERIES OF A MUSIC CRITIC

French *Meistersinger*, and thus potentially a warning to boys of other nations to beware! It is a brief but thrilling, racy, and triumphant reflection of powerful national forces in progressive unity as the completeness of the most intimate of experiences revealed them in the 1880's to a delicate, patrician French composer: the progressive unity of the forces of his native Cevenole mountains and of an aspiring, idealistic energy that all mountains sometimes free and make one feel, and of the virile people root-fast among them—here, by inevitable extension, those of all of France. It begins with a pure, nasal, lapidary expression of the surging force that is like the mountains' and makes one feel mountains. Like them, it rises from the dark depths of cool valleys, and climbing steeply, glows and glitters like rocky summits played upon by the light of rising suns. But from the first it is not only the feeling of the mountains that the scintillant expression conveys. There is also the fervid feeling of a beloved person amid them, and the tender second movement seems to bring us close to her, in all her reserve, beauty, and strength. This subtly varied theme is "she," as Mozart said of some of his own pieces: it is "Madame" —Madame and the relation between her essence and the virile force, here deeply passionate and almost soldierly, too, in the way of the French. And the joyous, popular third movement, in the terms of the old parlor game, is "the consequences." It expresses the life of the people themselves, with its sturdy, salty, humorous, rooty character: the continuous, progressive life of the race itself, in its men, its women and children; now felt and known, loved and shared. There are virile fellows here, salty, earthy, humorous mountaineers in hobnailed boots, men in a common march, and something that is like the moon and gives the feeling of mysterious seductive distances; and a fanaticism for *la revanche*; and piping children. There is a

D'INDY

dance of males, rough, positive, jocose—not without the triumphant crow of the cock who has achieved life and given and received it. The men draw the women with them in a waltz and whirl them toward an infinity. At the close there is a flourish of lusty fists, in concord.

But, of course, *diese schrecklichen Dissonanzen!* Yes, of course the style is dissonant, like that of the whole French symphonic school, the school of César Franck. They got the habit of dissonance and continual modulation largely from Wagner—Wagner who correctly prophesied that he would be understood best in France. Perhaps they abused the technique. But neither the music of the *Symphony on the Song of a French Mountaineer* nor that of D'Indy's other major works is about a disorder.

Still, we cannot afford to mock. The Germans were not the only ones who did not appreciate D'Indy. Not many did, anywhere; and their number still is small. Indeed, the musical world is still prone to perpetuate the old and hoary mistake that represented D'Indy as a sort of minor Franck and the relationship between him and his teacher as that of disciple and leader; and that is but another way of indicating ignorance of D'Indy's veritable and sizable and independent creative energy, and of the individual content of his expression.

True, as a young man, D'Indy for a number of years was a pupil of the venerable Belgian composer. True, he derived from his teacher a revelation of musical art and the spirit of the artist that was decisive; that awoke in him a love of his master and his master's work and an active sense of responsibility toward the two which ended only with his own life. True, also, that D'Indy developed in his own work forms he recognized and admired in Franck's. But it is no mere indication of this relationship that the musical world intends in calling D'Indy the disciple. The statement actually is a judgment of the relative merits of the work of the two men: one unfavorable to those of the younger man, deriving a specious support from the fact that D'Indy for a while was Franck's pupil, and always his apostle. And that judgment of ultimate value is a mistaken one.

It is not true that of the two men it was Franck who was the more creative and D'Indy the more assimilative: that Franck possessed the energy that brings forth new forms and styles freighted with new experience to a greater degree than D'Indy, or that D'Indy exploited the cyclic symphonic form and the trick of continual modulation which he found in Franck to the end of expressing experiences naturally much less interesting and vital than his teacher's—producing the less important, vital, durable work.

That D'Indy for his part did not dispose of an unlimited creative energy is undeniable. One cannot overlook the fact that he was at times incapable of dyeing his material with the clear quality of an experience. Some of his material remains reminiscent of Franck or of Wagner; witness the second variation in the first movement of the G Minor piano Sonata and the second section of the theme of the last movement of the violin Sonata. Other bits are quite banal: the coda of the first movement of the B Flat Symphony, the finale of the *Istar Variations,* the scherzo of the G Minor piano Sonata. His style was always heterogeneous, and there appear to have been moments when his feeling was actually nonexistent. D'Indy was a masterly though sometimes harsh contrapuntalist, but at instants, as in the slow movement of the *Sinfonia di Bello Gallico,* the melody disappears in a tangle of crabbed counterpoint; at others, it seems as though we were catching the composer, who detested the music of Max Reger, rivaling the German pedant in the production of paper music apparently designed for the entertainment of future analysts.

His form, moreover, does not always appear inevitable. That the cyclic symphony was germane to D'Indy is indubitable. His first symphony, the *Cevenole,* which was written during the years Saint-Saëns and Franck both were working at their more famous illustrations of the form, remains one of the happiest, freshest works in the cyclic category. And even the divertissements for small groups of instruments which the aging D'Indy wrote under the influence of the neoclassicism of the post-war years still combine their material in accordance with the principle. Yet there is reason to believe D'Indy to a degree superimposed it on some of his material, that of the B Flat Symphony in particular. That admirable composition suffers from the inclusion of passages of music based on the germinal themes and designed to unify the symphonic edifice, but actually so abstract as to be without meaning. The form of the symphonic variations, *Istar,* seems equally forced. The variations precede a theme, a scheme true perhaps to certain psychological situations, but not justified in this case by the musical result, a set of variations without augmentative interest and leading to the anticlimactic appearance of the motive.

Again, D'Indy's modulations, even more incessant than Franck's, prompt one at times to cry "Hold, enough!" They seem so habitual at moments, so unnecessary and unjustified. So, too, do his occasionally very laborious expansions of musical "cells."

As a whole, his work is a trifle one-sided, frequently wanting a popularity, a lightness perfectly balancing its austerity and heaviness, and an elementalism perfectly balancing its cerebral control. Nonetheless, its merits are multiple, and enormous.

It comprises a number of compositions, the G Minor piano

Sonata, at least in its exterior movements, the violin Sonata, the little *Cevenole* Symphony, and innumerable passages in many compositions including the B Flat Symphony and the tripartite symphonic poem *A Summer Day on the Mountains,* formed very largely of material beautifully modeled and infused with individually lofty and tender, magnanimous and sensuous thought and feeling. In these compositions the form is germane to the material. D'Indy for all his difficulties was a born symphonist; before his work the contention that the mold is foreign to French musicians falls to the ground. He had the quality of mind requisite to the symphony: the capacity to feel extremely intricate ideas, to organize and develop his material in harmony with them, and to control the intricate formal and tonal relation of part to part. Despite its evidences of the fetichistic superimposition of the cyclic idea, the B Flat Symphony remains an admirable piece of symphonic organization and the E Minor Sonata one of the glories of its class. It was that here his energy was free, and freely and completely materialized the subtle essences affinitive to himself, and gave him the power to grasp their intricate relationships entirely. And, like those of the *Cevenole,* these essences and ideas are those affinitive to very idealistic persons, kindred perhaps to the aristocratic bourgeoisie of the Third Republic, not altogether free of a slight vulgarity, but responsive upon very high levels. They have a certain narrowness and an involvement, as of things diffident and beset with doubts, and a certain stiffness and a monkish austerity; but they are also tender and rich, aspiring and idealistic, and in some sort of recurrent springtime break out, as in the marvelous last movement of the E Minor Sonata with its fresh and flowery material, and grow majestic and broad and passionate. The majestic, tremendously affirmative chorales that crown some of D'Indy's symphonic

D'INDY

edifices reveal like the little *Cevenole* Symphony their ultimate harmony and unity in faith and love. And the communicative forms themselves have their intricacy and their dignity, wonderfully clearly. The fabulously fine and perfectly structural detail has all the delicacy and firmness of the rarest goldsmith work.

If anything, the best music of D'Indy is superior to the best of Franck. The feeling of life communicated by it, true, is very like that communicated by the Belgian. It is the feeling of those who, fundamentally in harmony with the principle of things, and naturally possessed of faith in God and man and self and love of earth, and at odds with a dissonant milieu, are periodically inspired to the rapturous song of faith and love by surges of energy putting them in contact with the grand, faith and love begetting ideas and sensations, things and beings. But D'Indy apparently touched a world wider than Franck's, furnished with a greater number and a higher order of forces than his master's, furnished with high sensuous beauty, natural loveliness, and warmest love, above all with ennobled human substance and high goals that shed the power lifting the eyes to ever higher aims. To hear his firm, clear, serenely and passionately affirmative music is to feel the fire of courage recharging the spirit and the tongue unloosed in giving gravely fervent thanks for life and manhood, for loyal, chaste, deep love, and for a thousand natural beauties—the light on mountain tops, the friendly silent radiance of the moon, the peace of the tracts below, and the voices of sturdiness, gaiety and sweetness ascensive from Nature and her children. It is to know a cosmic order conformable to man's noblest capacity of response; to know, as one intimately connected with her, earth's perfect faith and love-engendering cargo of things: the tough, good, jolly underpinning of root-fast humanity; grand natural objects and high goals of life; and earth's loyalty to these high things and experiences and their full expressions.

This is not said to belittle the product of the composer of the *Prelude, Chorale, and Fugue:* merely to indicate how high among the composers of the second order the Frenchman's music actually stands. D'Indy's has all the virtues of Franck's, the sweetness, the subtle harmonizations, the deep sincerity, the clear ordinations; has them merely to a higher degree, for his harmony is if anything richer and less cloying than Franck's, his structure if anything more logical and complex. He has greater variety of expression. Altogether, his music is less heavy than Franck's, much more rhythmical and motory. His orchestra is not an exalted church organ but a true band, idiomatically treated, given a wonderful scintillance and a very individual, curiously French, pleasantly nasal tone. And his expressions are not, like Franck's, permeated with evidences of a latent, languishing eroticism, nor of an equally suppressed and disavowed arrogance and pride. Grand seigneur though he was, D'Indy was actually the humbler man of the two. Astringent in even the sweetest of its lyrical passages, dignified in its exaltation, tender and chaste and decent in its most passionate expressions, hard of edge like finely tempered metal, his music is really the more virile.

It would seem as though D'Indy actually fell very slightly short of gaining the front rank of musicians. What he probably lacked was the unlimited energy requisite to complete imaginative sympathy with all the essences of life, small as well as great, coupled with the clear perception of their relative places in the scheme of vital values, that is the secret of limitless creative power. For the possessors of that force, these essences exist mutually nonexclusively side by side, exerting various degrees of magnetism by virtue of their differences of gravity, intensity, luminosity, and inclusiveness. D'Indy's sympathy however was always somewhat partial—one feels it in the relative one-sidedness of his music; perhaps even at times nonexistent—one feels it in the bald and crabbed spots of his work. Nor was his hierarchy of values always natural. There would seem to have been a conflict in his mind between the claims of the smaller and the larger manifestations which was resolved only with the help of the illusion that a special sanction attached itself to the latter, that the expressions of the greater essences possessed truth and beauty exclusively as compared with light; that the work of Bach, Beethoven, Wagner, and Franck constituted eternal models; and that catholicism was exclusively the trait of Roman Catholics. Certainly the occasionally arbitrary character of his grandiose forms points to some such compulsive ideas, as does the dogmatism of the musical doctrines which he expounded at the Schola Cantorum, with their unfairness to Mozart, Schubert, Brahms, their damnation of light music, Protestantism, opéra comique, Berlioz, the compositions of Semites, and nearly all work not couched in the frequently heavy style derived from the four fathers of D'Indy's musical church.

And still, if he remains a French composer in the sense that Beethoven is not a German one, and occasionally was an aristocrat in the way the truest aristocrats are not, he still sympathetically expressed some of the noblest forces of French life and shared its sturdiness, its dignity, its fine earthiness and reasonableness and grace. And for all his conflicts he was a really austere artist, incessantly attracted from the meaner, smaller impulses and emotions and expressions toward the larger, more inclusive and illuminated ones, and worked in utter sincerity and conscientiousness.

DISCOVERIES OF A MUSIC CRITIC

His music would seem destined to endure as long as men with fine capacities for faith and love find the world a thicket. That its value has as yet not quite generally been recognized would seem to be due to the mere circumstance that it demands an unusual intellectual effort of its audiences, an unusual capacity to carry forms in the imagination, and that it makes considerable demands of technical prowess of its interpreters. And as both the intellectual capacity of musical audiences and the technical abilities of instrumentalists grow continually, it would seem that the very near future would definitely recognize the beauty of D'Indy's best music and its high message.

The Place of Ravel

NOT even at the time when his *Miroirs* succeeded Debussy's *Images*, his *Rapsodie Espagnole* the magician's *Ibéria*, and *Ma Mère l'Oye, Le Coin des Enfants*, was it discriminative to see the mere follower in Ravel. The Fincks did say of his work, "It's by Ravel; therefore it's like Debussy," while rival composers foresaw the future's label of "school of" upon his sober little pieces. The fact nonetheless was that from the first Ravel's sensitive, graceful, and ironic art had a personal profile. True, the composer began as a musical impressionist and symbolist, eloquent of the impact of a fluid, flickering, inconstant world upon his own psyche and of the mysterious gestures of the unconscious—*petites sensations,* as Leibnitz called them. And musical impressionism and symbolism were Debussy, their most richly gifted representative, to a degree that made late

THE PLACE OF RAVEL

adherents of the movement perforce appear his disciples. Yet the group as a whole flowed directly from Wagner. Several of its distinctest hallmarks, its feeling of the nervous movement of life, its sensitiveness to the latent, the indefinite, and the infinite, its delicate pantheism and responsiveness to the correspondences between the human psyche and the essence of inanimate things, and its excessively idiomatic use of orchestral timbres, particularly the luminous and opalescent ones, figured in *Tristan,* the *Ring,* and *Parsifal.* Ravel was as legitimately in the Wagnerian succession as Debussy himself or any other Frenchman.

True, Ravel's music, when it appeared, did exhibit the dominance of the harmonic over the melodic principle, the consecutive sevenths and ninths and the successive complex chords blent by the pedal, so specially typical of Debussy before Ravel reached the public. So too, however, did the pieces of the veteran Fauré and those of Charles Martin Loeffler, Cyril Scott, and the coeval rest of the musical symbolists. The traits were common property of the movement. And while perhaps none of the pieces of the other members of the group approximated the sensitiveness of form, the noble reserve, the penetrating sensuousness of those of Debussy and their feeling of enchantment and of doubt as closely as such compositions of our musician as his piano Sonatine, his String Quartet, and the latter and better two of the three numbers of the Suite for piano, *Gaspard de la Nuit,* the parallelism was to be ascribed to a certain similarity of temperament, an exquisiteness, a preference for the solitude of the ivory tower, a Latin reserve, rather more than to the younger man's discipleship; particularly in view of the fact that in certain regards the two bodies of work were sharply antithetical. Ravel's style, from the very commencement, had much more of classic rigidity than Debussy's excessively fluid, arabesque one. His preferences for the classic structures, the closed molds, over the freer, less formally textured ones, was promptly announced by his Sonatine, strict in its form, and inclusive of a minuet. And while the older man's art was markedly lyrical and tender, that of the younger, even in those days, was given to witticism and irony, and as the years passed, increasingly so. It can be said that Debussy was a sensuality and a sensibility: Ravel, a sensuality and a sensibility doubled by a sense of the ridiculous. Certainly we find the latter ironizing feeling in *Histoires Naturelles,* and almost more the slightly superior spectator than the dancer in *Valses Nobles et Sentimentales,* and cynical in that *Palais-Royal* Spanish scene, *L'heure Espagnole.*

No, the composer had a distinct individuality even before he entirely broke with impressionism and symbolism, as he did after the end of the war. Yet if it was rash to deny that independence, how much more rash it was to allow Ravel any great eminence or representativity, or to attribute a tremendous virtue and a high excellence to his product! And still, that is precisely what numerous musicians and members of the musical public, including the present writer, did do. Ravel, they said, was the bigger spirit: while Debussy stood upon the bank, Ravel waded in. And he was the sturdier artist, one of the company of the greatest French musicians with Rameau and Couperin. These judges must have been counting vague futurities when they spoke. A critical comparison of the work produced by the two men up to 1916, the year in which Debussy died, could not have been decisively favorable to Ravel. Let it be admitted, right off, that Ravel's Ballet Russe String Quartet is better sustained than Debussy's corresponding piece. Let it also be admitted that the Sonatine and *Le Gibet* and *Scarbo* are creations of moods perfectly worthy of standing beside the magnificent contributions made by Debussy to the literature of the piano. Let it be granted that a few pages of Ravel's, the passacaglia of the Trio for piano, violin, and 'cello, for example, and some of his songs with orchestra like "La Flute Enchantée," are impeccable. It still remains true that by and large Ravel's product is far more brittle than Debussy's. Debussy was not, for his part, heroically endowed with breath. But his effects come off, his forms convey his always genuine and oftentimes profound feeling. Ravel, on the contrary, frequently reminds us of someone talking with great charm and elegance but failing to make his point and communicate his experience. Take the *Valses Nobles et Sentimentales,* one of his most agreeable compositions. The coy and sprightly waltzes want relief and projection, and melt as it were from sight; only the penultimate one has swing, strikes sparks, and sustains its ecstasy. Other pieces, *Daphnis et Chloë,* for example, are overblown, iterative to the point of monotony and boredom. It is not that Ravel would seem to want feeling. He has feeling, even though it in instances approaches the insipid and the coquettish; he has intelligence, as well as charm, taste, elegance, métier. He does not want ideas. What he does seem to lack is power. There is a capacity for a nervous excitement at moments almost hysterical, but little or none for the living and complete transference of his experience.

Possibly we are unjust to Ravel's music in judging it by the standards of expressive art; for in many respects it is a sheerly hedonistic one and suggests that the creation of the sensuously delicious object with musical means has always, to a decided extent, been the composer's central aim. His pieces are extremely refined, sapient, and voluptuous exploitations of the elements of music and the timbres of instruments that, clotted sonorous pearls, tickle and ravish the ear as sweetmeats the palate. Certainly many of them, for example the *Ondine* of the piano suite *Gaspard de la Nuit*, are little more than prickling salon pieces, virtuosic exploitations of the musical medium in the interests of brilliance and glitter, perhaps more tasteful than their Lisztian forbears, but at times almost as empty. That is but another way of saying that they belong in a category of music distinctly below the one into which the art of Debussy fits. Debussy's, too, had its hedonism and *coté bijoux*. Nonetheless, Debussy was always the poet, reservedly but poignantly, and wholly communicative of his feeling of doubt and despair and of the rich and complex essences and ideas of a perpetually foaming, glittering, dwindling, and imponderable world.

Nor have the recent developments in Ravel's art materially increased its weight. Impressionism and symbolism passed from the center of the scene with the war, succeeded by the classical ideal of the self-sufficient musical object. In Ravel along with Strawinsky this new ideal manifested itself together with a growing tendency to take the works of former composers as points of departure. We find both as it were sitting before these old compositions, anatomizing them, and then reconstructing the particles into edifices satisfactory to their own states of mind. Were these composers' medium the verbal one, this process might readily be termed criticism. Strawinsky's *Oedipus Rex* could be called a criticism of the Händelian oratorio, *Apollon Musagetes* a criticism of the gallant ballet of Versailles, *Le Baiser de la Fée* one of Tchaikowsky. And Ravel's *La Valse* could be thought to constitute a comment on the Viennese waltz, the slow movement of the violin and piano Sonata a study of the blues, *Tzigane* one of the virtuosic gipsy fiddle piece, and the piano Concerto one of the "true concerto"—as one commentor says, "the brilliant work aiming less at profundity than at setting in relief the virtuosity of the pianist." But these "criticisms" of the later Ravel have a somewhat disagreeable feeling and in instances are inferior in quality. The best of them, *La Valse,* is a brilliant and effective but acid piece, and the worst of them, the *Bolero,* has the fault of vulgarity unfortunately capped by that of tediousness. *Tzigane,* for violin and orchestra, is neatly made, but fairly empty; and the little piano Concerto diverts, even dazzles, but excepting for the arialike theme in which, as in the violin Sonata, Ravel adroitly unites major and minor in the blues fashion, it is quite unsubstantial. The latest of his pieces, the one-armed Concerto written for the one-armed pianist Wittgenstein, is, as befits the exhibitory occasion, a circus piece, to the very point of containing a flourish of the sort that is sounded before the *saltomortale:* in this case the cadenza.

If Ravel survives, and it seems more than likely that to a degree he will, it would appear to be thanks to some of his piano pieces such as the Sonatine and *Scarbo,* to some of his songs with orchestra such as *La Flute Enchantée* and the *Chansons Madécasses,* perhaps the Quartet, the Trio, *La Valse,* and the *Rapsodie Espagnole.* There by virtue of his elegance, his charm, his taste, above all by his impeccable craftsmanship, he is one of his country's *petits-maîtres,* a captor like the Lancrets and Paters of some spirit of grace, a fixer like them of ravishing bits of color and of rare and improbable harmonies certain to charm future generations. Among musicians, his place would appear to be a little higher than that of Saint-Saëns, a little lower than Claude LeJeune and the other smooth melodists, clean workmen, recorders of bits of experience in elegant and transparent and delicate forms. He is a charming musician, and while the world has never much space for such as he, it needs them for the little sups of sensuous delight which they distill.

Scriabin Again

"SCRIABIN is one of the artists whose work vanishes with the time in which it was born!" This recent verdict by an earnest young composer is pretty generally that of his tribe. Scriabin's glory remains fairly completely in eclipse. From time to time a zealous conductor repeats the unfortunate *Poème de l'Extase*. And the programs of concert pianists occasionally include a Scriabin prelude, étude, even a sonata. Yet in the seats of the mighty the makers of opinion—and in this case, the conservatives sit with the radicals—you will find "none so poor to do him reverence." Scriabin, so runs the tune, is "romantic," "inflated," "mere color," "international in the invidious sense." In fine, he is tabu. If you, friendly amateur, happen to be one of those whom a number of Scriabin's piano compositions enduringly enthrall, and also one of those who have never found themselves compelled to seek an explanation for this constant enthrallment, you will doubtless have discovered a feeling of isolation the almost inevitable consequence of the act of sitting down at the piano to play some of his music for yourself. The sense that in playing it you are expressing feelings of something that is not a reality will have haunted you, so subtly does public opinion influence such naïve, uncritical admirers as ourselves.

SCRIABIN AGAIN

If such has been your experience, you would have been wonderfully delighted by the expert recital of Scriabin's First, Fourth, and Tenth Sonatas and a dozen of his Etudes, Preludes, and Poems ranging from Op. 8 to Op. 72, which the most faithful of Scriabin interpreters, Katherine Ruth Heyman, gave at the Town Hall in New York in April, 1934. The concert would have rekindled all your old enthusiasm for the Russian's piano compositions, backed by a new comprehension of the reason for their persistent hold on you. At the end you would have left the hall assured that the complete eclipse Scriabin's fame has suffered these latter years among "advanced" musicians, and one by no means honorable to the musical profession or advantageous to musical culture, was largely the snobbish concomitant of one of those changes in musical fashion with which every student of musical history is familiar. The perception that Scriabin was not perhaps the equal of such illustrious victims of the caprices of vogue as Rameau and J. S. Bach would not have affected the perception that in this matter, at least, he was sharing their temporary fate. The change of taste influential on *his* fortunes had involved an adversion from his romantic, idealistic, and exquisite music toward realistic, formalistic, stark and hard-boiled music like Strawinsky's. And as Mrs. Grundy is never satisfied with the mere possession of lions—she must always have ostracisms to content her—Scriabin's music, like that of Bach and of Rameau in their day, had not only been excluded from the category of the modern, a fate natural to all things in the course of time; it had been viciously depreciated. And musicians, especially chronically advanced ones, obey the Grundy far more obsequiously than they suspect they do; calling things "bad" often when the epithet should merely be "unfashionable."

That afternoon, Miss Heyman again disclosed the fineness

of Scriabin's art and the depth of the experience transmitted by it. To be sure, the truth that a little of the musical world's present antipathy to Scriabin's piano compositions might be ascribed to something besides snobbery was by no means hidden by the program. Certain of the compositions that figured upon it, a couple of them novelties to New York, remain as music the merest bits of color without substance. Scriabin was not one of those composers who are invariably free. The most audacious of harmonists, he sometimes lacked a feeling of form, or possessed only a rudimentary one. He had his periodic states of inflation, too: then he aspired to the freedom he did not possess, and exalted his feelings. Like most of his orchestral works, the poverty of certain of his piano pieces, *Vers la Flamme,* for example, reflects these intervals of inhibition. Again, the langor of some of his more substantial piano compositions unquestionably does belong to a period, breathing as it does of the overheated salon. Still, the recital by and large stressed the immense leaven of unsturdiness in the current attitude toward Scriabin, reclothing him in the dignified raiment of the exquisite, individual, perfectly conscious artist. The very sounds evoked from the piano revealed the man's profound relationship to his medium, his sense of its potentialities, an individual, scarce paralleled one. Not even Liszt sounds as rich and full as Miss Heyman's Scriabin; and certainly no composer ever used the piano trill as luminously and effectively as he. Again, one plainly saw the superficiality of the resemblance of his style to Chopin's that Cui once thought so fundamental: "bits filched from the trousseau of Chopin" was his wicked way of signifying it. Progressive from Chopin through the Russian salon school, Scriabin's early preludes doubtless are; yet even these early Chopinesque preludes are individual creations. They have the iron Russian clangor of the fullest Scriabin. And they have a

Russian concision. The conceptions are pithy, and the recapitulations are never literal and often extremely tactful. Again, even these early preludes are less monotonous than Chopin: they are rhythmically more alive. The obsessive rhythmical figures that become tedious in Chopin's piano sonatas rarely have their parallel in Scriabin, at least not in his piano works; and the latter are also far more vigorously polyphonic than their prototypes. Homophonist though he remained in practice, Scriabin developed a masterly capacity for combining various melodic strands in a way that gives his work an actual polyphonic character. Besides, the left hand in Scriabin is far less continually subsidiary to the right than it is in the pieces of his master. Less rich in ideas, Scriabin's temperament certainly was more active than Chopin's. And as the program advanced and the pieces grew more individual, the freshness of the composer's magnificent harmonies grew plain again, and what Miss Heyman has called his music's "subtle beauty of resonance" and "the accurate complexity of his rhythmic pattern." And again one recognized, together with the sense of his unfailing concision and his unfailing consistency of texture, the individual glamour of his now capriciously fluid, now broadly chanting, melodies. They seemed to rise from golden invisible tides, winglike, reflecting something of the magic of their mysterious source.

And while reclothing Scriabin in the raiment of the exquisite and conscious artist, the performance also hung him once more with the shining robes of the ecstatic seer who revealed his states and vision beautifully through the pianoforte. This latter reinvestment, curiously enough, was performed by what at first appeared the unfortunate aspect of the recital, its affinity with the theosophical séance. This affinity grew pronounced during the performance of the First Sonata, when the pianist's execution of the recitativelike section of the last movement made the phrases resemble, for all the world, those of an inexperienced medium experiencing for a first time a "control" and reaching out and imperfectly transmitting its messages. And throughout the recital, the half-deliberate hierophantic drama of the performer continued associating the music with the theosophic idea, to a degree that even the fact that Scriabin had been an informal theosophist, and in orchestral works like *The Divine Poem, The Poem of Ecstasy,* and *Prometheus* had provided the cult with something approaching a ritual music, did not quite seem to justify. Yet after the performance, this association of Scriabin with the theosophic world proved to have been not at all the unfortunate business it had at first appeared to be. It seemed actually advantageous, since it had referred one, even if extravagantly, to the category into which Scriabin's expression really fits and the idea his music actually expresses. In emphasizing both the ecstatic movement of the music and its ecstatic content, its aspiration toward diviner states of being and consciousness, its "shaking off of fetters," its "taking wings to higher spheres," and its imitation and celebration of "the forms that beacon humanity from the heights," Miss Heyman had actually indicated the Neoplatonic visionary in Scriabin, the Neoplatonist that the restless flighted movement and the ecstatic experience conveyed by his music ultimately reveals him to have been. To both theosophy and Neoplatonism there is common the belief that humanity possesses organs enabling it directly to apprehend and to approximate godhead, a spirit that resurges through ever more purely divinized and creative spheres to its own origin, the Father of Souls, and in its apotheistic movement becomes the source of ecstatic states which give men consciousness of its genesis, direction, and quarry. In fact, theosophy is a kind of popular Neoplatonism. And this ecstatic experience is the soul and the con-

SCRIABIN AGAIN

tent of Scriabin's music—diffusely, less attractively in the huge orchestral works, intensely, fierily in the Fourth Sonata and other piano pieces. For all its kinship with Chopin's, for all its kindred coolly aristocratic salon style, the music of Scriabin thus from the first was different from Chopin's in form and feeling, and grew ever more so the more completely Scriabin became himself. His feeling was not romantic or saturated with the brilliance of the world, the satin of flesh, the might and glamour of the temporal. It was otherworldly. Sumptuous though it is, his music is not sensual; elegant though it is, it is not mundane. A veritable ethereality pervades the best of it, and the experience it expresses is the experience of a very spiritual person who has his abiding-place in some heaven and into whose life that heaven periodically sends its fiery dews, reminding its son of his home, giving him wings to seek and touch and taste the eternal power and the glory. Hence one's assurance of that music's durability, of the permanence of such of the best of the Sonatas as the Second, the Fourth, the Ninth: in the very face of the eternal Grundy. The spirituality that takes the path of the Neoplatonic ecstasy has been found at all times among all people. It is one of the great forces enabling man to defeat materialism and make this world a harbor for idealistic persons. Among the artists who have shared it, Scriabin ranks high by virtue of the beauty of his art. To pretend that since his style was one confined to his epoch, Scriabin must therefore be expected to have nothing but a historical interest for future periods, amounts actually to placing oneself in the boots of a hypothetical sixth-century rationalist arguing that the writings of Dionysius the Areopagite had no future, since they were couched in fifth-century Greek.

DISCOVERIES OF A MUSIC CRITIC

Bloch and His "Sacred Service"

THE style of Ernest Bloch's latest work, the *Sacred Service*, here and there points back to that of the compositions constituting his *Jewish Cycle*. In these passages, it has the solemn orientalism that distinguishes as a whole the *Three Jewish Poems, Schelomo, Israel,* and the rest of the magnificent components of this late romantic group, and recalls their chromatic melismas, their harsh barbaric fanfarelike themes, and their other darkly gorgeous hallmarks and colors. And, here and there, the new piece expresses a bit of the old profound and passionate feeling that, intensely Jewish, seemed to identify the Jew anew and reveal the tanglement of his roots in the rich clay from which the passionate visions and expressions of the prophets rose. Yet all in all, this *Avodath Hakodesh* falls into a category of work other than that of *Cortège* and *Rite* and the first String Quartet and the other prime instances of Bloch's durable nationalistic Jewish music. A hope of joy was pretty definitely extinguished in Carnegie Hall in New York the evening Friedrich Schorr and the chorus of the Schola Cantorum sang the *Service* under the composer's baton.

It hadn't been exactly powerful, that hope of further revelations, nationalistic or catholic either, from Bloch's pen, long previous to the night of the performance. It was not Bloch's latter change of form and style that had discouraged one: the succession to the deeply sincere, glowing, lyrical music of his Jewish works—romantic in the sense that its formal interest was less than its expressive, that its colors were rich and exotic;

BLOCH AND HIS "SACRED SERVICE"

but nonetheless the romantic music of a thinker and a craftsman and both personal and nationalistic—with some music more classical in form and in style: notably the viola Suite, the violin Sonata, and the little Concerto Grosso. The feeling was still unchanged in these classicizing works; still that of the oriental rhapsode, and gold-dusted whether it embraced the sadness and the tragedy of life, or massively sensuous experience, or the promise of divine worlds to come. The forms had weight as of sturdy, stocky, sinewy limbs. What *had* discouraged was the fact that simultaneously with these last, more absolutistic, classical pieces, Bloch had commenced diluting his idiom in the shape of effective pieces for the violin and for string quartet; and the conviction that they indicated a spiritual decline began to lower. For Bloch had appeared in America as the representative of the highest level of musical endeavor.

The conviction that a declension was occurring, moreover, was fortified by the fact that after the appearance of the Concerto Grosso practically all Bloch's succeeding works, the major too, began showing a pallid substance. The second String Quartet was forceless, curiously vapid. The symphony *America* and the tone poem *Helvetia* were disappointments. Their material was tawdry: wasn't the choral finale of *America* distinctly reminiscent of that florid old favorite, *The Holy City?* And their effects were not only programmatic but theatrical, and the prophetic gesture of the *America* was pretty thoroughly belied by the slackness of its aesthetic quality.

Nonetheless, announcement of the completion of the new composition could not but stir some hope. Poor as they were, neither *America* nor its companions had provided a basis for a conviction that the composer's fire had definitely subsided; and the nature of the new work, an arrangement for baritone and chorus, supported by orchestra, of the Hebrew text of the

DISCOVERIES OF A MUSIC CRITIC

Sabbath morning service prescribed by the Union Prayer Book of the reformed synagogues of this country, suggested that the flame had rekindled. In the first place, one had long known that Bloch had long intended composing a choral work on a sacred subject—a mass of some sort—by way of concluding his *Jewish Cycle;* and the *Avodath Hakodesh* seemed likely on acquaintance to prove itself the realization of the idea the composer had so long carried about in his skull: the completion of *Israel* with a choral religious expression. And nothing forced his friends to think that the realization was impossible. In the second place, the nature of the work, a celebration, representation, communication of the Soul of the Jewish soul, the Jew's old, eternally enduring God, in still another way suggested a re-lumination. The service, though not an inevitable, is a very natural vessel for the expression of the fruit of the experience that is perhaps the inevitably Jewish one and predestinately Bloch's as every other sentient Hebrew's. To be a Jew and sentient is finally to be one who at some time, and in many cases many times, finds himself, amid a ruined, ashen universe, newly conscious of his deepest relationship: that with his old, eternally enduring God—now faintly glimmering there in the chaos—silent, incomprehensible, apart—God and still surrounded by deathly, destructive forces. For being a Jew is being one who, like the Michelangelo of Emerson, "from God—cannot free himself": and who, through travail of mind and spirit, and patient, humble surrender, finally succeeds in rendering his sense of this Lord pure and full again, and reconquering the fulfilling feeling of His omnipotence, sufficiency, and goodness, and the divine grandeur of the ends of life. To find Bloch turning toward the vessel suitable to the expression of this experience and its spiritual residue was therefore naturally to suppose that experience the cause of his orientation.

BLOCH AND HIS "SACRED SERVICE"

The performance of the *Service* had not, however, reached its conclusion before there had grown plain to us the fact that our expectations had risen up against reason, probably at the dictation of the insensate desire for repetitions of the past so persistent in all of us. That the composition was respectable, informed with thought, and thus distinct from *America,* was evident. The ancient prayers and expressions of the service had been effectively grouped in four sections succeeded by an epilogue into which the composer had injected a little sermon of his own. On the basis of the scheme of antiphonies of cantor and chorus to which the verbal expressions almost naturally yielded themselves, musical expressions influenced by an intelligent penetration of the text had been symphonically built up, the epilogue constituting a kind of summary of the musical substance. The style was concise and more classically sober and reserved than the vehement, highly colored, and sometimes a trifle lachrymose music to which Bloch had accustomed us, and aspired to the kind of universality, impersonality, conformable with its traditional, collective subject and its religious function. All the music was suavely cast for voices and instruments, and some of it was delightful; for example, the exultant little chorus "Adonai shall reign," for all its deployment in rather commonplace sequences: and, again, the tender, slightly Wagnerian interlude of the third section symbolizing the removal of the scroll from the ark of the covenant. The rolling theme underlying the chorus "Eternal God" was striking, significant of eternity, and deserving of fuller treatment. But as a whole, the composition was appallingly tame, resembling work one might have expected of an English Victorian. The "universal" style was hybrid, chiefly a dilution of the earlier Bloch; and the bland forms and expressions had all the old-fashioned character of things felt without warmth and intensity. The one "inspired" passage in the work, the "Rock of Israel," exploited a traditional melody. The conviction that the feeling underlying the work was passionless and tame was ineluctable: one had the sense that the composer was approaching his essence, the Eternal behind appearances, with the courteous kind of ardor characteristic of one's hospitable salutation of a distant, venerable relative of the family of one's wife, and that he was using the traditional form of approach to that distant, sympathetic relative in the way in which one might join in the ceremonies of a congregation whose faith one understood externally, intellectually, and whose feelings one preferred to respect. Nothing in the pretty, rehashed, and inflated music communicated strong emotion of any kind, let alone a feeling of "the unfainting Creator of the ends of the earth." And few notes of it revealed that profound, passionate devotion that unites the believer with his superessential Object and makes his own cries, words, songs, revelatory of His nature. Practically all were intelligent and dignified, but wanting freshness and poignancy. It was without a shock of surprise that one encountered, in the little sermon interpolated by the composer amidst the traditional text, the words "in the fulness of time, we shall know why we are tried and why our love brings us sorrow as well as happiness," and found that he had indicated his wish that they should be sung with "an expression of despair." They were but corroborative of our intuitions regarding the spirit of the whole composition, the feeling that it was basically incomprehensive of its subject. The poet really in touch with this subject, really moved by it, would we sincerely believe never have proclaimed that the fulness of time was necessary to man that he should understand why he was tried and why his love had brought him sorrow as well as happiness. Like Spinoza, he would have known that the knowledge of God possible to man immedi-

BLOCH AND HIS "SACRED SERVICE"

ately casts out feeling of self; and that if man suffers and finds his love bringing him unhappiness, it is for the reason that unlike the divine, his love is, humanly, limited.

The works constituting Bloch's *Jewish Cycle* are not, either, impeccable in form and feeling. Their stuff is not invariably choice. One hears Puccini here and there in them, and the recapitulation section of *Schelomo* is unfortunately lengthy. Their counterpoint, too, is not above suspicion. And the frequency with which expressions of lamentation appear in them makes them characteristic perhaps of a certain Jewish strain, but not of the spirit of the race as a whole. Still, these pieces have passionate necessity and cordiality and the revelatory beauty born of it, such of their number as *Israel,* especially the *Three Jewish Poems,* ranking high among the compositions neglected by our great orchestral organizations. Thus their category excludes pieces like the *Sacred Service* and the rest of Bloch's recent products, things without necessity and indicative merely of intelligence and tact and craftsmanship.

Will he revive? We cannot say, and somehow we do not expect it. It will, of course, be a bitter thing to have to accept the premature death of an impulse as creative as Bloch's once was: particularly one whose lyrical cast of expression made it a generous source of refreshment and of benefaction in this arid time. To us in America this loss will be a double one, personal as well as impersonal; for here he taught and worked; here he gave a young generation its first experience of that rarity, a vigorously genial musician who is also an able technician, and in many ways deserved the love which we felt and still feel for him. And in all our disappointment, we will have to be careful not to do him the injustice of considering his checkmate a monstrosity. The history of music exhibits many instances of similar suspensions among great musicians. Berlioz certainly had grown sterile long before his death. The freshness of his gift had long deserted poor Schumann before he sought to drown himself in the Rhine. Rameau himself summed up his own case, toward the end of his life, in the words, "My taste improves from day to day, but my genius is long since dead." Bloch's misadventure would seem not very different from these: and like these, will in no way affect the value of his earlier works. He will remain one of the permanent figures of the postromantic period; and compositions of his will long endure.

The Evolution of Strawinsky

THE lower part of the scene was wrapped in green darkness during the American stage première of the *Oedipus Rex* of Cocteau and Strawinsky, given by the Philadelphia Orchestra under Dr. Stokowski, with the assistance of the stage designer Robert Edmond Jones, and Mme. Matzenauer, Mr. Paul Althouse, and the Harvard University Glee Club, at the Metropolitan in the winter of 1930. Robed in blue, the chorus was massed upon a low grandstand rather to the left of the stage, with the soloists in their midst. The unseen Speaker commenced: "Without knowing it, Oedipus is at cross-purposes with the forces which spy on us from the further side of the grave. From the day of his birth they have been watching him to set a snare for him into which he shall fall." As the music began monotonously and hopelessly muttering a rune of the cruel Powers, into the luminous upper half of the scene there rose, as from out the humanity cowering at its base, a gaunt,

THE EVOLUTION OF STRAWINSKY

twelve-foot effigy of Oedipus the King. And in the course of the nightmarelike drama petrified in music, one after another equally tall and garish puppets of Creon, Teresias, Jocasta, and the other dramatis personae appeared beside it. At the moment of the catastrophe, the message of Jocasta's suicide, it vanished; then, while the orchestra and the chorus cried out of their darkness in horror and terror of the ferocious gods, a hideous effigy of the blinded, naked, outcast Oedipus rose on high, and dwindling beneath the weight of his pitiless fate, descended, extinguishing like a suddenly defective electric wire. For a last time the chorus and the drums monotonously muttered their hopeless rune.

No Greek drama had been presented to us. The antique tragedy had conceived of fate as a subtle concordance of character and circumstance. The classic Oedipus was not the puppet of an entirely external destiny. His catastrophe to a decided degree was the consequence of his own violence. The king who dashed out his eyes in his despair and shame was the violent son of a violent father, who had introduced sodomy into Greece, the offspring of an overbearing, high-handed family that disobeyed and sought to outwit the gods, and as little a passive victim as the Shakesperean Macbeth. If he walked into any "trap," it was one in no wise separate from himself. Certainly the antique destiny, in Aeschylus and in Sophocles, at least, invariably remained the daughter of the discords, the deceptions, and the ignorances of gods and of men, never the action of hostile powers upon helpless creatures.

No: what had been presented was a much blacker, more primitive conception of the relations of gods and human beings, one that, ever latent in the European mind, periodically rises from it in all its fearfulness. It represents gods jealous of and hostile to man, and man inevitably their enemy and their victim. Man has committed a sin, the original sin. He has been born: he has emerged from the night whose power he has defied and whose peace he has broken. But the gods are the stronger. Man is ultimately unconscious, and life involves him in evil upon evil: till at last, in awareness of his guilt, and broken in power and pride, he sinks, shattered, into the night from which he blindly rose. And behind the action of the Cocteau-Strawinsky *Oedipus Rex* one felt the ineradicable past deed whose inevitable consequence the catastrophe was, not half so much the blind parricide and incest as the event of birth itself; and read and heard from the forms the expression of the deep, irrational feeling of his original, inexpiable guilt that, lodged in man, mutters continually within him, and rises and overwhelms him in his hours of weakness and defeat; and the might of the Night itself that holds him by this hook.

The oratorio opera proved one of the most pessimistic and bitter of the messages of a composer who, distinguished by the pessimism and bitterness of his experience, is easily the greatest of personal forces in the contemporary musical world: the author of a mass of compositions extremely dynamic in form, including some of the world's most swiftly moving, starkly and intensely expressive pieces; of a half-dozen ballet scores which have restored to the choreographic form an importance comparable to that which Wagner returned to the music drama; and the immediate cause of a majority of the changes that have occurred in the cast and character of creative music during the last two decades. *Oedipus* also reinforced the feeling of disappointment the productions of Strawinsky immediately anterior to it had roused.

The very first of his individual compositions, the ballets *Petrushka* and *Le Sacre du Printemps,* which he composed during the milling period immediately preceding the outbreak

THE EVOLUTION OF STRAWINSKY

of the World War for the Diaghilev ballet, instantly had revealed the advent of a young composer with a fresh, very pungent, material sense. These extraordinary scores of the young Strawinsky, and to an extent the shortly subsequent *Renard* and *Les Noces,* were, partially, outcrops of the nationalistic movement of Russian music represented during the nineteenth century by the compositions of Glinka, Moussorgsky, Rimsky-Korsakoff and Balakirew. Like these, they too to a large extent were based upon the styles of Slavic folk music, pieces of which are interwoven in their fabrics; and they also groped for the meaning of the Russian soil and Russian nature and uttered its power and wildness. They had the family characteristics: brilliance of instrumental color, conciseness of expression, pantomimic spirit, animal vitality, and episodic structure; and their special multirhythmicality and partiality to humble material, and even their relentless polytonalism, must for all their indebtedness to Strauss' example be considered direct developments of certain of Moussorgsky's innovations. Simultaneously they were the offshoots of such elements of western music as the impressionistic harmonies of Debussy, the musical irony of *Till Eulenspiegel,* and the musical primitivism of *Elektra,* and nonetheless a merger of the two traditions in highly individual, powerful, epoch-making and -marking musical forms and expressions.

Petrushka and *Le Sacre* were not only "cubistic"; without the melting contours of the music of Debussy and Strauss, and bare of all silkiness and jewelry. Highly nervous in tension, they were robust, hard, plebeian, and struck one like hammer blows. And built up of stiff, angular phrases and often harshly harmonized melodic fragments and moving from massive block to block of color, they were above all distinguished by insistent, irregularly accented, but iterative rhythms abundantly emphasized by a percussion that kinged it over the entire orchestra. These rhythms of these frequently polytonic pieces were developed from the iterative rhythms of Russian folk songs. But they were also mechanistic, the full-grown children of the tendency to express the pulsations and spirits of mechanical things delicately begun by Beethoven in the allegretto of his Eighth Symphony and continued by Moussorgsky in the hallucination scene in *Boris Goudonow*. They were primitivistic to an equal degree: wild, orgiastic, brutal. And a new, an intense experience breathed harshly through these rigid forms, one radically opposite to the majority of those which for a century had been reaching the world through music. For this young Scyth the world was bare of the exquisitely sensuous, lovely, and delicious elements that had enchanted his predecessors down to Debussy and of the ideal elements that had caused composers from Beethoven through Wagner to Scriabin to feel its plenitude of glowing possibilities; above all, bare of the Idea, and of human beings potentially noble and free. Life for him was a stark affair, a cruel affair, and a gross affair: a thing earthy and tough, all thumbs, udders, and shaggy organs; full of pain, static, entirely mechanical. The human being at best was a feeble puppet dependent upon an energy entirely without him that played him in utter ruthless indifference. The music itself was apparently a strong and stoical, occasionally bitterly humorous, adjustment to this stark and fundamentally gross reality. The bubbling of the flutes beginning *Petrushka* introduces us immediately into this gimcrack world, with its quality of a gingerbread fair, and thorough mechanism. Human beings pervade this world, but their souls are automata: Petrushka, the ballerina, the sumptuous Moor; and barrel-organ tunes are the expression of the movement of the spheres. Prisoners and slaves of this external force, the puppets dance to music not of their making, and love and suffer and die with stiff, grotesque gestures; and in death mock their maker and owner. The entire wild and ironic score is full of the pain and the poetry of this mechanical world. The dolls and the instruments appearing upon the stage and their qualities and gestures have a counterpart in the music with its precise and iterative rhythms, its puppetlike, rigid, and angular phrases. The passage for the piano and other instruments accompanying the scene of the solitary Petrushka in his box, for example, is a strange miniature expression, a sort of music of little things, composed of whirring, purling, creaking sonorities delicately, mordantly related to the noises of intricate mechanism, watches, meters, tickers, dolls, and other devices.

And though no automata invade the stage in *Le Sacre* and the score is bare of the clockwork music of its immediate predecessor, it, too, with its dark and ferocious coloring, adjusts us to a mechanistic order of things. It embodies another intuition of the automaton in the human being. This ballet is a representation of instinctive and unconscious action. Its subject is the vernal rite of primitive tribes, the celebration and representation of the earth and its sovereign will by pagan Russians. But its feeling is a pessimistic one that not all primitive societies have shared. Cocteau found it "a symphonic expression of wild mourning, the labor-pains of the earth, farm and encampment sounds, little melodies that come from the depths of the centuries, the groaning of cattle, profound blows: a georgic of prehistoric ages." Through the idyllically piping but brutally polyrhythmic score, with its stamping rhythms, archaic modality, and heavily moving masses of sound, we feel the weight of the earth, its dark attractiveness, its everlasting voracity of tillage and blood, its domination of man with its sightless ineluctable will, its imperious exaction of his allegiance and self-sacrifice to the end of eternal reproduction. The second part of it, especially, is another poem of pain, the pain of parturition. In an ecstasy verging upon agony it sings the suction of the earth, the goodness of Dionysiac annihilation. There is only pressure of blind instinct here, the harsh urgence of overmastering biological impulse, the mournful, vuluptuous bath of slow craving. With a pistonlike iterativeness and relentlessness go the rhythms. The whole piece is full of the weight of slow-moving, dumb, irresistible mass.

Themselves progressive from cubism, these pieces in their turn influenced the whole course of music. The entire young generation of composers, under their spell, turned away from impressionism toward their kind of hard-boiled expressivity and began favoring irregular measures, demotic material, crystalline sonorities—and not only the young *composers*. One feels their influence in the, "I can take it" prose of Hemingway and his school. Meanwhile, Strawinsky had succeeded these two early masterpieces with several equally genial works in the smaller forms, three of them for the stage: *Renard, Les Noces,* and *L'Histoire du Soldat,* and a piece of absolute music, *Symphonies for Wind Instruments.* Products of the war years —Strawinsky was interned with his family in Switzerland— these pieces continue powerfully to express a painful and a pessimistic vision. *Renard,* an animal fabliau, followed *Petrushka* in presenting gross and cruel reality in the form of a grotesque. *Les Noces,* in the shape of a representation of a rustic wedding cortège and feast, embodies the relentless force that joins and sacrifices two human beings to the end of perpetuating the race. We feel it here as Schopenhauer felt it once, an unswerving dynamic urgence rushing ahead like an express train and carrying human beings ruthlessly along in its trajectory; and not a little through the painful expressions of the

THE EVOLUTION OF STRAWINSKY

bride and the women bidding farewell to youth, the iron determination in the voices of the men, the ribald cries of the drunken wedding guests, and the stern, gonging conclusion, fraught with a feeling of the impenetrable mystery of marriage. *L'Histoire* mordantly expresses, in the tale of an uprooted soldier damned by militarism itself, the mortgage the devil, here the material forces of creation, upon life; and the inevitable foreclosure of the mortgage. The score, like that of *Petrushka*, is humble and demotic in style. For a moment, after the soldier has restored the king's daughter to health with the music of his violin, the great chorale in tones recalling Luther's famous hymn expresses the victory of faith and unity and the ideal. But the victory is temporary only. At the end the devil wins. To percussive music that utters the omnipotence of the brute creation the soldier follows him down to hell. And the *Symphonies for Wind Instruments,* dedicated to the memory of Debussy, conclude with a stark dirge that, echoing the last chorus in *Boris Goudonow,* exceeds it in grim plangency.

These four pieces in many ways are Strawinsky's most perfect. Their forms are complete, their rhythms subtle; and certain in their effects, they completely and sustainedly express intense and deep feeling. Stark as it is, his music of *Les Noces* and *L'Histoire* is full of tenderness and revelatory of the considerable sensibility that he holds in check. The bone-weary *L'Histoire* even more than *Petrushka* shows the composer's feeling for the miniature. In other ways, too, these pieces differ from the ballets preceding them, and not only in the point of feeling or the obvious one of strict limitation of form and of material. While three of them, *Renard, Les Noces,* and the *Symphonies,* are built of material which, though stylized as in *Le Sacre,* is distinctly Russian—*Les Noces* actually contains a theme derived from the liturgy and constitutes a symphonic folk song—*L'Histoire* was anything but a nationalistic piece and represented a break with the nationalistic tradition and a redintegration in the catholic European one. The last three of the four works also exhibited a swing toward the linear principle of form. Strawinsky's early work, including *Renard*, had by and large conformed to the modified homophonic-harmonic principle of composition. From *Les Noces* onward it has conformed to the melodic-contrapuntal one. Effectively melodic, tellingly contrapuntal, swiftly moving, and firmly an entity, *Les Noces* is also distinctly less dependent on literary and mimetic associations than its predecessors, far more an absolute musical object in the mold of antiphonies of soloists and chorus. *L'Histoire* represents another step. It is extremely formally textured, cast in closed ancient and modern molds, marches, waltzes, chorales, and tangos, fox trots, and ragtime; and the music is frequently concertante in character. In the *Symphonies* we find Strawinsky studying his means, developing a form out of the impulse of the theme itself, and striving to discover what pure melody, harmony, and rhythm are capable of achieving. These three works are also distinguished by their novel sonorities. *Les Noces* is extremely percussive, metallic. The composer cast it for voices, four pianos, and a complex battery; and the powerful and melancholy music, almost Chinese in its melody, rings and chimes like sounded metal. *L'Histoire* ends with a virtuosic passage of percussive music; and the *Symphonies* are cast, as in stone, in the impersonal sonority of the thirteen wind pieces.

Strawinsky indeed had developed into a thoroughly neoclassic composer, and incidentally redintegrated the art of music with its great tradition. For the melodic-contrapuntal principle of composition and forms organically developed from musical ideas, the aim of the neoclassicist, themselves

THE EVOLUTION OF STRAWINSKY

constitute this great line; and while the movement toward it actually was initiated by composers other than and previous to Strawinsky, it attained its goal resonantly in his compositions and through them told upon composers everywhere, from Germany and Spain to the United States and Latin America, even influencing the most eminent of his coevals, Schönberg. And Strawinsky continued in this great tradition and continued to illustrate it: however, not altogether untroublingly. Since the *Symphonies,* his pieces had the hallmarks of a not altogether happy tendency. Strawinsky only too plainly was doubling neoclassicism with archaicism, reviving old styles and old types of pieces and mixing old material in with his own. In itself, archaicism is neither commendable nor reprehensible, the concomitant of the periodic "returns to the antique" to be found in all cultures. And the business of reviving old forms, at least that of imposing their limits upon new creations, is a kind of criticism in the medium of music, a manner of assimilating the ideas of former men and epochs. What is important is the method of this assimilation and the results. And in Strawinsky's case neither had been prime, or prime in only one instance. This was *Pulcinella,* a ballet built upon melodies of the eighteenth-century Neapolitan composer Pergolesi, and to a degree a leading cause of the revival among contemporary composers of the spry, lively, and brittle style of the Neapolitan classic opéra bouffe. Strawinsky had, it appeared, thoroughly felt himself into the idiom of the old master, and while introducing syncopations and rhythmic accents of his own into the adroitly composed score, maintained a unity in it. The succeeding pieces, the Concerto for piano and wind and percussion orchestra, the Octet for wind instruments, the piano Sonata and *Serenade,* however, were excessively heterogeneous in style. The material was a bewildering farrago of

DISCOVERIES OF A MUSIC CRITIC

Bach, Händel, Johann Strauss, jazz, and the kitchen range, all served up half baked together. Strawinsky, who had quit the Russian nationalistic basis, had not arrived at a catholic style, merely at a baroque composite.

Still it was not only the heterogeneity of the material that left one unsatisfied by these pieces. It was their relative sterility. One missed the powerful impulse of the preceding works and the expression of intense feeling through vivid forms. That the elemental violence, the garish colors, and the excessive dissonateness of scheme of the early works should in the course of time have been succeeded by a more contained, controlled, calm spirit, and more consonant harmony, seemed natural: one did not ask for continuous repetitions of *Le Sacre* and *Les Noces* in that sense, or repine that for Strawinsky every composition evidently exhausted the interest of its mold; and that his energy consistently redintegrated itself after every piece on a level other than the last and in connection with another form. What one did demand, however, was music that was fresh, the testimony of a convincing creative impulse: and what one got was dryly, elegantly percussive, and soberly colored music that was frequently twice-told, and entirely without sovereignly poetic passages like those that occurred in the cell scene in *Petrushka,* in the beginning of the second part of *Le Sacre,* in the close of the scene in *Les Noces* where the guests depart for the church and in the whole of the wedding feast, in the *Little Concert* of *L'Histoire,* and in the finale of the *Symphonies for Wind Instruments*. That there were striking pages in these archaicizing works was not to be denied. The second movement of the Concerto, with its Bach succeeded by a Russian-style melody, was lyrical. The first two little movements of the *Serenade* were stark and mobile. The Octet even as a whole was fairly diverting. The little one-act opera *Mavra,* composed during the post-war years in which Strawinsky was producing this almost sterile music, had a distinct charm and classic smoothness. But all in all, these pieces seemed perverse, the products of what appeared to be something persistently driven in a direction contrary to its natural one. The neoclassic discipline which Strawinsky was imposing upon himself, the objective architectural plasticity to which he aspired, all seemed willed.

It was this disappointment that the performance of *Oedipus Rex* finally crystallized. The opera oratorio was Strawinsky's first composition in the large forms since *Le Sacre,* for those of *Les Noces,* while bulky, are relatively limited both in scope and in material. In this work Strawinsky had sought to re-create the type of the Händelian oratorio: he had adopted its mold of numbers for chorus interspersed with solo pieces and striven for its grandeur and monumentality of style. He had had Cocteau's lines translated into Latin, to the further end of making his expression stonelike, severe, formal, archaic. In spots the score realized his aim. The ominous stoical drum beats, the square choruses and stark accents, all this virile expression of fatal knowledge, had archaic asperity and power. The arias were dramatically contrasted. Each was a portrait, executed with melodic lines often large and flowing, and strongly idiosyncratic and definitive of the character of the protagonist. The expressions of Oedipus were noble and revelatory of deep uncertainty; those of Creon, military, forthright, brusque. Teresias spoke in a priestly, evasive, mysterious manner, Jocasta in a sensuous and chromatic style. The changes of mood were definite; Oedipus' growing insecurity was marked during the suite of his arias, Jocasta's final terror expressed with all the vehemence of Italian opera. The chorus glorifying the queen at the moment of her appearance was strong, hard, barbaric, and terribly ironical. But while the dramatic tension was sustained, the total effect was not a happy one. The score, to begin with, lacks unity. The better part of the choral music has a severe ominous quality, Russian in essence, while Creon's diatonic aria is Händelian in its bravura, Teresias' Wagnerian in its exaltation and refinement, and Jocasta's has vulgar touches of Bizet and Verdi. The light Russian melody and rhythm of the shepherd and the messenger come like something out of *Petrushka* or *Renard*. And it remains a medley, from which the various kinds of material, especially the echoes of Italian opera, protrude, so many anfractuosities. And besides being eccentric, the music is oftentimes commonplace in quality. Next to the final outcry of the chorus, the most distinguished page of the score is Teresias' aria, with its melody overleaping intervals of sevenths and ninths. But the rest, including Jocasta's chromatic *de capo* aria, is curiously stale: and it is probable that not even Rossini or Donizetti would have been proud of the dreadful organ-grinder triolets of her second song. And music sung by the chorus and messenger before the recapitulation of the majestic initial chords and drum theme seemed a little absurd; it had apparently been lifted directly from the grandstands during a rousing intercollegiate match. In any case, for all its technical merits, the piece could not be compared with *Le Sacre,* or only to the elder work's advantage.

Strawinsky's own darkest expression of pessimistic feeling thus had become the source of dark and pessimistic feelings about Strawinsky; had become so before the night of the performance at the Metropolitan. Still an extraordinarily able musician, he seemed to have lost the better part of the genius and elemental power that had once thrilled us, and to have

THE EVOLUTION OF STRAWINSKY

become something of a crank to boot. The evening on Thirty-ninth Street had merely showed one the reason for one's disaffection.

II

Since that hour this disappointment has nonetheless considerably been modified. *Oedipus Rex* has not proved Strawinsky's final word.

The very piece immediately successive to it, the ballet score *Apollon Musagetes* for string ensemble, revived the hope of further benefits from the composer who, already superior in station to Berlioz, nearer that of the great innovators including Liszt, and only below the level of the major composers, had temporarily appeared to be threatened with a sterility quite as lamentable as that which finally overtook his noble French predecessor. *Apollon* is cast in the form of the classic ballet of Versailles, as *Oedipus* is cast in the mold of the Händelian oratorio. It includes several *pas de deux,* variations, and a coda, and the material suggests Lulli, Rameau, and Delibes: and essentially Strawinskian and Russian music appears in the *Variation d'Apollon.* Sometimes sweet and enervate in its French classicism, the score is redeemed by the syncopating coda and the apotheosis: the first, dance music tense with the old swell of forces; the second, a spacious concluding page impregnated with a calm and a melancholy that recall those of the majestic gardens of Versailles.

This ballet in turn was followed by another, *Le Baiser de la Fée,* "inspired by the muse of Tchaikowsky," and expressive, with a score built on melodies and themes of the Russian symphonist's and confined within their harmonic limits, of the unfortunate's tragedy. In this work, the muse of Tchaikowsky made another low in Strawinsky's work. While the score infuses the Tchaikowskian material with a characteristic Strawinskian stiffness, it approaches bathos, especially when at the climax it thunders forth the theme of the song "Nur wer die Sehnsucht kennt Weiss was ich leide." Intended as a criticism of a Russian composer to whom Strawinsky feels himself akin, and one whom he regards as misunderstood and neglected by the present generation, it actually brings to expression nothing that Tchaikowsky himself did not, and remains a curious but unnecessary gesture. But immediately after this redundant score, Strawinsky produced two others with distinct—one of them with great—formal and aesthetic interest. The old bole was evidently putting forth green shoots again, and the concert at which the Boston Symphony under Koussevitzky presented the two for the first time to an American audience was as joyful as any reconciliation with a temporarily estranged friend.

These pieces were the *Capriccio* for piano and orchestra and the *Symphonie des Psaumes*. The first represents the type of the Weberian *Konzertstück*. Essentially a divertissement, brilliant, whimsical, staccato, ornamented, basically consonant but typically Strawinskian in its crystalline sonority, it puts one again amid the lusters and the décolletages of an early Victorian drawing-room and again permits one to savor the charm and sparkle of pre-bourgeois manners. Possibly the piece is not much more than a grandiose parlor ornament: it certainly is without high specific gravity and merely aims at a social effect and pretends to nothing further. But it is easily the happiest of Strawinsky's eclectic compositions. While the material ranges from Bach to jazz and includes, in the middle movements, melismas in the manner of Liszt and *à l'hongroise,* these heterogeneous stuffs are fused in a form that actually combines the capriciousness and sparkle of the old brilliant salon music with the scintillance of jazz. It is indeed far superior to the piece with which one inevitably compares it,

THE EVOLUTION OF STRAWINSKY

the piano Concerto; for here the form and the moods are sustained. The first, exquisite in detail, works up gradually to the enchanting jazzy dancing finale which comes off with éclat: and the moods slowly progress from the sardonic initial one—in which one sees the face and the postures of a tragic harlequin—up to the climactic one, sparkling with malice and zest and, *mirabile dictu,* with genuine kindness and gaiety. It is as if Strawinsky had discovered the unseriousness, the joke of life, and were irradiating his audience with humor.

The second of the pieces, the *Symphonie des Psaumes,* is of sterner and stonier stuff. It is in the grand style, severe, architectural, lean and spare in sonority, and frequently abrupt and stark in attack. Its orchestra has been stripped of violins, violas, and clarinets, and the choral passages are bare of chromaticism and occasionally exploit the voices in unison. The three movements, connected by instrumental interludes, are rugged, simple, and somberly colored: only in the final alleluia does a kind of soft golden glow that recalls that of the mosaics in a Byzantine church suffuse the music; and even then the score is curiously rigid and hieratic. The mood is extremely elevated: the verses Strawinsky has set are taken from Psalms XXVIII, XXXIX, and CL in the version of the Vulgate; and the subject, beginning as a supplication to the Lord that he save his worshiper from the black pit—"I am a stranger with thee and a sojourner, as all my fathers were"—becomes a cry that "the Lord has put a new song into my bones," and ends in a solemn song of praise. The work assuredly is the strongest Strawinsky had produced since the *Symphonies for Wind Instruments.* Possibly it is a little less distinguished than the great ballets that towered like red girders against the melting impressionistic sky. The second movement, the fugue, with its modern counterpoint, is curiously indeterminate: Strawinsky, as if he could not achieve his original plan, lets it end somewhat lamely with a reaffirmation of the original subject in the bass. The main theme of the last movement, despite its loveliness, is a trifle commonplace: and all in all, the work is another illustration of the truth that Strawinsky's pieces in the large forms are less impeccable than those in the smaller. Yet it has much of the old feeling and power of expression. The feeling is stark and characteristically painful; while it is intensely that of the spiritual life, the raucous first movement seems haunted by the figure of the prodigal son in his degradation; and even if at the end the presence and the blessing of the Lord have become manifest, the composer does not seem to find himself in a world gladdened and saved by His presence. The Lord and His realm would seem to transcend it entirely and remain visible only through the gate of death: and the final mood, not entirely bare of agony, would seem to be that of patient expectation for release. To the world of *Oedipus* there has merely been added another in which peace reigns. This experience, however, is expressed with something of the old abrupt and elemental power: and in the third section, wild entries of barbaric music recall the early "primitivist." The first and last movements certainly have a grave beauty and the last a veritable splendor.

Was the experience a personal one or merely the result of some reference to the form of "sacred music"? It would seem to be the former, and not only because rumor has it that at some time previous to the creation of the *Symphonie* Strawinsky was converted to Catholicism, largely through the efforts of no less conspicuous a saint than Jacques Maritain. For the music itself is a gush of waters in a waste land, the end of a barren period; and as such the sign of some redintegration of

THE EVOLUTION OF STRAWINSKY

the personality that might of itself have sent the composer to the solemn verses he has set.

And from this time forward, Strawinsky's career has appeared not entirely to conform to the order of the three prehistoric ages which used to be attributed to humanity. For in his case it had been the age of iron that followed the age of gold, while the age of silver was following the age of iron. Silver doubtless is the little violin Concerto, the piece that followed on the heels of the *Symphonie* and was presented early in 1932 in New York by Samuel Dushkin at a concert of the Philadelphia Orchestra. It is modest in its proportions, but not at all the bad piece the New York critics found it: in fact it is as complete in its way as the *Capriccio*. Its two arias are austerely expressive of emotion. Their final measures are exquisitely musical, and the capricious finale sparkles and charms with its elfish sonorities. What appears to have happened is that some of the composer's remarks about his new piece, carried by the newspapers and the program notes and cast in the form of a comparison of his little Concerto with Mozart's, lent themselves to misunderstanding. Strawinsky was quoted as saying: "For Mozart the invention of the theme or themes represented the maximum effort: all the rest was made up of a certain formalism ... and with the developments of the theme, the repetitions, refrains and necessary 'cadenze,' the half-hour was soon reached.... But now that this development of the theme in a scholastic sense no longer exists, and still less repetitions (I am speaking, of course, of my own work); now that every measure is the result of an enormous condensation of thought (sometimes in a whole day's work I just manage to write one or two measures), porportions have changed, and a concerto of fifteen minutes is already a monumental work."

DISCOVERIES OF A MUSIC CRITIC

Now, Strawinsky's comment upon the conventional in Mozart's concertos and the comparison of their forms with his own is far from erroneous. But at the same time, the brief toccata that begins his own little Concerto contains a forty-bar recapitulation; and the second aria repeats its initial figure unaltered: hence the statement appeared a bit arrogant and sophistical. Thus, the exacerbation of the critical fraternity, who came to the performance spoiling for a fight, and the volley of Irish confetti which expressed their greetings to the poor victim.

Silver, too, is the latest of Strawinsky's major scores that have been presented to the public, the "melodrama" *Perséphone,* upon a text by André Gide, performed in concert form by the Boston Symphony under Strawinsky himself in March, 1935.

The deeply moving Gide-Strawinsky creation itself is a sort of Eleusinian mystery.—The mysteries yearly performed at Eleusis in ancient times in connection with the nine-day worship of "the Mother" and "the Maiden," Demeter and Persephone, were dramatic representations, resembling the medieval mysteries, of the events in the stories of the two "holy" and "pure" savior goddesses. Developments of the primitive worship of the spiritual forms of the earth and of the seed, these representations and some of the other exercises of the festival came, under the presidency of the Eumolpidae and members of other sacerdotal families, to express certain of the deepest and most consoling conceptions of the Greek religion. Men like Pindar and Sophocles derived from them immutable convictions of their eternal welfare in this world and the next. Like the bas-relief of Demophoön or Triptolemus between Demeter and Persephone now in the museum at Athens, the mysteries conveyed these goddesses' loyal guardianship of their human

THE EVOLUTION OF STRAWINSKY

nurseling and the inalienable blessing laid by them upon him.

And the new Franco-Russian "melodrama" imparts in the form of a mystery of Persephone, freely conceived in the manner of the Eleusinia, modern intuitions similar to those allied in the minds of the ancients with the myths of the Mother and the Maiden. The Persephone of Gide and Strawinsky is a divine person, at once the spirit of the spring and the seed and the unfailing human Lover: "She who if men go down into hell, is there too." She is also the human heart, the creative spirit that—periodically drawn by pity into the realm of death and dreams and "the shades of men outworn," temporarily held there and eventually reborn like the springtide, in love and greater consciousness to the earth and breathing men—lives not unto itself.

The poet and the composer have intended their work—a "melodrama" in so far as it associates the speaking voice with choral and instrumental music, but one that partakes of the nature of the ballet and of the oratorio—for the stage. The part of Persephone is written for a chanting mime—actually Ida Rubinstein; that of the Eumolpidus—simultaneously the interpreter of the mystery and the counselor and companion of Persephone—for a singing actor. The chorus participates in the action. And the first performance of the work was dramatic, forming part of Mme. Rubinstein's season at the Paris Opéra.

The representation, like one of the evident guides of Gide's conception, the Homeric hymn to Demeter, begins with the scene of the rape. The stage represents the precincts of a temple. It is "the first morning of the world," and the great heart of Persephone, who is playing among the nymphs to whom her mother has confided her, is moved to love. As in the hymn, the rape is precipitated by her discovery of the sweet and deathly narcissus. But in *Perséphone* there is no Aïdoneus with his chariot and black steeds. The motive of the descent is the compassion aroused in Persephone by the flower's odor. Eumolpus and the nymphs tell her that whoever looks into the narcissus sees the unknown underworld, and, gazing, Persephone views "a people wandering hopelessly, sad, restless, discolored." Advised by Eumolpus that "her youth will lighten their distress, her spring charm their endless winter," and already "married to Pluto by her compassion," she bids the nymphs farewell and takes the springtime with her from the earth.

In the unending night of the underworld, she lies clasping the narcissus, seeing the host of those who "pursue—what dwindles and glides away" and, in a death of time, "recommence without end the incompleted motions of life." Eumolpus tells her that it is her destiny to rule; that she must forgo pity. They offer her cups of Lethe and the treasures of the earth. She rejects them. At length the gods send Mercury, who offers Persephone the pomegranate; and "finding in the darkness a relic of the light above," Persephone eats. The savor of the lost earth returns to her, and gazing once more into the narcissus, in anguish she sees the world in its winter and her mother wandering in rags among briars, sharp stones, and tangled branches. She calls to Demeter, but her voice does not carry. Then Eumolpus declares that the winter cannot remain eternally; that in the palace of Celeus in Eleusis, Demeter is nursing Demophoön who will be Triptolemus. Persephone sees the Mother leaning toward the child over a burning brand and carrying him in the salt breeze; she perceives the noble lad, "radiant with tawny health, rushing toward immortality." She greets him who will "once more teach man to plow." Reviving, she sees the day; with love, in joy, she salutes the earth, and her earthly husband, Triptolemus. A chorus, including children's voices, hails the returning queen as Persephone falters forth from the gates of the tomb. She dances; she plights her troth to the hero; and once more, of her free will, prepares to return to the unhappy underworld:

> Je n'ai pas besoin d'ordre et me rends de plein gré
> Où non point tant la loi que mon amour me mène;
> Et je vois pas à pas descendre les degrés
> Qui conduisent au fond de la détresse humaine.

The chorus celebrates the departing Lover, and Eumolpus delivers the precept of unselfishness derived, as at the Eleusinia, from the mystery:

> Il faut pour qu'un printemps renaisse
> Que le grain consente à mourir sous terre
> Afin qu'il reparaisse
> En moisson d'or
> Pour l'avenir.

But though the performance of *Perséphone* in Boston, like that in London, was in concert form, even in this partial shape the work is solid and very affecting: in Boston, for instance, critics and public were quite in accord respecting its impressiveness. The first reason for this effectiveness is that the poetic work is narrative and dramatic; the second, that Gide and Strawinsky have transmitted the idea through their mediums so clearly and fully that it touches one without the aid of the pantomime. Strawinsky in fact has transmitted the general sense and mode of the piece with extraordinary depth and warmth. His method is the classical one: that is to say, he neither has described with music, nor attempted the cosmic, nor stopped to illustrate the word. He has written pure music, letting the general mood of the music, or the speech-recitative of the soprano—which resembles the arialike delivery of

DISCOVERIES OF A MUSIC CRITIC

Racine at the Comédie Française—express his subject. But the expression is there, fully; we feel the sorrow, the suffering, the grayness of the underworld, the divine goodness of Persephone, the ecstasy of rebirth.

Indeed, the eminently religious atmosphere of the work flows chiefly from his setting. Elevated in style and mood, silvery and reserved, and with something of a starry brilliance, it is also strong and austere and even ascetic, like a Russian ikon; indeed, Strawinsky's Persephone has somewhat the quality of a Byzantine Theotokos. Where Gide has apparently, as in the opening scene, given him an opportunity for graceful and voluptuous music, Strawinsky has written music (the *Ländler* of the nymphs, for example) that is willfully uncouth and banal. This is not because he cannot write a beautiful melody, for he can: one has but to hear the second eclogue in his recent *Duo Concertante* to be assured of it. The reason for these banalities is probably either a fierce contempt for the senses, or a sense of the impropriety of an appeal to them in a work of religious mood. The score contains severe and ascetic instrumental combinations: oboe and tuba; flute, tuba, and timpani. But it is also full of thrilling music, such as that expressing Persephone's new vision of the light . . . it is spiritual light for Strawinsky, the light from the sphere transcending that of the underworld that is our earthly home . . . or the gorgeous, Russian barbaric chorus hailing the reborn queen, with its festive drum beats; or the final chorus. Not a reconstitution of music, the work is nonetheless very satisfactory. The style, the diatonic one of the latter Strawinsky, containing elements ranging from the Italian operatic to the Russian primitive, is more unified than in *Oedipus Rex*. The work stands high among his best later things with the *Symphony of the Psalms* and the *Duo Concertante*.

THE EVOLUTION OF STRAWINSKY

III

Strawinsky's general figure and position have meanwhile been growing ever plainer: it would appear as if we were commencing to see him with more than merely contemporary eyes.

He stands before us as the inventor of a new kind of music, an extremely virile kind, the healthy antithesis of the later romanticists' excessively feminine music: and the composer of work essentially religious, not only in the sense in which all art is religious, insomuch as it expresses the meaning and the value of life, but in the sense that it expresses the relations of God and man, oftentimes in forms recalling the liturgical; and, finally, the author of pieces that, high in endeavor and couched in the grand style, severe and great and classic in their orderliness, convey a great experience, and one ultimately weightier than that of any other contemporary composer. At the same time he appears to us as one who, destined to remain conspicuous among the composers of the last centuries, will never, except with a very few of his pieces, probably the very early *L'Oiseau de Feu*, and *Petrushka* and *Le Sacre*, find widespread favor, and not because of any limitation of his art's emotional scope or of his craftsmanship. The cause of this prelimitation of appeal, which even today renders his work the possession of a relatively small section of the musical public, lies for us in the circumstance that Strawinsky is the great reactionary; and the great reactionary is never a popular spokesman.

We use the epithet "reactionary" in the sense in which it was employed in Thomas Mann's recent paraphrase of Nietzsche's characterization of the work of the romantic school of 1800 in Germany, and by inference, that of this group's western allies, De Maistre, Chateaubriand, Montalembert, and the youthful Victor Hugo. This imaginative work Nietzsche, and Mann after him, called "progressive in the form of a reaction," and its creators "powerful and infectious and at the same time anachronistic spirits, who for a last time conjured up a past epoch of humanity, as a sign that the new tendency of things against which they strove was not yet sufficiently strong victoriously to withstand them." Brilliantly expressive of the whole prescientific, medieval, Christian world-idea, it contributed to the experience of the race precisely by virtue of its illuminativeness.

And in Strawinsky we feel a spirit very like that of these poets of the early nineteenth century, challenging the feeling men have had in the last centuries and conjuring up past epochs of humanity as a sign that the new tendency is not yet sufficiently strong victoriously to withstand them. Strawinsky has not only given us a series of musical pictures of the past: that, after all, is what many artists do. He has been re-expressing past ways of feeling and world-ideas very much at variance with those of the great composers who have created our music. These great composers, as we have said, felt idealistically and found a world full of ideal elements and glorious possibilities, containing above all the Idea, and human beings potentially noble and capable of freedom. Their work expressed a grave optimism, a feeling of the real presence of God in the world, and a world all-identical with the godhead. To this idealism, Strawinsky has opposed the pessimism that informed the world-pictures of earlier societies, and societies even more primitive than the medieval one evoked by the reactionaries of 1800. The first of these world-pictures were nihilistic, expressive of a cosmos oppressively a senseless mechanism, and also troglodyte. In *Le Sacre* Strawinsky asso-

THE EVOLUTION OF STRAWINSKY

ciated his musical ideas with a pagan ceremonial representing the primitive religious complex of ideas about the earth, night, the dark side of nature and the human psyche, and death: a complex of ideas very much in line with those of the German "romantic" school. And with his archaicizing works—in contradistinction to his neoclassicism, which is progressive, Strawinsky's archaicism may be explained as symbolic of his reactionary tendency—with these post-war works, he began giving us world-ideas which may even be pre-Christian, and certainly are very primitive. And while a benevolent God appears to throne over the *Symphonie des Psaumes,* the composition seems to posit him entirely removed from the bitter and painful cosmos and in a realm approachable by man only through the gate of death. In *Perséphone,* too, the underworld would appear to be the earth, or at least the earth deprived of the divine light; and this light would appear to fall into it from without, and not to be, as the great idealists would aver, an element of the creation itself, if not its very essence.

That to a degree the whole phenomenon of Strawinsky's contribution is closely connected with the phenomenon of the war and its consequences is undeniable. One recognizes in his amazing compositions the images of a world dictated by materialistic science and the feeling left by the catastrophe. Nonetheless, we do not see the relationship as one of cause and effect, rather more as one resulting from the circumstance that the war gave the genius of Strawinsky a particularly brilliant opportunity for realizing itself. The feeling of life which Strawinsky has conveyed would have materialized itself even without the war. Its idealistic antithesis had grown rhetorical in inheritors of the Beethovenian tradition such as the early Strauss, Mahler, and the Scriabin of the orchestral poems; and itself and its pessimism and feeling of a static and painful world is permanent in the race, and periodically eloquent. Precisely what its source is, we cannot say. It would appear kin to that fatalism, that feeling of oppression and contraction and of the world-cave—very different from that expansive feeling of limitlessness of the great Europeans, and periodically releasing itself in fanatical outbreaks like that of *Le Sacre*—which Frobenius and Spengler have named and attributed the one to the Semitic and the other to the Magian worlds. Probably there was nothing fortuitous in the circumstance that the *Symphonie des Psaumes* called to our mind the mosaic-gilded interior of one of the Byzantine domes that for both these critics represent this eastern world-idea: one of those domes from whose vaulting the Christ and his Mother gaze pitilessly down upon the accursed human race. What is curious is that Strawinsky is not a Semite, and thus we must attribute this fundamental primitive, pessimistic, and fatalistic feeling conveyed by his music to a source in Russian nature, itself in many respects Asiatic and oriental, an attribution made easy for us by the fact that the Russian fatalism we hear in the music, say, of Moussorgsky, would appear to be very closely related to the "kismet" of the Levantines. But that is but another way of saying that Strawinsky is one of the great, the representative, Russian composers; and one who through the power of his genius as well as circumstances will stand among the great representatives of a world-idea that has long haunted and continues to haunt the race of men.

BARTÓK

Bartók

BELA BARTÓK'S music has a powerful urgency, one of the most powerful that contemporary music shows. It is the urgence of the primitive, of the child and the child of the skyscraper period: a wild, intolerable tension bringing him to his instruments as to drums, and releasing itself through their beats and rhythms with fire and fury. It is like Strawinsky's: in fact, the whole of Bartók's work parallels the Russian's to an amazing degree. And as it does so honestly, in instances anticipating that body's deviations, and where it keeps pace with it, doing so in perfect independence, it provides another proof that the developments in the art of music incidental to the present generation's life are due not to individual willfulness, but to the Zeitgeist. For, confronted with this honest parallelism, we cannot but recognize the agency of a commonly informing spirit.

Like Strawinsky—his junior by a single year—once his academic period was over, Bartók began composing in the spirit of nationalism; for his part, as one of the musical representatives of the particularist or separatist movement in Hungary. Two immature works, *Kussuth,* a tone poem for grand orchestra, and the *Rhapsody,* Op. 1, for orchestra and piano, convey, like *The Firebird,* their junior by a few years, a sense of the national identity through more or less traditional forms. *Kussuth* and the *Rhapsody* move indeed as fully in the wake of Liszt, Brahms, Wagner, and Richard Strauss as *The Firebird* in that of Rimsky, Scriabin, Moussorgsky, and Wagner. But shortly Bartók's individuality projected itself clearly in the little piano *Bagatelles,* in 1908, much as Strawinsky's in his brilliant *Petrushka* in 1911, both compositions constituting original nationalistic music.

Still, in Bartók's far more than in Strawinsky's case, this original nationalism was intwined with a thoroughgoing folklorism of which it was both the cause and the consequence. Strawinsky had used popular Russian music, as the good nationalist, the pupil of Rimsky, that he then was; and his style was modified in accordance with this material. But the folk material he had used was fairly familiar: if he had gone to the people, it was much more for the color of their music, its rhythms, instrumentation, robust spirit, than for its actual melodic substance. Bartók, however, had begun, out of nationalistic love of local Hungarian man, collecting actual Magyar folk music—not the songs and dances the musical world had hitherto considered the actual Magyar folk music; that was merely the deformed and vulgarized version of the actual thing exploited by itinerant gypsy musicians. The music Bartók found in use among the country people was a much more distinct, dignified, juicy one than the Hungarian-gypsy and was based on scales that pointed to its partly Byzantine, partly Asiatic, origin. And in the course of the next two decades he helped collect many hundreds of Hungarian and Rumanian and Wallachian folk songs, and recorded and published, and harmonized and even incorporated in the forms of original compositions, many of them. The *Bagatelles* indeed represent only the first of the far-reaching effects that the acquaintance with the actual musical lore of his people and the solution of the problems of the stylistically correct harmonization of its melodically and metrically subtle songs, was to produce on his imagination.

BARTÓK

At the same time both the *Bagatelles* and *Petrushka,* anticipating their younger brethren, contain passages frankly, unequivocally bitonal. Music in two simultaneous tonalities, like that in the *Bagatelles* and in *Petrushka,* had probably been made not only possible but natural, according to the law of progressive evolution, by the chromaticism of the late romantics. That had broken down the walls between the various tonalities. There had been suggestions of bitonalism in Moussorgsky, in the original version of the polonaise in *Boris;* and Strauss in *Also Sprach Zarathustra*—a work that had deeply impressed the young Bela Bartók—had ended the piece in two different keys and in the finale of *Salomé* had most effectively superimposed a chord in F on a chord in C. Over in America, Charles Ives had in his total solitude actually been writing polytonically since the early 1900's. But the bitonal *Bagatelles* and the extended bitonal passages in *Petrushka* were the first of their kind to reach the public—and reached it with a vengeance, since the very unimpressionistic robustness, earthiness, and what Van der Null calls the glassy precision of these new works, set their revolutionary methods and expressions in "the most glaring light." Meanwhile, they coincided more or less with another revolutionary step in harmony, also the consequence of the thorough chromaticism of Wagner and Rimsky and the impressionism of Debussy—the atonalism of Schönberg.

Again, directly after their respective passages of the tonal Rubicon, Bartók and Strawinsky both developed into thoroughgoing "primitivists," the first in the little *Bear Dance* and in the *Allegro Barbaro,* the second in the mighty *Sacre.*—To a degree, this "primitivism" of the two composers was also made not only possibly but natural by the law of progressive evolution, through developments in the immediate past of music. It is an outcome of the "barbarism" of the late romanticists, especially that of the Liszt-born Russian Five; of their exploitation of wild and frenetic rhythms, of oriental monotony and color, and of other effects antithetical to the elegance and grace of salon music. Yet the short, rigid phrases reiterated with hammerlike regularity, so characteristic of "primitivism," constitute a realization of the possibilities of static music far more extreme than any attempted by the "barbarians"; indeed, they seem to have appeared in Strawinsky's music as much in consequence of intuitions of the life of mechanisms as of any others. And Bartók, too, has had his "mechanistic" fantasies, most notably in the idea of the ballet *The Wooden Prince,* although to a lesser degree than his great coeval. Both composers meanwhile have remained "primitivistic" throughout their careers, Bartók somewhat more, Strawinsky somewhat less. Primitivism ceased to dominate Strawinsky after *Les Noces* and appears only episodically in *Oedipus Rex,* in the *Symphony of the Psalms,* and in *Perséphone.* But all through Bartók's music, from the early orchestral *Two Impressions* through the second string quartet to the very latest pieces, you will find passages in which rigid phrases are repeated with very slight variations with almost hammerlike emphasis and insistency and wild frenetic rhythms; and feel a familiar impulse, something like a wild man's and nonetheless modern, expressing itself vividly, through instruments sounded as are drums.

The parallelism has continued up to the very present hour. In complete independence of each other—unlike Picasso and Braque, the two composers have never worked together—and still as though shoulder to shoulder, they have been leading music ever further away from Wagnerism. For Bartók, representative of a small nation though he is, has none of the provinciality of outlook that is so frequently the defect of such representatives; he is as much the good European, as much in the van of life, as though he lived in one of the major capitals. And progress from Wagnerism (in the sense that Wagnerism and poetic or expressive music are synonymous) toward pure music is the achievement of the day. They have also been developing a classic-dynamic music, classic inasmuch as it is conceived in the closed classic schemes of the suite, the sonata, the concerto, dynamic insomuch as it contains a continuously evolving, progressive material. They have furthermore been eschewing harmonic methods in favor of contrapuntal ones and also reviving old ecclesiastical modes and making original mixtures of major and minor keys, and latterly have reverted from bitonalism toward a new sort of diatonism—pan diatonism, in Nicholas Slonimsky's happy nomenclature. And they have been producing music bonily structural in the spirit of the day, and both in structure and content expressive of the present hour. That hour's tempo, its nervousness, its strain, its stimulation, its lassitude, all are here; its energy without grace, its excitement without passion; its irritations. Grotesque, mordant, even scurrilous feelings come certainly very frequently to expression in both men's compositions: feelings of revolt, of exasperation, of satire, in Strawinsky with something of the irony and caricature of the clown, in Bartók with more of the wit and mischievousness of the kobold. (Or is it the child's? There are pieces of Bartók's, the second movement of the Suite, Op. 14, that recall the demonry of a child, determined to be impossible to his heart's content.)

Still, these two parallel bodies of work are perfectly distinct. We never, for instance, find Bartók archaicizing, like Strawinsky, recalling now Bach, or Händel, or some other eighteenth-century composer, now Italian opera from Pergolesi to Verdi, or forming a compost of these idioms blent with Russian primitivism and with jazz. Bartók's style-feeling is more consistent than the mercurial Russian's. He has pretty faithfully continued to cast his thought in the style developed by his treatment of the old Hungarian folk music. Nor does he ever verge upon the neo- or the pseudo-classic. Besides, the piano is Bartók's medium to a degree that it is not Strawinsky's. Bartók, too, has composed for the orchestra—the *Images* and the *Dance Suite;* and for the stage, an opera, *Bluebeard's Castle,* and two ballets, *The Wooden Prince* and *The Singular Mandarin*—the latter one of his most significant works. And he has written five string quartets, and a violin sonata, and a number of songs. Still, it is in piano music that he has worked out most of his cardinal problems—first in the little *Bagatelles,* then in the *Nenias* or laments and in the *Rumanian Dances,* then in the Suite, Op. 14, and later in the piano Sonata and in the great piano Concerto. Bartók himself, incidentally, is a most distinguished pianist, a fine interpreter of Beethoven sonatas.

In fact, it would be impossible ever to confuse the works of the two composers: they are two branches that have grown close together but separately from a single bole. Bartók, to begin with, is more the miniaturist: despite the Concerto and the Sonatas, huge structures in the grand style like the *Sacre* or the *Symphony of the Psalms* figure less frequently in the roster of his works than in that of Strawinsky's. Again, Bartók is by far the more subjective and lyrical of the two men; and his music reflects brooding states of which Strawinsky's gives little evidence. The essential quality of his music is also extremely individual: finely dry like a wine very moderately infused with liqueur and without sweetness and fruity flavor. One is tempted to say it has a nutty taste, for it is frequently dark of timbre, gritty, earthy, acrid, bassoon-colored, or silvery.

BARTÓK

All in all, Bartók's music is by far more special, like Debussy's, than Strawinsky's is—reflecting a life somewhat withdrawn, outside the forum and the market, shy, sober, aristocratic, and indifferent to the floodlights.

Bartók is also the less powerfully gifted of the two men, more restricted in his somewhat more subjective, lyrical scope of life than Strawinsky in his distinctly objective one; less varied in mood. The first movement of a work by Bartók is very likely to be an *allegro barbaro;* the second, a *nenia;* the third, one of his characteristic scherzolike dances. His mind has gone into subtlety and intricacy more than range and scope of experience. He is less evenly inspired than Strawinsky and has given fewer perfectly sustained works. Works as representative of Bartók as the piano Sonata, the Second and the Fourth String Quartets, all contain powerful, completely distinguished and fascinating movements that exhibit his singular power of combining immobile harmonies with developing melodies, or his gift for varying rhythmic patterns or exploiting the color of the stringed instruments; and yet the *nenia* of the Sonata, for all the effective relations of the reiterated plangent *E,* is somewhat static; and the first movement of the Second Quartet is somewhat "out of style" and reminiscent of Scriabin; and that of the Fourth Quartet far less pointed and significant than the other, fabulously pungent movements. In matching perfect pieces like *L'Histoire du Soldat* or *Les Noces* among Bartók's compositions, one finds oneself somewhat restricted, and turning to some of the smaller piano works, particularly the Suite, Op. 14, of the mounting excitement sustained through three contrasted movements, and after a tragic fall, beautifully dissolved in the ethereal finale. But these are the negative aspects of an extremely positive achievement. Like Strawinsky again, Bartók has written powerful and subtle and solid original music, powerfully articulative of the tense, nervous feeling of the age of steel; and timeless too. One has the impression that the piano Concerto is among the greatest of modern pieces, worthy to stand beside *Le Sacre,* and that the musician who after hearing it cried, "Grand; like a new Vittoria," was not far from the truth.

"Gurrelieder"

AN artist's expression infrequently is completely individualized by the time of his twenty-seventh year, and that of Schönberg was not exceptional. When in 1900 he began to set the poetic cycle which the seraph of Danish literature, Jens Peter Jacobsen, had formed from the legend of King Waldemar I of Denmark and the fair Tove and called the songs of Gurre, the castle with which the legend associated their tragic love, the future heresiarch still was, regularly enough, under the domination of the expressions of his immediate predecessors. These were the Wagnerian, the Straussian, the Brahmsian, and the Mahleresque. His setting of *Gurrelieder* for giant orchestra, choruses, and solo voices thus is largely traditional; like the youthful work of other gifted composers, say, the Wagner of *The Flying Dutchman,* the Strauss of *Don Juan,* the Strawinsky of *L'Oiseau de Feu.* The giant cantata recalls the general romanticism of the late nineteenth century, in particular the rapture and the harmonic system of Wagner, the vasty means of Mahler's choral symphonies and something of his melodic architectural form, Strauss' beefy contrapuntal effects and dramatic em-

"GURRELIEDER"

phasis, and Brahms' rich *Lieder* style. It actually is a sort of Wagnerian music drama cast with Strauss' and Mahler's symphonic means in the form of a song cycle, for soloists and chorus, preceded by a prelude and inclusive of two sizable orchestral transitions, and not without distinct Brahmsian characteristics.

One tenor represents Waldemar, another Klaus the fool. The soprano represents Tove; the mezzo the little wood dove; the bass the peasant; the four-part male chorus, Waldemar's ghostly henchmen. The work falls into three parts, lightly corresponding to the three parts of a symphony and the acts of an opera. The first includes the songs of Waldemar and Tove expressing their longing for each other, the songs vocal of their joy in reunion, their nocturnal dialogue and premonitions of death and of resurrection, and finally, after the first orchestral interlude, the song of the wood dove lamenting the death of Tove at the hands of the jealous queen. The second part contains Waldemar's denunciation and rejection of God. The third embodies the demonic nocturnal hunt to which Waldemar and his henchmen have been condemned, the choruses of the men interspersed by the song of the frightened peasant, the jittery soliloquy of the fool, the ghostly Waldemar's expression of his sense of the dead Tove in the voice of the woods, in the regard of the lake, in the laughing light of the stars: and finally the play of the summer wind and the resurrection of the lovers in the life of nature.

The composer of *Dreimals Sieben Lieder des Pierrot Lunaire* is nonetheless clearly heralded, nay actually present, in *Gurrelieder;* as definitely present there as the composer of *Die Walküre* in *Der fliegende Holländer,* the composer of *Don Quixote* in *Don Juan,* the composer of *Les Noces* in *L'Oiseau de Feu.* The work, naturally enough, is unequal. The first four songs in the first part have far less quality than the later ones; and pages such as that of Waldemar's blasphemy, the macabre hunting chorus, and the final salutation of the sunrise, reveal more of ambition and striving than of power. The dreaminess and the sweetness of some of the music is occasionally cloying. And still, for all its weaknesses, its Wagnerian, Straussian, Brahamsian echoes, *Gurrelieder* is a creation, the sonorous, sumptuously colored embodiment of an original idea, full of glowing poetic music, and doubtless has a future. The conception, to begin with, is a formal one. Each of the nineteen songs composing the whole, a simple or double *Lied* form, is built up structurally from its own melodic germ and is organically related to the rest by the cyclic use of themes, by contrasts of tonality and character, and by orchestral transitions of various length. The work actually concludes with the chord in the tonality with which it began. And Schönberg's form is already distinctive: and when we speak of his form as being already distinctive, we are referring to the form of the older, the main part of the *Gurrelieder,* written between 1900 and 1902, and not that of the close of the last section, including the *Sprechstimme,* the melodic use of the celesta, and the high, shrill, piercing sonorities; for that dates from 1910 and is therefore contemporaneous with the *Three Pieces,* Op. 11, and the work of the middle Schönberg. Here, in the earliest parts of the score, we find him melodic and contrapuntal to a degree, even on the simplest and most Wagnerian pages. While his harmony is fairly Wagnerian, it is anything but slavishly so, displaying a considerable sensitivity. As for his melodic line, it frequently leaps over wide intervals, as in Tove's third song, and skips about nervously in the songs of the peasant and the fool. Instrumental sonorities are often used thematically, from Tove's second song onward. The instruments themselves frequently are employed soloistically, and examples of the oppositions of the sonorities of various orchestral families are anything but uncommon. And the individualized constituent forms and the grand one they build up communicate individual moods and an individual experience. If these moods and this experience are "romantic"; if *Gurrelieder,* like *Tristan,* constitutes with surging, rapturous, and dreamy page after page a "climate of love," it does so unhackneyedly. The erotic moods are tenderer, more penetrating and spiritualized than Wagner's relatively simple ones. Schönberg's heroine, too, possibly in conformity with Jacobsen's idea, is much more feminine and shy than Wagner's heroic amorosa. The range of the moods also includes such fantastic and original variants as those of the bedeviled peasant, the dislocated and grotesque agonies of the fool, the Puckish humors of the *Summer Wind's Wild Chase.* The very implicit experience, the vision of a vital progress by stages of personal love and personal loss to a selfless victorious absorption in the divine breath, the "life" of nature, while essentially romantic, is individual. And while the entire expression, like Wagner's, is rapturous and subjectively lyrical, it is rapturous to the verge of the ecstatic; and its psychographical and subjective lyricism borders on expressionism, on the ecstatically confessional. And it is a magical score, rich in the elusively mysterious, sensuous, melting, and bewitching sort of expressions which, drawn with a fineness no completely waking condition can achieve, flow from some enchantment in the subject itself and, abundant in the music of Schumann, of Wagner, of Debussy, are called poetical.

Need it be asseverated that these distinctive characteristics of *Gurrelieder* are the germs of those completely distinguishing and characterizing the later work, at least that part of it previous to the systematization of the twelve-tone technique?

DISCOVERIES OF A MUSIC CRITIC

The plasticity of the *Gurrelieder*—what is it but the adumbration of the extraordinary plasticity of those later works, indicative of an intuiton always connected with a form-feeling that works itself out with utter relentlessness, compression, and logicality, whether in the molds of the *Lied* form or in those of contrapuntal forms, the passacaglia, the canon, the inverted canon, or the *motus cancrizans*? The harmonic sensitivity, what is that but the indication of the sensitivity that was to produce the bewitching harmonic beauty of the characteristic atonal pieces, the third of the Five Pieces for orchestra, *Der Wechslender Accord* in especial. The wide leaps and skips of the melodic line, are they indeed anything but the annunciation of the melodic line of the scherzo of the first *Kammersymphonie* and of *Das Buch der Hängenden Gärten,* the chamber operas, the song "Herzgewächse," the *Three Times Seven Songs of Pierrot Lunaire*? For us, they are nothing if not prophetic; and for us, the thematic use of instrumental sonorities is equally so; also the soloistic use of instruments, triumphant first in the *Kammersymphonie* and then in all Schönberg's instrumental pieces. And the oppositions of the sonorities of various instrumental families seem anticipatory of one of the traits of style most distinctly Schönbergian. Equally so is the feeling communicated by *Gurrelieder*. The feelings expressed by the later music are those of exquisite, idealistic, not so largely neurotic as neurodynamic modern people—people who make tremendously prompt, deep, intense nervous responses. Tove herself is but an earlier version of the exquisite essence figuring in *Pierrot* as "eine weisse Wäscherin." And the ideas which compose and relate these essences are those of the erotic experience. More consistently and continually than any other contemporary composer of worth, Schönberg is the musician of the exquisite, the deep, and also the bitter and painful erotic adventure: a circumstance which connects his art with that of Beardsley, of Strindberg, of Rodin, and that of other great "decadents." Op. 15, the cycle of songs on poems derived from *Das Buch der Hängenden Gärten* by Stefan George, creates a "climate of love" even more subtly, more poignantly and inclusively than *Gurrelieder*. The monodrama *Erwartung* brings to biting, almost madly intense, expression the experience of the modern woman who, wandering beyond the walls of her little garden in search of her lover, finds him dead for the sake of another. And the other little music drama, *Die Glückliche Hand*—the hand of Venus—conveys the experience of an enamored artist who, physically disgusting to his partner, is crushed by her efforts to escape him. The *Serenade,* Op. 24, also expresses, with the help of the words of Petrarch, the experience of the rejected lover. Again, the moods of the later Schönberg include many that, extensions of the tortured ones of the latter sections of *Gurrelieder,* approach the extreme of uneasiness, of torment and dolor; and the cantata's peasant, Klaus the fool, and the Puckish summer wind attain a kind of apotheosis in the extremely bizarre moods of the "youthful idealist," the moon-drunken dandy *Pierrot Lunaire* of the fantastic twenty-one songs. The later forms of expression are also extremely ecstatic, almost supremely so, and supremely confessional. Psychographical, subjectively lyrical music would seem to reach its most exalted pitch in these works: they make the composer seem one determined not to shrink from the most audacious articulations of inner movements, those of the unconscious itself, and the ultimate secrets of his own soul. And the whole of the later music, with its many passages of the purest lyrical expansion—for all its inclusion of pages of paper music—constitutes the most poetic, glamorous music produced by any living composer. That poetry is a fragile one, an exquisite one, a sort of expression of the gleaming, evanescent moment of feeling. *Pierrot Lunaire,* which contains this "Celtic magic" perhaps more abundantly than any other one of Schönberg's works—it is perhaps its apex and one of those of modern music—may even seem, with its elusive lights, surges, ecstasies, aromas, a sort of Chinese jar filled with conserved flower petals, and thus something of an anomaly in the present world. But it is not certain that succeeding times will find it so and may not conceive it as the crystallization of the finest Viennese, the *fin-de-siècle* European sensibility, and find the place of the composer close to that of the other exquisite musical poets, Schumann, Wagner, Chopin, and Debussy.

Indeed so clear a prefigurement of the composer of all these magical pieces does *Gurrelieder* give that it is difficult to understand how musicians whose interest in their art in a serious one could have contrived to assist at the first American performance of the revelatory piece, under Stokowski's baton early in 1932, and continue, for all the grossness of the production, unconvinced of the integrity of Schönberg's entire output up to the time of his systematization of the twelve-tone technique. That they should have come away as puzzled by the system-making Schönberg as they were before they heard the cantata, is not a wonder. For *Gurrelieder* casts no light on him. But that it should have failed to make them conscious of the one man present from first to last in all of Schönberg's pieces confessing the dominance of sensibility, and failed to make them recognize in the later atonal works, up to the *Serenade* and the Suite, Op. 25, the logical developments of the germs stirring in this first experiment with the larger means if not the larger forms, verges upon the miraculous. For us, Schönberg's declaration at the time of the first performances of his songs on George's poems is unsurprising: "In these *Lieder* I have succeeded for the first time in approaching an ideal of expression and form that have hovered before me for years. Hitherto, I had merely not sufficient strength and sureness to realize that ideal. Now, however, I . . . have definitely started on my journey." For if we ourselves see anything in Schönberg's career, it is nothing if not the development of a man according to the law of life which compels us, if we would live and grow, to become ever more fully and nakedly what we essentially are.

"Wozzeck"

THE musical world may think to perceive in the isolation in which members of the Viennese group about Schönberg have been living with their intimates and their pupils, acquainted each, it has been asserted, with at most eleven persons outside his actual family, the sign of their divorce from common humanity and self-indulgent concentration of interest in a private world; and choose to detect in the apparently fantastic monotonal system, the twelve-tone technique original among them, the proof of a retreat from life. Yet it is a fact that out of this secluded group there has come a dramatic work beautifully and broadly expressive, through the new musical form developed among its members, of the psyche and the world of one of the most tragic of contemporary human types. This is the *Wozzeck* of Alban Berg,* himself one of the principal creators in the *cénacle,* and indubitably Schönberg's most gifted pupil. And the piece proves that the insulation of the components of the Viennese coterie is merely apparent and actually

* This essay was written before Berg's death.

the state of self-sufficiency, of indifference to the politics of art, and of utter concentration upon the formal and aesthetic problems crowding in upon them, in which the complete feeling of life leaves pure artists.

The book of this deeply moving musical drama is made up of fifteen of the twenty-three brief scenes of the tragi-grotesque play of *Woyzeck* or *Wozzeck,* the little masterpiece in which Georg Büchner, a prematurely deceased member of the Young German school of the 1830's and a revolutionary who expressed the tragedy of revolutions in his drama *Dantons Tod,* arraigned the existing social idea through sympathy with the under dog. The action half realistically, half symbolistically, represents the catastrophe of a poor soldier in a provincial German garrison during a time of peace; but the relation of the crude action to the facts of poverty, of human savagery and stupidity, generalizes it into a symbol of the experience not only of the "little man" but of the fine but incomplete and defenseless individual in an unspiritual society. Franz Wozzeck, the protagonist, is weak not only because of his ignorance, his poverty, and his low social status, but because of the circumstance that his sensitive mind is a half-developed individual's. As Dr. Willi Reich points out in his excellent analysis, Wozzeck has an unclear sense of the primeval unity of his being and a childlike intuition of the life of the all-mother, and he has begun to judge for himself and to judge himself. But his half-awakened individualism only renders him helpless against the humiliations he has to endure from the powers of the world and the repressions of military servitude; and under his humiliations and repressions, assisted by his own inner weakness, his intuitions become delusions, and he ends as a murderer and a suicide. These oppressive half external, half internal powers are satirically represented by Büchner in the form of a caricature of a captain, a

"WOZZECK"

military doctor, and a drum major, so that the whole of Wozzeck's spiritual as well as material environment appears in a grotesquely comic light. Through the figure of the captain we perceive the force of a fear-engendered Philistine morality; through that of the doctor, the inhuman coldness of materialistic science, inimical to man and his soul; and through that of the drum major, the brute in the male. All these part real and part symbolic as well as half external and half interior forces grind Wozzeck under and deride him. The military doctor, a scoundrel, performs medical experiments upon him—Wozzeck submitting because the few groschen the doctor pays him help support his girl and their illegitimate child. The drum major seduces the girl, actually half abandoned by the helpless Wozzeck. The captain, himself tormented by the military doctor, maliciously opens Wozzeck's eyes upon the intrigue. Faced with the final humiliation of having to share the object of his love with another, the desperate soldier stabs the girl and drowns himself in a pond.

The fifteen scenes drawn by Berg from this mordant little tragi-grotesque have been organized by him in the form of three acts of five scenes apiece, constituting respectively an Exposition, a Crisis, and a Catastrophe; and in this shape they have been made contributory to a music drama intensifying Büchner's idea with a power that sets the product beside the most aesthetic works bequeathed the lyric theater since Wagner —*Pelléas, Le Coq d'Or,* and *Elektra*. The composer has freshly felt the oppressive world of the under dog. His atonal material is deeply infused with the terrible experience and its tormented moods. And he had conceived his score in sympathy with the dramatist, reinforcing *his* work in the way permitted by it. The dramatist had called for incidental music in the forms of military marches, folk songs and choruses, and dances of various kinds. Again, his play is episodic, inviting musical connections of the short scenes. And its realism, in spirit not so much that of the nineteenth as of the expressionistic twentieth century, almost invites a musical reinforcement of the action itself. For, figurative of inarticulate characters, it allows these personages to exhibit their feelings and their conscious, semi-conscious, and wholly unconscious motives in brittle, ejaculatory, sometimes entirely irrational, words and phrases and sentences resembling those of persons under fearful emotional stress, thus by its very illyricality offering music the opportunity of purveying lyric and choragic expressions and augmenting the dramatic expression in the way most naturally its own. And Berg's score performs the three chores consciously and unconsciously left to music by Büchner. It supplies the realistic incidental music. It connects the little scenes with interludes. It supplements the verbal and dramatic expressions with music that lyrically expresses the tormented feelings and states of the protagonists and that choragically renders the sentiments of an ideal spectator moved by the vision of their unnecessary suffering; particularly in the great orchestral epilogue, which, placed before the final scene and recapitulative of the thematic material of the score, seems to cry to the heavens the pity of the waste of the human being, and to men the need of a humane world.

And it presents its entire contribution, popular incidental music and all, in the shape of formalized symphonic music. Retaining to a certain extent the Wagnerian technique of the Leitmotiv, Berg has rejected the porridgelike Wagnerian form of the music drama, conceiving his score in the framework of forms drawn from absolute music—suites, passacaglias, themes with variations, fugues, sonata forms, inventions, etc.—and integrating his material in these traditional molds solidly, sustainedly, sometimes with a refreshing musicianly length of breath. Perhaps not all of these formalizations of his are equally distinguished or unified among themselves from the point of view of style. Berg is one of the genial contemporary Europeans, a student of Schönberg's quite worthy of comparison with his puissant teacher. All of his works, his String Quartet and Chamber Symphony no less than his *Wozzeck,* introduce us to expressions of a live sensibility, a genuine lyricism and eloquence, and a fire nobly held in rein: the possible effect of the combination of Germanic feeling and fervor with Viennese elegance. One is tempted to call Berg's temperament simpler than Schönberg's, more sensuous and warm and romantic: and he is armed with a deal of this master's prodigious technique. But he is also a little less powerful than Schönberg, and his expression tends more to run in grooves dug by the music of Debussy and *Tristan* than Schönberg's does. He is less sure of his style than his master, less evenly inspired. Thus, just as in the material of *Wozzeck,* one sometimes hears echoes of the *Ring* and of *Pelléas,* one sometimes finds the score recalling, as in the great orchestral epilogue, the mannerisms of Puccini and Strauss. Still, these pages are venial sins, not really blemishing. The music as a whole sounds very rich; and the innumerably many fruits of exquisite feeling and discretion audible in it, to a degree amply compensate for the occasional secondary passages. Besides, much of *Wozzeck* is prime: the passacaglia, for example, the variations, indeed the majority of the scenes and interludes; and all of it with sure eloquence reinforces, interprets, and generalizes the dramatic idea. We never find the composer sacrificing emotion or the interests of the drama to the traditional musical organisms in which he has cast his score. The vocal medium, a mixture of song proper and Schönbergesque speech-song, conforms realistically to the drama of the words and situations. And through Berg's constant application of the musical principle of variation in conformity to the dramatic movement, the traditional forms remain sensitively, pointedly psychographic and representative of the developments of the tragedy. The score as a whole is capitally expressive, particularly in the soft, descending, dragging progressions accompanying the deep depression into which the laden Wozzeck is thrown by the voices of nature at twilight, in the stuttering rhythm to which the horrified tavern guests awaken to the blood stains on the deranged man's hands, in the sibilant chromatic harmonies in sevenths that follow the suicide in the stilly pond, and in the dance scene with its unforgettable communication of a world from which all color and joy have fled.

Besides, the various absolute musical forms have been applied to the text with a sense of their dramatic relevancy. The five-part binary form, a symphony, underpins the entire second act, itself representative of the growing difference between Wozzeck and Marie. The music of the first act, exposing Wozzeck's relationship to his environment, begins in the form of a suite, continues first as a rhapsody, then as a military march and cradle song, then as a passacaglia, and ends as an *andante affetuoso quasi rondo;* and each of these forms, too, has its dramatic symbolism. The suite, for example, which is made up of archaic dance patterns such as gavottes, gigues, and sarabandes, underlies Wozzeck's conversation with the captain, the representative of church and state. The passacaglia mordantly intonates the scene exposing the doctor and his fixed idea; the military march and cradle song, the scene exhibiting Marie's excitement over the soldiery and her loneliness with her child. The last act, again, is made up of five inventions, through which a reiterated low B♭, an organ point, accompanies the mounting obsession of the murderous impulse; and like the preceding forms, the *inventions* are appropriate to the action. The very final scene, where Marie's boy innocently plays while other children run in with the news of the discovery of her dead body, is coupled with a *perpetuum mobile,* itself poignantly expressive of the sense of the unending meaningless motion called "life" with which the tragedy leaves one. Thus a pronouncedly successful attempt to solve the problem of form in the musical drama with the means of absolute music, an important proof that a large work can be built up atonally and with the twelve-tone technique of the Viennese group, and one of the solid achievements of modern music, *Wozzeck* has expressed the gray and terrible world where the "little man," the under dog, lives, suffers, and perishes alone, unseen, unheard: and thus idealistically given the modern world a potential social ligament. For the essence of the character himself, we repeat, is the under dog's in the widest sense. It is that of half the fine people we know. And it is that of all the people all over the world who, half-individualized members of an unspiritual society, suffer, break and perish, struggling to hold the bit of infinity that is the patrimony of the human creature.

Neoclassicism and Hindemith

THE most fruitful of contemporary German composers, Paul Hindemith, is one of the most conspicuous representatives of what is perhaps the most sharply defined movement in contemporary music. This is the neoclassical, an evolution that during its course recruited a formidable faction in many parts, inclusive of the most considerable and sensational of living talents—those of Strawinsky, Prokofieff, and Markevitch among the Russians, those of Ravel and Auric among the French, of Berners and Walton in England, Malipiero in Italy, Chavez in Mexico, and Copland, Harris, and Sessions in the United States. Like several other recent musical streams, the atonal, for example, it owes its inception very largely to Ferruccio Busoni and ultimately to his fondly quoted Nietzsche, who first called to music to rid itself of the incubus of the "actor," the man of the theater, the dramatist. This in any case is certain, that about the turn of the century Busoni, then as later a resident of Berlin, began rejecting in his own practice the programmatic forms—which during the ascendancy of Richard Strauss had been accepted to such a degree that a composer wishing to direct critical attention to his work had perforce to give it a program—in favor of forms entirely developed out of the purely musical substance itself, out of motion; and simultaneously, cultivating the linear, melodic, contrapuntal principle of composition in preference to the homophonic-harmonic one to which musical art had been true for almost a century and a half. This revolution or, better, reformation of Busoni's, named by him *neuer Klassizismus,* acquired an independent strong adherent in Max Reger. Reger not only wrote absolute music, principally in the chamber forms, but also essayed the linear, melodic, contrapuntal style: at least, harmony no longer figured in his works as the prop of melody. Reger also experimented with the infusion of a modern feeling and content into the old contrapuntal forms and the *stilo concertante*—the style of the old concerti grossi, with their soloistic and formal concertante exploitation of in-

NEOCLASSICISM AND HINDEMITH

strumental sonorities, their contrasting sections for the tutti and for solo groups. He even began the "archaicism" so very characteristic of the entire movement, reintroducing old technical devices such as the chord of the Neapolitan sixth, and others derived from composers even as very early as Dufay and Binchois. Another equally independent supporter of the movement appeared in the person of Gustav Mahler. Beginning with his Fourth, all Mahler's symphonies more and more fully embodied the linear, contrapuntal principle. In his very last works, *Das Lied von der Erde* and the Ninth Symphony, his clearly interweaving melodic lines have the lightness, and his structures the transparency and the aërialness, of chamber music. Even Richard Strauss may be said to have participated, in a limited way, in the reformation. Like some of that of the later Wagner, much of his music had had a certain polyphonic and contrapuntal cast; and in *Ariadne auf Naxos* he gave his orchestra a chamber-musical cast as well as proportion, and in this opera, its predecessor *Der Rosenkavalier,* and its successor, the ballet *Josephs Legende,* played with seventeenth- and early eighteenth-century idioms.

Still this stage of the new movement was chiefly precursive. The linear mold of all the pieces of the pre-war musicians, even those of Reger, the most thorough neoclassic of them all, were, as the musicologists are prepared to prove to us, compromise formations: a basically harmonic feeling was still strong in the composers. Neither was the abandonment of the program a complete one. Programs certainly haunted Mahler's Ninth and even peered through certain of the later pieces of Reger, the *Romantic Suite,* for example. Nor were the patterns of experience, conveyed by these neoclassicizing forms, to any great extent distinct from those conveyed by their immediate predecessors. The whole creative equipment of Busoni, Reger, and

DISCOVERIES OF A MUSIC CRITIC

Mahler was insufficiently powerful, and possibly too prematurely deprived by their deaths of its highest development, to complete a veritable reformation. That achievement had to wait upon the ripening of the fresh talents and new experiences of the pre-war neoclassicists' kindred among the members of the immediately post-war generation, those of Strawinsky and of Hindemith in particular.

Hindemith for his part definitely began producing the type of new music Busoni dreamt of—the new music, thoroughly contemporary in feeling, composed without reference to models derived from either nature or literature, conforming to the melodic form principle, spun entirely out of material inherently musical and in the *stilo concertante*—around the year 1923, his own twenty-eighth. It is possible he was stimulated to it partly through acquaintance with certain neoclassical works of Strawinsky's dating from the last years of the war, *L'Histoire du Soldat* in particular. Hindemith's later work suggests a certain attentiveness on his part to the innovations of the great Russian composer: the consonant basis of his *Neues vom Tage* follows somewhat abruptly upon that of *Oedipus Rex:* it is not at all incredible that, in lifting the curtain upon the music-making contained in *L'Histoire* as well as in *Renard* and the *Symphonies for Wind Instruments,* the armistice helped the young German to himself. But at most, it could merely have pointed him more intensely in the direction he was naturally taking. Hindemith is no follower, like Casella, who usually tags a Strawinsky piece for four instruments in five movements, say, with one for five instruments in six movements. He has his own broad approach; and his pioneer neoclassical piece of 1923, *Das Marienleben,* a powerful song cycle on poems by Rilke, in which the melodic line of the voice is entirely independent of the piano's, and the polyphony com-

NEOCLASSICISM AND HINDEMITH

prises polytonality, and the expression of the rhapsodic, ecstatic moods is entirely achieved by the character of the melodies and their progress, constituted only a stage in the plainly discernible series begun by his preceding compositions. Hindemith's early violin and viola sonatas, string quartets and songs, were neo-classical in Reger's sense, for all their slight reminiscences of Brahms and Strauss, though with considerably more melodic breath; and the polyphony inclusive of polytonality, thoroughgoing in *Das Marienleben,* is clearly heralded by them. It was an equally consequent step that Hindemith took in composing the important works, the products of the years 1924-7, that succeeded the song cycle: the polyphonic concertante concerti published as Op. 36 and 38—one for piano and twelve solo instruments, another for 'cello and ten solo instruments, still another for violin and large chamber orchestra, and concertos for viola and chamber orchestra and for grand orchestra. For all Hindemith's preceding orchestral compositions, in particular the half-parodistic *Kammermusik 1921,* with its haunted "nocturne" for four instruments, one of them a bell, and its madly seething finale on a fox trot and other jazz themes, were to a large degree cast in the chamber-musical, the concertante style. Again, Hindemith's first full-length grand opera, *Cardillac,* which succeeded the first series of his concerti, had its forerunners among his works, unique though it is by reason of its thoroughgoing application of the style and the forms of instrumental music to the matter of a music-opera. (Not only is the action frequently interrupted by set numbers, duets, sextets, and other concerted pieces—proceedings, as is well known, foreshadowed by the later operas of Strauss, *Der Rosenkavalier* and *Ariadne,* and by those of Busoni, *Dr. Faustus* in especial—but the different scenes are conceived as independent fugues, canons, and passacaglias.) In the little one-act comic opera "for

DISCOVERIES OF A MUSIC CRITIC

Burmese marionettes," *Das Nusch-Nuschi,* which dates from the days of the armistice, we find a similar reversion not only to the forms of dramatic music which temporarily suspend the dramatic action, but to sheerly instrumental forms. The second act of this amusing affair is a series of dances.

Besides, the style and quality of *Das Marienleben* and the series of concerte op. 36-38, like that of the later ones, massive products of his very recent years, would prevent even an inattentive critic from confusing them with other music. They are very personal and original. If these fine works shared their polyphonic polytonalism and their ruggedness with other neoclassical works, those of Strawinsky, for example—as the later ones their manifestation of a new harmonic tendency and a tendency to loosen up the strict polyphonic forms with other recent compositions—both their polytonalism and their ruggedness unquestionably are distinct and individual: to a degree because of the relentless uncompromisingness, verging almost on brutality, of the former, the Germanic quality of the latter. Hindemith's way of building up his works is also quite his own. Each is laid out in broad blocks that contrast with one another because of their different tonalities. What, however, most thoroughly distinguishes his pieces is the quality of the melodic lines that compose them. In instances made of material that verges on the commonplace, or reflects Bach servilely, they are nonetheless almost invariably extraordinarily powerful. As we see them from our vantage-point over the whole of Hindemith's product, they appear angularly excursive lines harnessed in regular, sometimes obstinate rhythmic patterns, oftentimes marches and courantes, and swiftly, vigorously progressive within their harnesses. Heavily, irregularly accented; impetuously overleaping intervals of fourths and fifths; characterized by brutally abrupt re-entries of themes; and periodically pointing out of the harmonic planes on which they lie toward other harmonies, they stretch out, oftentimes at a mad pace, steadily renewing themselves and oftentimes attaining great, in some cases prodigious, lengths. Still another feature distinguishing Hindemith's music is the clarity and originality of its sonority. Like that of all the neoclassicists from Mahler onward, his instrumental color is relatively uniform, unmixed, sustained and "conditioned," to adopt words of Egon Wellecz's, "not by a striving for sumptuosity and differentiation of timbre, but by a will to clearest contour and the most distinct architectonic structure." But Hindemith also writes exquisitely idiomatically for his instruments, particularly for the viola, his personal instrument. Thus his works are remarkable for single pages extremely novel and brilliant in their sonorities, like the second movement of the Concerto for orchestra, with its marvelous buzz and susurrus of the string choir, and for their thoroughgoing interfusions of color. The Concerto for organ, wind orchestra, and 'celli and bassi, is a good instance of sonorous relation, balance, unification. The orchestration balances and composes the timbres of the organ and the other instruments with an extraordinary richness.

Again the moods conveyed by Hindemith's music have extreme individuality. Their roguishness and irony and occasional feelings of nihility, their robustness, restraint, and freedom from the distinctly romantic expansivity, even their occasionally expressionistic, ecstatic elevation—especially in certain of the numbers of *Das Marienleben*—may possibly be shared by them with those of several contemporary composers. The smoldering passionateness, sober plaintiveness, deep inquisitiveness and broodingly analytic cast they have, nonetheless, are quite unique, for all Reger's shadowy anticipation of their tempers: particularly the Ragnorok moods, wild with a sense of the catastrophic inclination of things, that are conveyed by some of Hindemith's wild, whistling, fatalistic marchlike finales. Unique, too, are their ordonations, that associate and combine, as in the impassioned chamber cantata *Die Serenaden,* lighter moods, and very intimate ones—rapt, poetic lover's moods—with sentiments and intuitions of human destiny, and with a complete coherency. What, however, most thoroughly individuates Hindemith's work, well-nigh assigning it to a special category, is the circumstance that, in nine out of every ten of his compositions, the principal source of the auditor's tension and interest is the movement itself, the melodic line's sheer manner of progress. The interest is never entirely unrewarded by aesthetic gratification, it is true. Frequently lyrical, the dynamic-motory lines express moods and attitudes. Yet constant and adequate as it is, their expressivity somehow provides a minor gratification aside from the main one. That remains the melodic line's excursive way of running out, leaping, and renewing and extending itself, its "quality and coherency, variety, character." The pieces thus endow the mind principally with objects of fascinated observation and with a business of attention and of objectivation which, as it were, takes it away from personal concerns, and calms, rests, and re-equilibriates it. Several attempts on the part of German musicologists to name this possibly conscious, possibly unconscious, specially interesting form of new music have given us the novel terms *Motorik,* roughly to be translated as "motorism," also the word *Bewegungsvorgang*—"movement-event," and *Ablaufsform*—possibly "outflow-form."

Suffice it us, while the musical world ponders the merits and decides upon the final form of the new names, to notice to what a degree this peculiar, peculiarly interesting, and peculiarly rewarding music of Hindemith's they are intended to signify

NEOCLASSICISM AND HINDEMITH

integrates the impulses of the post-war generation. That generation was strenuously motory and strenuously observant, but, perhaps for traumatic reasons, strenuously motory and strenuously observant without complete emotional participation in matters, tending to solve problems by intense but sheerly muscular and nervous activity, like that of sport and the dance —a circumstance that impelled Honegger to dub a certain one of his expressions *Rugby*—and simultaneously given to exquisite, analytical inquiries into the mechanism and processes of things that are not entirely identical with a feeling-perception of them. And Hindemith's music provides, with its swiftly, ruggedly moving, prodigiously sustained lines that somehow remain coolly objective to the auditor, a form integrating, by the metaphysical miracle that is always art's, this generation's spirit of physical and of mental action and contemplation. Since we are on the subject, let us also remark to what a degree the whole neoclassical musical achievement, including Hindemith's, appears a consequence of the peculiar temper of this post-war generation of which he is so shining a member. In pointing to this connection, we do not refer only to the patterns of experience communicated by this new music, in their frequent jocosity and mordant irony, their restraint and freedom from romantic expansivity, obviously those of these disabused coevals. Nor do we refer particularly to the new varieties of surface form through which some of these patterns are communicated: *Gebrauchsmusik,* didactic works, pieces for amateurs, aural dramas for the radio, and others: plain consequences on the one hand of the generation's need of a new cult music and on the other of the new means for music provided by its apparatus (all of them have, incidentally, been exploited, often with success, by Paul Hindemith). We refer to the neoclassical form itself, the strict embodiment of the linear, melodic, contrapuntal principle in concertante and contrapuntal molds—referring to it in the very face of a consciousness that this connection with the post-war world very possibly was not the sole condition under which the restoration of the form might have been achieved; that it might very well have been effected during a time in which the general temper was other than it was during the last two decades. The linear is the major principle of musical art. Climaxes of cultures or possibly the sheer periodicity of all forms probably help to make for its periodical resurgence, and it is likely that it was they who did so in the post-war era and that the neoclassic forms themselves may well have helped call out the feeling the members of the new generation brought to it. Nonetheless, the evident peculiar favorableness of these forms to the expression of the way of being and feeling of the new composers, together with the fact of our own firm conviction that it is always the period's peculiar feelings of life which select and develop the forms it exploits—that "interior nature models all of life"—impels us to hold the victorious neoclassicism, if not a consequence, at least a concomitant of the post-war tenor of life. That period triumphed in a certain technical, mechanical precision: and the transparent, aërial neoclassical and concertante style opens the musician's way to a preciseness, a purely structural beauty, like that of machine-cut objects and edifices of steel, concrete, and glass. Again, the time had an aversion to subjectivity, to personal lyricism, in Eliot's words to "an excitement over its own feelings and a passionate enthusiasm over its own passions." Rightly or wrongly, it believed that "one is prepared for art when he has ceased to be interested in his own emotions and experiences except as material." And counterpoint, of course, tends to make a pattern of the lyrically as well as of the specifically expressive, to generalize and stylize it, as it were.

NEOCLASSICISM AND HINDEMITH

Besides, the period had, if not a distinctly anti-nationalistic, at least a liberal-catholic tendency, and talked of "western culture" instead of German *Kultur* and "the Latin genius." In the musical world, one composer who had originally gained fame as the author of a rankly nationalistic score called *Pictures of Pagan Russia,* and another who had written a piece called *Italia,* and a third who had been hailed as the pure Aryan German composer of Brahmsian, Regerish sonatas and quartets, suddenly found themselves standing shoulder to shoulder, since not only ward politics make strange bedfellows. The neoclassic form had probably offered them not only a catholic style in the place of one built on the folk song and the idiom of their various lands, but, through its reflection of the common antiquities of western musical culture, a mold itself symbolic of catholicity. Even the curious archaicism of its handling of these molds may have been emblematic, an attempt to connect with the spirit of a prenationalistic Europe; and emblematic, too, the group's attraction to jazz. For jazz is the product and the expression of cosmopolitan populations.

A recent incident certainly brings to light the profound kinship between Hindemith, at least, and the liberally, catholicly feeling group until lately at the head of west European affairs —reinforcing our contention. This is the incident of the intervention of Nazi officials in the matter of the production by the Berlin Opera of the composer's new grand opera *Matthis der Mahler* (Matthias Grünewald), with the consequence that the work was *verboten,* that Conductor Furtwängler temporarily resigned his post, and that Hindemith, who had already, despite his immense craftsmanly knowledge, been deprived of his post of teacher in the Berlin Normal School, the Hochschule, withdrew from Germany to Switzerland. The public reason for the interdiction was the opera's unromantic sonority;

DISCOVERIES OF A MUSIC CRITIC

"Hindemith," one heard loudly declared, "was a mere noise-maker." The very truth, however, is that the libretto, the author's own, is a tragedy of German democracy, somewhat parallel to Hauptmann's noble *Florian Geyer,* insomuch as it too expresses this tragedy in the form of a picture of that first terrible defeat of German democratic aspirations in the Peasants' War. Hindemith, thus, represents the unhappy German Republic; one might almost say that he is the German Republic.

As for *Matthis der Mahler,* it ought, judging by the three symphonic excerpts from it performed by Klemperer during his season with the New York Philharmonic during the fall of 1934, prove to be the great recent opera, far above the class of a *Lady Macbeth of Mzensk* or *Lulu.* Irrespective of their terrific communication of the experience of life during the Nazi terror, especially in the sections entitled *The Entombment* and *The Temptation of St. Anthony*—the titles being adopted from those of certain sections of the famous altarpiece of Grünewald in Colmar, which in some way not yet disclosed figure in the opera—the excerpts are singularly powerfully sustained, sonorous, and expressive contrapuntal pieces in the grand style severe; and their grandeur of form and depth of meaning leaves no doubt of the largeness of the composer's personality and the immanence of his recognition as the leading composer in Central Europe, if not upon the entire continent. He is already conspicuous to us as one of the few individuals who have made the contemporary evolution of music a matter of general importance and added materially to the world's store of chamber music; and if one still finds his place a little below that of Strawinsky—for us, the leading composer of the time—it is only for the reasons that the substance of his music is less varied, more uniform, and most of his compositions less distinct than his elder's, and that the kind of music he frequently writes, the music that interests us principally with the movement of its line, is ultimately not the most supremely interesting and rewarding. To be sure, it has great value; still, this value is perforce inferior to that of art which integrates all our faculties and impulses, placing us as it were on or in the movement of things, perhaps because it integrates a spirit of action and of contemplation, both surcharged with feeling. Strawinsky, for his part, never leaves us merely observant. But it must be remarked that Hindemith has contributed distinct and completely engaging compositions, too: among his earlier works, *Das Marienleben;* the String Quartet, Op. 22; the solo Sonata for viola, Op. 25, No. 1; *Die Serenaden,* and the little Concerto for orchestra; among his later ones, the Concerto for woodwind, with its moving feeling of the stern old Prussian soldier life, Op. 41; the brilliant Concerto for piano, harp and brass, Op. 49; and so, it appears, parts of his oratorio *Das Unaufhörliche*—the absolute conceived in a myth—and the fragments from *Matthis der Mahler*. And as he is slowly but steadily maturing as an artist—a fact declared by the greater distinction and significance of the later concerti as opposed to the earlier, and the inclusion of a deeply affecting music in his last works, and is "but young in deed," it is most likely that should nothing interfere with his development, we shall find him standing on a level with the great contemporary composer, if not upon one actually superior.

DISCOVERIES OF A MUSIC CRITIC

Milhaud

EDENIC calm and warmth and luxury stole on the staid Town Hall the evening in the season of 1933-4 when the New Chamber Orchestra under young Bernard Hermann presented one of the masterly items of the music of the 1920's for the first time in New York. This aromatic work was Darius Milhaud's music for the ballet *La Création du Monde;* it probably is the most perfect of all pieces of symphonic jazz, excelling even such very brilliant jazz symphonies as Copland's piano concerto. A subtle, wonderfully singing, vigorously contrapuntal, richly orchestrated, and completely satisfactory score, it tensely, sustainedly, savorsomely expands the germs of the style fathered by W. C. Handy of the "St. Louis Blues" in a large form and with the characteristic means of the jazz banditti: harmonic orchestra, saxophone, and multiple percussion. And it gives a rich and full expression to the peculiar feeling of the "blues."

That feeling is mainly nostalgic. What softly and infectiously moans in the notes of our melancholy sort of jazz is, ultimately, homesickness, the perennial human longing for Eden and its vanished ease and warmth and peacefulness—more realistically, man's lost condition of animal freedom, gaiety, irresponsibility, and desire unshadowed by self-consciousness and pain. The American Negro, perhaps, first found the contemporary childish-primitive musical idiom crudely voicing and stilling the ancient nostalgia with its sensuous plaintiveness. But the whole world, never entirely free of the recessive yearning, and

MILHAUD

wearied, disappointed, and demoralized by war, promptly chimed in with him and joined him in some of his practical efforts to recapture the lost paradise.

Harlem arose, a city such as vision could never have conceived. And hither, in 1917 and again in 1922, came Darius Milhaud, chief member of the scandalous Parisian *Six*. He had previously with felicity exploited the Brazilian music-hall idiom in his polyrhythmic and polytonic piano tangos *Los Suadades do Brazil* and in his music for Claudel's ballet *L'Homme et son Désir* and, following Satie's lead, the cognate popular American idiom itself in his music to Cocteau's ballet *Le Bœuf sur le Toit*. And, possibly because he himself was full of the universal nostalgia and possessed the artist's power of developing the means necessary to the expression of his feeling and the realization of its object, he was deeply penetrated by the "blues" idiom, impregnated with its spirit, and moved to expand its style and idea into the sustained and waking dream that alone can satisfactorily retrovert men to their primitive condition.

The completed score was coupled by him with the ballet *La Création du Monde,* by Blaise Cendrars, and was produced in Paris by the Swedish Ballet in 1923, very considerably in advance of the appearance of Gershwin's *Rhapsody in Blue*. The action of the ballet, derived from an African legend of the formation of the universe, portrays the progressive ordination of the cosmos and the perfection of the Edenic condition by the three giant deities of creation. Obedient to their spells, movement commences in the confused primeval heap of things. Trees emerge from it, and various beasts. The stage grows luminous while the animals turn in a dance about the bodies of the African Adam and Eve issuing gradually, limb by limb, from the central mass. The pair perform a dance of desire, while the remainder of the mass resolves into other human beings. All join in a delirious round. The crowd eventually dissolves into little groups, leaving the original pair alone and embraced in a lasting kiss amid eternal May. And Milhaud's music not only sings the song of the frabjous garden. It laps and cradles people in the warm magic tides they crave. The solemn overture with the gravely singing saxophone rocks us on primordial waters. Animal gaiety shakes itself free in the subsequent monkeylike fugue on a jazz theme. Pan himself seems to call through the tender, tenderly harmonized melody in the second part, softly, sweetly, insinuatingly luring birds and beasts and men to move harmoniously with him in his perpetual spring. The sumptuous syncopes of the brass in barbershop harmonies sing the splendor of paradisiac reversions. After the sublime last honkey-tonk, all is "luxe, calme et volupté." In the spirantlike tones of the flutter-tongued flutes which conclude the score, life has become the sweet bubbling of cane within a hazy land and the sounds on baby lips.

In the face of this virtuosic and poetic score, one again asks oneself why not only it but all of Milhaud's music continues to suffer neglect at the hands of American conductors and their instruments? That neglect is severe: like *La Création du Monde,* the whole of Milhaud's art possesses, to a degree rare in contemporary music, together with a French grace and clarity, the quality of sensuous enchantment, of witchery and mysteriousness—once one of the special qualities of modern Parisian music, from that of D'Indy through Charpentier to that of Debussy and the earlier Ravel. And, a very lyrical musician, a singer like most composers who have Jewish blood, he is somewhat less subjectively lyrical and psychological than the members of the French school who immediately preceded him—much more the pure musician. The earliest of his interesting larger works, the lyrical drama *La Brebis Egarée* on a text by Francis Jammes, pendant to *Pelléas* though it very largely is, and the product of the immediately antebellum years, has a musical texture much more consistent than that of its great prompter. And Milhaud's later, much more characteristic works have continued along the route of pure musicality. They are also less precious than those of his predecessors: more taut and active in movement; more frequently popular in accent, swing, and grace; and also more acrid in their elegance; and in instances mordant, brutal, brutally polyphonic. But they have considerable métier.

Among Milhaud's many original compositions there is a grand opera *Christophe Colombe,* on a text by Claudel; three short three-act operas, *La Brebis Egarée, Les Malheurs d'Orphée,* and *Le Pauvre Matelot;* three chamber operas; half a dozen ballets; numerous orchestral works and songs. And either they have reached us ten years late, like *La Création du Monde,* or for the most part not at all. With the exception of *La Création,* the only major piece of Milhaud's presented to New York during the last decade was his delightful little Concerto for percussion. And after asking oneself the reason for this neglect, one reaches conclusions similar to those reached after similar former queries. They are double. One is that while the critical statement that "there is at least one good idea in everything Milhaud writes" was a jest and intended as one, it contained the jest's necessary modicum of truth. Milhaud's production not only is prolific, but shows a touch of routine; and in consequence, the number of his quite sincere, completely satisfactory works by no means equals that of his compositions. One comes upon somewhat commonplace pages in even some of the most attractive of these, *Christophe Colombe* and *Les Malheurs d'Orphée.* And still not a few of them, including *La Création, Le Pauvre Matelot,* and the Concerto for percussion, are little master works.

The other reason for the neglect, the more serious, is that most of Milhaud is comprised in the music of the 1920's, and that at the moment it ought to have been received and installed in the concert repertoire, the mass of that music met a condition of dry rot in the American public and its conductors. But it is the conductors, the musicians most of all who have "declined the gambit, shown fatigue." It is they who have turned aside toward the second-rate, in especial toward the music of that overstuffed bard Jan Sibelius, unto the latest bray.

Auric

A RADIATION of highly tonic crystals, real French salts, was the first of the two effects of the Monte Carlo troupe's New York production of the ballet *Les Matelots,* choreography by Massine, decorations by Pruna, music by Georges Auric. With each of its means, *The Sailors* freshly communicated the lightness of temper persistently characteristic of the French and perennially bestowed upon us by their artists: the peculiar ironic buoyancy nourished by their relish of human nature in all its amorality paired with an acute sense of its inner contradictions. The action of the blithe little ballet conveyed the happy humor with a half jocose, half tender representation of the facile adjustments popularly associated with the waterfronts. In flinging, loose-limbed masculine dances interspersed with coquettish, formal, feminine ones, and in staccato pantomimic play, three gobs and their girls swiftly enacted a gay tale of partly serious relationships. While the lasses pined in port, the jolly tars sketched unconventional "designs for living." Later, the leading jack jealously returned to his patient little Penelope. The others cheerfully circulated their fair. The couple embraced comfortably, in the middle of the floor.

Meantime, the gay, witty curtains, scenery, and costumes heightened the mood with their harmonies of crude, clear tints of a watercolorlike brightness; while the other component of this delightful, delightfully presented little work of art, the music, puissantly reinforced the concept. Auric's pungent, scherzando score is not only perfectly in the picture. Quite in the Chabrier tradition, it is one of the most vigorous items of the newer French music. It is light "vulgar" music insomuch as it requires small effort of its auditors, gives immediate pleasure, exploits music-hall material in the forms of waltzes and other popular dances, and remains fairly uniform in rhythm and consonant in harmony. Also, it is neoclassical. But it is quite dissimilar from such spineless affairs as Virgil Thomson's score for *Four Saints*.

Auric has taken an energetic hold upon his medium. His expressions are smart, rounded, organic, and balanced. While the character of the score is mainly burlesque, in the spirit of the subject, lyrical passages, the exquisite, poignant *Solitude,* played during the scene of the two lonely girls, and the romantic nocturne, set to the scene of the temptation, do contrast with and give value to the harder expressions. They also figure as the moderato and the trio of the scherzo of the five-part symphonic mold—allegro brillante, moderato, theme with variations, scherzo, and rondo—into which the work is cast: archly cast, too, since the solos of the three sailors and their ensemble are matched with the "variations," and the scene of the circulation with the rondo.

As for the second of the two consequences of the performance, it consisted in the agreeable recollection of an old promise and flowed directly from the perception of the brilliance and gallic saltiness of the score. The pledge remembered, dated from the days of the armistice, when young Auric, as a member of the famous, short-lived Parisian Group of Six, loudly along with his confrères advertised his intention of producing a music robuster, brinier, more crude-colored *à la française* than that of the impressionists. Auric's first experiments, the three *Pastorales* and the settings of Radiguet's *Les Joues en Feu,* had been interesting though brutal: the brutal harmonies of the pre-war Strawinsky, and Satie's demotic music, had here been combined by a talent that was expressing itself in gamin-like irony. Then, after some incidental music, came the ballet after Molière, *Les Fâcheux,* less brutal, more elegant, recuperative of the tradition of good "vulgar" comic music, but somewhat too obedient to the musical post-war fashion for archaicism, and too weak in its sentimental passages, to be entirely satisfactory. After that, for us over here in America, in any case, the curtain fell on Auric; for though *Les Matelots* was composed in 1925, no conductor troubled to perform it for an American audience. Our musicians were not to be deflected from their interminable Beethoven, Brahms, and Wagner rackets; nor had we an institutionalized ballet. Thus, only such charming but unassuming compositions of Auric's as the incidental music to René Clair's *A Nous la Liberté* managed to cross the ocean.

It was impossible not to suspect the composer of graceful defalcation. Hence the revelation incidental to the performance of *Les Matelots.* For here with a vengeance was the fulfillment of the old promise, "vulgar" music, sentimental on the level of comedy, with form and substance, not facile like Poulenc's, and salty with the humor of the French man of the people. Plainly, the "bad boy" had long since "made good."

Shostakovich

UNTIL quite recently, it was well-nigh as dangerous to deny the genius of Dmitri Shostakovich in orthodox Communist society as to deny the omniscience of Marx there. The young Russian composer was a sort of uncrowned composer laureate to the Soviets. After writing a somewhat traditional but vigorous and terse First Symphony he had embraced the revolutionary cause and striven to put music in its service in the manner in which the old composers had striven to devote it to the interests of the church. He had written *May Day,* a symphony evidently intended to form part of a revolutionary ritual; and he had written music for a number of propagandistic Soviet films. *May Day* is clangorous but not very good, a kind of musical illustration. The body of it is marchlike and processional. The steely themes have a certain unmistakable proletarian cast and so to speak wear caps. There are assemblages for popular tunes for the brass. And at the end, after trombone solos dogmatize somewhat in the manner of speakers addressing gatherings in squares, a hymn hails the world revolution. But the musical medium is most dependent on the idea: it is bare of an intrinsic interest. In form it is tremendously pretentious. It is bold, harsh, unsentimental in its idiom: uncompromisingly contrapuntal; steely in sonority. The composer has aimed at a somewhat Strawinskian, swiftly evolving form: as the critic Victor Belaiev has put it, "Shostakovich has not only refrained from repeating a theme in its original or in a transformed version, but in writing a theme he has avoided even the repetition of identical motifs and melodic turns of phrase: and one gets the impression that he wants every bar to be different from the rest." But essentially the work is quite academic, conventional in its developments, juiceless almost to the point of desiccation, and excepting a few passages, in particular the lyrical commencement with the two woodwinds, rhetorical and unconvincing.

Yet some of Shostakovich's movie music was ingenious: and besides, he was obviously very young, and quite orthodox and outspoken in his contempt of nonrevolutionary composers and other bourgeois; and somehow to doubt his geniality was to attack the revolution, Russia, the proletariat, Communism, Marx, Lenin, Trotzky, and Stalin.

Suddenly, then, the situation changed. Shostakovich no longer was the holy of holies. One no longer hears much about him. True, he still figures in the world of music and of revolution. (There are the movies.) But scarcely as a god.

The rock on which his reputation noisily foundered, for the present at least, was the production of his opera, *Lady Macbeth of Mzensk*, in Cleveland and New York in the winter of 1934-5 by the Cleveland Orchestra under Rodzinski, in conjunction with the League of Composers, and by a Russian cast.

This opera belongs to a recent genus of works for the lyric stage. It is a didactic piece, a manipulation of the musico-dramatic form in the intention of making that form bring home certain abstract truths; and in view of its four-act length, and its conception for a sizable vocal ensemble and a grand orchestra augmented by extra brass and percussion, the bulkiest example of the new species. Its fellows and predecessors, for instance the *Lehrstück* of Paul Hindemith and the *Jasager* of Kurt Weill, are relatively short pieces for modest ensembles.

The particular truths which Shostakovich wishes the work to impress upon us are twofold. The first of them, in his own words, is "the position of women in old, pre-revolutionary Russia," especially that of those who, "set by fate in gloomy and miserable surroundings and belonging to a merchant class which was hard, greedy, and small-minded," led "sorrowful and pitiable lives." (Succeeding operas are to show other aspects of the general position of woman under the old régime.) The second of these truths, unconfessed by the composer but plainly proclaimed by the work itself, is the nastiness and ludicrousness of life under the old bourgeois economic and social system: not only the stupidity and hypocrisy of priests, police, and capitalists, but the ludicrousness of the serious feelings of these people about death, sexual intercourse, and other matters that seemed important to them. The opera aimed to deflate bourgeois feelings and values.

To gain this end, Shostakovich, in collaboration with an author named Preis, has set before us a drama derived from the famous novel of Nikolai Lesskov, *Lady Macbeth of Mzensk District,* better translated as *A Small-Town Lady Macbeth.* The heroine of this novel is a powerful woman who, demoniacally possessed, generates death wherever she turns; and this terrible figure Shostakovich and Preis, to begin with, have transformed into that of a "social victim." They have eliminated the woman's devilishness. They have stressed her helpless subjection to the males of her family and her maternal love for her lover. And, concentrating their by no means abundant store of human sympathy entirely in her, they have surrounded her with grotesques of low-class persons in bourgeois clothes. Thus their Katerina Izmailova is an ignorant but richly fibered creature, clever, gifted, and interesting, helplessly enmeshed in a deadly environment and "driven to crime" by it. We see her married to a weak member of a mercantile family, childless, and tyrannized over by a jealous and lecherous father-in-law, bored to death by her idle, empty existence, and readily succumbing to the assault of an ambitious clerk. After her father-in-law has got wind of the intrigue and had the clerk lashed within an inch of his life, we see her vengefully feed the old man rat-poison in a dish of mushrooms and stonily watch his agony. When her husband discovers her lover in her bedchamber, we observe Katerina help the latter strangle the intruder, hide the corpse, and return to bed with the clerk. The corpse is discovered by some carousing peasants who run to the police, and Katerina and her paramour are arrested during their wedding and sent to Siberia for life. On the eastward march, the man turns from her with loathing, takes up with a prostitute, and robs and humiliates Katerina for the girl's sake. The merchant's wife, in utter despair, seizes the strumpet and drags her down with her into the river.

In this way, Shostakovich and Preis created a figure which by its very existence indicts its milieu and with it the prerevolutionary literature which saw in its Katerina Izmailova, in the words of the young composer, "a cruel woman—who 'wallows in fat' and murders innocent people." "Lesskov," says Shostakovich, "gives us no illuminating interpretation of the incidents which are developed in his story."

Let it here be stated that not everyone shares or has shared Shostakovich's conviction of the failure of the author of the exquisite *Bogeyman* to give an "illuminating interpretation of the incidents which are developed" either in *Lady Macbeth of Mzensk District* or in any other of his stories. Hear Leo Tolstoy: "It is singular that Dostoievsky is read so much: I do not understand why? Nor do I understand why Lesskov is read so little." And the painter Repin, who portrayed the sage of Iasnaya Poliyana, reported that Tolstoy frequently of evenings read tales by Lesskov aloud in his family circle, and often was scarce able to finish them because of the intense emotion they roused in him. The truth is that Lesskov had published a bitter attack on the journalistic world of the Russia of his day, and from that hour was a doomed man.

But this is beside the point, which is that in this Katerina Izmailova, Shostakovich had acquired a figure able to impress on us "the unhappy condition of women under the old régime," especially those "belonging to a merchant class which was hard, greedy, etc."; and, not content with this "social victim," has, the better to flay the old prerevolutionary Russia and its prejudices, transformed the Lesskov tragedy into an action often resembling a Punch-and-Judy show, or a biological exhibit, or something far apart from ourselves, in which grotesques dressed in the civilian and clerical and military togs of the 1840's reveal greeds and lusts more or less ludicrous and nasty, through expressions and actions more or less abrupt, ridiculous, and ugly. And not even content with this transmogrification, Shostakovich has coupled to this half pathetic, half satiric drama a score which takes sides against the figures of his violently possessive bourgeois puppets. To only one soloist has he assigned a few lyric expressions that touch our emotions sympathetically—the prima donna. To the rest he has given expressions that, ironic, burlesque, humorous, move us to laughter or contempt, but never to emotional participation. If emotion threatens to overtake his expression, he rapidly deflates it, and now humorously, now cruelly, the passionate, erotic, religious, tragic expressions of his characters. Take the musical representation of what is going on behind the bed curtain in Scene III of Act I. The situation concerns two healthy human animals in rut. But Shostakovich's musical characterization of the event, with its repeated trombone glissandi, is not only brutally realistic. It is cynical to the point where it makes that other musical description of a similar event, the comic introduction to *Der Rosenkavalier,* appear almost idealistic. For Strauss is laughing with the business, Shostakovich at it. Not content with the cynical hubbub, he succeeds it with flatuslike sounds from the brass. And at other times, too, his orchestra makes loud, contemptuous fun of the characters and their situation, till we feel we are observing the antics of curious rodents in a trap, and find our own feelings deflated. In fact, only during Act IV, the scene on the border of Siberia, does the composer entirely quit his externality and let himself fully feel the situation. And that is, as he says, to "arouse sympathy" for the broken people who, in the dark old days, "moved under guard through the far-off expanses of the former Russian empire to penal servitude." It is possible the gods judge differently: it is possible that they see the reason for this final diastole, his relative expansive feeling of life, in the circumstance that at this point his picture presented Shostakovich not only with figures of the suffering under dog, but with figures of bourgeois people—the merchant's wife and her ambitious lover—in the degraded position where he wanted them.

But that, too, is neither here nor there. Nor does it even matter that the doctrine the opera is supposed to inculcate is essentially an ugly one, bare of natural feeling, and suggesting a malodorous combination of the dirty little boy and the priggish theorist, and also pretty generally suspect and promptly awakening skepticism. The conception of a "social victimization," to the extent where the milieu can be held responsible for such crimes as murder, is repellent to decidedly individualized existences and the feeling born of them, since it is a rationalization impelled to remove from the individual's shoulders his greatest pride, his self-responsibility. The conception of the humorousness and inanity of the importance attached by the "bourgeoisie" to such affairs as the sexual act is equally subject to immediate challenge, since that importance, too, is connected with the individual's self-respect; while the whole view of the triviality and contemptibility of the lives and feelings and expressions labeled "bourgeois" meets the challenge of all persons who, having felt and experienced life, know that nothing is ever trivial or inane when completely seen and felt, and that nothing not completely seen and felt can be said to have been seen. One is tempted to believe that even in the U.S.S.R., where Shostakovich's "truths" are said to have a sort of official sanction, they are not widely accredited. And, finally, not even the fact that the lesson of the opera is a self-contradictory one, since we cannot feel sympathy for a single character in a situation where sympathy is denied that character's relations with others, since the parodization of these relations and subsidiary characters and the entire milieu degrades the "sympathetic" character too—not even this fact is of prime importance; much as the jumble itself may prove the externality of the idea itself. What alone remains important is that as in *May Day,* the music to which this abstract idea is coupled remains dependent upon the idea for its meaning and interest, and that this opera, like the symphony, proves Dmitri Shostakovich a musical illustrator, a composer without integrity who adapts himself and his medium as best he can to external ideas. That was what was perceived by the intelligent who assisted at the performances; and the perception is the actual cause of Shostakovich's recent eclipse. Certainly the score is less arid than that of *May Day*. We find some melodies of considerable length in it. And passages such as the heroine's soliloquy at the beginning of the third scene in Act I, or the tender music at the close of the hallucination scene, or the *hopak* of the drunken peasants, charm us musically. But even these passages at best are theater music, depending to some degree upon the drama for their effectiveness; and in the one act where the music does generate the drama, in the last, the Siberian act, the composer nonetheless reveals his dependency on externals—in this case, the music of the Russian composers whose plangency he reflects. And the rest of the score is ancillary. The medium has no real life of its own: never does it generate the drama out of itself, and all in all derives its meaning from the literary ideas and the clever drama with which it is associated. Who, for example, would listen with interest to the interludial passacaglia, which like practically all the sustained passages of score shows a weakness of impulse, and amid all its vehemence grows static and monotonous and tedious well before it is over—the one exception to this rule being the fugue which accompanies the hazing of the cook in the second scene—who would listen to them were it not felt that this "monumental" music was the author's comment upon the action? To be sure, the score is very virtuosic: Shostakovich is a brilliant and tellingly lapidary, steely orchestrator, and he has an extraordinary ability to point and characterize, clearly and effectively, with the wide musical means at his disposal, the situations and motives of his drama. But of creative power there is little evidence. The majority of the characterizations in this opera are not musical in the word's prime intention. One does not make music by characterizing cheap sentiments, such as those which Shostakovich has attributed to some of the personages, the old man and the clerk, for example, with cheap valsiform music. The long and complex score is actually poor in either fine or powerful ideas or long musical breaths and, in spite of the evidence that the composer has sought out a stripped, hard, modern style and striven for strength and severity of outline, a crazy-quilt in material. One meets with Prokofieff, with Strauss, with Borodin (particularly with Borodin), even with Moussorgsky, and not only in the last act. This weakness one might be able to overlook, in view of the composer's youth—he is still under thirty, and many composers, Wagner for example, were still unorganized during their twenties—were it not for the fact that in tonal scheme, *Lady Macbeth* is so confused that it is almost impossible to credit the man with any real power of musical organization. Without point or reason, the score is now atonal, now polytonal, now flatly diatonic; and this in view of the fact that Shostakovich is by no means chary of theorizing, especially as regards some of the more obvious problems of his art. "I do not agree," he writes, "with the theories, at one time current among us, that in the modern opera the vocal line must be absent, or that it should be no more than speech in which the intonations are to be accented. Opera is above all a vocal production, and singers should occupy themselves with their real duty, which is to sing, and not to speak, recite, or intone. Thus I have built all my vocal parts on a broad cantilena." But where his ear and sense of order should have been his guide, he remains confused and incoherent, and in a score whose development, he boasts, "progresses constantly, and in a symphonic form—flowing unbrokenly, interrupted solely by the ending of each act, and resuming its course in the following one, not piecewise, but by further development on a grand symphonic scale."

DISCOVERIES OF A MUSIC CRITIC

The tragedy is actually Communism's. Communism looks for music not only morally effective in the proletarian direction, but capable also of "unifying broad stratas of people" in the Communistic idea, and in so doing on no account seeks the impossible. That music can fortify a natural direction of the will is an old truth, long since expressed by the Greeks in their story of the lame Lacedemonian schoolmaster, and indubitable by anyone who has ever experienced and reflected upon the force of military marches and of dance music. The potentiality of moral effect is not even exclusively confined to pieces which, like those of military bands and dance orchestras, address themselves primarily to the physical man. Compositions of high quality and level of appeal possess it also, and not only in the invidious sense of the Kreutzer Sonata. The great masses and other ecclesiastical compositions of the old masters moved and still move their audiences in the spiritual direction; and works like the *Egmont* Overture of Beethoven, the *Ruy Blas* Overture of Mendelssohn, the *Rienzi* Overture of Wagner, the Rakoczy March of Berlioz, even the *William Tell* Overture of Rossini, strike the fire of the democratic revolution in the brain today as much as when they first were played. *Masaniello* once actually fired a revolt, in Belgium in 1830. And music can equally well, sometimes actually without assistance from the word, communicate Ideas. The old masses and motets certainly conveyed by their movement and the relations of tone to tone the static world-order perceived by the church; and music like that of the dionysiac finale of Beethoven's Seventh Symphony seems not only to contain a democratic revolution, but to impart the dynamic order that is its aim. There is indeed no valid reason for doubting that a great composer who was also a sincere Communist could produce music of high quality and appeal making for the proletarian goal.

SHOSTAKOVICH

But as yet Communism has got almost none of the music it requires, at least very little high in quality and appeal and moving on mental and spiritual levels. The best of Communism's musical acquisitions lie pretty much on the plane of march and other kinds of songs. Many of the better of these songs are curiously enough of German origin, and also, curiously like the "Marseillaise," contain passages in minor keys without thereby attaining that terrible somberness and menace which, as Goethe observed, inheres in the French revolutionary song by virtue of *its* minor passage. The most musically vigorous and effective of these German Communist songs remains probably the "Vorwärts!" by Kurt Eisler, sung in the film *Kühle Wampe*. Its only drawback flows from its *preussischer Kommanodoton*—its Prussian hortatory inflection —which probably will render it effectual solely among populations composed of German Aryans.

The sad truth would seem to be that the Communist faith and idea is not an actual part of any genial living composer! Were it, Communism would be receiving what it requires in the way of music morally and ideally infectious in its sense; for all music morally and ideally infectious is the consequence of the existence, at the very center of some creative musician's being, of the attitude, the direction, the idea, which his music conveys to its audiences. It was the permeation of their lives with the Christian spirit and idea that placed the gifts of great masters like Palestrina and Bach so tellingly in the service of the Catholic and of the Protestant churches; it was the permeation of Beethoven's with the democratic that made his music so revolutionary. Such music may be externally spurred, but not induced, even by the best and most pressing of reasons, the most cogent senses of purpose and effect, the most attractive prizes. It is born freely, out of the composer's feeling of life, coming like "Dian's kiss" in the poem, and with just the content of meaning and tendency naturally infused in it by the composer's quality of energy and attitude and way of living. Thus it may be truly said the old great composers of masses and motets "placed their gifts at the service of the church," for what they gave to religion was given freely, out of the deepest impulse of their beings, and only incidentally because it procured them a living.

But the composers who thus far have sought to furnish Communism with the higher sort of music it requires seem to a man to belong to that type of artist which attains a false conspicuity during the first years of every new régime. It is the type of those who, because they are either young and unformed or weakly equipped with an individual impulse, vision, and way of expression, or both, readily accept and accommodate themselves—half consciously enough, in all probability—to the ideas and theories and formulae in the air about them—precisely as they accept and accommodate themselves to the ideas and theories and idioms of other composers, possibly for the reason that these ideas and theories fill the void in their own minds, or for the reason of the various material advantages connected with the adoption, or for both. At best they are illustrators who use their means to elucidate more or less literary or extrinsic ideas: and by the degree to which their medium fails of functioning independently, quite unconsciously indicate the degree to which these literary and extrinsic ideas have failed to become merged with their own being. In Shostakovich's work, certainly they fail of independence; and that is what makes us feel that he deserves the brutal characterization of his kind of activity voiced by a very great Russian

SHOSTAKOVICH

composer who was an inconspicuous part of *Lady Macbeth's* New York audience. It is a pity we cannot report that characterization verbatim: it was a terribly just one. But it was excessively free, and we shall have to content ourselves with a bowdlerization and merely recount that what the great Russian composer remarked was: "Shostakovich! First he licks the boots of the Soviet government, and then he licks the boots of all Russian Music!"

And if we feel Shostakovich, this most promising, most daring and able of Soviet Russian composers, this brave, hard, and utterly superior and unsentimental young revolutionary, one of the noble company of the illustrators, where shall we place poor Mossolov—Mossolov, whose *Steel Foundry* is a dull replica of the stamping of a steel mill and suggests that he used his powers to disadvantage; that they would have been far more effectively and triumphantly utilized had he brought a real foundry on to the concert platform?

Of course it will be said that *Lady Macbeth* is a success in Russia and interested audiences in Cleveland, New York, and Philadelphia. Earnest critics certainly ascribed a sense of humor to the composer—even if only one of the sort that finds its objects in the erotic adventure—and preferred the work to so real a composition as *Wozzeck;* and it will be said that one does not please to such an extent without reason. To which the reply is, that the drama of *Lady Macbeth of Mzensk* was clever, that the dollhouse settings were amusing, and that the satire, the hard realism, the ideology, all were interesting. But that was all; certainly, if we look forward to the further music dramas in which Shostakovich is going to illustrate for us the condition of women in Russia throughout the nineteenth century, it is entirely out of curiosity about the kind of ideas he will find to illustrate. In fact, it is for every reason save the anticipation of a work of art: since the creation of a work or art, even one of such an inferior category as the didactic, pre-requires a certain integrity.

Weill and "Gebrauchsmusik"

THE word *Gebrauchsmusik* is the latest stimulant of the unsleeping temptation of the musical Mrs. Malaprops. It means ritual music, and useful music, and conventional music. But the definiteness of their meanings do not save novel musical terms from misapplication, least of all those whose noble detonations appear to express deep and mysterious matters, such as musical things perhaps are, and commonly are conceived to be. The recent flourishes with the word "musicologist" have provided some charming instances of this law. Signifying one who believes in, and practices or tries to practice, the application of scientific method to musical studies, the word has been conceived to denote "one possessed of a profound understanding of music and its rules." "One great accomplishment cannot be denied Mr. ——," we read, recently, at the end of a critical article; "he certainly is a musicologist." And a colleague of the gentleman so praised has already conceived of *Gebrauchsmusik* as signifying "commanded music."

Luckily we are going to be saved from succumbing to the temptation provoked by this new name and slogan by the circumstance that several examples of the kind of music that caused its coinage, or flowed from it, have recently been presented to us; and the objects have defined the meanings of the

WEILL AND "GEBRAUCHSMUSIK"

generic term. Among these are two little operas by the Berlin composer Kurt Weill, one of the bannermen of the movement: they are works which have attracted our attention with their originality and musicality no less than their illuminativeness. One of them indeed is a bull's-eye of recent musical endeavor. This is the mordant social satire *Die Dreigroschenoper, The Threepenny Opera,* a very free and squalid and savage modernization of *The Beggar's Opera:* the score even includes one of the tunes from Gay's old piece. Ineffectually produced at the Empire Theater in New York during the season of 1932-3 in an English translation that almost completely dimmed the brilliant irony of the lyrics of the librettist, Bert Brecht, it presented us with a significant little score made of converted and specially turned conventional music. A majority of the songs of the grimy "operetta" are actually based upon and cast in the general forms of organ-grinder melodies and fox trots and marches grown threadbare in the service of forgotten musical comedies. But the old song and ballad stuffs used by Weill have been divested by him of prettiness and banality and cleverly and vigorously re-formed, barbed, and accented with subtly expressive intent. The music of *The Threepenny Opera* is a doubly ironic beggar music. The persistent Yiddish minors and archly drooping melodic lines of the renovated ancient tunes, and the wheezing instrumental effects of the tiny orchestra, render the whole score eloquent of the post-armistice depression, cynicism, distress, but also ridiculous and ironic of it, and the only respectable "twentieth-century blues." This is Berlin and its "let-down" state after the peace, and the "let-down" of every high tradition. But it is also Berlin having a last laugh at its own sorry circumstance. This two-edged musical expressivity conveys the idea of the libretto perfectly. For Brecht's savage reconstruction of Gay's beggar opera idea, too, is "such a piece as

DISCOVERIES OF A MUSIC CRITIC

beggars might conceive and beggars enact": one of those social exhibitions of rags and sores and crippled members, and of threats and fists, that constitute the pauper's time-honored "weapons in the struggle for survival"; and simultaneously an irony of the low spirits of the beggarly and the weak that only during blue moons impel them to make a demonstration against their oppressors and get themselves a morsel of meat.

As regards the problem of the meaning of *Gebrauchsmusik,* this biting little score enables us to define it in part as music that, while making a wide appeal through the conventionality, popularity, and simplicity of its means, simultaneously bends them to communicate a new content or feeling. And the fact that the shabby songs of *The Threepenny Opera*—with their ancient burdens of the ship which almost invariably figures in the dreams of oppressed persons and their hoary retorts to those who preach morality to the poor—"First comes fodder, then morality!"—and their well-worn refrains, "Man lives but by misdeeds!" and "He only who lives 'well' lives pleasantly!" are especially appropriate to the particular context in which we find them, need not discourage us from accepting them as representative, to some extent, of the aesthetic of the entire movement, itself an offshoot from *die neue Sachlichkeit.* The examination of other of Weill's scores—*The Lindbergh Flight* (a cantata for radio, composed in collaboration with Hindemith) or *The Rise and Fall of the City of Mahogany*—will prove that repointed conventional and jazz forms are common to all of them. The reason for their appearance is said in certain quarters to be Communism, which wants a style accessible to the masses. Brecht, Weill's constant librettist, was something more than a poetic fellow traveler of the Communist movement in Germany.

Persons reading this account of Weill's music will not fail

to recognize that, whatever its rationale, the movement it represents exhibits, in the manner of other contemporary movements in music, the general leadership of Strawinsky, in this instance the Strawinsky of *Petrushka, Renard, L'Histoire du Soldat*, and other pieces which created new ideas for old and conventional musical objects. In fact, the music of *The Threepenny Opera* represents a logical extension of the Strawinskyan irony which influenced the Six in Paris and their English parallels at the time of the armistice.

The spell of the Russian original is equally manifest in the other of the two Weill operas which gave us the sense of the more important meaning of the slogan of *Gebrauchsmusik*. This second piece, the thirty-minute opera, *Der Jasager (The Yea-Sayer)*, intended for presentation in schools and by young people and actually given at the Playhouse in Grand Street by the Music School of the Henry Street Settlement under the direction of A. Lehman Engel in the spring of 1933, does not, however, proceed so directly from the earlier as from the later Strawinsky. Conventional music figures in this poignant, slightly lachrymose little work, especially in the song of the mother in the first act and the trio of students in the second. But it is not so preponderant as in the squalid operetta. Simple, anything but revolutionary, and characterized by the harsh contrapuntalism of Hindemith and other German moderns, the *Jasager* score is relatively more original in manner, as in substance; and the Strawinsky who influences it, the Strawinsky of *Oedipus Rex*, is more Strawinsky the dramatist than the composer. As in *Oedipus*, only the center of the stage is devoted to the action, which is stylized. And like *Oedipus, Der Jasager* presents us with a masked and stationary chorus which flanks the scenery on either hand and comments upon the action, and from time to time sings a refrain, in this instance to the words, "Highest in value, in wisdom and understanding!"

The Yea-Sayer indeed exhibits a sort of morality for students and other young people. It values the self-sacrifice of the weak for the sake of the strong, of the individual for the sake of the group. Derived from the Japanese, the action represents the crisis in the life of a small boy, a rôle, incidentally, sung by a boy soprano. For the sake of finding aid for his sick mother, the lad joins a party of older students who are climbing a mountain range to arrive at a city of wisdom. On the ascent the lad's strength gives out, and rather than force the party to retrace its steps and fail of its objective he freely consents to let it rid itself of him by casting him from a cliff, thus achieving the sole greatness accessible to the weak.

Precisely this inculcation of morality by operatic means, which is the aim of the little piece, an affecting one for all its banalities, clarifies for us the second meaning of the word *Gebrauchsmusik*, which, of course, literally means cult or ceremonial as well as conventional music. *Gebrauchsmusik*, therefore, is music which is not *Kunstmusik*—i.e., art with no end outside itself and existent in its own right as the absolute expression of an idea. It is music which largely with the aid of literary symbols serves an end other than the absolutely artistic one and is useful in rituals, in ceremonial occasions and exercises, and even helps, in the manner of the old church music, to exhibit an ethic and teach a lesson. The celebrations and rites that it assists are not religious in the old sense but those of the state and of humanity. This conclusion, again, seems to relate the German movement of Communism, with its particular preference for art that is propagandistic, indoctrinating, a "weapon in the class struggle," and serviceable in the rituals of the religion of humanity.

In view of the circumstance that the *Gebrauchsmusik* move-

WEILL AND "GEBRAUCHSMUSIK"

ment was dying in German even before Hitler restored the worship of the Teutonic divinities, including Wagner, it may be said that our illumination is a trifle tardy. But the word has a future other than that of designating a small category of works inclusive at best of a few pieces by Hindemith, Weill, and poor Comrade Shostakovich. In the first place, the tendency to create new ideas for conventional and popular musical forms and expressions remains a pretty universal one: one learns of its widespread existence from the pieces of the Englishmen Lambert and Walton and from such hopeful young Americans as Moross. In the second, composers who deeply feel the spirit and symbols of social rituals will continue to provide those rituals which can be enhanced with music with *Gebrauchsmusik,* possibly even with music that without literary aid conveys an ethic, and the term will continue to designate this sort of work, itself but one of the many forms in which music proves "useful." For all music is useful. All works of musical art express essences and ideas and thus, with their symbols of the inner truth of life, provide the best of bases of social relationships.

In fact, the kind that is least useful is a certain kind of *Gebrauchsmusik* itself, the kind which does not convey an individual interpretation of the meanings of the ritual it is intended to express, but provides general and conventional symbols and a sort of collective expression. Thus it devitalizes the individual, who lives through individual expressions and interpretations and finds his relationship to others through them. It is anti-social, since all societies are ultimately dependent for their existence upon leaders, and none but an individual can lead. It also makes for division within the individual himself and generates social menaces in the forms of schismatics, heretics, witch-hunters, fanatics of this religion or that, reformers, and other agents of unrest and disorder. Let us by all means have *Gebrauchsmusik*. But let it be the work of artists, not of "revolutionary" academicians.

"Ionization"

IN this, one of his most recent compositions, Edgar Varèse has given us a complete piece of music for the "nonmelodic" components of the battery. The feat indubitably is marvelous, and still no bolt from the blue. Varèse has always, to a singular degree, thought in terms of the percussion instruments and leaned toward expression through them. His scores have usually called for unusually complex and active batteries: in composing *Hyperprism* in 1923 he even set up an orchestra in which the percussion predominates over the melodic band in the proportion of seventeen to nine.

Besides, as it is now constituted, the pulsatile and frictive choir is perfectly capable of functioning as a sonorous unit. The newer composers have not only immensely augmented and diversified it; they have included in it instruments corresponding to the high and low string and woodwind pieces. The slightly enlarged normal battery which composes the orchestra of *Ionization* contains definite soprano, alto, tenor, and bass groups, susceptible of combination in four-part harmonies. It also contains two sirens—instruments which are capable of running continuous ascending and descending scales.

Thus the production of a piece such as *Ionization* was indubitably in the evolutionary order of things, predestined both

"IONIZATION"

by the direction of Varèse's own development and by the development of musical feeling and musical resources during the last century and a half. Since Mozart, indeed, composers have almost steadily been exhibiting an increasing sensitivity toward and an increasing appreciation of the musical possibilities of percussion and exploiting them ever more frequently and weightily. The romanticists laid ever larger quantities of pulsatile instruments under contribution. They associated snare and bass drums with the regular tympani and introduced xylophones, tom-toms, gongs, and bells of various kinds into the classic orchestra, steadily augmenting the once minute percussion choir in a ratio greater than the choirs of strings, woodwinds, and brasses, till at last it became the equal of the other three. The motive of this exploitation was first of all a desire for color. It was the desire for oriental and barbaric color that impelled some of the French and Russian composers to multiply the number of drums in their orchestra. It was also the desire for realistic effects: for this reason, Mahler introduced cowbells into his Sixth Symphony and Strauss whips into the orchestra of *Elektra*. Again, the motive for the augmentation of the percussion choir was the desire for dynamic expansion that culminated in the titanic ensembles of Mahler and Strauss, Holst, the younger Schönberg, and Varèse. Still, almost from the beginning, the composers of the last century were tending to use nonmelodic pulsatiles as the means of producing something more than coloristic effects or accentuating rhythms: and by nonmelodic pulsatiles we mean instruments of percussion other than pianos, xylophones, celestas, bells, and other pieces usually considered capable of playing tunes. They began introducing their sonorities into the melodic line: first Beethoven in the Fifth and Ninth Symphonies, later Wagner in *Das Rheingold*

DISCOVERIES OF A MUSIC CRITIC

and *Die Walküre,* then the rest. The moderns but capped the entire tendency and made the pulsatiles play not only melodic but, episodically, solistic rôles as well: actually for the first time in Strawinsky's *Petrushka,* with its celebrated interlude for snare drums alone, later in some of the interludes of Milhaud's setting of *The Libation Bearers,* and still more recently in some of Shostakovich's movie music and in the interludes and stage music of his incidental pieces for Gogol's *The Nose.* And the battery as a whole began to king it, as it were, over the other instrumental choirs, and to function ever more independently and absolutely. Events of this sort took place, probably for the first time, in the largely noise-making bands of Pratella and the rest of the Futurists. But as the compositions of this Italian group were purely brain-spun and empty, they do not concern us here. What does concern us is the fact that in 1917 Strawinsky gave the instrumental portion of his score of *The Little Wedding* with telling effect to an orchestra composed entirely of pianos and an aggregation of nonmelodic bars and surfaces. A year later he assigned with equally telling effect whole blocks of *The Story of the Soldier,* the diabolic finale most notably, to the battery alone. Some time after, Milhaud, the score of whose *Man and His Desire* and *Creation of the World* are full of the pulsatile effects of the Brazilian and Harlem jazz bands, wrote a charming little concerto for orchestra which originally gives the leading rôle to instruments of percussion. We have already spoken of the novel orchestra set up by Varèse in *Hyperprism.* The step from this point to the apparent prodigy of his piece for nonmelodic instruments alone is thus plainly a logical one, particularly so when one takes into account the motive for the whole ultra-modern musical assault on the battery.

This motive rose from the feeling of the individual composers

"IONIZATION"

and that of our whole time, precisely as the motive for the incorporation of percussion instruments in the orchestra sprang from the romantic feelings of the late nineteenth-century and early twentieth-century composers. That the ultra-moderns' intensive exploitation of the battery has also to an extent been externally conditioned, it would of course be foolish to deny. The romanticists had indicated the possibilities of percussion to their successors; in fact, they had laid the battery in the moderns' path. And the virtuosic exploitation of percussion in post-war jazz bands had further demonstrated the hitherto unsuspected potentialities of this component of the musical means. Material considerations, decidedly pressing since the world catastrophe, undoubtedly also helped influence the orientation toward the pulsatiles, since percussive means are economical of man-power, one player being sufficient to several instruments in the percussion orchestra. The forty-two pieces called for by Varèse's score for *Ionization,* for example, require only thirteen executants. Still, without an inner feeling not only adjustable to these external conditions, but able to adjust them to its own ends and in sympathy with its own idea, they would never have been fruitful, at least not in musical form. Authentic creativity is neither apish of the work of others nor impelled in any great way by external conditions and considerations but by feeling and spirit. The feeling actually determinative of the general assault on the battery was, to begin with, primitivistic. An after crop of late romantic "barbarism," born both of the divided culture-being's yearning for the unindividualized, will-less condition of unity with nature which the European associates with the state of pre-Christian barbarian or African life, and of the threatening eruption of raw forces which culture subordinates or sublimates, it engendered dreams and ideas and pictures of Scythian and Negro worlds that, for reason of the excessive, subhuman indeterminacy of the sounds of percussive instruments, naturally found expression through frenetic and monotonous rhythms of the pulsatiles. Another source of the feeling making for the predominance of the battery lay in the astringent quality of life itself, creating an unlyrical disposition in composers as in other artists, a natural aversion from the more excessively vibratory and humanly singing instruments toward the both more brutishly and more mechanistically expressive ones. Still another is to be found in what may be termed "skyscraper mysticism." This is a feeling of the unity of life through the forms and expressions of industrial civilization, its fierce lights, piercing noises, compact and synthetic textures: a feeling of its immense tension, dynamism, ferocity, and also its fabulous delicacy and precision, that impels artists to communicate it through the portions of their mediums most sympathetic to it, and through forms partly imitative of those which excite their intuitions.

Varèse in particular among composers would seem to be subject to this feeling: he is somewhat the mystic of the sounds of sirens, horns, gongs, and whistles afloat in the air of the great industrial centers, in the sense in which Picasso is that of the city landscape with its house-wall, billboard, newspaper textures; and the pre-war Strawinsky, of the machine and its rhythms. That the other feelings, the primitivistic, the unlyrical, are also his, is not to be doubted: the first of his important compositions, *Amériques,* has affiliations with the extremely primitivistic *Sacre;* and, excessively austere, his music as a whole is almost bare of cantilena-like passages. But, himself one of the surviving members of the Guillaume Apollinaire group moved almost as a whole by this skyscraper mysticism, Varèse has pretty consistently retained its feeling; and thus spontaneously become one of the most audacious exploiters of the pulsatile and friction instruments, and of the medium's possibilities for high and piercing and shrill and brute dynamic sonorities. In this, he has undoubtedly been influenced by still another intuition, his vision of the perspectives of modern science. Those perspectives have been comprehending mind-stuff in what hitherto had appeared the inanimate regions of life; events in the physical realm having come to show greater and greater resemblance to human expression and events in the psyche. The old antithesis between mind and matter has been proving more and more illusory; and Varèse, who was trained for engineering, would seem to have been standing before this new reality; finding it charged with emotion and generative of feelings of the relation between the forces known to physics and chemistry and those of the human psyche, and of ideas in the form of complexes and relations of the sounds and timbres of the instruments related to the whole realm of the semi-material. It may even be, as has been suggested, that he has in him something of the alchemist; that like the medieval scientists, he is moved by the desire to unveil god-nature and its divine or diabolic springs. Probably no chance cause is responsible for the affixion to his *Arcanes* of an aphorism of Paracelsus of Hohenheim's.

In any case, his music gives us an overwhelming feeling of life as it exists in the industrial sites, and of the perspectives of recent science. Not that his art is in any way illustrative. His medium is independent, and if his expression is "metaphysical," like Wagner's and Scriabin's and Mahler's, and musically mythological, like theirs it addresses the senses, possibly with an unparalleled dynamism and aggressivity, but nonetheless beautifully and completely. Each of his pieces can be enjoyed sensuously for reason of its new, fabulously delicate and fabulously dynamic sonorities, its terrifically telescoped, concentrated, telegraphic form, its hard outlines, cubic bulks of brassy sound, powerful dissonances, subtle complex rhythmicality, golden screams; above all, for reason of its incredibly emotional tensity, that of the most characteristically modern life. He is thus the actual creator of the music the Futurists theoretically projected, but could not, for reason of their personal unmusicality, achieve. For what was theory in them, in him is feeling, and a musical one.

Take *Ionization*, the work for percussion alone. It is, as we have said, a complete piece of music: one is never conscious, during performances of it, of the limitation of the special medium the composer is exploiting. The performance creates, sustains, and finally releases a high nervous physical tension. The form which comprises the inordinate, delicate, overwhelming volumes of the piece is clear, apparently that of a three-part song, with distinct themes, developments, recapitulations. And still it is a myth: the representation of processes and the immanent creator. Subjected to it, one feels life wonderfully afresh in one of its apparently inhuman, excessively dynamic changes. By reason of their extreme hardness, extreme indeterminacy, and other points of dissemblance from the more humanly vibrating sounds of string and wind instruments, the tones of the forty-one percussion and friction pieces for which the composition is cast—triangles, Chinese blocks, rattles, snare drums, cymbals, lion roars, gongs, tom-toms, bells, piano (nonmelodic, playing only tone clusters), and the rest—in themselves somehow suggest the life of the inanimate universe. The illusion, if illusion it is, of an analogy between the subject of the music and events or processes in the physio-chemical fields, is reinforced by the volumes of the extremely simplified, extremely skeletonized form, which, explosive, curiously timed and in-

"IONIZATION"

terrupted, and curiously related and responsive to one another, further suggest incandescent manifestations of material entities in stellar space. And the terrific conciseness of the style, telegraphically succinct in its themes, rapid in its mutation and developments, overleaping connective steps, and nervously alive with dialectically generated new ideas; and the acute high timbres, the abrupt detonations and tremendous volumes of sound which figure almost incessantly, quite specifically suggest the spirit of some intensely dynamic process of the sort imperceptible to the senses but not to the penetrating organs of science: say the famous one by which gas is transformed into a conductor of electricity, with its separation of neutral molecules into ions by the impact of the swiftly mobilized ions originally present in the gas subjected to the electrostatic field, and its mobilization and generation of further ions by the newly formed particles. Thus one felt oneself identified anew vis-à-vis the cosmos of the physicists, amid and still upon the surface of some new ocean of heaving, bursting, strangely sensitive matter, and filled with power and preparedness by this new experience of the intense way and orderliness of things.

As for the process of the elevation and coronation of the battery as the king of the orchestra, leading to its autonomy, that may well have attained its term in *Ionization*. In music, we know how not only fashions but feelings change, and even if the skyscraper mysticism of Varèse should persist, as undoubtedly it will in himself, it may never again lead him to write for percussion and friction instruments alone. His very latest piece *Equatorials* is cast for an ensemble not wholly percussive in character, and the other composers who have recently taken to producing pieces for the battery alone have no claim on our consideration. But even if *Ionization* should prove a unicorn it would still maintain its place in the ranks of music. It is a little work of genius, born of the evolving life of music and its means, and the spirit of an individual and an epoch, a credit to its mother and its father. And it is both an individual and an epoch that are being denied in the stupid, extreme, entirely undeserved neglect—the most stupid, extreme, and entirely undeserved of all that are being inflicted by the musical world upon any living composer—that is still the part of the brilliant composer of *Ionization,* of *Hyperprism* and *Intégrales* and *Arcanes* and all the rest of his powerful music.

Gershwin

GEORGE GERSHWIN'S rhapsodies and other pieces in the symphonic forms have inspired certain critics to classify him as a good "vulgar" composer. They mean to indicate that he is a composer of the class represented by Chabrier: that, like the exuberant author of the *Espagna Rhapsody* and the *Suite Villageoise,* he organizes musical motives popular in origin or in character and infused with the lighter essences, in light symphonic molds, and while conserving the original salt and earthy charm of the material expresses all the common man's humorous, ironical, buoyantly erotic, and sentimental feelings of life with it. *Notre Chabrier à nous,* one critic, adapting D'Indy's epithet for Debussy, affectionately called him.

This judgment is extremely uncritical, exhibiting a defective vision of good "vulgar" music and of Gershwin's ambitious product and the difference between them. That many of the expressions found in our Broadway paladin's two Rhap-

GERSHWIN

sodies and his piano Concerto, his *An American in Paris* and his *Cuban Overture,* formerly the *Rumba,* are popular and American, is certain. Not the earliest symphonic works merging or attempting to merge the expressions of Broadway with traditional and personal expressions—for Satie's *Parade* and a number of the pieces of the Parisian Six represented this tendency before the *Rhapsody in Blue*—Gershwin's absolute and programmatic compositions are distinguished by their frequent, sometimes vivacious and adroit, at other times coarse and brutal, exploitations of the jazz idioms, rhythms, and colors. That the result is representative of a certain kind of American is also certain; their immense popular success is one proof of it. Yet to qualify as a vulgar composer and rank with Chabrier, Albeniz, Glinka, and even with Milhaud and Auric at their best, a musician has to "compose" his material, to sustain and evolve and organize it to a degree sufficient to bring its essences, their relationships, their ideas, to expression. And that Gershwin has accomplished to no satisfactory degree, at least not in any of the larger forms he has up to the present time given the public.

Take any one of his ambitious products. It is only very superficially a whole, actually a heap of extremely heterogeneous minor forms and expressions. Individually these minor forms and expressions, themes, melodies, rhythms, harmonies, figures, ornaments, are frequently piquant and striking, and richly dissonant, and brilliantly colored. But they are extremely disparate, first of all in point of freshness. Some are the raciest of rhythmic and coloristic neologisms, effective exploitations of various elements of the jazz idiom or original material. Others are very worn and banal. Again, they remain equally disparate in point of style, some of them being popularly American in essence or gaily, brightly Yiddish, and others impressionistic, or vaguely grand-operatic, or reminiscent of the melodramatic emphasis and fioritura of Liszt, or Chopinesque. And they also remain disparate in point of quality, since a number of them have sharpness, jauntiness, dash, indicating a perhaps shallow but distinct vitality, while others are weak, soft, cheap, representing a vitality duller and lower than that at which interest commences—so soft and cheap indeed that in comparison with them the best of Gershwin's ideas, mauger the fact that very few of them have the delicacy and power of first-rate stuff and that his treatment of jazz is by no means highly sensitive, appear almost the expression of another man.

Too, these expressions, for the most part, are insufficiently extended and frequently fizzle out. By and large, the Gershwin symphonic piece is a lot of preluding, a succession of fairly unrelated advances toward a whole that, if at times it appears to come into being, never sustains its existence very long. The composer introduces subjects upon subjects, mostly short ones. But rarely does he do anything with them, rarely relating them to one another so that they complete each other and advance the interest of the whole piece. Most of them remain static, mere phrases, which he either ornaments with Lisztian fioritura, or repeats with ever greater dynamics, or sets soaring in a series of sequences that, ascending by half-tones, recall the worst of Wagnerian *Steigerungen*. Long rhythms rarely appear. Gershwin at best has what might be termed merely "local" rhythm, due to his keen ear for irregular popular dance measures, especially the Charleston beat. But of actual movement, actual organization, his compositions are pretty bare. Whether this is due to the extreme heterogeneity of his material, so extreme as to prevent co-ordination, we cannot say. It must suffice us to remark that no integrating principle has borne on them, bringing them into relationship with one another, establishing with them a moving, developing form made up of emotionally related parts. Upswells of creative energy momentarily manifest themselves, it is true. Yet they seldom break over and flow into new developments, variations, ideas. Sometimes, for periods, wholes with some direction, some determination, make as if to appear. But they never sustain themselves.

Take the juiciest and most entertaining of Gershwin's concert works, the F Major piano Concerto. It commences with a number of disconnected flourishes. At length the composer comes to grips with his material: the first original theme enters, syncopated, impassioned, on the piano. It is repeated by the saxophone in a low register and by the piano, and after short divertissements, twice by the tutti, the last time with decided dash. A certain tension has been created, impelling one to look forward to some sort of contrast and development. What now follows, however, is an irrelevant theme, very popular, and in a Charleston measure. For a period the music flows. Sometimes lyrical, sometimes merely rhetorical, the page is one of Gershwin's most sustained and charmingly orchestrated expressions. But it, too, stops short of completion. And after a brief polyphonic passage the first theme is restated with inflations recalling some of the grandiose effects of the Capitol Theater, and the movement ends inconsequentially with more irrelevant flourishes, leaving one with the feeling that something which started to happen has not come off. Still, tension sufficient to make one look forward to the second movement hangs over from the composition's beginning. Again, for a minute, one is engaged. The second movement begins with an interesting, muted, atmospheric treatment of a blues theme; but after the melody has been stated and we have been led to look forward to some inevitable development, the composer introduces some more material which one would call similar to the original

DISCOVERIES OF A MUSIC CRITIC

blues theme were it not so very much more inferior to that original theme in quality. All tension has disappeared. The impulse of the beginning is entirely let down. The weak material grows pathetic amid strains of the *Liebestod*. And the movement is concluded with a nostalgic little coda made from the "blues" theme. Hope that the composer is going to get somewhere or can get somewhere has entirely dwindled, and though the last movement begins vigorously with a good scherzando theme for the xylophone, one is not surprised to find the movement largely a recapitulation of old material, leading up to a restatement of the original theme more grandiosely inflated even than any of the preceding ones and concluding inconsequentially with further flourishes.

While the succeeding composition, the tripartite *An American in Paris,* starts somewhat more energetically, it, too, has no real movement. Somewhere during the second section the composition stops advancing, and it too concludes with mere meaningless recapitulations; and with the exception of the amusing passage imitative of French motor horns, the material itself is less attractive than that of the Ritzy concerto.

Thus, deficiently expressive of essences and of ideas, even the lighter, saltier, more comic ones that are the vulgar American composer's objects, these strings of melodies and rhythms put one in touch with little that is real. Momentarily we feel the forces of ambition and desire: imperious, unmitigated appetites, yearnings for tenderness, intoxications flowing from the stimulation of novel, luxurious surroundings, Parisian, Cuban, Floridan, from the joy of feeling oneself an American—Americanism apparently conceived as a naïve, smart, inept, good-natured form of being, happily and humorously shared by other good fellows like oneself—and from a gaminlike eroticism. But neither they nor their relations are explicit or steady. True, at moments in the piano Concerto and *An American in Paris,* an idea, curiously enough a tragic one, of an inevitable chaos, a predestinately incomplete and unsuccessful connection between complementary forces, feebly glimmers on one. But its glimmer is fickle and disappears as the form itself loses its impulse and falls into idle repetitions and meaningless flourishes. The whole, if it points to anything, points to a creative energy too feeble and unenduring to afford sustained contact with reality and a mind that, lacking creative power, remains the prisoner of by no means idealistic dreams. It is impossible to hear Gershwin's symphonic music without being from time to time moved by its grandiloquences to conceive—with the aspect of things having some immensely flattering, glorifying bearing upon ourselves—of towers of fine gold rising amid Florida palms, splendiferous hotel foyers crowded with important people and gorgeous women *décolletées jusqu' à là,* and immediately contingent upon paradise; or rosy banks of nymphs amorously swooning amid bells of rose-pink tulle. A tawny oriental city acknowledges us as its conqueror in the sundown, and the superb naked woman who stands above the city gate, starred with the diamond in her tresses, descends and advances toward us with exalted words and gestures, hailing our peerlessness while we ourselves recognize in her the one we have always sought and loved. Are these atrocious dreams our own? Possibly, but they have grown articulate through this music.

That these pieces are characteristic American productions is not to be doubted. Their spirit unfortunately makes them so, since weakness of spirit, possibly as a consequence of the circumstance that the new world attracted the less stable human types, remains an American condition. It makes of the American business man often a poor organizer and the American artist frequently an advertising man. With spirit, both types would create a material and a spiritual order, based upon human relationships, the one with practical, the other with aesthetic, means. For spirit apprehends actual forces and their ideas and creates a human relationship, a society, with them. But materialism sees nothing but its personal objects, and investing them with bogus glamours and glitters, perpetuates the disorder, the waste, the anarchy, the solitude, that are favorable to its limitless expansion and gratification. Thus, most American art is advertising, glorifying the material objects and fanning up the appetite directed upon them; and this category of aesthetic products is dangerously close to that of George Gershwin. Indeed, we are tempted to call Gershwin the laureate of musical advertisers, perhaps the most genial of them all, but the head of their company: the musician of the materialistic age that saw the bloom of the worst business and best advertising America has ever endured, the jazz age. True, one of that materialistic period's most poetic representatives, the mercurial Zelda Fitzgerald, has with indubitable authority declared in *Save Me the Waltz:* "Vincent Youmans wrote the music for those twilights just after the war. They were wonderful. . . . They lay above the streets like a white fog off a swamp. Through the gloom, the whole world went to tea." Nevertheless we still dare call Gershwin the typical jazz musician.

Of course it is possible that the idea of the musicians who called him our vulgar composer was entirely prophetic and that Gershwin is not yet but will be the musical interpreter of what the ordinary American feels in his genuine living moments. The event is certainly not without the bounds of possibility. Gershwin is still a relatively young man. There is no question of his talent. The musical language is natively his own: one can see he was not introduced to it yesterday, that he knows it and feels and likes it, and has a decided knack with it. He has spontaneity, an ear for complex rhythms, a feeling for luscious, wistful, dissonantly harmonized melodies. Above all, he has a distinct warmth; and if the main honors for the symphonic exploitation and idealization of jazz have gone to Milhaud for *La Création du Monde,* to Honegger for his piano Concertino, and to Copland for his piano Concerto, rather more than to himself, he at least stands almost gigantically among the other sons of Tin-pan Alley, Bennett, Levant, Grofé, who have grappled with more or less symphonic forms. At least he has a veritable urgence and a spirit of endeavor that commands sympathy.

Only, we remain unconvinced that he has sufficient of the feeling of the artist. The artist's remoteness from material objects, his suspended, selfless, aesthetic touch of them, his tension and experience of order, and his impulse to organize his material in conformity with that experience—we have not as yet caught more than a fleeting glance of them in Gershwin's products.

We remain obliged to him mostly for *Funny Face* and his other smart musical shows. His talent burgeons in them.

Porgy and Bess, produced since this book passed into the hands of its publishers, but fortifies one's conviction of Gershwin's shortness of the artist's feeling. The score is a loose aggregation of somewhat heavily instrumentated numbers in many instances conforming to the style of American Negro music, especially the blues, and in others to that of the Puccini grand opera. Some of these pieces, for example the entire thunderstorm music, are very bad and empty; others—one thinks particularly of the lullaby and the fugue in Scene I, the antiphonies of chorus and solos in the scene of the wake, the street calls in Act II, and certain popular numbers like Porgy's song, "I got lots o' nuttin," embody musical, melodic, or rhythmical ideas, and have a quality and sensuous charm and flavor. An aggrandized musical show, the opera contains triple the music of the ordinary one, even the ordinary one of Gershwin's make, and in some spots music of triple the interest of the best of the species. But the score sustains no mood. There is neither a progressive nor an enduring tension in it. The individual numbers spurt from a flat level, and ending, leave one largely where they picked one up. Nor do they communicate a reality, either the rich, authentic quality of the Negro or the experience of Porgy the pathetic cripple who unexpectedly gets his woman and rejoices and suffers with her and then at last loses her, or of Bess, the weak victim of the flesh and the devil. It would seem as if Gershwin knew chiefly stage Negroes and that he very incompletely felt the drama of the two protagonists. At moments there is a warmth and emotion in the expression that indicates some sense of the experience. Ultimately, nonetheless, the expression lies in conventional patterns, as if the feeling of the composer had been too timid to mold musical forms in accord with itself and had succumbed to conventional and, alas, sure-fire gestures of the musical theater. Long before the conclusion one feels the music has got one nowhere new and true. What endures is largely the splendid sense of the artistic spirit of the Negro singers and dancers, who give themselves 100 per cent.

Cowell

HENRY COWELL'S fame as the inventor of something called "tone clusters" had preceded his memorable first appearance as a composer pianist in New York. Nobody knew exactly what these "tone clusters" were. Everybody knew merely that they were something invented by a young musician in California named Cowell, and the size of the audience that assisted at the first of the composer's local demonstrations was probably the result of a general determination, on the part of the musical, to find out. At last the inventor appeared upon the platform, a little man with a small, bright, egg-shaped head. Waddling with terrific velocity toward the grand piano at the center of the stage, he promptly sat down at it and applied his entire forearm to the ivories of the dignified instrument. A roar arose from the piano, followed by one from the audience, which in its turn was followed by still further roars from the piano as the composer again and again struck and released masses of keys now with an arm and now with a fist.

These stunning effects were the tone clusters. One of the compositions exhibiting them was called by Cowell *The Voice of Lir*. Lir was an Irish deity whose tongue, according to legend, had been cleft, and whose speech in consequence was half comprehensible, half inarticulate. The piece was supposed to represent Lir's language. With his right hand, the young Californian played the beginning of a phrase which, for the reason that it was in the pentatonic scale, sounded like a bit of Gaelic folk song; with his left arm he concluded the phrase

DISCOVERIES OF A MUSIC CRITIC

with a tone cluster. This was one of Lir's difficult sentences, and the piece consisted of a series of them. Faster and faster came the melodic phrases, faster and faster the complementary roars, till it became apparent Lir's messages were filling the whole world with MacDowell and with elemental bellowings.

Another of the pieces was called *Anger Dance*. Before playing it, the composer rose and addressed his audience, explaining that he wished to inform them of the origin of this particular composition. A few years ago, he angrily said, he had developed a severe pain in one of his legs and had consulted a physician who told him that he would do well to have the leg amputated. The doctor's brutal advice had so infuriated him, he continued, that he was almost beside himself when he left the fellow's office; and the piece was an expression of what he had felt. Before playing it, Cowell continued, he also wished to inform the audience that instead of taking the doctor's advice he had gone to an osteopath, who in a few weeks had driven the pain away. With these triumphant words the composer sat down again at the keyboard and let the piano dispel all doubt in his listeners' minds as to his own and its ability to boil.

Still another piece was called *The Banshee*. It contained no tone clusters or any other keyboard effects. To play it, the composer rose from his stool, and stepping resolutely behind the piano, thrust a hand inside its open queue and started to pluck the wires. The moment was tense. Few members of the audience could help feeling that if they were the piano, they would certainly get up and sock the fellow; and everybody glued his eyes upon the venerable instrument, expecting at any moment to see it rise on its hind leg and deliver a swift one to his jaw with one of its fore paws. But either because it was helpless or because it had a greater confidence in the integrity of the composer's intentions than his audience had, the piano submitted. From its sounding strings there arose a series of weird glissandi which any theatrical producer mounting a play about a haunted house and wishing to suggest the spook by musical means could not possibly have improved upon.

These simple, home-made effects had apparently been perfected by Cowell on the ancient upright piano on which his musical education was started. As a baby in Menlo Park in California, where he was born in 1897, he had attracted the attention of his elders by forming entire musical phrases well before he could speak; but when he had grown to boyhood, his family was too badly off to be able to afford music lessons for him. His mother, an intellectual, after separating from her husband and taking herself and her boy to Kansas, found herself unable to support either him or herself. So the boy began getting the bread for the pathetic little ménage by working twelve hours a day in the fields for wages amounting to twelve dollars a month. Later his mother took him back to California, and Henry found a new and better means of getting a livelihood. There was a market for young trees and plants at a town some four miles away from his dwelling; and so, three or four times a week, the embryonic composer marched himself into the mountains that lay some four miles in the direction opposite to that of the town, filled a bag with saplings, carried it to market, and then walked back home. It was at this time that he got hold of the old upright. He taught himself to play on it; he even began to compose; and as he was without inherited prejudices in regard to the instrument's uses, he began experimenting with it and discovered it could be used both as an instrument of percussion and as a harp, particularly in the absence of music teachers. Later, after he had got some musical training first at the University of California and then at the Institute of Applied Music in New York, and had got his definite direction, these little percussive and harplike effects became the basis of numbers of his compositions.

But with few exceptions the New York critics were unkind to the composer, his tone clusters and his pieces, which was short-sighted of them. The tone clusters were legitimate and by no means despicable effects: it was perfectly conceivable that they might figure compellingly in the compositions of the future. The business of plucking the strings of the piano produced a queer rich dead sonority, something like that of a harpsichord. As for Cowell's little compositions, while they were somewhat monotonous and distilled a watery poetry, they had a certain musicality that should have prevented anyone from brusquely dismissing their author.

And Cowell was not to be discouraged. He came back by immediately re-engaging Carnegie Hall for a second concert and placarded the place with announcements: "Cowell Plays Again!" Later he reappeared in New York, again as a composer performer, at one of the experimental concerts of the International Composers' Guild. The composition he presented was a quintet for string quartet and thunderstick. The thunderstick is an instrument employed by the Indians of the American Southwest in their religious ceremonies. It is shaped like a small paddle, and when attached to a string and whirled about, it produces a sound resembling that of a small electric fan capable of considerable regulation. That evening Cowell himself manipulated the thunderstick. Standing behind the quartet of viols and reminding all the world of a sort of musical bacillus (possibly for the reason he was so virulent, so infectious), the intrepid little composer vigorously swung the instrument about his head, letting its now soaring, now diminishing sound provide the exciting background that the extremely mild string music decidedly required. All went perfectly until suddenly the composer lost his grip. Off the thunderstick flew into the parterre, narrowly missing the stately heads of several members of the audience. But Cowell was not embarrassed, the merest reddening of his countenance alone indicating his displeasure. He had, in fact, faced out worse situations. His first concert in Leipzig had necessitated a call for the police, and while the quarreling factions of the audience dragged each other about the platform, he had calmly continued striking out his tone clusters. There had been riots in Munich and Vienna as well, and none had fazed him, either. So, quickly recovering his ethonological instrument, he easily recaptured his place in the music and resumed the whirling activity that gave his music and himself their necessary wings.

And, ever gyroscopic and original, the activity represented by these first and memorable appearances of the California lyrist has, if anything, during the more recent years redoubled and tripled in character, velocity, conspicuity, and scope. Its scene has not been confined to Carnegie, Town, or Aeolian Hall. Its scene, so to speak, has been the whole world, from China to Peru. It has included concert and lecture tours of the United States from coast to coast every year since 1920 and five concert tours in Europe and the U.S.S.R. It includes perseverance as a composer, a pianist, an editor of new music, both in score and in record form, a promoter of performances of music, a director of musical activities, a lecturer, an author, a teacher, a musicologist, and the inventor of a new musical instrument, a "rhythmicon" which can perform triplets against quintuplets. A very sizable brochure, compiled by Olive Thompson Cowell, his lady stepmother, and entitled *Henry Cowell a record of his activities,* gives in its twenty-odd pages but the merest skeletonized outline of his busy bustle, and most of the pages are given over to this outline, only the last few containing citations of all the references to this activity in the lectures, books, and magazine articles of his fellow musicians and musicologists and of the comments it has generated in the press. Its instrument has long since ceased to be the piano or the thunderstick and its end the communication of the composer's feelings and experiences. Its instrument has become the new American music and its end that music's life. What he now strikes are the chords of Chavez, Copland, Piston, Riegger, Weiss, Ives, Roldan, Antheil, Donovan, Moross, Ruggles, Varèse, etc., and those of such European contemporaries as Webern, Weisshaus, and Schönberg. And what he now waves is the gonfalon of the contemporary, the new, the progressive. Wherever in his steady whirl he has set foot on earth, from Los Angeles in the west to Vladivostok in the east, concerts have sprung up, like flowers about the feet of Flora, and they have invariably included performances of the works of the leading American moderns. And he has got these revolutionary scores not only played, but printed and recorded as well. And he has been writing about this music and getting his articles published in important organs, and interesting colleges, forums, and clubs in it, and making fruitful contacts with musical people in Russia, Germany, and for all one knows in Kamchatka and at home, and in the meanwhile composing. He has indeed become very influential, and if in person he is still as little and rapid and shiny as of yore, you will find him—should you seek him out in his den at the New School in New York, where he teaches and lectures and performs—amid an imposing litter of African war drums, ringing telephones, grand pianos, heaps of new music in printed and manuscript form, collaborators and copyists of all ages and sexes, adorers aged from fourteen to eighty, electrical musical appliances of his own invention, and philosophizing musicologists; and after speaking with you for a few minutes about "creative music" and "indigenous music," two mysterious terms frequently on his lips, he will probably dash away—in so doing giving a few last touches to an acid Virginia reel for *theremin* or an atonal sinfonietta for classic orchestra—probably to give a lesson at the Christadora House or some university.

True, this whirling activity to a degree still conforms to at least one of its pristine patterns, insomuch as it rivals that of a small electric fan and provides somewhat more fun, interest, and benefit to the perpetrator than to his audience, and verges on murder as on life-giving, and in the last analysis remains a little less than musical in the deepest sense. In other words, the constructive effect of this restless bustle of Cowell's remains disappointingly small. While he has succeeded in getting many very important works performed, some of the performances make one wonder whether the volatile impresario is after all not more fully concerned with getting the names of compositions on to programs than with getting the pieces themselves faithfully presented. As for the pieces Cowell has chosen to champion and to publish and press, they are almost as frequently sterile as fertile; and despite their frequent reasonableness, his choices on the whole make manifest no particular values, saving perhaps the intrinsically insignificant ones of American birth, technical oddity and unconformativeness, and, as a friend of ours cleverly remarked, "an incessant exhibition of major and minor seconds, sevenths, and ninths." If his *Modern Music* editions are handsome and for all one knows correct, the phonographic records he has issued are not to be recommended for their technical quality. His own compositions are frequently rhythmically inert. It is as if only the outer voices and not the interior moved.

And take the symposium, *American Composers on Ameri-*

DISCOVERIES OF A MUSIC CRITIC

can Music, edited and to a considerable degree written by Cowell himself. It is a typical production. It is instructive enough, including several penetrating criticisms—Seeger's of Ruggles, Copland's of Chavez, Cowell's own of Ives, some of Slonimsky's bright interpretations, and suggestive general articles by Ives and Harris. It also contains much that is picayune, like Chanler's article on Copland and Cowell's on Harris, and redounds in meaningless technical "criticism" and evidences of an obsession with the means of music and a neglect of its substance. And as the thirty-one separate pieces which compose it—many of them reprints—have no relation to any common standard and are not even homogeneous in method, it merely substitutes another critical confusion for the one it pretends to abolish.

And yet it has value, distinct value, and so have a fair number of the effects of Cowell's incessant "activity." In the last years, besides increasing in character, velocity, conspicuity, and scope, Cowell's business has actually increased in effectualness. Together with much that is sterile, he *has* performed, got into print, and pressed music of the sort that the present shies from and the future battens on; and half loaves are not to be despised in these hard times. Cowell, to his everlasting credit, has no fixed ideas. Perhaps he has no ideas at all, but no idea and a lot of mercuriality are better than a fixed idea that music is excellent in proportion to its resemblance to that of Brahms or Strawinsky or in proportion to the degree to which it makes its audience "see red." American culture is substantially indebted to his mental fluidity. His persistent and very practical championship of radical and unpopular work, too, has provided steady encouragement to those with something individual in them to give. And his compositions, at least his *Synchrony* for large orchestra, and his piano Concerto, would lure at least this reviewer to making a small pilgrimage to the end of hearing them again. Indeed there is something almost saintlike in this activity. Cowell is after all quite disinterested. He has always been, and he remains, a poor man. What little money he has derived from this concerts, his symposiums, his critical articles, has immediately been reinvested by him in new concerts, new symposiums, new musical publications and recordings. He doesn't even push his own work forward at his recitals. He usually gives the *pas* to compositions of others, nor does he ever print or record his own work. It is entirely the work of his contemporaries that *New Music* and the New Music Records have been streaming out into the world, and almost invariably the work of unknown strugglers. The greater the pity, of course, that this play of energy has occasioned such waste and spilt milk. But it is useless to regret it. It is apparently the inevitable consequence of one like Henry Cowell's, very American in its pioneering initiative, its freedom from the constraints of authority and tradition, and its diffusion and tendency to find egress a little too regularly through an enthusiastic scratching of ever new virgin surfaces rather more than through sustained penetration of them.

Recent American Operas

SEVEN new American operas reached the public during the seasons 1931-35. They are *Peter Ibbetson, Jack and the Beanstalk, The Emperor Jones, Four Saints in Three Acts, Merry Mount, Helen Retires,* and *Maria Malibran.* Let us pass them

DISCOVERIES OF A MUSIC CRITIC

in review. None of them is entirely bare of interest; and various in origin and in form and feeling, all significantly reveal a family likeness and lead the mind to two definite conclusions.

1. PETER IBBETSON. *Play from the novel of George du Maurier, music by Deems Taylor. New York: The Metropolitan Opera, February 7, 1931.* This opera is the Metropolitan's outstanding American success. Applauded more warmly by its first audiences than any American work previously mounted by the old institution, its periodic revivals continue to please; and the indications that it may find a place in the company's repertoire are definite.

The causes of this success, as far as it may be attributed to the composer, appear double. The first of them would seem to be his musical competence. His score is sufficiently mellifluous, fluent, well orchestrated, bare of desert spots, to gratify the lightly critical ear. And it is dramatically relevant, and occasionally, especially in the dance numbers and the parlor ballads and the little military march, very pretty. In Taylor, America, for better or worse, has produced an operatic composer the equal of the Mascagnis, the Wolf-Ferraris, and other European makers of effective operas.

The second of the causes of *Peter Ibbetson's* success would appear to be the music's augmentation of the play's comfortableness to persons unable to live out their own lives.

It will be remembered that the play presents two characters whose principal actions are the dream-form revivification of the state of familial identity, and the dream-form erotic relationship with more or less tabu persons, that provide outlets for the dammed-up and regressive libido. And it will be remembered that it presents their pathological actions not in the light of truth but colored by a false poesy and glamour, rendering these figures attractive subjects of personal identification for actual people who, like themselves, cannot live; and thus the means of a social, flatteringly poetically tinted alleviation of the painful condition. One of these characters, Peter Ibbetson, is introduced to us as a charming and Chopinesque young man in a world bare of young girls and men of his own age—the ward of a spiritual impostor, the caddish and libidinous Colonel Ibbetson. Under the lusters and amid the crinolines and glacé gloves of a London ballroom of the 1850's, Peter relates the story of his life to his motherly friend, Mrs. Deane. Ibbetson is not his name. His name is Pasquier, and his happy childhood was spent in Passy with his father and mother and with a little girl named Mimsy. But this childhood circumstance disappeared, and with it father, mother, and Mimsy; and Peter was taken to England by Colonel Ibbetson and given the Colonel's name. The old circumstance still haunts his feelings; he can even hear the silenced voices. The other of the two protagonists now enters, the lovely youthful Mary Duchess of Towers. Peter stares bewilderedly at her and she at him, each of them stricken by some vague familiarity in the other. And as the Duchess is carried off to waltz, Peter lifts the bouquet which she has unconsciously left behind her to his lips and murmurs, *"L'amour!"*—The consequence of this infatuation seems to be a reinforced attraction to the vanished world, for the next act shows us Peter at an inn in Passy. An ancient man enters the room: it is a military man, not Colonel Ibbetson, but an old Napoleonic soldier who formed part of the old family group. Feeble, he does not recognize Peter, who tries to kiss his hand; and he goes away regretfully murmuring the names of the persons of the old circle.—From a window Peter now spies Mary Duchess of Towers descending from her carriage and immediately throws himself on a couch. The scene darkens. In the place of the rear wall we now see Peter's vision, the old childhood garden in the apricot light of an eternal afternoon. Under a tree, in the costumes of the past, the elders sit silently while the little Peter and the little Mimsy sport under their benevolent regards. Suddenly Mary Duchess of Towers enters, and following her, the adult Peter. She tells him that she has drawn him hither and that he is free to observe the inhabitants of the old garden but not to speak with them. Colonel Ibbetson now enters. Peter observes his advances to his mother, but as he springs forward to protect her the garden disappears. Once again we see Peter in his inn, and the Duchess enters, driven to this refuge by a storm. Peter now definitely recognizes Mimsy in her, and she her old playmate in him; but when he seeks to take her in his arms she tells him that she is not free and that he must not attempt to see her again. In the next scene, Peter murders the Colonel for having told Mrs. Deane that he, Peter, is the Colonel's bastard; and thereupon we see Peter awaiting the moment of his execution, in jail, reconciled to quitting a prisonlike world, and addressing trinkets to the Duchess and Mrs. Deane. Reprieved but condemned to life imprisonment, he receives Mary's message that his life has just begun. She bids him "Dream true!" and once more the rear wall vanishes, revealing the old family group picnicking beside the *mare d'Auteuil*. The adult Peter again appears in the dream world, calling upon his mother, complaining of his unbroken loneliness; but though neither she nor the others hear him, his cry is heard by Mary, who, entering, holds out her arms to him. In the last act Peter as an old man is dying on his prison couch, after having spent each night in the dream tryst with Mary. He knows that she is dead, and her spirit appears to him, telling him "life is but a dream," calling him to even better things. Once more the rear wall disappears, and

RECENT AMERICAN OPERAS

now the ever-youthful Mary steps toward the prisoner with extended arms; and from the couch of the dead man there arises a charming and Chopinesque youth. In the middle of the stage the couple embrace.

The score meanwhile augments this comfortableness to those moved to the regressive revivification of childhood or familial states by reviving, in the guise of new work, musical forms and musical modes of expression developed by the generations immediately preceding the existing ones. Dominant during the period when the present generation was as yet unable to develop its individual feelings and their appropriate means of expression, they actually constituted the ground from which this generation finally advanced or should have advanced in its own direction. And their revival sets the auditor back in what, musically at any rate, corresponds to his familial environment. Not that the score of *Peter Ibbetson* is deliberately imitative. But it adds nothing to experience, uttering nothing new, not even within the limits of the pretty and the light, presenting no individual solutions of musical problems in conformity with individual adventure. The music is ably but undistinguishedly traditional, inclusive of dissonant waltzes in the *Rosenkavalier* style, of a somewhat Parsifalesque prison scene, and of other passages vaguely in the manner not only of Strauss and Wagner, but of Tchaikowsky, Debussy, and Bizet.

The score has still further kindnesses for the blocked individual impelled to revert to the familial situation. With its prevalent, extremely melting, pink and Huyler's essences, it both dissolves the last obstreperous particles of will still moving the individual to meet his own objects and master them and gratifies the largely infantine yearnings that again are his. Orchestral passages like the one during which Peter "dreams true" on the couch in his French inn room—passages that have no momentum and neither move anywhere nor attain anything but merely soar spasmodically—but express the attitude that is less aggressive than resorbent and ingestive. And what projects itself saccharinely in the ensuing dream scenes provides the object fulfilling this passive yearning. It is perfectly appropriate that at the commencement of one of these scenes we hear "poor Peter" crying for "Mimsy," which sounds so much like "Mumsy"; for if any passages in the literature of opera, and perhaps in tone itself, have the essence of the mimsy or the mumsy, it is, one fears, the soft syrup-sweet pages answering his cry and accompanying the milkily lit dream scenes of the opera. It is not the Mother that meets us here, in this piece by this adult, technically competent American. That is what is projected and achieved mightily, magically, in the second act of *Tristan*. Here, the prettily erotic ululations of off-stage women's choruses give us something that is distinctly "Mamma." It heals sore spots with comforting applications of sweets. It sinks us in warm water.

2. *JACK AND THE BEANSTALK. Libretto by John Erskine, music by Louis Gruenberg. New York: The Juilliard School, November 19, 1931.* The spirit of this clever little *Singspiel* places it in the category of things illustrated in the theater by the half playful, half ironic fairy-tale comedies of Gozzi and of Tieck. It is that of romantic wit. The world unfolded by Erskine's libretto is enchantingly irrational and childlike and atrocious. It contains a cow which not only talks but infers and thinks more sensibly than the human characters. It contains an old woman gradually transformed into a ravishing young princess. There is also a young lad in it who outwits a bloodthirsty giant, bringing the ogre's magic harp, his hen that lays golden eggs, and his captive princess back in triumph to

RECENT AMERICAN OPERAS

his home. Again, like its great patterns, the farce ironizes from some superior viewpoint the actual world, rational philosophy, and the naïve conceptions animating the race's fantasies and dreams of victory. The giant bristles with platitudes concerning the sanctity of the home, uttering his banalities in a balmy falsetto. But he cannot control his appetites for flesh and for gold and comes to grief through his incapacity to check his tendency to slumber off at crucial instants. Jack and the cow philosophize together. He patronizes her with the wisdom of the schools, informing her that animals are incapable of making moral choices. The cow patiently, stoically demonstrates the fallacy of the rationalists and sighs over the brutishness of human beings. At the end, during the universal jubilation following the giant's sudden death, she warns Jack and his princess: "What do a bag of gold, and a hen that lays golden eggs, and a harp that plays magic tunes, amount to, as things to begin life on? The giant was a failure. I nearly fell into the hands of the butcher. And all I can tell you, gold and hen and harp notwithstanding, is, you'd better look out for yourselves!"

And, essentially dramatic, the little libretto fails of brilliance only because of the immelodiousness of some of the lyrical lines in which its wit is couched. Just how arhythmical the whole of the lingual material is, could not be gathered, for much of it was unarticulated, and from time to time one recognized the composer's responsibility for some of the muzziness. His declamation was inexpert: for an impenetrable reason, and with monotonous regularity, he had coupled a long note to the first syllable of almost all the polysyllabic words! Indeed, if we are convinced of the wit of the libretto, it is very largely thanks to the fact that, as a *Singspiel, Jack and the Beanstalk* contained passages of spoken dialogue amid thoroughly intoned scenes;

and they suggested that what was too very clever to be sung was being spoken. Still, in spite of Erskine's dryness, the libretto provided the composer with an excellent opportunity for producing a bright theatrical score. It is spectacular, calls for formal music—songs, dances, and choruses—as well as dramatic, and offers a frame for a charming mixture of playful and ironic expressions in the spirit of romantic wit.

To a degree, Gruenberg's score tastefully expresses this ironic idea. It has a certain jocosity, particularly in the thunderous, beautifully *frightful* introduction to the second act, the land of the giant, and in the scene of the giant's entrance into his castle. It also is charmingly ironic in spots. The three occasions on which the magic hen noisily prepares to lay her egg and anticlimactically deposits it are represented by satiric passages of cutely "mechanistic" music of the sort familiarized by Strawinsky's *Petrushka*. Portentously initiatory, they get nowhere, falling humorously flat, and slyly recalling the indeterminacy of the entire mechanistic musical movement. There are even lightly poetical pages in the score, the chiming music for the beginning of the scene on the road to the market, in particular. At the same time a deal of the score is hollow. The jazzy song of the magic harp is utterly vulgar. The expressions of the old woman gradually transformed into a beautiful young princess do not at all give the feeling of a princess, wanting as they do the glamour that in all lightness they ought to have and remaining merely characterless: thus depriving the score of a primary value necessary to its effectiveness. And the market music and that of the ironically joyful finale are empty and tinselly where they should be solidly satiric, high-spiritedly mocking. Thus, despite its ingenious passages and its "tastefulness," its high technical competence in

RECENT AMERICAN OPERAS

the matter of orchestration, and all its surprises, Gruenberg's little score is only half satisfactory.

Before quitting the subject of *Jack and the Beanstalk* may we be permitted a word also motivated by an interest in the progress of the Opera, but regarding the theory of the ideal libretto stated by John Erskine in the program books of the little work? This hypothesis—which was threefold and contended (1) that the ideal libretto should be comic; (2) that it should be based upon a plot with which the audience was already familiar; and (3) that it should be a bare outline, an unadorned structure of words chosen not for their own sake but merely as supports for music—was largely a work of imagination. But as it was the basis, or the justification, of the book of *Jack and the Beanstalk* and was, or appeared to be, given practical proof by the relative success of the Erskine-Gruenberg production—after the generally pleasing performances before invited audiences up in Claremont Avenue, the little *Singspiel* had a short run on Broadway—this theory might reasonably be conceived to be in a position favorable to its ascendancy over the growing body of ambitious American composers.

Certainly it was conceived in complete disregard of experience, of the facts of the fortunes of the Opera. In the first place, there is no good reason why composers should choose comic libretti in preference to tragic ones. Erskine says that "most operas survive, if at all, in spite of dull and gloomy stories." Now there is no doubt that many excellent operas which survive do so in the face of the poor, the "dull and gloomy" literary quality of their books: *Fidelio,* for example, and in even greater degree *Euryanthe*. But Erskine's identification of tragedy with dullness and gloominess is an entirely arbitrary one. It has still to be proven that as far as the opera goes, a tragic action is necessarily less interesting and exalting, and popular, too, than a comic one: certainly *Tristan* and *Carmen* and *Rigoletto* have held their places quite as stubbornly as *Die Meistersinger* and *The Marriage of Figaro* and *Falstaff*. It has also still to be proven that a comic action cannot be quite as dull and gloomy as a tragic one; certainly Broadway yearly supplies manifold evidences that it can. Nor has the best dramatic music invariably been allied with comic libretti; indeed, it has most frequently been allied with tragic, at least with extremely serious, subjects. And to take from music its opportunities to interpret and heighten tragical texts would unnecessarily deprive it of at least half its theatrical effectiveness.

Nor is the difficulty of following the plot of an opera to which one comes unprepared—Erskine's reason for his second hypothesis, the advisability of the selection of familiar plots—a valid excuse for depriving future operatic work of the interest accruing from an unhackneyed subject or a familiar one subtly expressed and motivated. (Even the most traditional or legendary subject, freshly treated, would bristle with subtleties.) That opera and opéra comique labor, by reason of their very nature, under difficulties regarding specific intelligibility, and that this drawback almost balances the form's immense emotional effectiveness, is not to be questioned; but it is also true that these obstacles to communication are not insuperable. Many composers have surmounted them to shining degrees: the leading Frenchmen with their exquisite declamation, Wagner and his school by the use of leitmotivs and fluent psychological modulation of the musical expression. In any case the impurity of the bath water is no good reason for throwing out the baby. As well deny Shakespeare the stage for the reason that the full appreciation of his poetry requires extra-theatrical study, or Dante the style of poet because the full enjoyment of his *Commedia* prerequires considerable philosophic thought. One can of course say with Strawinsky that music is *trop bête* to express anything, but that feeling merely points the operatic composer to highly transparent subjects, not necessarily to banal ones.

As for the plea for the bareness of the structure of the libretto and the complete subservience of words to music, it appears equally ill taken, unsupported as it is by past experience and wanting sufficient point to recommend it to composers. We all know how many of the most entertaining and most popular operas are based on libretti intricately worked out and on words marshaled with considerable literary skill, from Wagner's to Sullivan's, from Mozart's and Rossini's settings of the comedies of Beaumarchais to Strauss' settings of the tragedies of Wilde and Hofmannsthal. Even the ultramodern composers who would seem to be most completely in agreement with Erskine on this point, composers like Strawinsky and Hindemith who have seemed to require only bare structures for their operas and oratorios and used the word as the merest of props for music, have, like the old setters of the opera poems of Metastasio, almost regularly turned to the productions of subtle poets for their libretti. Strawinsky's *Oedipus Rex* is based on one of the most intricately worked out of dramatic plots, and Hindemith, who experimented with an extremely "bare" book in *Neues vom Tage,* did not hesitate to turn to the poet Gottfried Benn for the book of his oratorio *Des Unaufhörliche.* And it is significant that the better the literature employed by these composers, the better the music, the *Psalms* of Strawinsky and his *Perséphone* on Gide's text excelling his Cocteau music and his *Mavra,* and Hindemith's music to words by Brecht and Benn surpassing that of his deplorable farce. Indeed it is almost safe to say that the literary quality of the

DISCOVERIES OF A MUSIC CRITIC

libretto, often the immediate precipitant of the score, is almost regularly one of the best agents of the composer's inspiration. True, instances of musical triumphs over the incompetence of librettists dot the literature of opera; and many nineteenth-century Italian operas do submerge the word pretty cavalierly under the tides of music. Still, *The Magic Flute* and *Fidelio* and *Euryanthe* are really the exceptions among operas; even Gluck's most moving pages, the second act of *Alceste,* for example, are married to the more affecting expressions of his librettists: and the Italian "concerts in costume" are an inferior genus. Besides, Mr. Erskine is extreme: he would rule literature out entirely. "If a libretto were self-sufficient poetry," he says, and it is hard to see how anything with a literary quality could fail of a certain self-sufficiency, "to add music would be an impertinence." The world may smile to learn that it owes *Boris* and *Pelléas* to impertinences.

Thus these theories prove themselves quite untheoretical, in fact so plainly that they seem almost foolish, a circumstance surprising in the work of so invariably clever a writer as Erskine. What prevents them from seeming completely so is the fact that they actually are reliable bases for construction as far as one particular sort of musical expression is concerned. This is expression in the spirit of romantic wit: here, they provide the correct ally. The ironic perception naturally battens on a comic libretto, on a situation both the source and the object of mirth, the happy feeling of superiority being possible only *vis-à-vis* an expressively limited world-picture. It also battens upon a plot already familiar and entailing the pleasure of recognition, for the reason that the harmless, the predictable, and the banal excite the feeling of distance and the levity of the spirit. Bareness of structure and insufficiency—but witty insufficiency!—of poetry are equally favorable to the ironic perception, affording as they do an external view of the poverty of our imagination.

And this relevancy to works in the category into which *Jack and the Beanstalk* wholly falls reveals the reason for the extravagant theorem. It was a justification of the little opera, of the spirit in which Erskine and Gruenberg collaborated, intended perhaps not only as a defense against the heaviness of the public, but as a stimulus to critical publicity. Whether the little opera required this defense and this interested challenge is open to question. There can, however, be no question that the form of the defense and challenge was an irresponsible one.

But, to our mutton!

3. *THE EMPEROR JONES. Libretto from the tragedy by Eugene O'Neill, music by Louis Gruenberg. New York: The Metropolitan Opera, January 8, 1933.* The play, you will remember, ended with the daylit scene outside the forest, surely the little tragedy's finest one. After having exposed at length his crazing protagonist's expenditure of life in the struggle with humiliating phantoms of his personal and racial past, themselves progressive projections of his false and easily undermined and swiftly dwindling self-confidence, the playwright here gave a most exquisite twist to his aesthetic knife. He let us observe the disproportionateness of the Emperor's fatal, curiously artistlike internal conflict to the external reality from which he was fugitive. In a daylight effectively banal in contrast to the hysterically tormented night, we saw a few bush Negroes crouching attentively. Suddenly a shot rang out. Paralyzed by the unavailing struggle with his own deep weakness and submissiveness, Jones had made an easy mark. A few soldiers quietly emerged from the woods carrying his limp body.

DISCOVERIES OF A MUSIC CRITIC

A feeble, low-class Briton stepped over to the corpse and mocked it.

Instead of this ingenious, profoundly significant scene, Gruenberg's music-drama has as its finale an operatic transmogrification of the penultimate one. The phantasmal witch doctor and his crocodile god, symbols of the exhausted man's overwhelming tendency to renounce existence under the spell of the illusion that his death is acceptable to an implacable deity demanding human sacrifice, have been transformed into actualities. The witch doctor is the head of the ex-emperor's real pursuers, and finally subjects the broken fugitive by his incantations. Low in the background an immense voodoo moon presents the horrid mask of a Central African Moloch. A multitudinous human pack rushes in. Jones, with a last, unmotivated spurt of self-preservative will, shoots himself with his silver bullet. And orgiastically stamping and intoning a fierce paean, the horde of blacks triumphantly carry his body out.

The bulk of the opera follows the play with greater faithfulness. But the grossness of the finale is characteristic of the level on which the work may be said to succeed. It is that of very ordinary operatic effectiveness. Ably put together by a musician possessed of considerable technical facility, selectivity, theater-blood, and orchestral mastery, the score places O'Neill's play within the scope of the opera house, endowing dramatically gifted baritones like Lawrence Tibbett, the hero of the Metropolitan performance, with an immensely grateful rôle. Only the Nazi revolution would seem adequately to explain the fact that a half-dozen German opera houses have not promptly mounted this musical version of *Kaiser Jonas,* as the Teutons prettily call their favorite O'Neill play. That in itself is a kind of victory, especially for an American composer, member of a tribe, as he is, regularly unsuccessful in the grand operatic field. Yet if it is a victory, it is scarcely one which shines. It is only very remotely due the methods of the artist.

The score has no valid raison d'être. If it places the play within the opera house's scope, it does so without adding anything essential to O'Neill's sympathetic tragedy of the representatives of delusional, handicapped, victimized races and minority interests—not even to the play's chopped, altered, theatrically grossened form. It does not add a new dimension to that of its literary subject, in the way that the scores of *Pelléas* and *Elektra* and *Wozzeck* and some minor works do, seconding the experience of the poet with that of the musician, achieving with musical means the expression which music is excellently fitted to achieve in the theater, the expression of the inner world of the protagonists. Gruenberg's competent score has no decided life of its own. The best of the ideas exposed in it, the fanfare connected with the Emperor's superficial conceit, for instance, lack a strictly individual color; and the worst of them, the bad *Sacre du Printemps* rhythm of the final orgy, are almost embarrassingly cheap. The interludial outcries given the chorus which spies upon the action from stockades on either side of the stage are largely noise, and the most effective orchestral passage in the opera, the sibilant chromatic music accompanying the white rising of the moon over the woods, remains queerly twice-told. In instances, the vocal medium, which fluctuates between song and speech as in the dramatic works and songs of Schönberg and his group, is telling; one remembers with pleasure the intonations of the Emperor's despairing "O Lawds" at the commencement of the fifth scene. But all in all, Gruenberg's song-speech lacks the shape and logic that legitimize its prototypes in scores by the members of the Viennese coterie. And all in all, the outstanding music of the piece is to be found in the setting of the spiritual "Standing in the Need of Prayer," which Gruenberg lets his agonist sing. And that is an interpolation.

What the music actually does is externally to accentuate what was already given by O'Neill, to work theatrically on the spectator while leaving the playwright perform the veritable labor and touch the emotions. The more or less derivative eerie, shivery, and lugubrious orchestral colors which Gruenberg has sapiently exploited: the creepy sibilation of the strings, the spookish rattling and tintinnabulation of the percussion, the moans and hollow brooding sounds of the horns, and the blood-curdling shrieks and bellowing of the chorus, by and large constitute a kind of superior bogey music which plays wholly on the nerves, reinforcing the work of the stage machinist more thoroughly than that of the poet. Whether it performs its function more efficiently than the instrumental sound which O'Neill incorporated into his play, the beat of the drum which starts toward the end of the first scene and slowly and terrifyingly accelerates throughout the action, remains open to doubt. The drum beat was more organic and necessary than the music. Gruenberg has retained the instrument's pulsation in his score. He lets it sound periodically from behind stage and has striven to heighten its effect by giving it successive entries in progressively faster tempi and heavier volume. But, forced to rival a lot of other and similar sounds, the drum note is far less impressive in the opera than it was in the play.

The music only gilds the lily, but the question whether any score written for the play by any musician was a priori condemned to do so, must be allowed. In materializing his hero's visions, O'Neill partially projected the inner realm whose externalization in music drama is usually the business of the musician; and this performance of his apparently lends color to the contention that, unlike Hofmannsthal's, or Maeterlinck's, or Büchner's dramas, *The Emperor Jones* condemned each and every kind of score that might have been combined with it to superfluity. But the corroboration is purely illusory. With his organic drum sound, O'Neill not only exploited a musical means in the form of his drama, but unconsciously indicated the rôle the score could legitimately enact in a musico-dramatic conception of his tragedy. It was that of the representation of the drum itself and its effects. Performing the realistic function of the pulsatile, possibly even featuring its timbre, the orchestra might very effectively express the effects of the drum sound upon the fugitive, the modification of his feelings beneath its impact. Thus it would be playing the dramatic rôle assigned to music by the playwright, projecting the struggles of the spirit in progress in the hunted and self-tormenting man beneath his very hallucinations.

Whether such a score can ever be written is uncertain. In any case it would seem as though Gruenberg's work might, for various good reasons, remove *The Emperor Jones* for a long period from the ranks of the libretti at the disposal of composers. The potentiality of the real music, however, endures in the play.

4. *FOUR SAINTS IN THREE ACTS. Poem by Gertrude Stein, stage version by Frederick Ashton, music by Virgil Thomson. Hartford: The Society of the Friends and Enemies of Modern Music, February 8, 1934.* The curtain rose on a stage backed by cellophane shaped in prisms that shimmered like ice and like candy, and on a colored cast dressed like saints and novices in popular Catholic prints. To a kind of slow barrel-organ tune, the chorus began singing: "Four saints pre-

pare for saints. It makes it well fish." A compère and a commère advanced across the stage rapidly, colloquially intoning: "We had intended if it were a pleasant day to go to the country. It was a very beautiful day and we carried out our intention," etc. The action, a loose ballet-form string of significant gestures, commented upon by the compère and the commère and reinforced by Gertrude Stein's lazy verbal expressions and Thomson's simplicistic score, began with the entrance of St. Therese No. 1, impersonated by a buxom black singer in a cardinal red, ecclesiastical velvet robe, and a cardinal's hat. While she stood, dominating the scene with her bulk and voice, and the music suggested burlesqued Anglican chants suddenly turning into "My country 'tis of thee," a curtain was quietly withdrawn from a small gilt bower at the rear of the stage, discovering another St. Therese, costumed precisely like the first but seated in elegant privacy. And while the external representative moved about the stage and was saluted and enthroned, the interior one had vapors and then started painting and then cradling the infant Jesus; and we began to divine the idea, to some extent because we had previously read the libretto and taken note of the words, "Anyone to tease a saint seriously" and "St. Therese in a storm at Avila, there can be rain and warm, snow and warm, that is the water is warm, the river is not warm and if to stay is to cry," and perceived that one of the things the opera was about—all in Gertrude Stein's half serious and half impudent, half lyrical and half satiric spirit—was the famous temperamental instability that had gained for the "undaunted daughter of desires" among very devout Catholics the nickname of "the little gadabout."

The divided saint meanwhile had continued true to form, "half indoors and half out of doors," and invariably self-important and self-engrossed. Then the stage began to draw our attention. It looked like the scenes of pink and blue crystals one used to see, gazing through the peepholes of the sugar Easter eggs, or the little snowstorms inside old-fashioned glass paperweights, also like a concentration of the strange, pretty, and mysterious impressions that an imaginative child taken by its Irish nurse to a Roman Catholic religious ceremony at which little girls were confirmed might derive from the ceremonial movements, seatings, and reverences, the chants, the robes, the decorations, and the lights. And Thomson continued very smart and slack with his musical medium, making a few bimbamlike imitations of church chimes without intensity, picking at the beautiful medium of music in a very bland, very funny, "quite" deflowering kind of way. At length Ignatius of Loyola, impersonated by a short young Negro in a green robe, appeared and reverentially kissed the hand the interior St. Therese languidly extended to him; and two figurines in tulle carrying palm branches extended themselves before the threshold of the bower, while against the cellophane prisms the choir looked precisely like angels in a child's heaven or tinsel-fringed upon a Christmas tree; and there was a sort of trio, and St. Therese was photographed and the act at last came to an end, leaving more than one spectator sorry he possessed more than an ocular sense. The eye had been amused by Florine Stettheimer's elfish half jewel-box, half candy-box set and costumes. But the ear had been exposed to a vacuum utterly empty of tension and ideas and musical quality and containing somebody being tediously "gay."

The decoration of the second act further suggested the ambiguities of baroque religion and art, so voluptuous in their ecstasies. A lacy opera box occupied the extreme left of the stage, which, with its elegant palms and pyramids and putti, altogether evoked the half boudoirlike, half operatic atmosphere of the particular Roman church—Santa Maria della Vittoria—specially connected with the cult of the great Spanish woman saint. It was not difficult to gather that the "teasing" was intended for the entire period and that the performance itself aspired to the baroque, famous for its habit of freely mixing the comic and the sacred. For a while the second act proceeded much like the first, but gradually it grew serious. Compère and commère, who had begun by waltzing across the stage in evening clothes, singing "One, two, three, four, five—saints," became progressively more and more engrossed in the action, the commère spying sympathetically upon it from the opera box. The prose grew exalted. The composer began giving a little music, in the same sense in which a scraggly tree in an open field may be said on a hot day to give shade. More moving things began occurring on the stage, the scene of the dance of saints with electric candles, the scene of the ecstasy vis-à-vis the great golden disk that glowed in the depths of the scene. The third act, in Ignatius' monastery, was also serious in tone (although a ballet of sailors compromised that, too). Inside the wall that excluded the curious Therese—much as the action from this time on excluded her—the disciples sat weaving a net, while the saint speculated whether he had or had not seen the Holy Ghost. ("Pigeons in the grass alas," etc.) At last there was a dead march on the words "Wed is dead" and a glorification of the Jesuit. And the idea, or rather more the ideas, of the whole show grew plain. The first, more important, of these ideas—almost exclusively that of Gertrude Stein—is the relation, part humorous, part serious, part definite, part vague, between two essences which the author claims to have discovered in the Spanish landscape—one of them more feminine, the other more masculine—and which she has identified as those of two great baroque saints, Theresa of Avila and Ignatius of Loyola. The relation is an antithetical one, and the contrast reveals the superiority of the more masculine of these two very special forces. For during the drama, and particularly through her inner division, her sexual confusion, her self-engrossment, the feminine one "loses the show" and comes to nothing in life, while her opponent, because of his masculine concentration and will, achieves certain ends, founding an army, perceiving the Holy Ghost, attaining glory. That the two antithetical figures have a personal reference is also probable; surely the St. Therese resembles a certain lady in her Picasso-hung salon on the left bank of the Seine in Paris and the Ignatius some one of the artists who, at one time or another, kissed her hand and afterward deserted her.

The second idea, to a degree that of the librettist and the decorator, concerns the relation of these three bright moderns to the Catholic religion, attesting the sempiternal power of that religion, its mysteries, its ritual, and the figures of its illustrious champions over their reluctant wills, assuring that religion a future which present conditions might appear to belittle. Half attracted, half defiant of those mysteries, that ritual, those figures, and attracted and defiant of the very material that gave them a chance to express their mixed feelings, their combined work attests a sense of the inexplicable, irreducible magnetism of the solemn stuff initially approached so debonairly by them.

If Thomson must be said to have helped establish these ideas, credit for their establishment nonetheless belongs more largely to the two ladies with whom he was associated, than to himself. His score is very little, does very little. Said by his friends to conform to an aesthetic of lightness, of urbanity and ele-

DISCOVERIES OF A MUSIC CRITIC

gance, it evidently starts a new and not particularly important category of light works, since it takes the feeblest hold of the lighter essences and lacks both the inventiveness and the levity, the gaiety, the high spirits, of the light music of the past, from Offenbach's and Suppé's to Johann Strauss' and Sullivan's. Certainly this score provides none of the intoxication this music hitherto has provided. It is perhaps witty. But that is all. It has been called instrumental in getting the ladies Stein and Stettheimer "on" the stage. The truth is that it was they who got it "on," not vice versa. Without Gertrude's humorous and significant verbalizations few could have tolerated the vapid music, and without Florine's settings and the handsomeness of the Negro cast the show would have had almost nothing for the senses.

The last act was gay, on the level of musical comedy, and concluded the work in the tone of an airy mundanity and cynicism. The music was quite folky here in an American idiom and somewhat better than in the other acts, perhaps for the reason that, unconformably enough, it was brightly orchestrated in this section. Before the conclusion, the producers had the bad taste to introduce, in the scene of reconciliation between Therese and Ignatius, a golden chalice surmounted by a golden circle looking exactly like the Holy Grail in the old pictures. At last the opera came to an end, a tidbit for "sophisticated" audiences of the sort which we have recently begun developing, just the right thing for Hartford's Society of the Friends and Enemies of Modern Music, and a thirty-minute vaudeville stunt stretched out to the length of eighteen saints in four acts and two and a half hours.

5. *MERRY MOUNT. Libretto by Richard L. Stokes, music by Howard Hanson. New York: The Metropolitan Opera,*

RECENT AMERICAN OPERAS

February 10, 1934. In 1627, Miles Standish at the head of soldiery descended upon Thomas Morton's trading-post at Ma-re Mount or Merry Mount. Morton had erected a maypole at Merry Mount; he had brewed beer; he had sent word to the Indian girls:

> Lasses in beaver coats, come away,
> Ye shall be welcome to us night and day;

and with these consorts he and his companions had "danced and frisked together," as one of the old chroniclers put it, "like so many fairies or furies—as if they had anew revived and celebrated the feasts of the Roman goddess Flora or the beastly practises of the mad Bacchinalians." Morton had, "likewise, to shew his poetrie, composed sundry rimes and verses, some tending to lasciviousness, and others to the detraction and scandall of some persons, which he affixed to his idle or idoll Maypolle": and together with his companions, men, like himself, awaiting wives from England, he had escaped marriage by "playing Proteus with the help of Priapus." Morton was placed in the stocks at Plymouth and later sent foodless back to England.

All American historians before William Carlos Williams have called Morton a "vulgar royalist libertine," "an amusing old debauchee and tippler," though some had glimpsed in the conflict between himself and the Plymouth colony the struggle between two rival business firms; for Morton was selling firearms as well as brandy to the Indians. Williams was the first to let us see into this apparently sordid affair and recognize the struggle between two eternal human spirits, the Puritan and the Cavalier; the revelation is one of the multiple virtues of his extraordinary *In the American Grain*. The maypole intrinsically was but a sign of the old pagan sympathy with unregenerate human nature at the basis of Cavalierdom, at least of a compromise with it; for it permitted periodical indulgence and dissipation, at the risk of encouraging the heterogeneity, the confusions, the wastefulness, of the human being. Thus Morton was semi-consciously the standard-bearer of a profound feeling, and the fire he drew upon himself from the direction of Plymouth essentially the expression of the feeling eternally opposed to his, the one that allowed no compromise with the flesh and expressed itself in attempts forcibly to purify human nature and completely unify it in the austere, efficient likeness of the Most High. Williams also indicated that this spirit, too, like the Cavalier, ran the risk of involving the human being in confusions and dissipations at least as dangerous and probably more destructive than those the maypole brought in its train. Directly after the story of Merry Mount, he introduced Cotton Mather's hideously credulous accounts of the witchcraft hysteria in Salem and let the inevitable consequences of the forcible repression of the playful and apparently wasteful activities of human nature rise clearly before our eyes. Thus the extinction of Merry Mount came to represent the tragedy of New England, since the compromising Cavalier spirit at worst leaves the human being in a kind of accord with himself and the universe and thus sets him free spontaneously to aspire to unity and perfection, while the Puritan at best intensifies the inner warfare to which all human nature is subject, making unity with the creative principle of things almost impossible of realization.

Mr. Stokes in the libretto of his historical opera has tried to derive a poetical symbol from the business at Merry Mount, and one somewhat resembling Williams'. To point the picture, he has idealized Morton's rough trading-post into an elegant Cavalier colony and the motive of the erection of the

RECENT AMERICAN OPERAS

maypole into the wedding rites of a beautiful aristocrat, Lady Marigold Sandys, come with a gay party to America to espouse a noble groom amid dances, games, and other aesthetic expressions of the love of life. To deepen it, he has, like Williams, further combined the subject with episodes from the witchcraft hysteria, drawing imaginatively too upon Cotton Mather's *Wonders of the Invisible World,* in particular the passage from it constituting the *Account of One Joseph Ring.* He lets his chief protagonist, a bedeviled Puritan minister, who, enamored of the Lady Marigold and party to the murder of her lover, repair in dream to a "hellish rendezvous" where, amid Babylonian orgies, he sees himself ecstatically signing the devil's book and cursing New England for the sake of the Astarte-like figure of the great lady who has spurned him. But Mr. Stokes' libretto is a nonetheless sad affair. It has certain merits, no doubt; it provides its composer with plentiful opportunities for choral, dance, and processional music; and the scene of the "hellish rendezvous" is grand theater. But Mr. Stokes is not much of an artist. Feebly a poet, inexpertly a dramatist even in some of his most dramatic scenes, and guilty of a meaningless concluding one, he has not fully felt his material. While he has idealized the Cavalier spirit he has not opposed the Puritan idea to it, with the consequence that his Pilgrim Fathers appear, dramatically ineffective, as mere sadistic spoil-sports, and his minister remains a sex-enfevered weakling; and his drama verges on the ridiculously inferior.

To this grotesque libretto, the first distinctly bad one our résumé has re-introduced to us, Mr. Hanson coupled a score which, save in certain choral passages, is heavy and soft. It, too, has certain merits; it has wisely been kept in large blocks. But these merits are minor, the music almost uniformly lacking quality and expressivity. The music projecting the minister's passions and distraction is very weak. The maypole music rather flatly exploits some English folk dances. And while the intermezzo before the big and Babylonian act begins interestingly, for all its redolence of Debussy's *Sirènes,* it ends by reminding one of Mr. Hanson's *Romantic* Symphony. For here, too, one finds him repeating his ideas over and over again as though he could not get from the spot. If *Merry Mount* indicates anything, it is that his medium remains the chorus.

6. *HELEN RETIRES. Libretto by John Erskine, music by George Antheil. New York: The Juilliard School, February 28, 1934.* John Erskine had a bright idea. John Erskine is always having bright ideas, and very naturally, too, for he makes flatteringly much of them, and the little things know their friends. This particular one communicated to him the truth that while men's lives come to an end, women's never do. Women remain open to new experiences to the very last at least. And possessing a peculiar gift of gab and smartness, and having the cause of American opera at heart, he materialized his conception in the form of an operatic libretto about the latter days of Helen of Troy. Its first act presented the embodiment of ungovernable and ultimately destructive Beauty's gay return from the inhumation of Menelaus and the subsequent scandal—to the elders—of her resolution to voyage alive to the Isles of the Blest in search of the still virginal soul of Achilles. Its second displayed the apathy of the heroes in Hades, stirred only by remnants of their ancient rivalries over Helen; the confusion that followed her descent among the unwilling shades; her rape of the big bully; and her reascent to earth in his embrace. Act III exhibited her waxing boredom with the later repetitious stages of the amour, Achilles' eloquent

disappointment and voluntary return to Hades, the interruption of Helen's preparations for death by the appearance of a dumb and desirous young fisherman who couldn't talk but danced for her, and the divine one's wondering gift of herself to the worshiping boy.

Placed by royal fiat in the hands of George Antheil, this libretto assured the composer of performances by the Juilliard School of Music. Antheil, for his part, was not deeply involved by the Erskine idea, possibly because of the utter absence of quality from the verbal expressions in which it was couched. But he had an operatic formula which he had worked out under the influence of certain modern German composers, Weill and Krenek in particular. (For after Strawinsky there came Weill, and after the aesthetic of the Ballet Mécanique that of music calm, melodious.) This formula prescribed a lyric opera, with an overture, and dramatic music uncorrelated to particular situations and merely matching with a fitting atmosphere the general disposition and overtones of the action. Any musical style, from that of the polyphonic classicists to that of the homophonic Broadwayists, was to be introduced by the composer at his discretion, nor was he to shrink from treading upon the heels of any of the past masters, neither Puccini's nor Strauss' nor Meyerbeer's, saving those of Wagner alone. The chorus was to be stationary, as in *Oedipus Rex* and *Der Jasager,* and masked. And he set to work.

At least, this is the history one infers from the result of the collaboration, produced by the pupils of the Juilliard under the baton of Albert Stoessel. *Helen Retires* is diverting enough, an affair very pleasing in many ways, and one of the triumphs in American opera, especially in view of the fact that with the possible exception of *Mona,* by Horatio Parker, American opera has almost no triumphs to celebrate. The little piece's idea, as we have indicated, is bright; and everything that the composer has supplied in the way of music, for all the vague familiarity of some of it, exhibits taste, alertness, and intelligence, and has a certain quality. Some of it, the playful flute solo and the big chorus in the first act and the polyphonic duet in the last, for example, is very charming. The last act is distinctly dramatic. The score has a pleasant, present-day terseness and hardness; and in spots, particularly in the scene preceding Helen's descent among the unwilling ghosts (themselves, according to some wag, all members of the Columbia University Faculty Club), it makes a heartening presage of a good loud "Hail Columbia" kind of American musical style. One wishes Antheil might give us more of *that*.

Structurally, nonetheless, the score is quite unstrung. And much of the "harmless" music has a curious saplessness, a thinness as of something untimely spent. There was absolutely no tension save toward the end of the excellent third act; and of real vibrance and passion, even such as was congruous with a comic work, *keine Spur*. The orchestration was noisy, without sonority.

7. *MARIA MALIBRAN*. *Libretto by Robert A. Simon, music by Robert Russell Bennett. New York: The Juilliard School, April 8, 1935.* The subject of this little opera, produced with charming sets and costumes by Frederick J. Kiesler, is the wisely truncated amour between Maria Felicita García Malibran, the operatic comet of the 1820's, and a poetic young man of her Manhattan. The upshot of the production, in one mind anyway, was considerable impatience with the composer. For the piece is flat, and the fault is his.

Mr. Simon's libretto is no jewel. A good idea, it is unpretentiously but somewhat tenuously dramatized. It reaches us

RECENT AMERICAN OPERAS

studded with amusing gags in the style of the captions in *The New Yorker,* but others of its features (for instance, its inclusion, by way of daring satire, of a grotesque of a stout dowager) recall the more insipid aspects of the gay weekly. The book's serious weakness, however, is traceable to its want—in dialogue and lyrics at least—of the poetic note, even to the modest degree compatible with a lightly sentimental, sophisticated subject. But since the cause of the flatness of *Maria Malibran* is the incompleteness of most of its music and since, in the past, complete musical forms again and again were projected through lines and figures thinner even than are those with which Mr. Simon provided Mr. Bennett, we are obliged to lay the burden of the blame upon the latter's want of urgency.

The score does reveal anew the minor virtuosity of the composer of the *Lincoln* Symphony. The orchestration is expertly brilliant. The harmony is unhackneyed, very modern, and in places subtly managed. There are even evidences of an original dramatic feeling, most notably in the melody with gaping intervals played by a single woodwind after Maria has sent her Philip away the first time, before the first curtain. But in most cases the germinal ideas fail to develop or expand, and the numbers hang fire, leaving the drama to its own devices. The possible exception to this rule are the two buffo arias for baritone and Maria and Philip's frostily delicate duet on a somewhat Coplandesque theme in Act I. But these do not make a summer, particularly since the baritone aria in the third act is very ordinarily popular. Nor can it be said that the demands of the opera taxed the composer's inventive powers, for the three acts are very short, and the librettist called for three interpolations: one of "Home Sweet Home,"—which Mr. Bennett has harmonized most spicely—another of "Una voce poco

DISCOVERIES OF A MUSIC CRITIC

fa" from the *Barbiere,* and the third of the beginning of a vapid air from Zingarelli's *Romeo e Giulietta.* The sum of what was required of the composer was three or four numbers in each act and the running musical plinth which he has fairly ingeniously supplied to the spoken dialogue. All in all, *Maria Malibran* constituted a decided decline from the plane of *Helen Retires,* the Juilliard's novelty of the previous year. And that was by no means an exalted one.

THE CONCLUSIONS. Our first is that *Mona,* by Horatio Parker, remains the great American opera—the strongest, most significant, most rewarding. This conclusion is inspired not only by favorable memories of the music drama dating from 1912, the year of its performance at the Metropolitan Opera House, and by subsequent commerce with the piano score, but by the audition of three major excerpts from the work lately performed with voices by the New Haven Symphony under Professor Smith. This proved to persons who had never doubted its solidity and importance that the piece was even better, even more of a living issue, than they had believed it to be; and made the public utterance of a plea to the managers of the Metropolitan Opera that they revive it appear a duty unquestionably owed *Mona,* Parker, and American music and culture in general.

That *Mona* somewhat owes its eminence to the insignificance and unsturdiness of most of its successors—their lack of weight and quality—one cannot deny. It is by no means a perfectly satisfactory work. The interest of Brian Hooker's poetic libretto about the early Britons depends unhealthily upon the abstract truth—the disaster consequent upon woman's masculine protest—it is intended to body forth. And Parker was no great dramatist; he was much more the pure musician who late in life turned to writing music dramas. Thus, while he accepted the musico-dramatic form and even the system of leitmotivs, he never wrote in the extremely rhetorical, mimetic manner of the born musical dramatists; and his dramatic effects were few and stiff. He was a somewhat short-breathed melodist, too, and his ideas sometimes lack distinction. The beginning of the second act of *Mona* (specifically Nial's scene and dance with his shadow) is musical commonplace in what verges upon waltz time. Besides, there are reflections of *Tristan* in the score, one particularly plain one unfortunately near the climax of the love duet.

Still, *Mona's* eminence derives as largely from its intrinsic virtues as from the shortcomings of its rivals. Anything but poor in musical beauties, it is a virile work, in the grand style, utterly bare of cheapness, awakening admiration for itself and the composer. An individual experience communicates itself sincerely, directly, forcibly here through means definitely mastered. Austere in temper and stiff in his opinions, Parker was nonetheless a natural musician, with a decided urgency, who had "learned his trade." He was an originally subtle harmonist if not a fluent melodist, and in *Mona* his harmonic sense proved itself invariably unpredictable and pungent. He was a masterly orchestrator: the instrumental fabric of *Mona* has a fine consistency without turgidity or cloudiness, and in several respects curiously anticipates ultramodern methods of orchestration: much as we might expect to come upon them in Strawinsky, for instance, we find in Parker's score cool passages for woodwinds alone and for brass alone.

There are many magnificent pages in *Mona,* notably the heroine's grand arioso-style account of her dream in Act I, the wild battle chorus at the end of Act II, and the introduction to and the scene of the stabbing in Act III—bitten, like some pages of Hardy's, with the tragic feeling of the northern peoples. If in *Peter Ibbetson* America has contributed an opera ranking with those of the Mascagnis and the Wolf-Ferraris, in *Mona* it contributed one actually able to stand beside *Pelléas* and *Elektra* and the great operas of the post-Wagnerian period. And this "music by a professor," with its purely musical beauties, its austerity, its severity of style, was perhaps further in advance of its time than they were.

The second of our conclusions is that while Americans have not as yet revealed a talent for opera any larger than that of the English, the English critic's "The history of British opera is the history of a tragedy" may not as yet be supposed to provide a model for a concise summary of the fortunes apparently in store for the American species.

True, after a quarter-century of serious struggle by Americans with the operatic forms, from the efforts of Walter Damrosch, Frederick Converse, Horatio Parker, to those of Deems Taylor, and a quarter-century of persistent presentation of American operas by the Metropolitan Opera, we have seen the high and palmy days of the movement arrive. Seven new operas have approached the footlights inside of five years. Yet the total gain, so far as art and music are concerned, besides such mere box-office successes as *Peter Ibbetson, The Emperor Jones,* and the sensational *Four Saints in Three Acts,* are, all in all, the mediocre one of *Helen Retires.* Thus the supposition that, like the English, the Americans cannot develop a gift for dramatic music and are hence predestined to failure in the lyric theater cannot lightly be dismissed.

The decided artistic successes of American music, like those of English music, lie in the absolute forms. Excepting *Mona,* they remain pieces such as Ives' *Concord* Sonata and other

RECENT AMERICAN OPERAS

works by Copland, Harris, Sessions, and still other symphonists. Even in the theater, it is the relatively absolute forms, the dances, songs, and choruses, that most attest our composers' abilities. It may be that in the theater, as we have suggested in another connection, their affinitive form is the modern equivalent of the masque, the musical comedy, the pageant opera—anything but the theatrical form in which music functions as the projector of the interior drama.

And still, if this hypothesis is inevitable and to be considered, it cannot yet be made into a reason for discouragement; even for prejudice regarding the possibilities of fine American work in operatic form. For it is not sufficiently strongly founded to justify any attitude toward the future other than an open one.

In the first place, if the dramatic music of the Americans is all in all inferior to their absolute music, it is not so to any enormous degree, at least not to a degree sufficient to make the absolute forms predeterminately American to the exclusion of all others. This is not to say that American operas are not for the most part poor art, often half, a third, a quarter achievement as far as music goes—dependent upon their libretti, without individuality of idea or expression, only very infrequently the consequence of sonorous material manipulated in accord with an individual experience, feeling of life, idea. It is merely to say that the achievements in the absolute forms are still small in spiritual as in material bulk and that if one sets American opera with its triumph *Mona* against their mass, the difference will not be sufficiently great to justify a conviction that the absolute forms have the gods entirely with them, and the operatic, entirely against them. The two bulks have the likeness that might exist between two members of a single family.

In the second place some of our operatic composers have written absolute music, too—Gruenberg, Hanson, and Antheil

—and have been no more creative in this medium than in the dramatic, in fact less creative, for *The Emperor Jones* is more impressive than Gruenberg's symphony, and Antheil's *Helen Retires* more impressive than his *Ballet Mécanique*—a phenomenon that would not be possible were absolute music particularly affinitive to American composers. Here is another disproof of the contention that Americans are fated to fail with opera.

Indeed, it would seem reasonable to suppose that if American opera to date has been something of a tragedy, it has been such because, with the exception of Parker, quite as much the composer in his oratorio *Hora Novissima* as in *Mona,* our most gifted composers have avoided the field, perhaps for no better reason than that, as Antheil has claimed, American music has grown up prejudiced in favor of the abstract forms by the German musicians who educated the country musically; and that, rid of their prejudice in favor of the abstract, our composers might be as productive in the operatic as in the strictly symphonic field.

It would be without trepidation that one would hear that a Copeland or a Sessions was at work upon an opera. One would be conscious of the possibility that they might be essaying the form in vain, merely for the reason that it is possible theater-blood cannot run in American veins. But we repeat: that is a mere guess, and there is nothing to prove that it is a correct one and that a creative American composer with a strong orientation toward the opera cannot appear even at the present hour.

Ives

THE earliest of his compositions Charles E. Ives has chosen to preserve for us are a couple of quicksteps, one of them an arrangement for "kazoo" orchestra of "The Son of a Gambolier." Dating from his undergraduate days at Yale, juvenile and pretty thoroughly in the conventions of the brass band and college glee club music of the period, they nonetheless stand prophetic of the composer's highly individual, mature, important works.

They are the expressions of the experiences of a callow American youth of the period through forms scarcely distinguishable from the simple, limited ones habitual in the composer's native Danbury and New England of the '70's and the '80's, with its little church choirs, town bands, dance and theater orchestras. And the later works by Ives, the glorious *Concord* Sonata, the *Three Places in New England*, the *Suite for Theater Orchestra*, and the happy rest, are expressions of an almost national experience, the relations between the essences affinitive to the American people past and present through forms in some instances partially, and in others almost wholly, evolved from those of the American tradition.

Nearly all Ives' characteristic work abounds in minor forms derived directly from this store. In the second number of the orchestral suite *Three Places in New England,* we hear "The British Grenadiers"—actually one of the marching songs of the American revolutionary army, which sang it in superb indifference to its text. In the first movement of the Fourth Sym-

DISCOVERIES OF A MUSIC CRITIC

phony, "Old Hundred" sounds; and favorite Virginia reels and other old fiddler tunes in the second number of the theater suite, *In the Inn,* and in *Barn Dance;* and "Are You Wash'd in the Blood of the Lamb" in the little cantata *General Booth Enters Heaven,* to Vachel Lindsay's words; and "Good Night, Ladies" in *Washington's Birthday*; and various patriotic tunes in the song "In Flanders Fields," etc. Their function is always a thematic one, sometimes a symbolical and an ironical one, too. But in many of these compositions—curiously abrupt in their contrasts, full of lines finely drawn, and despite their frequent brevity large in their scales of values and deeply expressive of essences and ideas clearly, boldly felt—the grand forms themselves are plainly developments and enrichments of the rudimentary musical forms favored by American society. *Putnam Camp* is first a waltz, then a fox trot, and last—horridly polytonically and polyrhythmically enough—a military march. *In the Inn* and *Barn Dance* partake of both the jig and the reel—indeed may be said to be jigs and reels; in these instances wonderfully shrill, jagged, and rich of substance. The song "Charlie Rutlage" is an expanded frontier ballad; the adagio of the Fourth Symphony a hymn tune developed in fugal form. The Hawthorne movement of the *Concord* Sonata has nicely been called "proto-jazz" by John Kirkpatrick.

It is even possible that Ives' complex harmonies and rhythms are the development of germs latent in those rudimentary forms. We refer to the clashing harmonies and polyrhythm of his entirely characteristic pieces. . . . Ives in fact is not only one of the most advanced but one of the earliest polytonalists and polyrhythmicalists. Aesthetic radicalism was in the air of his home. His father, his first teacher, experimented continuously with acoustics in the conviction that only a fraction of the means of musical expression was being used by musical art, and even invented a quarter-tone instrument; and during his own undergraduate days Ives, it seems, was already experimenting with new chord structures. Ten years in advance of the publication of the score of *Salomé*, he began a composition for the organ with a chord in D Minor superimposed on one in C Major. These experiments, not only with chord structures but with exotic scales and harmonic rhythms, too, met with the disfavor of his professor in music, Horatio Parker; still, Ives persisted in them, and is said to have tried out his innovations with the help of the orchestra of the old Hyperion Theater in New Haven. And in 1903, the year of the inception of the sketches for certain of his very personal orchestral pieces, he was already writing completely atonally, thus anticipating similar European innovations; for the atonal passages in Mahler's symphonies are of later date, and the famous *Three Pieces for Pianoforte*, Op. 11, by Schönberg, the first European pieces completely beyond the tonal system, were published only in 1911. And he has persisted upon his course. The close of *Putnam Camp,* for example, combines contrapuntally two march tempi in different keys: the one 25 per cent, too, faster than the other. The third and wonderfully fresh section of *Three Places in New England* entitled *The Housatonic at Stockbridge*—a sonorous cataract, easily the jewel of the suite and one of the thrilling American orchestral compositions—includes a rhythm for a solo violin quite independent of that of the rest of the orchestra, and atonal and polytonal figures that clash with the tonic harmonies of the brass and the woodwind. The third of the three pieces comprised in the *Suite for Theater Orchestra,* the magical, sensuous *In the Night*, exhibits another instance of Ives' extreme polyrhythmicality in its combination of a definite rhythm played by horn, bells, and celesta with an extremely indefinite, almost unnumbered one carried by strings and other instruments, and seems to call for the installation in the conductor's stand of a mechanical robot able simultaneously to beat the two extremely distinct and varied measures. Well, these revolutionary forms of Ives' were actually adumbrated by the practice if not by the theory of traditional music. The American composer very early began observing that the melodic, harmonic, and rhythmic distortions of traditional music —frequently of English origin—produced under the stress of excitement by church organists, village bands, country fiddlers, frequently initiated forms truer to their feelings and to the essences and ideas they apprehend than the more regular performances. The untuned organ, the choir soulfully soaring "off key," an organist excitedly striking "false" notes in his musical élan, the members of a rural orchestra embroidering individually on the rhythms and wildly playing simultaneously in different tonalities, the clashing bands at Fourth of July celebrations, were actually initiating living forms certainly possessive of a freedom the cut and dried originals did not have, and of a truth of their own. And they actually were, in spite of the fact that the descriptive terms had not as yet been coined, polytonic and polyrhythmical. And in many of Ives' complexly tonic and rhythmical pieces, notably *Putnam Camp, In the Inn,* and *Barn Dance,* we seem to find not only realizations of these types of forms quite unconsciously suggested by the excited musicians, but of certain of those they shrilly initiated.

This peculiar form of Ives', and its idiosyncrasies, would appear to be the direct consequence of the nationalistic bent of his mind. We have defined the nationalist as the emergent individual who, in becoming conscious of his own essence, simultaneously becomes conscious of the essences of his nation and its soil, and, put in touch with national ideas by his experience, invests them with worth and realizes them with love. In most instances the musical nationalist apprehends these forces in part through the traditional musical forms of his nation, often the folk music; and often spontaneously expresses his idea with a form inclusive in warp and woof of these traditional bits for the reason that he has long since absorbed them, and that the idea to which they are related calls them forth again. Now Ives is nothing if not a nationalistic American composer. The forces conveyed by his music are deeply, typically American. They are the essences of a practical people, abrupt and nervous and ecstatic in their movements and manifestations—brought into play with a certain reluctance and difficulty, but when finally loosed, jaggedly, abruptly, almost painfully released, with something of an hysteric urgency; manifested sometimes in a bucolic irony and burlesque and sometimes in a religious and mystical elevation, but almost invariably in patterns that have a paroxysmal suddenness and abruptness and violence. We recognize their kin in American humor, in political and revival meetings, whenever and wherever a wholeness has existed in Americans. We have seen their likes through much American literature; one frequently thinks of Twain and Anderson in connection with Ives, as well as of the New England writers whose ideas his music has interpreted. They are curiously like the forces of the abrupt, fierce American Nature herself, who is vernal overnight and summery two weeks after winter has passed away; like the moods of her spring freshets and the floods that pour from the porous soil; and the moods of the vaguely, confusedly, voluptuously sonorous, suddenly swelling night over the towns. Ives has indeed felt the spiritual and moral forces of America past and present not only through American folk music, but through literary and other artistic expressions,

DISCOVERIES OF A MUSIC CRITIC

too. Perhaps the richest, most inclusive, most beautifully formed and drawn of all his pieces, the Sonata, *Concord, Mass.*; *1840-60,* apparently flows from an experience including a discovery of the spirit of transcendentalism as it was contained in the prophetic Emerson, the fantastic Hawthorne, the sturdily sentimental Alcotts, the deeply earth-conscious and lovingly submissive Thoreau. Another piece, the scherzo of the Fourth Symphony, flows from an experience inclusive of another sense of Hawthorne, derived in particular from *The Celestial Railroad*; while the cantata *Lincoln*, on Edwin Markham's words, indicates a creative comprehension quite as much of the figure of the great commoner as of the spirit of the swan of Staten Island; and the many songs on the words of American poets from Whitman down to Louis Untermeyer and Fenimore Cooper, Jr., and prose men including President Hadley and even obscure newspapermen, the connection of experiences with their verse and prose. And further works demonstrate a stimulation through still other media than musical or literary ones. There is the first of the *Three Places in New England*; called *The Shaw Monument in Boston Common,* it conveys a feeling partially crystallized by the St.-Gaudens. And there is the third of them, *The Housatonic at Stockbridge*; and it refers to a crystallizing object neither artistic nor human: the sweep of the vernal river.

Thus, musically gifted, Ives has been put in the way of the sonorous expression of American life, paralleling—possibly because of the circumstance that he was used, from boyhood up, to expressing himself in terms of the traditional forms—the Russian music of Moussorgsky, the Magyar of Bartók, the Spanish of De Falla. His characteristically American, jaggedly ecstatic, variously electric and rapturous, almost invariably spasmodic sonorous forms are criticisms, like theirs, of the folk music and the folk itself. Humorous to the paroxysmal point in the cast of *Barn Dance, In the Inn,* and the Scherzo of the Fourth Symphony; traversed by an acute sensuousness and voluptuousness in the case of *In the Night;* cataclysmically passionate as in *The Housatonic at Stockbridge;* or rapturous with the quality of slowly groping, reaching intellectual processes (*The Shaw Monument*) or with those of religious, prophetic, mystically intuitive moments and their ingredients of insight, faith in the human impulse to perfection, knowledge of the breath of earth (*General Booth Enters Heaven, Emerson, The Alcotts, Thoreau*)—his whole so very American expression puts us in touch and harmony, like prose by Twain and Anderson, Cummings or Thoreau and all who have conveyed American essences with fullness and love and beauty, with forces constant in our fellows, selves, soil, and thus with the whole American idea. We feel its parts and their connections, and the breath of the whole.

And the fates have been very generous. They have not even preconfined Ives to a single medium of expression. He has been able to represent his feelings of American life in a prose that, manly as it is racily American, conveys them if not as broadly, nonetheless as truly as the musical medium does. *Essays before a Sonata,* reading-matter intended primarily as a preface or apology for his second piano sonata, the *Concord,* but isolated in a small companion volume for the reason that inclusion with the notes would have made the musical volume as cumbersome as baroque, contributes, together with the composer's very interesting assertion of and generalization about sound's much-questioned ability to convey material, moral, intellectual, or spiritual values, four most poetically penetrating criticisms for the "subjects" of the four movements of the work. Another juicy essay of Ives' is suffixed to the volume in which

DISCOVERIES OF A MUSIC CRITIC

he has collected a hundred and fourteen of his two-hundred-odd songs. Like *Essays before a Sonata,* it also is a sort of smaller twin to the work it is intended to illuminate. This particular one, privately printed too, and now, also, the lucky windfall of second-hand music shops, is one of *the* American books: not only for the reason that it contains most of Ives' first-rate lyrics, among them "Evening" (Milton), "The New River," "Charlie Rutlage," "Like a Sick Eagle" (Keats), "Walt Whitman" and others, but equally for the reason that its very form expresses a distinctly American mode of feeling. That form is extremely miscellaneous. It juxtaposes within a narrow compass—indeed, the volume is a sort of record of Ives' entire development—one hundred and fourteen songs very heterogeneous in point of size, since some are but a few measures long and others cover pages; very heterogeneous in point of idiom and style, for some are based on borrowed and others on original material, and some are diatonic and others impressionistic and others atonal; very heterogeneous too in point of spirit, since certain are homely, certain racy, certain humorous, and others delicate, or intimate, or spiritual; and in point of value, too, since certain are crudely or lightly drawn, and others finely, poignantly, and powerfully. But out of that miscellaneousness, extreme for all the visibility of the personal thread in the intensely disparate fabrics, an idea greets us: the idea that all things possessing breath of their own, no matter how dissimilarly and to what differing degrees, are ultimately consonant. That is good Americanism, and the postscript but re-expresses that feeling and that idea in the maxim, "Everything from a mule to an oak, which nature has given life, has a right to that life; whether they [its values] be approved by a human mind or seen with a human eye, is no concern of that right." And when the prose runs: "I have not written a book for money, for fame, for love, for kindlings. I have merely cleaned house. All that is left is on the clotheslines," we merely recognize anew the American speaking with the spirit of the Artist.

That is Ives: the American as an artist, as a composer, and the foremost of the Americans who have expressed their feeling of life in musical forms; for even Parker's substance is not as mature as some of Ives', itself unexcelled as yet in point of maturity of substance and richness of feeling by that of any of the younger men. The *Concord* Sonata indeed remains the solidest piece of piano music composed by an American. Its beauty and its significance still surprise us; they still are one of the wonders of the last years, which have revealed them. For Ives had been forced to create in a complete solitude, without external support or recognition. Though individuals able to appreciate the works of literary and pictorial artists as fresh and as significant as his musical ones were not lacking during the first quarter of this century, the musically highly cultured individual was still extremely rare in the American ranks. Lucky for the composer that he was the manager of an insurance company! What porridge he would have had had he been a professional musician can be discerned from the fact that only yesterday one of the white-headed boys of American music, a voice of the official musicality and its conventional criteria, publicly affirmed that those composers who wrote atonally or polytonally did so merely because they were too untalented to compose in the old tonal schemes. But with the multiple appearance of the musically highly cultured individual—composer, performer, or amateur—in the United States a phenomenon one of the most happy of all of those of the last decades, the raising of the curtain on Ives' long-obscured works became almost inevitable. Some intelligence seems to lead the individual almost somnambulistically toward the food he requires for his existence and to bring it toward him, and what comes into the world as an idea does not go lost. In any case, up the curtain went on this good "business man's" music. Henry Bellaman wrote about it and called it to the attention of the Pro-Musica. The Pro-Musica and later Nicholas Slonimsky, the Pan-Americans, and Copland had some of his pieces performed at their concerts. Henry Cowell began publishing and recording others. The discovery is still an esoteric one. No conductor of a major orchestra has still either seen fit or been able to perform Ives' orchestral pieces. The second Sonata has never yet been heard in its entirety. And only a few of the songs have as yet figured in song recitals. Still, the curtain *is* up. The music is beginning to be accessible not only in printed but in record form, to the benefit of a world larger than the narrowly musical one.

For artists such as Ives can help enormously to create a democratic society in America. In investing American essences with worth and presenting them with beauty, they help to convey the national idea as it actually relates these warring and still cognate forces: thus providing a matchlessly practical basis for mutual adjustment.

Harris

ONE of the events of the last decade indicative of progress is the emergence of composers of the first rank among the American people. (The activity of spirit is an infallible sign of health.)

HARRIS

And one of the most fecund of the composers whose emergence has constituted this inspiring recent occurrence is the Cimarron Roy Harris. His work, to be sure, is quite unequal. There are holes among some of his melodic lines, and some of the forms are incomplete: the fugue, for instance, in the little Concerto for string quartet, piano, and clarinet. The thematic material is occasionally dowdy, vaguely reminiscent of Tchaikowsky, Debussy, or Beethoven; and some of the climaxes labor terribly for the summit; and no work of his, with the possible exception of the piano Sonata, Op. 1, is thoroughly sustained, for each contains at least one movement inferior to the others in force or quality or workmanship. But the value of works of art, in the words of some wise Frenchman, doesn't derive from their freedom from defects, but from their comprehension of positive qualities: and since that is the case, Roy Harris' may be said to have great value, for they not infrequently exhibit the characteristics of great art. They are lofty in plan and endeavor, cast in the larger and the contrapuntal forms, classic music in the sense that they embody organically developed musical ideas, and rugged and frequently sublime in style for all their gray and humble color. But their dignity is frequently not only a matter of grandiose endeavor. It is one of actual substance. The forms are oftentimes very broad and the volumes that compose them oftentimes stark, powerfully expressive, and energetically driven. It has been said that some of the massive volumes of sound which Harris produces with few instruments, particularly in the last movement of his Concerto and in the first and last movements of his string Sextet, are orchestral in effect and merely physically overwhelming. With this judgment the present writer ventures to disagree: for him, they are legitimate, powerfully expressive, the fruit of skillful exploitations of the sonority of the instruments in sympathy with powerful feeling.

Another quality typical of great art that is frequently exhibited by Harris' compositions is lavishness. He is not only a prolific composer and never a trivial one: his music almost regularly has a will. It "pours," warmly and densely. One feels involuntarily that the man *must* sing, and recollects the words of Sachs in *Die Meistersinger* about another bird whose bill was well grown. This lavishness not only of output but of expression comes surprisingly in music signed, like his, with a good American name. That of most American composers of high endeavor, deep sentiency, and strong personality, is after all a relatively measured product; and we have with reason come to associate fullness and generosity of output and expression, and fervor and passionateness of accent like that of the fantasia and andante of Harris' Concerto and the andantino of his Variations for string quartet, with European music.

His music, too, has a strong individuality and a happy originality. Many of his rhythms—they have been said to "shift nervously from double to triple time and vice versa"—are delightfully novel and vigorous. They have a queer American quality, something jogging and loose-jointed that recalls the gait of cowboys. Many of his plaintive, originally modulated, bitter-sweet melodies—distantly related, for their part, to the Scotch-Irish frontier folk songs and the Moody and Sankey hymnody—are equally distinctive; and all through his music one finds a deep individuality of accent—now grandiose and now abrupt—and an original rugged and wrenched sonority and somber coloring. Nor can we allow that he is not an original harmonist, that his music, while apparently frequently polyrhythmical and polytonal, is neither to any valid degree. The interplay of the rhythms of the last movement, the scherzo, of the piano Sonata, seems to us too effective to permit its composer to be ruled out of the good company of the polyrhythmical composers. The polytonal basis of the effective andante of the work also cannot be denied. After all, in order to exclude from the polytonal category a piece which, though constructed on two different chords, nonetheless leaves us conscious of a tonal center, one would have to exclude from it both *Petrushka* and *Le Sacre*. And that would tend to leave the category *Hamlet* without the Prince of Denmark.

Besides, you will find a grave poetry in these forms; they express feelings always warm and frequently deep. They are feelings of American life itself in all its sadness and gaiety, humorousness, nostalgia, and tragedy. Homespun and homely and humble in quality, the pieces oftentimes have epic breadth and accent: they taste and breathe of the vast and sorrowful American soil. Harris was born in Oklahoma, on the last American frontier—the son of a farmer and of an English girl of humble origin who had come out to America to work as a waitress in a Harvey restaurant; and over the biggest of his pages, the bell-like opening and coda of the Sonata, the wild preludes of the Sextet and the Variations for string quartet, the almost meterless commencement of the Sextet's finale, and the plangent, deeply affecting slow movement of the *Symphony 1933,* there seems to float, gray, far-spreading and silent, and almost symbolic of national experience, the infinite and inscrutable dome overarching the plains and the lives of the millions who have hoped and struggled and suffered on them. He himself appears a kind of rhapsode of the American migrations and pioneer existences: several of his works, especially the Sextet and the *Symphony 1933,* seem to us ideas exhibiting the relations between various American forces, or between different American modes of the force of life itself, as it has been represented and experienced by the pioneer. In both these works one feels a peculiar American energy, muscular, spare, adventuresome, starting off with a tremendous brio, and then, as if baffled and short of its goal, becoming passive and dolent, and at last slowly regaining its temporarily lost momentum and self-confidence. The *Symphony 1933* conveys this idea very powerfully, the Sextet a little less so, for while the prelude and the finale with its fine fugal exposition of the vehemently rhythmic theme are among Harris' best achievements, the intermediary chorale is comparatively weak and dull. The symphony—the first tragic American symphony, according to Dr. Koussevitzky—begins with a wildly percussive motive recalling with its irregular rhythms the excited mood and gestures of some Celtic bard. The heroic, rugged, abruptly accented, almost guttural—and curiously American—first theme makes its appearance in the windy horns; and its marchlike progress on the horns and trombones conveys to us the content of the rhapsode's vision. It is the spirit and force of "adventure and physical exuberance" indicated to us by the composer's own program, and the peculiar movement, the epic and homely American quality of the expression, and the wrenched sonorities momentarily conjure up before us the picture of an American caravan impetuously pressing forward, to the cracking of whips and the cries and jocosities of teamsters, into new western territory. The picture quickly fades as the music grows more abstract. Still, the agitated developments of the material clearly continue to embody and convey to us the spirit and the force of the pioneer on all American frontiers. But in the movement's middle section the marchlike progress dies away. The music seems to reflect the feeling of fathomless distance and of human aspiration toward some ever-retreating spiritual goal; and moods of bafflement and of vital suspense like those of the prelude of the Sextet begin to govern it; and in the long coda the temper is already predominantly tragic. And the second, the main, movement of the symphony is entirely melancholy and gentle and dolent in character, and its subdued plangent tones and somber color, its brooding, alternately stern and tender figures, voice a universal and still fresh sense of the dark end of human aspiration and endeavor: in Harris' own words, "the pathos which seems to underlie all human existence." In this free rondo, with its long pastoral melody in the Aeolian mode, its four-voiced chorale and other contrapuntal figures, its unforgettable dramatic episode for the horns, trombones, and low woodwind, and its long coda with low strings pizzicato, as in another of Harris' great slow movements, that of his piano Sonata, we feel this human tragedy, as it were—God help us, but we cannot otherwise—in connection with the American plains. We feel the faint lights in melancholy skies over gray rolling earth. We feel an expanse full of the graves of human hopes. We feel humble lives, an infinity of bafflement, patience, loneliness. Doubtless, if we should look behind this strong and reserved and moving expression of protracted sorrow, we would find it eloquent of the hereditary melancholy of the northern peoples, and a mirror of the old experience of the "lone prairie" on which the composer was born. But we would also find it eloquent of some new and more universal experience and one which, taking a hint from the symphony's subtitle, we may safely identify with the national experience of the last years. This music sings a sympathy with the spirit of "adventure and physical exuberance" modified by a fresh acquaintance with and compassion for man's ineluctable destiny; and that is the feeling not only of the pioneer but of an America that has as a whole experienced disappointment and grief and been a little matured by its experience. And the last movement of the work communicates a slow recapture of a lost momentum and confidence, working up slowly as by intense effort to a new affirmation of life and its possibilities for perfection. Near the close, the melody gives a queer little cheer, that is like a new thrill of life and courage, an encouraging call from a height and the wave of a ten-gallon hat.

Harris is beyond all question the dynamic potentiality of a wholly satisfactory, major composer. True, he has not yet given us a perfect work and has let down somewhere in every one of his pieces. We are not referring to his failures of technique, his occasionally awkward counterpoint, his harmonic dullness; we are referring to his periodic descents from high levels of style and expression to soft and sentimental ones. A certain staticity spoils the first movement of his very latest work, the Trio for piano, violin, and 'cello, in certain respects his most mature one. And yet, together with this persistent incompleteness, each of his rapidly successive pieces has exhibited first-rate qualities in fuller measure and to the greater exclusion of all others than has its immediate predecessor. The piano Sonata, Harris' Op. 1, has much power and nobility and poignancy; but the substance is not entirely fresh, stemming from the modern French and Debussy. The admirable little Concerto immediately subsequent to it has more of virtue than the Sonata, for it has the Sonata's power and warmth and grandeur, and its material is more personal and its scope of emotion larger. And the Sextet and the Symphony are improvements on the Concerto; Harris' individually rugged and melancholy idiom appears relatively unmixed in these works, and the melodic lines are longer and in many passages attain epical sweep. The values flowing from the relation of note to note, too, are larger. And the little recent Trio contains, after all, what is perhaps Harris' most magnificent piece of music, the superbly, glowingly, powerfully unfolding final fugue. Besides, the later pieces are stronger of form than the earlier—to the degree, in any case, to which form is a matter of vital contrasts, of correlative oppositions of objective and subjective expressions and complementary forms and figures representative of the antithetical feelings and experiences of the race. In the earlier pieces, the faster movements, particularly the motory, humorous, ironical scherzi, are almost regularly superior to the more lyrical, subjective slow movements, which tend slightly to sentimentality. If the *andante ostinato* of the Sonata is deeply felt, it certainly is far more repetitious than the polyrhythmic, polyharmonic scherzo. Only the substitution of a new andante for the old one of the Concerto succeeded in balancing the work. But in the andantino of his Variations for string quartet, Harris at last gave us a slow movement that is on the level of liveness with the best fast movements that he has written, and another in the *Symphony 1933*.

And this continual and advancing purification has been a matter of a relatively few years. Harris had a late start. Born in 1898, his Op. 1 was composed as recently as the year 1926. As late as 1925 he was getting his living as a teamster; only from 1926 onward did the spirit of an individual, and then of the Guggenheim Foundation, enable him to go abroad to study with the inevitable Nadia Boulanger and then set to work freely. We have Henry Cowell's word for it that he "began by writing in the crudest manner he [Cowell] ever remembers seeing from anyone who thought that his products were compositions: unbelievable commonplaces of harmony, like a schoolboy's first exercises; melodic fragments of no distinction; rhythms all half-note blocks in 4/4 meter. But Harris would point them out with the firm conviction that they were potential masterpieces." And Harris has remained humble toward his art, for all his boundless belief in his own possibilities. He is still sure of each new work he offers the public, now as then, and still defends it hotly against its critics; and he has had critics, and good ones, some who sang, "Unto us a man is born," or "O Harris, O mon Roy," while others, like Walter-à-Piston and Henry Cowell, challenged his pretensions and put his works under the magnifying glass of technical criticism and said, "Thou ailest here and here." And he has had important presentations of his music both in America and abroad. But he has made the most of all his opportunities, listening apparently critically, humbly to his own pieces, and has invariably ultimately rejected the inferior among them and put compositions ruthlessly back on to the stocks when they needed reworking, and cut away whole movements and substituted better, and furiously labored at the improvement of his style and form. Thus his music and his figure fairly glitter with the signs of his capacity to develop fully into the great thing of which he is now the impressive potentiality, and of the relative briefness of the period which the process will have to consume.

Copland

ULTIMATELY one of the solid achievements of recent musical art, Aaron Copland's work is a troubling one. It is excessively austere, in places very bare and bleak. The thematic material is oftentimes dynamic but extremely laconic and unpromising. The grandiose forms in instances get very slowly under way and at times have the monotonousness that flows from an absence of strong contrasts. Passages of an almost unrelieved and well-nigh intolerable strainfulness, of "reiterated and uniform motion" in which no progress of experience seems to be taking place, figure not entirely unfrequently in them. The sonorities are almost exclusively lapidary and metallic, very rarely flowery and rich. Even where it is speedy and gorgeous, the music remains a little hard and rigid.

And it conveys an experience that for all its clarity and largeness remains bitter and rasping to a distinct degree. There is a feeling of Waste Lands in this music, of the stony and steely desert which New York includes. The moods are frequently those of persistent yearning, relieved by satiric humors in which the material very eloquently makes the sign of the thumb and nose; and by wild laughter and frenetic motion, and tragic and rueful retrospects (the piano Concerto, *Music for the Theater*). In instances we imagine walls which, no matter how long and how high we climb beside them, offer no aperture (*Symphonic Ode*); in others, cruel and implacable gods, Rhadamanthi unpityingly judging and mocking their human subjects; and a blasted and cindery world, good for destruction (piano Variations). Until very recently, the trio *Vitebsk* on a Jewish theme remained a kind of anomaly among Copland's pieces because of its sweet and joyous song. Even there, the feeling was that of the world of childhood.

This work is an expression—one of the very leading ones—of the immediately post-war generation and its large but cramped and half-crucified energy, its cocksureness, rasp, smothered desire, and its challenge of all things. But it is an expression! A member of this generation from birth, Copland is an artist, and despite the narrowness of his range and scope,

DISCOVERIES OF A MUSIC CRITIC

possibly a major one. His energy is ultimately free, and his experience musical and pure, intense and profound. It has engendered original sonorous material deeply dyed with the quality of his oftentimes tragic feeling, including plaintive melodies as pure and limpid as the songs of white-throat sparrows, scherzo-like passages of extravagant and adagio passages of sultry and smoldering lyricism, germinal themes as shrill and triumphant as the crows of giant metallic roosters, flinty, lithic harmonies and sonorities that, both grim and rich, are veritably dusky jewels of the age of steel. The volume of certain of the climaxes is brutal and brilliant like cubes of brass. Some of this material is finely Hebraic, harsh and solemn, like the sentences of brooding rabbis. Some of it, rhythmically in particular, is jazzy and distinctly American: the material of which Copland's brilliant piano Concerto is constructed is a musicianly development of the nostalgic blues idiom and of the typical Charleston polyrhythm. Nearly all of it is powerful, bold, and hard of edge.

This material, eloquent of a generation's experience, reaches us fused and expanded and worked up in big musical forms. They are in the grand style severe, often very large in scale. They are architectural, the organic developments of material without literary intention, frequently broad in style, built up of large blocks and severely without ornament, elevated and even impassioned in emotional pitch, and lengthily sustained on that high level. And they are severely unified: it is evident that Copland feels organically, since the material in each of his works is strongly related and expanded in various and exhaustive developments. He is indeed extremely economical and conservative of material: while in the earlier pieces, the Symphony, the piano Concerto, and *Music for the Theater,* the themes are still multiple, in the later pieces, the Ode for orchestra, *Vitebsk,* and the piano Variations, they are single;

and the pieces are expansions of characteristically Coplandesque laconic, defiant, heraldlike calls. In the case of the Ode, the frugal theme, a projective sequence of four notes, in its now buoyant, now contemplative, now scherzando and jazzy and finally grandiose metamorphoses, yields five consecutive movements of no mean length, among them the slowly blooming middle section with the slow syncopation of the theme by the English horn, and the pert scherzo; and only during the commencement of the grandiose finale does the material commence to wear dangerously thin. In the case of the piano Variations, the projective, shrilly crowing five-note theme yields eighteen minute but different variations, all dissonant, with wide melodic intervals, all extremely percussive, some accusative, some plangent, some bitterly, brokenly questioning, some shattering as the yelps of hounds, some denunciative, leading up to a tragic peroration that seems to tear the whole edifice of things apart.

And for all their periodic inertia—sometimes under conditions of fast tempi—and their monotonousness, lack of strong contrasts and uniform somberness of coloring, Copland's forms eventually release the tension they create. At moments the auditor gets a painful sense that nothing is moving and nothing is going to move. There is a wild beating of unflying wings. And still, very subtly and almost secretly, the periods fully round themselves; and at last, after some progress that resembles the staggering journey of an exhausted traveler over burning sands or the negotiation of endless rocky ledges, the oasis and the summit is attained; the work mounts to its climax, and gains its goal of God-feeling. And like spiritual needle baths, these works wake the hearer to sometimes terrible but always fresh and strong feelings of life. One feels the struggle of the forces of life to pull together, to adjust themselves to the stone of giant cities. One feels the struggle of "the barren staff the pilgrim bore" to break into flowers; one feels the struggle of energies to divert and loose themselves. And one feels a final success, as of a wounded thing that regains its strength and comes to something at last; and of energies that, captive, badly shattered, fragmentary, incoherent, after writhing and suffering, finally through much wrestling and travail break madly out of their separate cells and their isolation and find their way into a new day and union and harmony.

The very latest of Copland's pieces, the still unperformed *Short Symphony* and the *Statements for Orchestra,* indeed, reveal considerable recent growth. They seem superior in form to any of his preceding compositions and representative of maturer experiences. The bounding melodic line of the *Short Symphony* has great vitality, jumping and moving strongly and precipitously: the first two movements are extremely direct and round; and while there is a passage of the old airless kind of music at the beginning of the finale, the work eventually marches to its conclusion. The whole gives the feeling of stoical but heroic strength, of a high and heroic will; and spontaneously one puts this little Symphony in the category presided over by the *Eroica.* The *Statements,* as their name would indicate, are very concentrated brief pieces, dogmatic in manner and tone. They are extremely original and extremely simple, and one or two of them have a new depth of mood and feeling verging on the prophetic. Others are more programmatic, apparently a kind of propagandistic music which Copland has written in the enthusiasm of his recent swing toward the left. Another recent piece, a sort of overture on Mexican themes entitled *Salon Mexico,* belongs among Copland's *burlesques,* with the second and fourth movements of *Music for the Theater* and the second of the piano Concerto. It too is very brilliant, and like Chabrier's *Espagna,* a splendid joke.

It is a formidable little array of pieces which Copland has already given us. They may never have a wide audience, because of their extreme austerity and the severity of their forms. But they stand with but few American rivals in the front rank of contemporary musical production and perhaps in an even wider rank, for they are uncompromisingly and idealistically lofty in endeavor and accomplishment, deep in feeling and ultimately expressive of an experience: and they have more than one touch of the sublime.

Chavez

THE important Latin-American composers appear to us five in number. They are Hector Villa-Lobos in Rio de Janeiro, Alejandro Garcia Caturla and Amadeo Roldan in Cuba, and Carlos Chavez and Silvestre Revueltas in Mexico. All of them are nationalistic, insomuch as their work is somewhat a symphonic equivalent for the folk music and an idealization of it; and this circumstance is one of the sources of the dissimilarities of their products. For in Brazil and in Cuba the folk music is basically African; in Mexico, Amerindian: thus the pieces of Villa-Lobos and the two genial Cubans could not but help tend toward the sensuous and the opulent and that of the two Mexicans toward the austere and the astringent. But the spiritual and stylistic differences of the folk music whose character these five composers have as it were re-expressed is not the only source of the dissimilarities between their creations, which range from good vulgar music to music in the grand style. There are dissimilarities due to different degrees of endowment with energy and spirit among them, and for this reason the music of the Brazilian composer and of Caturla and Roldan remains in the good vulgar category—and brilliantly illustrates it, too—while that of the two Mexicans, in particular that of Chavez, for the Rabelaisian Revueltas is, as it were, his second, figures in the highest order of contemporary work.

Chavez indeed is not only the most important of the living Latin-American composers. He is one of the very important ones native to the New World and representative of it.

His highly original work is part of the culture of modern Mexico. In classical, architectural, and at times severely contrapuntal forms, Chavez' music interprets the forces of the Mexican soil to man and expresses the attitudes, the temper of feeling, the vital balance that permits man to live in partnership with it. It is an austere music, robust, oftentimes joyous, but reserved, terrifically held in, impersonal, and flinty and sometimes abrasive. The forms are oftentimes very laconic, concentrated and foreshortened, and generally have more intensity than dimension, and high specific weight. The fugue of Chavez' piano Sonata might stand for them all, it is so telescopic and condensed. His idiom, too, is laconic, bare, brutal, and at times scratchy. Some of it is traditional: classical, Spanish-American, Indian, jazz. We find huapangos and zandoungas in the great *Sinfonia de H.P.,* the music for the ballet *Horse Power* created by Chavez in conjunction with Diego Rivera and produced in Philadelphia in 1932: while some of his piano pieces are couched in fox-trot measures and one of them in the scheme of a blues. But under his treatment all traditional stuff becomes individually robust and lean and austere. The melodies, most of them modal, oftentimes approach savage singsongs, recalling the tunes of the Amerindians. Tattoolike themes, made of dry, sere staccato volumes and brittle pizzicati, and drumlike in their effect, prevail; and he is much given to sudden astringent hesitations in his melodic flow, to suspensions and pauses: the third bar of his early piano Sonatina supplies a characteristic instance of one of these curiously brutal indeterminations in the arrest of a bit of three-part counterpoint in quavers, on a sudden crotchet. Dry and staccato volumes, essentially percussive, prevail, and he is very partial to hollow octaves and unisons. In the piano pieces, flinty and martellato sounds appear, like sparks struck from the keyboard. In its many scherzolike movements this music has an original susurrus, a buzzing, rustling, cackling quality that evokes the desert, the rattling of dry pods, the cackling song of the red man in his dusty pueblos. The rhythms are brusque and curiously impassive, and the color new and rough. Chavez has a penchant for *guiros* and *claves* and other instruments of hard and dry percussion.

But there is a dance in it all, a dance of life, a feeling of virility and sun. There is unity here, unity with a harsh and difficult but austerely beautiful and sufficiently generous and loyal earth, and a dance of the male, in the plenitude of liberated energies, in athletic reserve, in derisive impenetrability.

No musical forms quite like these have appeared either in Latin or in Saxon America or on the rest of the earth. Traditional and original elements are merged in them into a newly vital expression. Pieces like the piano Sonata, *Energia, The Four Suns,* the *Sinfonia de Antigona,* the *Sinfonia de H.P.,* move energetically in paths of their own, with a life, a fire, a momentum of their own. At a first hearing they may seem impossibly wry and perverse. But at a second they will open up, displaying an individual form and a logic. To hear a piece like *Energia,* with its terrific high tensity, its daringly timed and spaced buzzing, rasping string sonorities, and its queer new astringent sensuosity, color, raciness, earthiness, is to feel music beginning anew as in the young Strawinsky, and more freshly and more potentially. This is really New World. It is still a *little* music, a body small in bulk and in weight, this new classical music of the Mexican culture world. It includes as yet scarcely more than a baker's dozen of first-rate pieces. Among these must be counted some of the products of Chavez' probationary years. The early Aztec ballet, *The New Fire,* is notably bare of pictorial pretensions; but it is still Debussyan. But the three little Sonatinas, respectively for piano, for piano and violin, and for piano and 'cello, and the racy little improvisation entitled *36,* are rich in intimations of the stringent style of the future robust, dry, impassive pieces, and masculine in quality. The short, compact, forceful little piano Sonatina, for all its reminiscences of Ravel, has a fine savage singsong, Amerindian in its monotony and rigidity and piercing earthiness. The piano and violin Sonatina for a few measures recalls the pentatonic pomp of Moussorgsky; then suddenly a characteristically Chavezlike turn intervenes, and as the song of the two contrapuntal voices swells and the full reiteration of the theme announces an approaching climax, the violin voice precipitously drops into a new key while the piano continues in the old. Uttering its cry a semitone below the expected tone, it continues flatting through the succeeding cramplike measures. The polytonic effect is simultaneously brutal and powerful, strangely miserable and immensely gratifying, like a muscular contraction. And the scherzo is a typical bit of wild, dry, gibbering, and mocking music.

As for the sere, offhand little piano piece *36,* it is all drumlike effect, brittle pizzicati, informal rhythm, a bit of the debonair, burlesque, crude-colored sort of music projected by the Parisian Six during their heyday. If one associates it with the less important of Chavez' pieces, it is largely because, composed near the beginning of his still relatively brief career, it is less substantial than its successors in the pianistic medium, the Sonata and *Unidad*. Still, it is all Chavez in a nutshell.

More fully representative are pieces like *Energia,* the Sonata for four horns, the piano Sonata, the *Mexican Pieces,* and the Aztec ballet *The Four Suns*. The piano Sonata is dry as a plant lost in the sands. The leanness of the sonority, the uncompromising harshness of the counterpoint, the strictness of the beat, at first are intolerable. The themes are at once childlike, precise, drumlike, and decisively rhythmical. The treatment of the piano is essentially percussive. The four compact, boldly contrasted little movements are predominantly staccato and martellato, moving in vigorous abrupt rhythms, and prolific of jerky accents and flinty sounds. Hollow octaves and single unsupported voices are prevalent; so, too, Chavez' favorite suspensions, brutal deceptions and interminations. The impressionistic pedal does not figure. There is no voluptuousness in the score; at moments, when the composer himself is at the piano, we seem to be hearing modal, polytonic music executed as if the piece were Bach and the performer a student of the French Conservatoire. The fugue is bald; the scherzo, a savage, dusty bit, another of those flighty, glittering, rhapsodic passages in which we hear an echo of the atrocious rattlings and scratchings of the Aztec instruments. Yet the piece has a powerful lyricism, strength, and a deep and austere beauty. *Unidad,* the most recent and the most important of the *Mexican Pieces,* has an élan and high spirits like those of the youthful Schumann, all in the form of a characteristically earthy Chavez composition.

And its form is more completely articulated than that of some of its predecessors. Chavez' weakness was in his form: his forms were oftentimes made up of repetitions. But *Unidad* has an unflagging line and streams ahead like a pennant in a wind.—As for the "four suns" of the Aztec ballet, they are the four geological periods of the Aztec codices: worlds of water, of wind, of fire and lava, and of earth; and the dances represent them ritually, in the form of a primitive rite. The music is iterative, Amerindian, full of shrill and piping tones, and simultaneously ferocious and reserved. It has an almost frescolike quality, as of something entirely formal and objective: it is as if inscribed on a temple wall in Chichen Itzá. While the score might not have found its present shape had not the ballet movements of *Petrushka* and *Le Sacre* preceded it, its primitivity and austerity are entirely distinct from the Russian music.

The latest of Chavez' compositions given concert performance in New York is the overturelike *Sinfonia di Antigona;* it is classic music in the grand style severe. What nonetheless seems to be his best work is the definitive version of the *Sinfonia de H.P.* This is a curious piece, a kind of cross-section of Chavez' entire product. Parts of it actually date from the time of the Sonatinas; others are very recent; and the whole contains several different sorts of music. For example, it contains popular tunes, a commonplace huapango and a zandounga cast in the style of Bach's two-part inventions; the brilliant first movement is in the form of the classic sonata, polyphonic in style and elevated in feeling; and introductory to the brilliant finale, a marvelous and poetic page of metallic timbres on a par with the best of Varèse and Prokofieff and Antheil's exploitation of these sonorities out of a feeling of the magic of the industrial scene. Some of the miscellaneousness was very possibly due to the idea of the ballet *Horse Power* itself; it involved a contrast and an interfusion of the characteristics and powers of northern and industrial and tropic and primitive America. But the mere miscellaneousness of styles is not the only defect of the score. The folkloristic portions are inferior to the rest, especially to the brilliant exterior movements, and to the massive and austere slow movement, the third, and the cracking and luminous scherzo, the fifth. And still, for all its inequalities and its overloudness, the score is marvelous. It is full of musical expressions of a puissance and a joyousness unmatched in American music and conveyed by forms that have great vitality and blaze with sun and laughter. And listening to certain of the movements, one seems to be hearing a kind of American *Die Meistersinger* prelude, a polyphonic piece that in an American classic style, and through original and western forms, expresses with a magnificence like that of the German the forces of America and the vital attitudes that make life possible upon our soil.

The piece is but repeating, in a grand way, the burden of all Chavez' pieces. For his art is a reflection of forces by no means confined to Mexico. It is a reflection of the soil of the continent; it is a communication of the attitudes and tempers of feeling that it demands of its children, and that make life upon it possible. Chavez is not a Mexican so much as a North American composer.

DISCOVERIES OF A MUSIC CRITIC

Riegger: A Note

THERE would be little profit in leaving the field without attempting to make amends, to the full extent of our small powers, to an American composer stupidly neglected by the musical press. This composer is Wallingford Riegger, and the poor treatment he received at the hands of the professional critics incidental to the performance of his *Rhapsody* for orchestra early in the winter of 1932 by the Philharmonic under Kleiber was characteristic. Some of the writers gave him space while others did not, but none gave him any of the applause his piece richly merited; and evidently for no better reason than the one that, with the exception of an episode in the middle of the *Rhapsody,* which was chromatic in scheme, the whole composition was atonal, or rather, free of diatonic tonality. Yet it was evidently the work of an excellent musician, magnificent in texture, consistent in idea, grateful to the ear and lucid in form.

One might suppose that the fact that the author was several times a prize man, having gained the Paderewski award in 1921 for his piano Trio in B Minor, the Coolidge award in 1924 for his cantata *La Belle Dame sans Merci,* and the honor of Doctor of Music from the Cincinnati Conservatory, would have helped our friends over their prejudice against the "modern" style, by showing them that at least it was not helplessness in the older styles that had impelled Riegger to essay the new one. And there were other proofs of his integrity to be had with little expenditure of energy. A comparison of his

RIEGGER: A NOTE

works in the older, chromatic style with those in the more advanced styles would have revealed that, greatly as the idioms might differ, the spirit and feeling of all were related. Whether indeed the style, as in the piano Trio and other early works, is thoroughly chromatic; or whether, as in the piano piece *Blue Voyage,* inspired by Aiken's novel, it is impressionistic, without definite tonality; or whether, as in the best passages of the *Rhapsody* or in the more recent *Sonority for Violins,* performed a few years ago by Stokowski, or the Suite for flute solo, played last season by Barrère, it is built on arbitrarily selected tonal centers—the world-feeling underlying all Riegger's delicate compositions is single. It is a very restless one, appropriate to worlds unstably shifting from position to position. It is also the feeling of one himself searching for some firmness in the oceanic flux: gently, quizzically, incessantly questioning. Riegger to some degree seems to be continuing the expression of the spirit we have come to associate with Debussy and impressionism, even though his idiom is perfectly distinctive and his interest more in thematic development than in tone color.

But the atonalism seems to have obstructed the critics, to a man. The fact is curious. If indeed one is unable to hear the relation of note to note freshly in every composition, whether it be tonal, bitonal, or without any tonality whatsoever, what indeed can one be said actually to be hearing?

DISCOVERIES OF A MUSIC CRITIC

"Union Pacific"

WE cannot be enthusiastic about *Union Pacific,* the new American ballet by Archibald MacLeish and Nicholas Nabokov which the Monte Carlo troupe mounted with decorations by Albert Johnson in Philadelphia, Chicago, and New York in the April of 1934. All in all it failed of being the good and important American myth it might have been. The completion of the transcontinental link was assuredly the most important American event immediately subsequent to Appomattox: and it provides artists with an opportunity for the creation, through a representation of the process by which the completion was achieved and the experience of that achievement, of a picture of the creative American force and of a bond like the actual railway. But the representation of MacLeish and Nabokov was incomplete and at moments trivial. True, a few expressive images did appear during the pantomime. The somewhat Sandburgian best of these significant figures occurred a trifle anticlimactically in the first scene. It was composed by dancers representing one of the Irish construction gangs which helped extend the railway westward across the plains and through the Rockies in the latter '60's. Serially, the laborers carried on to the stage other dancers stiffly stretched out and cased in dark-colored cerements and laid them upon the boards in the forms of ties and rails. Again, at the close of the second scene, a vigorously rhythmical counter dance movement of the Chinese construction gang and its surveyor, supposed to be extending the line eastward through a brilliantly blue Utah, indi-

"UNION PACIFIC"

cated a relentless, almost ecstatic, concentration of brain and brawn upon the completion of the far-flung structure. The final picture was happily ironic: after the representation of the linking of the two sections at Promontory Point and the confrontation of the heads of locomotives pointed east and west, several mimes impersonating financiers advanced to the center of the stage. And pompously driving in a golden spike and expressing their emotions to the strain of "Old Hundred"—as the bankers in Wall Street, complex American creatures that they were, actually did on the day in 1869 when word of the completion of the road was flashed to all parts of the Union—these dancers finally self-complacently posed for their photographs against a background of grinning coolies, Paddies, greasers, and whores.

That was all, somewhat less than we might have expected from the talented, earnest author of *Nobodaddy* and *New Found Land*. Nor was the Nabokov score entirely above the sketchy MacLeish libretto and its choreographic realization. It was more poetically expressive, certainly more serious. Nabokov probably is the livest of Russian composers younger than Prokofieff—in point of emotional capacity and healthiness and sweetness of spirit he is easily the superior of the somewhat overadvertised Markevitch. He had been living in New York during the previous year, and he provided *Union Pacific* with a score which, though it remains theater music, reflects the constructive process, the experience and the creative force, more vigorously than does the work of either the American librettist or the American decorator. Never, perhaps, either profound or exquisite, the lusty, melodious, agreeably solidly colored composition, for a space at least, represents fresh masculine energies and the zest of enterprise. It has *joie de vivre*, and it sings out as from a pair of virile lungs the homely songs of the period, such, for instance, as "Lady Gay," "I Am a Gambling Man," and "Oh, Susannah." Nabokov exploited these tunes with considerable skill and feeling for their character and pathos and only occasionally oversweetened them in the Russian fashion. In fact, his score indicates a sincere, lifting feeling of constructive force and American daring. Yet in the middle of the third part, the big tent scene, a tableau amplified out of all proportion and beyond dramatic necessity in order to permit the *corps de ballet* to perform some characteristic dances, Mexican and so forth, and give Massine a chance to do a truly sublime cakewalk, it loses its élan, its meaning, and its freshness. Then for a while in the fourth and final part it takes hold of the idea and becomes poetic again, but again it peters out with the satiric close. By and large, the ballet amounted at most to a garishly colored, faintly ironical animated print, quaintly representative in the flat manner of Currier and Ives of the completion of the transcontinental link, the itinerant barrooms that followed the construction gangs, and other specialties of the place and period.

But that is not poetry. It would seem as though MacLeish, to begin with, had been somewhat confused and uncertain in his feelings, that he had not given Nabokov the libretto that would have permitted the composer to represent the creative event that attracted them both, and that the traditions and requirements of a decadent choreographic organization had further interfered with both their ideas and their expressions. One regrets the abortion, since MacLeish and Nabokov had the subject for a very fine and important American myth—a transcontinentally connective instrument more important even than a railway—and had, both of them, although to slightly varying degrees, some real feeling of the American creative force. And one hopes that they can contrive to put their work back on the stocks again—for they have the talent—and complete and render it the real *Union Pacific*.

Epilogue: The Land Awaits

WHILE the machine carrying a pair of my friends and myself to the first festival of American chamber music at Yaddo in Saratoga was traveling up the Hudson Valley north of Red Hoek that afternoon late in the April of 1932, I was haunted by mixed feelings of freedom and suspense. The freedom I felt was my own, for the much-desired liberty to assist at and report the little fête and make the trip up the lordly river in the company of my friends had but very recently been assured me—actually only on the previous evening. I had been spending, and wasting, the past three weeks far from my work-table, as a member of the jury of an exceedingly sordid and apparently interminable business case. I had been released from the drudgery yestere'en by an entirely unanticipated and costly declaration of a mistrial. And during the first stages of the little journey on a suburban Albany Post Road bordered by the yellow greenery of early spring and glistening stone walls and festooning jasmine, the mere eagerness to make our aim had possessed all our minds.

But after the mastery of the familiar Highlands and the old Poughkeepsie streets, I found myself as it were in sight of my recently threatened goal. The attendance of the distant purplish chain of Catskills in the west; above all, the changed, rela-

DISCOVERIES OF A MUSIC CRITIC

tively northerly aspect of the country and the day, announced its proximity and assured me of my good luck. Where previously rocky hills and a smoking small industrial belt had met my eyes there now lay, to either side of the car, fields of rich, damp, furrowed chocolate-colored earth, indicative of the old and careful human culture of a loyal substance; and the peaceful valley whose eastern rim the machine was taking, spread out below, a broad, rich farmland swelling up on either side of the deep-lying ribbon of water. The overarching sky was clouded—that of the lower Hudson had been sunny and clear. The tones of the landscape were dark, bluish, and cool. And over the line of craggy Catskills—a receding series of flowing crests of an ever less substantial blue—the clouds were slashed by streaks of the orange and apocalyptical light of the westering sun that turned the rain falling on the mountains into faintly gilded curtains and distinguished mysterious warm pockets amid their bluish planes. Close at hand, by the side of the motor road remotely accompanied by the chain, slender budding fruit trees shivered in the cold spring breeze.

But while the feeling of freedom that now possessed me was plainly my own, the feeling of suspense mingled with it seemed that of another and of no human being. It came as from the vernal, beautiful, beloved land itself. It had a character and an identity; and in the old patroon estates, the outspread valley with its individual and northern physiognomy, the mysterious westerly mountains, and the immense continental expanse they indicated and secreted, I recognized anew the vastly, half-known and half-hidden but whole entity America. And it definitely evoked the feminine pronoun. The entire land, the cultured territory, its towns and rocks and the very skies behind them, was She. The phenomenon undoubtedly had several causes—one of them the season—but none so influential as the

EPILOGUE: THE LAND AWAITS

event of the immediately preceding days, the suicide of Hart Crane. The figure of the unhappy poet was very prominent in all our minds; and with it a sense of the pity of his untimely death. And Hart Crane had felt the life of the American soil in the figure of Pocahontas; and for us his idea had passed into objective reality. Over the furrowed earth beside the roadway and by the blossoming fruit trees, there seemed elusively to hover the essence of the little Indian princess he had touched in the soil; a tawny aboriginal girl, of elfish grace, untamed for all the labor of the centuries of the white man. Over in the mountains "wisped of azure wands," her life was intensely concentrated, and strong, majestic, spiritual, sacred; and she herself a priestess, godly of race and limbs. And with her whole farspread being, this terrestrial entity seemed to wait expectantly, in this undecided spring, most, perhaps, in the mysterious mountains. It was as if her entire being were vigilant. Only what she waited upon with all her soul, could not be divined.

Was it a material fruition, that of summer? It did not seem to be such: the spirituality of the vigil suggested a person, a gesture, an event. But the nature of the person, gesture, event, eluded me. Was it some spiritual plowman? Puzzled, troubled, I searched the great attentive form for some revealing sign of its desire and saw a mountain chain mysteriously pointing northward. The far purple tip of its fingers seemed to extend toward the northerly vacation land where I strove o' summers with a rebellious novel-stuff; and a craving for the *villegiatura* and its circumstances propitious to production grew strong in me. At the same time the goal of Saratoga and Yaddo, the hospice of the next couple of days, took on a new magnetism and a sanctitude. The waiting entity seemed to point thither, too, as to some place where her expectation to some degree might be fulfilled.

At twilight, on the wet pavement of the desert main street of Saratoga before the grandiose and gracefully built very American piles of the hotels, the feeling of the land's mysterious desire had grown half joyous, like one promised a proximate though still unrevealed fulfillment.

The next morning it was temporarily abeyant and remained so throughout almost the entire two-day festival. The first view of the company of musicians, amateurs, and critics who had traveled to Saratoga in response to the invitation of the hospitable artists' foundation under whose patronage the fête was taking place drove it from my mind. In the chapel, the assembly room, the nature of the company indicated that the occasion was not so much a festival of American music as a battle. Challenge was what was most definitely in the air, the silent but incisive defiance of the major music critics and professors.

No representative of a great New York morning paper had arrived. The *Boston Transcript* had Meyer there, but the most influential of the New York musical reporters present was a second-string man. The critical ranks were filled by the musical writers of the two liberal weeklies and young Berger of the *Mirror*. Later a United Press man put in an appearance. As for the academic gentlemen, none but Donovan of Yale honored the exercises, and Donovan is himself a composer.

No mass demonstration on the part of the musical public had been anticipated. Several hundred invitations had been issued by the foundation, but the relative remoteness of Saratoga from the great rookeries and the other obstacles to the pilgrimage had dampened hopes of a large attendance. The appearance of the critical and academic powers was expected

EPILOGUE: THE LAND AWAITS

nonetheless. The number of the works of the newer American composers played by live musical organizations and the amount written in all earnestness about these works and their authors were sufficient to prove to anyone of open mind that the new American music was a living issue. Works by a number of the men given special attention by the leading conductors and hailed as leaders by the younger composers and their critics figured upon the programs sent out with the invitations. And it was not unreasonable to suppose that those professionally concerned with the welfare of musical art would jump at the opportunity for judgment of disputed matters offered by conditions favorable to receptivity.

Consciousness of the snub was ineluctable. For a moment it was possible to believe the great men kept off by the fragility of their honesty, incapable of exposure to the presence of composers, or by the pressure of their affairs. One could conceive Gilman busied with the confection of purple wisecracks and Pateresque turns of phrase destined to cast the light of culture on some matutinal grapefruit and coffee and subway ride, and gently perspiring over a little badinage meant to serve as program notes for the *Manzoni Requiem.* These hypotheses nonetheless evaporated in view of the ineluctable fact that a very definite faith had brought the persons gathered in the chapel through spring to Saratoga: a faith in two things, the liveness of recent American music and the leadership and breadth and soundness of Aaron Copland, director of the festival. Various degrees of faith, of course, were represented. Some of the pilgrims were assured of the presence of the forces of life in the music of contemporary Americans. Others were more skeptical of it but willing to be won to conviction. Certain had come because they felt that the institutions which presented the newer music during the New York season were in irresponsible hands and welcomed the Yaddo festival because it took the introductory function from the control of third-rate composers and shoddy politicos and assigned it to a first-rate artist. Others, again, were merely eager to see what, if anything, Copland had to offer under conditions making for concentration and freedom from the hurly-burly of New York and the inevitable interference of the public in search not of vision but of entertainment.

All, nonetheless, were prejudiced to some degree in favor of the cause and the leader; and it was plain that those who conspicuously absented themselves and whose absence was not due to irresponsibility in the conduct of the critical and professional functions were letting their nonappearance express their skepticism, distrust, disdain.

Thus the Yaddo festival began, another battle of Saratoga. The critics and professors had put both the new American music and the composer-impresario on trial before their own partisans. For all the faith of the assemblage, these had to some degree to demonstrate their worth; and it cannot be said that a preliminary inspection of the three programs gave an overwhelming assurance of their ultimate acquittal. Recent American chamber music was evidently entering the lists under a handicap. Copland had clearly not made his selections on the basis of originality and force and in impersonal disregard of the incongruity of certain aesthetics with his own. The names of Ives, Sessions, Harris, and Copland himself appeared on the programs. But those of Ruggles, Weiss, Cowell, Ornstein, and several other interesting composers were missing, the names of a number of composers of smaller figure appearing in their stead. Nor was any other objective principle of selection demonstrable. The program was composed of a number of pieces receiving their first performance, and a number of others

EPILOGUE: THE LAND AWAITS

which, like Harris' piano Sonata, Riegger's Suite for flute solo, Copland's own piano Variations, had previously met the font. It was plain that with a certain pardonable cocksureness Copland had preferred, to an impersonal basis, the basis of his own personal enthusiasms, and in all sincerity had placed on his programs only what conformed to his own taste. Still, American music might conceivably appear no worse for the narrowness of the basis of selection. What it lost in front it might easily gain in intensity, provided only that the works isolated were clearly representative of some creative principle. All depended on the depth and purity of Copland's own point of view and his faithfulness to it.

It cannot be denied that the progress of the festival gave the skeptical critics and professors some show of right. The young American music did not as a body attest any special heroism at Saratoga, in spite of the care and ingenuity expended on the preparation of the concerts. This was due not so much to the defects of the new American music as to those of the direction. True, the young American music is not so rich in noble chamber works that it can give the audiences of three concerts completely ecstatic or interesting hours. But it sports more live works than the festival showed, none of them so overplayed that it could not bear repetition. And it cannot be said that Copland availed himself of the best or demonstrated entirely superior or even consistent taste as impresario. His programs revealed errors and inconsistencies of judgment. Pretentious sterility and sterile lack of earnestness both took up too much place.

The merits and the defects of his generalship were clearly displayed by the first concert. It began with an important revelation, that of the musicianship of a young New Yorker, Israel Citkowitz. He had appeared before the public as the

DISCOVERIES OF A MUSIC CRITIC

author of a graceful sonatina and some songs a few years since. But the three movements for string quartet performed at Yaddo were the vehicles of a wonderful fervor, part Shelleyesque, part Hebraic; and the workmanship was characteristically limpid. A real discovery, a true spirit! Immediately after, Chavez' latest piano composition, *Unidad,* made its bow and associated itself with *Energia,* the piano Sonata, and other of the fiery Mexican's superior works. It is a dance of the male on the American soil, astringent, mocking, impenetrable; and, perfectly representative of Chavez' dry, laconic style, is distinguished by unflagging length of line and breezy impetuosity. But the next number, four polyphonic pieces by Vivian Fine, was irritating. Three of the pieces were extremely amateurish, one was clever and slight, and none clearly justified its place on the program.

The climax of the first concert had now been reached. It was made up of three units. The first, Virgil Thomson's *Stabat Mater* for voice and string quartet, on a poem of Max Jacob's, proved the smooth, agreeable work of an elegant tinpot. The little cantata is neoclassic in politics, Catholic in ideology, royalist in style, and most effective theater. What deeply charmed in it was the voice of Mrs. Ada MacLeish, one of the brilliants of the festival. She sang twice more and displayed exceedingly pure and pearly tones, effortlessly produced. But for a very slight inaccuracy of attack in the upper registers and a muffled English diction her performance would have been perfect. Nor was her artistic performance solitary. The festival was rich in exquisite performances, particularly the piano playing of Jesus Sanroma, the performances of the flutist Georges Laurent, and Copland's own work as composer, pianist, and accompanist.

After the Thomson came what was in fact the *pièce de ré-*

EPILOGUE: THE LAND AWAITS

sistance, Sessions' Sonata; and it proved an error of judgment, placed where it was. This Sonata is not a whole, but two fragments, one composed of the first three movements, the other of the finale. It is the deeply inward expression of an aristocratic musicianship, beautifully written and original in parts. But spiritually it fails, since the sparkling last movement does not release the tension created by the others: in fact it constitutes a red-hot musical *non sequitur.* The charming songs of Paul Frederick Bowles were scarcely solid enough to retrieve the concert, lyrical and discreetly written as they were. And at the end, the false note of the *Four Diversions* for string quartet, by Louis Gruenberg, was acutely discouraging. Intrinsically cheap, these pieces were only too evidently selected in infidelity to the director's own taste.

The remaining concerts were somewhat similar. The second descended from the heights of Harris' Sonata, the inspired work of what is probably the greatest natural talent in American music, to the Serenade for string quartet by Mark Blitzstein, evidently the one "which the starved lover sings to his proud fair, best quitted with disdain." Composed of three largo movements, it three times attains what appears to be the ultimate in lethargy. Berezowsky's Quartet was also ripe for Koko's little list. Oscar Levant's jazz Sonatina called for Gershwin, who does that sort of thing brilliantly. And the third concert began encouragingly with Piston's Sonata for flute and piano, beautifully articulated work of a musical stylist, and took a nose dive in that curious combination of youthful pedantry and aged smart-Aleckism, the Suite, also for piano and flute, by Henry Brant.

But it was during the second concert that the tide of battle definitely had turned and all skepticism of the reality of the forces at work in American music quit the minds of the better part of the audience. The climax supervened toward the end of the evening. The place of vantage had been reserved for George Antheil, due to play three Sonatas and a Sonatina. But at the eleventh hour he fell sick, and Copland, who had placed his own piano Variations on the last program, substituted himself and his composition for Antheil and his, and looking prodigiously like business, marched up to the keyboard and attacked the Variations. In a minute the critics were repulsed.

Many of the members of the audience had previously heard the bitter and gorgeous, stark and structural piece. No previous performance, nonetheless, had revealed its greatness as fully as this at Yaddo, and the power of its contracted, slowly progressive volumes with their flinty, metallic sonorities. Music of the depths, built out of sonorous characteristics of one of the world's saddest hours, bitten in tone, iron of clangor, brooding, savagely philosophical, with at times a bark like that of hounds, it seemed to pull that agonizing world slowly up toward a new birth in a new bare day. The piece fairly towered, hard, nakedly structural, maximally expressive, the black menhir of an age. One felt its author the composer of the coming decades.

After that all was well with the festival and well with all beyond it. The happy effect of the Copland Variations was duplicated on the next, the last, day. The morning had been lost in a conference between "critics and composers." It would have been lost even if the critics with whom the composers wished to confer had been present, since the composers evidently were under the illusion that the minds of critics closed to *their* worth as artists would have been susceptible of aperture to them with the can-opener of personal persuasion. But on the final program there figured a small but finely selected group of the songs of Charles E. Ives, and they revealed the presence of a first-rate composer of *Lieder* in the ranks of American

EPILOGUE: THE LAND AWAITS

music. A deeply sentient New Englander, somewhat of the type of Robert Frost, Ives in his songs expresses a deep and wise and very American feeling of life through little forms of perfect design, original in color and individually realistic. "Serenity" to Whittier's words, "Maple Leaves" on words of Aldrich's, and the version of the cowboy ballad "Charlie Rutlage" are all prime compositions of their sort.

So one forgot the mistakes, the failures, the disappointments. One only knew that there were artists in America.

And that was curiously satisfactory, curiously exciting. But not only satisfactory to oneself, fulfilling one's own self. Even as I walked out of the door of the chapel at Yaddo that dark spring Sunday afternoon and in the porte-cochere stood looking at the background of pines, I realized that the assurance of the presence in America, in the ranks of the American composers, of a human greatness working itself out through form had an importance for something vast, entirely transcending, entirely without, me. Then, in the car once more and headed for New York and the work-table, the feeling of the land I traversed conveyed to me the truth that the entity for whom this presence of human greatness expressing itself through form had an importance, and was the agent of satisfaction and fulfillment, was the soil itself. Satisfaction and fulfillment had evidently taken place within her. In the dusk the low, cool and brown and rolling forms of earth, were pacific. The feeling of tension in any case no longer was acutely present. And swiftly I divined what the object for which She had been waiting actually was. It was the artist; and she had lately felt and found him: at the Yaddo festival itself.

Was it all illusory? I thought not. Something had definitely happened, out there in the landscape, as well as to me; and the two events, I knew, were one. What if the event in her bosom had been but the definite triumph of the sun and the season and the plowman, and the event in mine, spirit's triumphant manifestation of its existence in America? Dimly I knew them related, even more identical than I could grasp and capable of further relation and of ultimate unity. The spirit, too, was the giver of light and life, and the work of pure art its medium potentially able to minimize the exploiter in man and maximate the husbandman. Through men, the work of art could touch the earth with loving hands. And as in the last light the mountains came mistily into view again, I knew now very fully that what the land, concentrated and mystic and spiritual among their crags, awaited ceaselessly, was ever more of the spirit I had lately enjoyed and toward which I myself was hopefully directed, in the very machine bearing me toward New York: the spirit of the guardian, the lover, the laborer, the interpreter, the spirit of the artist.

Biographical Appendix

THE COURT MASQUE

Jonson, Ben, *Masques and Entertainments,* ed. by Henry Morley, Routledge, 1890; Milton, John, *The Masque of Comus,* arranged by Sir Frederick Bridge, Lane, 1908; Campion, Thomas, *Works,* ed. by Percival Vivian, Oxford Press, 1902; Rolland, Romain, "L'opéra anglais au XVIIe siècle," Encyclopédie de la musique; "The French Ballet and the English Masque," *Sewanee Review,* 1896; "Notes on a Collection of Masque Music," *Music and Letters,* 1922; Prendergast, A. H. D., "The Masque of the 17th Century," Musical Association, London, *Proceedings,* 1896-97.

MONTEVERDE

Claudio Monteverde was born in Cremona in May, 1567, and at an early age entered the service of the Duke of Mantua as a violist. The Duke's maestro di capella, Marc Antonio Ingegneri, instructed him in counterpoint. His first works, *Canzonette a Tre Voci,* were published in 1584. In 1602, Monteverde became maestro di capella in Mantua: and in 1607 his music drama *Orfeo* was produced there, followed the next year by his *Arianna.* In 1612 he entered the service of the Venetian Republic, and in 1613 became its head musician, at a salary of 500 ducats, enormous for the time. He composed masses for St. Mark's, and dramatic interludes for concert performance. He was admitted to the priesthood in 1633; his wife had died in 1607. For the first Venetian Opera House, opened in 1637, he composed *Adone; Le Nozze di Enea con Lavinia; Il Ritorno di Ulisse in patria;* and the first historical opera, *L'Incoronazione di Poppea.* He died November 28, 1643, the most famous composer in Europe.

Music dramas: *Orfeo; Arianna* (a fragment); *Il Ritorno di Ulisse*

BIOGRAPHICAL APPENDIX

in patria; L'Incoronazione di Poppea. Three volumes of church music; eight books of madrigals; a volume of *Canzonette;* two of *Scherzi Musicali;* several ballets; etc.

Goldschmidt, Hugo, *Studien zur Geschichte der italienischen Oper im 17. Jahrhundert,* Leipzig, 1901-04, 2 vols. in 1; Prunières, Henry, *Monteverdi, His Life and Work,* Dutton, 1926; Rolland, Romain, *Les origines du théâtre lyrique moderne,* new ed., Paris, 1931; Schneider, Louis, *Un précurseur de la musique italienne au XVIe et XVIIe siècles: Claudio Monteverde,* Paris, 1921.

J. S. BACH

Johann Sebastian Bach was born in Eisenach March 21, 1685, of a family of distinguished musicians. His father, Ambrosius, and his eldest brother, Johann Christophe, were his first teachers. At fifteen, he entered the convent school of St. Michael at Lüneburg; at eighteen, he was a member of the band of the brother of the Duke of Weimar; and in the same year (1703) organist of the new church at Arnstadt. In 1705 he visited Lübeck to hear Buxtehude, and remained there three months as an organist. From 1707 to 1708 he was organist at Mühlhausen, and from 1708 to 1717 court organist and chamber musician at Weimar. Much of his organ music was composed during these years. From 1717 to 1723 he was capellmeister to the music loving Prince Leopold of Anhalt-Cöthen at Cöthen: most of his works for orchestra and chamber ensembles date from this happy time. On the death of the Prince Bach became director of the St. Thomas School for Choir Singers in Leipzig and organist of the St. Thomas Church, where he remained till his death on July 28, 1750. The larger number of his chorale works date from these years. He was married twice, and had twenty children, of whom only five survived him. Three of them were important composers—Wilhelm Friedemann, Carl Philip Emanuel, and Johann Christian.

Works: B Minor Mass; four small Masses; five Passions (of which only two survive); five sets of Church Cantatas; Christmas Oratorio; two Magnificats; *Well-tempered Clavichord* (forty-eight

BIOGRAPHICAL APPENDIX

preludes and fugues); six French Suites; six English Suites; six Partitas: Aria with thirty-two Variations (Goldberg): *The Art of the Fugue; Chromatic Fantasy and Fugue;* Concerto in the Italian style; six Sonatas for violin and piano; six Brandenburg Concerti; numerous works for organ, harpsichord, violin solo, etc.

Dilthey, Wilhelm, *Von deutscher Dichtung und Musik,* Leipzig, 1933; Forkel, J. N., *Johann Sebastian Bach,* tr., notes, and appendices by C. S. Terry, Harcourt, Brace, 1920; Parry, Sir C. H. H., *Johann Sebastian Bach,* rev. ed., Putnam, 1934; Pirro, André, *L'esthétique de Jean-Sébastien Bach,* Paris, 1907; Schweitzer, Albert, *J. S. Bach,* Macmillan, 1923, 2 vols.; Spitta, Philip, *Johann Sebastian Bach,* Gray, 1884-85, 3 vols.; Terry, C. S., *Bach, The Historical Approach,* Oxford Press, 1931.

MOZART

Wolfgang Amadeus Mozart was born at Salzburg January 27, 1756. From the age of three he showed an aptitude for music. His first teacher was his father, Leopold; later, he had some instruction from Padre Martini in Bologna. For several years, beginning in 1762, his father exhibited him in several European capitals as a child prodigy: in 1769 they went together to Italy, where Mozart found some success not only as a pianist and composer for the pianoforte but as a composer of opera. From 1773 to 1777 Mozart had a small appointment at the court of Salzburg: then he set out with his mother to secure himself employment. He was unsuccessful in Munich, Mannheim, and Paris: in the latter place, his mother died, possibly because of improper medical care. From 1779 to 1780 Wolfgang was back in Salzburg, and then tried his fortunes in Vienna as a free-lance composer, with varying success. He married in 1782; then, when in 1789 Frederick William II of Prussia offered him an appointment at Potsdam, Mozart refused to quit Vienna. During these years he went on several concert tours, but found no greater financial support in Vienna than an insufficient annuity from the Emperor. In 1791 his health rapidly deteriorated; and on December 5 he died, apparently of malignant

BIOGRAPHICAL APPENDIX

typhus fever, a pauper, and convinced that his career had merely begun. His body was thrown into an unmarked grave.

Operas: *Bastien und Bastienne; Idomeneo; La Finta Giardinera; Die Entführung aus dem Serail; Don Giovanni; Le Nozze di Figaro; Così Fan Tutte; Die Zauberflöte.* Fifteen Masses; Requiem (concluded by Süssmayr); forty-one Symphonies; thirty-one Divertimenti, Serenades, Cassations; twenty-five piano Concerti—one for two and one for three pianos; six violin Concerti; Concerti for flute, harp, horn, and clarinet; twenty-six String Quartets; seven String Quintets; Quintet for clarinet and strings; forty-two Sonatas for violin and piano; seventeen piano Sonatas; three Fantasias; fifteen Variations; five Sonatas for four hands; organ works; arias; songs, etc.

Bellaigue, Camille, *Mozart,* Paris, 1906; Bekker, Paul, *The Changing Opera,* Norton, 1935; Dent, E. J., *Mozart's Operas,* McBride, Nast, 1913; Dilthey, Wilhelm, *Von deutscher Dichtung und Musik,* Leipzig, 1933; Ghéon, Henri, *In Search of Mozart,* Sheed & Ward, 1934; Jahn, Otto, *Life of Mozart,* London, 1882, 3 vols.; Rolland, Romain, *Some Musicians of Former Days,* Holt, 1915; Sitwell, Sacherevell, *Mozart,* Appleton, 1932.

CIMAROSA

Domenico Cimarosa was born December 17, 1749, at Aversa, Naples, and was trained at the Conservatorio Santa Maria di Loreto. His first opera, *Le Stravaganza del Conte,* was produced with great success in Naples in 1772. From 1772 to 1780 he resided in Naples and in Rome, and composed twenty operas for these two cities. Between 1780 and 1787 his operas commenced to conquer the European stages. At the invitation of Catherine the Great he went to St. Petersburg in 1787, and there produced most of his chamber compositions. A few years later, he succeeded Salieri as court capellmeister in Vienna: it was there he composed *Il Matrimonio Segreto* (1792). Later he returned to Naples, and was appointed capellmeister to the King. When the French took Naples in 1792, Cimarosa expressed his republican sentiments in so enthusiastic a manner that he was imprisoned and condemned to death. His life was spared, but he was banished; and he died in Venice January 11, 1801.

Works: Sixty-six Operas; several Oratorios; Cantatas; Masses, etc.

Cambiasi, Pompeo, *Notizie sulla vita e sulle opere di Domenico Cimarosa,* Milan, 1901; Vitale, Roberto, *Domenico Cimarosa,* Aversa, 1929.

BEETHOVEN

Ludwig van Beethoven was born in Bonn December 16, 1770. He began music in his fourth year; he had lessons from his father, from Neefe, and later from Haydn and Albrechtsberger. In 1784 Beethoven received an appointment as organist from the Elector of Cologne; he had begun publishing compositions of his own a year previously. In 1787 he journeyed to Vienna, and played before Mozart. Returning to Bonn, he found a patron in Count Waldstein: and with Waldstein's assistance, transferred his residence to Vienna. He was cordially received by the Viennese aristocracy, who generously patronized him. In 1795 he published his Op. I. Three years later, the first symptoms of his deafness appeared; by 1803 they were very pronounced; and by 1816 he could hear only with the aid of an ear trumpet. In 1805, the failure of his opera *Fidelio* turned Beethoven almost completely to instrumental music. It was revived in 1815, at about the same time that Beethoven achieved his great popular success with his *Battle Symphony* on the national anthems of the Allies. During the years from 1812 to 1817, his production was sparse, but resumed lavishly again after 1818. In 1809 the Princes Kinsky and Lobkowitz and Archduke Rudolph had agreed to pay Beethoven a pension of 4,000 florins annually, but due to the depreciation of the currency, Beethoven found himself from 1811 onward in financial straits: during his last years, his financial worries were augmented by his desperate attempt to provide for his nephew Carl, whom he had ill-advisedly adopted in 1820. His last years were extremely lonely and extremely unhappy; he had resigned his hopes of marriage—possibly because of a

BIOGRAPHICAL APPENDIX

syphilitic infection—before 1814. He died in Vienna March 26, 1827.

Works: Two Masses; Oratorio *Mount of Olives;* Opera *Fidelio;* Ballet *The Creatures of Prometheus;* nine Symphonies; eight Overtures; five piano Concertos; violin Concerto; *Choral Fantasy; Triple Concerto;* sixteen String Quartets; *Grand Fugue;* eight Trios; five Sonatas for piano and cello; ten Sonatas for piano and violin; thirty-two pianoforte Sonatas; twenty-one Variations; two hundred and fifty Songs; one hundred small pieces, etc.

Bekker, Paul, *Beethoven,* Dutton, 1925; Busoni, Ferruccio, *"Was Gab Uns Beethoven?" Die Musik,* 1922; Dannreuther, E. G., "Beethoven's Works," *Macmillan's Magazine,* 1876; Indy, Vincent d', *Beethoven,* Boston Music Co., 1913; Lenz, Wilhelm von, *Beethoven et ses trois styles,* Paris, 1909; Mason, D. G., *Beethoven and His Forerunners,* Macmillan, 1904; Nottebohm, M. G., *Beethovens Studien,* Leipzig, 1873; and *Ein Skizzenbuch von Beethoven,* Leipzig, 1880; Rolland, Romain, *Beethoven the Creator,* Harper, 1929, Vol. I, and *Goethe and Beethoven,* Harper, 1931; Schauffler, R. H., *Beethoven,* Doubleday, Doran, 1929, 2 vols.; Sullivan, J. W. N., *Beethoven, His Spiritual Development,* Knopf, 1927; Thayer, A. W., *The Life of Ludwig van Beethoven,* Schirmer, 1921.

GLINKA

Michael Ivanovich Glinka was born June 2, 1803, at Novospasskoi in the government of Smolensk. As a child, he was much affected by the Russian folk music which he heard a band, made up of serfs from his uncle's estate, perform. His first piano teacher was his German governess; his second, John Field. After his schooling, and a trip to the Caucasus, he studied the classical masters by himself and wrote pieces for his uncle's band. In 1824 he entered the Ministry of Ways and Communications and settled in St. Petersburg: four years later, on medical advice, he resigned his post and traveled to Italy. It was there he decided to compose a national opera, and in 1833 he went to Berlin and took lessons in composition from Dehn. *A Life for the Czar* was performed for the first time in 1836. For the next three years Glinka was choirmaster in the Imperial Chapel. *Ruslan and Lyudmila* was performed in 1842. It was a failure, and in disgust, Glinka left Russia for a tour in France and Spain in 1844. Berlioz introduced him to the Parisian public. In Paris he wrote the incidental music for *Prince Klomsky:* after collecting material in Spain, he went to Warsaw to live. Here he composed *Kamarinskaya* and *A Night in Madrid.* A second visit to Paris was terminated by the outbreak of the Crimean War. Glinka went to Berlin, and was busy on his autobiography, and studying the music of the Western Church for the purpose of discovering the correct method of harmonizing Russian folk songs. He died February 15, 1857.

Operas: *A Life for the Czar; Ruslan and Lyudmila.* Incidental music to *Prince Klomsky.* Also two Spanish Overtures; fantasia *Kamarinskaya; Valse Fantasy;* forty pieces for piano; numerous vocal duets, quartets, and trios; chamber music; etc.

Calvocoressi, M. D., *Glinka,* Paris, 1911; Montagu-Nathan, Montagu, *Glinka,* Duffield, 1917; Riesemann, Oskar von, *Monographien zur russischen Musik,* Munich, 1923, Vol. I; Newman, Ernest, "Glinka," *The New Witness,* 1917.

WAGNER

Richard Wilhelm Wagner was born May 22, 1813, at Leipzig. From his eleventh year he showed an aptitude for literature: during his sixteenth year, an audition of Beethoven's symphonies turned him toward music. His first musical master was Gottlieb Müller, his second and last Theodore Weinlig. At nineteen he wrote a Symphony; during the same year he wrote his first opera libretto (*Die Hochzeit*). Engaged as chorus master at Würzburg in 1833, he there composed his first opera, *Die Feen.* Next year he was music director at Magdeburg, and in 1836 finished his second opera, *Das Liebesverbot.* After engagements at Königsburg and Riga, Wagner went with his wife, Minna Planer, to Paris, where he struggled desperately for opportunities to do his work, and actually composed his Faust Overture. After three years he went to Dresden, where in 1842 *Rienzi* was performed with great success, and where

BIOGRAPHICAL APPENDIX

next year Wagner became royal music director. *Der Fliegende Holländer* had its première in 1843, and during the next five years Wagner wrote *Tannhäuser* (Dresden, 1845; Paris version, Paris, 1860) and *Lohengrin* (Weimar, 1850). Embroiled in the political unrest of 1848, he had to flee Germany, and went first to Paris and later to Zurich, which he made his headquarters till 1859. Here he composed two-thirds of the *Ring* and most of *Tristan*. During the next two years he was in Paris, where at the instance of Napoleon III *Tannhäuser* was mounted at the Opéra: due to the machinations of a cabal, it had to be withdrawn after the third performance. In 1861 Wagner went to Vienna; two years later Ludwig II of Bavaria called him to Munich. Here, *Tristan* was performed in 1865, *Die Meistersinger* in 1868; also, the first two parts of the *Ring*. In 1865, however, Wagner had again to withdraw to Switzerland; here, in 1870, he married Cosima Liszt von Bülow. In 1872 the couple moved to Bayreuth, where in 1876 the *Ring* was given in its entirety at the Wagner Festspieltheater; and *Parsifal* was given in 1882. Wagner died in Venice February 13, 1883.

Operas and Music dramas: *Die Feen; Das Liebesverbot; Rienzi; Der Fliegende Holländer; Tannhäuser; Lohengrin; Das Rheingold; Die Walküre; Tristan und Isolde; Siegfried; Die Meistersinger von Nürnberg; Götterdämmerung; Parsifal*. Symphony in C; *Eine Faust-Ouverture;* Overtures *Polonia* and *Columbus; Siegfried Idyl;* Huldigungsmarsch; Kaisermarsch; etc. Eleven songs; numerous arrangements. Ten volumes of literary works.

Adler, Guido, *Richard Wagner,* Leipzig, 1904; Baudelaire, Charles, *Richard Wagner et Tannhäuser à Paris,* Paris, 1894; Bekker, Paul, *Richard Wagner,* Norton, 1931; Chamberlain, H. S., *Richard Wagner,* Bayreuth, 1894; Lichtenberger, Henri, *Richard Wagner, poète et penseur,* new ed., Paris, 1931; Mann, Thomas, *Past Masters and Other Papers,* Knopf, 1933; Newman, Ernest, *The Life of Richard Wagner,* Knopf, 1933, Vol. I; Nietzsche, Friedrich, *The Case of Wagner,* Macmillan, 1896, and *Götzen-Dämmerung,* Berlin, 1906; Rolland, Romain, *Musicians of To-day,* Holt, 1915; Shaw, G. B., *The Perfect Wagnerite,* Scribner, 1899.

BIOGRAPHICAL APPENDIX

COSIMA WAGNER

Cosima Liszt was born in Bellagio December 25, 1837. She was married to Hans von Bülow on August 18, 1857; to Richard Wagner August 25, 1870. She died in Bayreuth April 1, 1930.

Chamberlain, H. S., *Briefe 1882-1924 und Briefwechsel mit Kaiser Wilhelm II,* Munich, 1928, 2 vols.; Du Moulin-Eckart, R. M. F., Graf, *Cosima Wagner,* Knopf, 1930, 2 vols.; Seillière, E. A. A. L., Baron, *Le néoromantisme en Allemagne,* Paris, 1928-31, 2 vols. in 1.

MOUSSORGSKY

Modeste Petrovich Moussorgsky was born March 16, 1835, in Karevo in the government of Pskov. His parents were members of the lesser nobility. His mother gave him his first piano lessons. At the age of ten he was sent to the school of St. Peter and St. Paul in St. Petersburg. He took pianoforte lessons from a Professor Herke or Gerke. At the age of twelve he played a *Rondo de Concert* by Herz in public. In 1852 he matriculated at the School for Ensigns, and in the same year his first composition, a polka, was published. While serving as an officer in the Preobrajensky Guards, in 1856 he made the acquaintance of Borodin. Soon after, he met Dargomyjski. In his own words, "for the first time, he lived the musical life." Later he made the acquaintance of Cui, Balakirew and Rimsky-Korsakoff; it was Balakirew who inferred Moussorgsky's dramatic gift, and set him to work on an *Oedipus,* and gave him lessons in composition. In 1859, a nervous malady prevented him from working. Directly after his convalescence, Moussorgsky resigned from the guards and set earnestly to work. To support himself, he took a position in the government service; and shared his quarters with several friends. In 1865 he was once more attacked by his nervous malady, and had to retire to his brother's in the country. In 1869 he returned to St. Petersburg, and lived with his friends the Opotchinines. His hour of success came in 1874,

BIOGRAPHICAL APPENDIX

with the performance of *Boris Goudonow*. In 1879 he resigned his post, and sought to support himself by playing accompaniments. He died in 1881 in a military hospital.

Operas: *Boris Goudonow; Khovanstchina; The Matchmaker* (one act only); *The Fair at Sorochinsk* (fragmentary). For chorus and orchestra: *The Destruction of Sennacherib; Joshua Navin;* orchestral fantasia, *Night on the Bare Mountain*. Numerous songs. For piano: *Pictures from an Exhibition* (orchestrated by Ravel).

Calvocoressi, M. D., *Musorgsky,* Dutton, 1921; Riesemann, Oskar von, *Moussorgsky,* Knopf, 1929; Rivière, Jacques, *Etudes,* 7th ed., Paris, 1924; Rosenfeld, Paul, *Musical Portraits,* Harcourt, Brace, 1920; Wolfurt, Kurt von, *Mussórgskij,* Stuttgart, 1927.

STRAUSS

Richard Strauss was born in Munich June 11, 1864. His father, Franz Strauss, was first horn-player in the Munich Court Orchestra, and a pronounced anti-Wagnerite; his mother was the daughter of the brewer Georg Pschorr. Strauss began composing at the age of six. From 1870 to 1874 he attended the elementary school at Munich; from 1874 to 1882, the Gymnasium; and during the next year, the University. From 1875 to 1880 he studied harmony, counterpoint, and instrumentation with Hofkapellmeister F. W. Meyer. His compositions were performed publicly from 1880 onward. In 1885 he made the acquaintance of Alexander Ritter, who, together with Hans von Bülow, is said to have converted young Strauss, until then a good Brahmsian, to modernism and Wagnerism. In 1885, at Bülow's invitation, Strauss conducted a concert of the Meiningen Orchestra, and in November of that year he succeeded Bülow as conductor of the organization. In 1886 he became third kapellmeister at the Munich Opera; in 1889, director at Weimar. 1892-93 was spent by him in Egypt and Sicily after an attack of inflammation of the lungs. In 1894 he became chief kapellmeister in Munich: in 1895, his extensive European concert tours commenced, Strauss conducting in Budapest, Brussels, Moscow, Amsterdam, London, Barcelona, Paris, Zurich, and Madrid. In 1898

BIOGRAPHICAL APPENDIX

he became conductor of the Berlin Royal Opera. In 1904 he came to America to conduct at four festival concerts given in his honor in New York. In one month he gave twenty-one concerts in different cities with nearly as many orchestras. The tour ended with an hubbub over the fact that Strauss had conducted a concert in the auditorium of the Wanamaker store: the world had come to consciousness that the most original of living German composers saw no conflict between art and commercialism. From 1898 till 1918 Strauss resided chiefly in Charlottenburg and in the summer at Marquardstein near Garmisch. After the war he became general music director in Vienna; and once again in 1921 toured America.

Operas and Music dramas: *Guntram; Feuersnot; Salomé; Elektra; Der Rosenkavalier; Ariadne auf Naxos; Die Frau ohne Schatten; Die Aegyptische Helena; Intermezzo; Arabella.* Ballets: *Josephs Legende* and *Schlagobers.* Orchestra: *Burleske; Aus Italien; Macbeth; Don Juan; Till Eulenspiegel's Lustige Streiche; Also Sprach Zarathustra; Don Quixote; Ein Heldenleben; Sinfonia Domestica; Eine Alpensinfonie.* Choruses: a melodrama, *Enoch Arden;* numerous songs; early Sonatas, Concertos; several arrangements.

Finck, H. T., *Richard Strauss,* Little, Brown, 1917; Gilman, Lawrence, *The Music of To-morrow,* Lane, 1906; Gray, Cecil, *A Survey of Contemporary Music,* Oxford Press, 1924; Huneker, J. G., *Overtones,* Scribner, 1904; Mason, D. G., *Contemporary Composers,* Macmillan, 1918; Pannain, Guido, *Modern Composers,* Dutton, 1933; Rolland, Romain, *Musicians of To-day,* Holt, 1915; Specht, Richard, *Richard Strauss und sein Werke,* Leipzig, 1921, 2 vols.

D'INDY

Paul Marie Théodore Vincent d'Indy was born in Paris March 27, 1851, of an old noble family originating in Hérault. Having lost his mother in infancy, he was educated by his grandmother, who was his first music mistress. He studied for three years under Diémer, attended Marmontel's class, and learned harmony and the

BIOGRAPHICAL APPENDIX

elements of composition under Lavignac. During the Franco-Prussian War he served with the Garde Mobile; after the war, in the hope of overcoming his family's objection to his choice of the musical profession, he submitted a quartet to César Franck. Franck recognized his gift, and accepted D'Indy as his pupil in his organ class. In 1874 D'Indy obtained a second *accessit* from the Conservatoire, and a first the following year. In 1876 he attended the first performance of the *Ring* in Bayreuth, and traveled to Vienna to present to Brahms a dedicated copy of Franck's *Redemption*. His own *Piccolomini* had been presented in Paris by Pasdeloup. Beginning in 1875 he became chorus master of the Celonne concerts, and later of the Lamoureux. In 1884 he won the prize of the musical competition of the City of Paris with his dramatic legend *Le Chant de la Cloche*. With Guilmaunt and Bordes, in 1894 he founded the Schola Cantorum, which rapidly rose to an institution of tremendous influence under his leadership. He visited America several times as a conductor, the last time in 1921. He died in 1932.

Operas: *Attendez-moi sous l'Orme; Le Chant de la Cloche; Fervaal; L'Etranger; La Légende de Saint-Christophe*. Orchestra: *Wallenstein Trilogy; Saugefleurie; Symphonie Cevenole; Istar; Variations Symphoniques; Symphony in B Flat; Jour d'Eté sur la Montagne; Sinfonia Brevis de Bello Gallico*. Incidental music for *Karadec* and *Medée*; Sonata for violin and piano; piano Sonata in B Minor; two *String Quartets; Cours de Composition Musicale;* songs; etc.

Aubry, G. J., *La musique française d'aujourd'hui,* Paris, 1915; Bernard, Robert, *Les tendences de la musique française moderne,* Paris, 1930; Borgex, Louis, *Vincent d'Indy,* Paris, 1913; Cœuroy, André, *La musique française moderne,* Paris, 1922; Cortot, A. D., *La musique française de piano,* Paris, 1932, Vol. II; Gilman, Lawrence, *The Music of To-morrow,* Lane, 1906; Mason, D. G., *Contemporary Composers,* Macmillan, 1918; Imbert, Hugu005, "Vincent d'Indy," in Gray, *Studies in Music,* Scribner, 1901.

BIOGRAPHICAL APPENDIX

RAVEL

Maurice Ravel was born in Ciboure, Basses-Pyrénées, March 7, 1875. Shortly after his birth his family moved to Paris. His first piano teacher was Henri Ghis, his first teacher of composition, Charles René. He received piano lessons from Ricardo Viñes, and in 1891 was awarded a "première médaille" in piano-playing at the Conservatoire. In 1897 he entered the class of Fauré; his *Sites Auriculaires* were publicly performed in 1904. In 1901 he failed for the first time to gain the Prix de Rome. His quartet was performed in 1904; and a year later he failed for the fourth time to gain the Prix de Rome. *Histoires Naturelles* were performed in 1907, the *Rapsodie Espagnole,* in 1908; *L'Heure Espagnole,* at the Opéra Comique in 1911. *Daphnis et Chloë* was given by the Russian Ballet in 1912 and by the Opéra in 1921. During the war Ravel served as an ambulance-driver, and was wounded before Verdun. He was dismissed from service. At present he lives near Paris. In 1928 he made a tour of the United States.

Opera: *L'Heure Espagnole*. Ballets: *Ma Mère l'Oye; Daphnis et Chloë; Adélaïde; L'Enfant et les Sortilèges*. Orchestra: *Rapsodie Espagnole; La Valse; Boléro*. Piano Concerto; piano Concerto for the left hand; *Tzigane* for orchestra and violin; String Quartet; pianoforte Trio; Introduction and Allegro for harp. For piano: *Sonatine; Miroirs; Gaspard de la Nuit; Valses Nobles et Sentimentales; Le Tombeau de Couperin* (arranged for orchestra); Sonata for violin and viola. For piano and violin: songs with orchestra: *Scheherazade; Histoires Naturelles; Trois Poèmes de Stéphane Mallarmé; Chansons Madécasses*. For voice and piano: *Cinq Mélodies Populaires Grecques; Sainte;* etc.

Aubry, G. J., *La musique française d'aujourd'hui,* Paris, 1915; Bernard, Robert, *Les tendences de la musique française moderne,* Paris, 1930; Cœuroy, André, *La musique française moderne,* Paris, 1922; Cortot, A. D., *La musique française de piano,* Paris, 1932; Gray, Cecil, *A Survey of Contemporary Music,* Oxford Press, 1924; Manuel, Roland, *Maurice Ravel,* Paris, 1914; *Revue musicale,* 1925

BIOGRAPHICAL APPENDIX

(articles by Suarès, Klingsor, Manuel, etc.); Pannain, Guido, *Modern Composers,* Dutton, 1933; Shera, F. H., *Debussy and Ravel,* Oxford Press, 1923.

SCRIABIN

Alexander Nicholas Scriabin was born in Moscow in 1871 of aristocratic parents. In his tenth year he was placed in the Second Moscow Army Cadet Corps. His first piano lessons were taken from G. A. Conus. Musical theory he studied with S. I. Taneieff. While continuing the Cadet courses, he matriculated as a student of the Moscow Conservatory of Music. Here he studied pianoforte with Safinoff, counterpoint first with Taneieff and later with Arensky. His studies both in the Conservatory and in the corps were completed by 1891. In 1892 he toured Europe for the first time as a pianist, playing in Amsterdam, Brussels, The Hague, Paris, Berlin, Moscow, and St. Petersburg. The next five years Scriabin devoted both to concert tours and to composition. In 1897 he became professor of pianoforte at the Moscow Conservatory, remaining such for six years. In 1903 he resigned from the post in order to devote himself entirely to composition and concertizing, and made his residence in Beattenberg, Switzerland. It was during this time that he was converted to theosophy. He spent 1905-06 in Genoa and Geneva. In February, 1906, Scriabin embarked on a tour of the United States, and played in New York, Chicago, Washington, Cincinnati, and other cities. The next two years he spent in Beattenberg, Lausanne, and Biarritz; from 1908 to 1910 he lived in Brussels. Then he returned to Moscow, and toured Russia in 1910, 1911, and 1912. In 1914 he visited England for the first time. Returning to Russia just before the outbreak of the World War, he set to work on a piece involving the unification of all the arts, entitled *Mysterium.* He died on April 14, 1915, of blood poisoning.

Orchestra: Two Symphonies (the first with chorus); *The Divine Poem; The Poem of Ecstasy; Prometheus;* Concerto for piano and orchestra. Piano: Ten Sonatas; numerous poems, preludes, mazourkas, études, etc.

BIOGRAPHICAL APPENDIX

Bauer, Marion, *Twentieth Century Music,* Putnam, 1934; Gray, Cecil, *A Survey of Contemporary Music,* Oxford Press, 1924; Heyman, K. R. W., *The Relation of Ultramodern to Archaic Music,* Small, Maynard, 1921; Hull, A. E., *A Great Russian Tone-Poet: Scriabin,* Dutton, 1917; Montagu-Nathan, Montagu, *Contemporary Russian Composers,* Stokes, 1917; Rosenfeld, Paul, *Musical Portraits,* Harcourt, Brace, 1920; Swan, A. J., *Music 1900-1930,* Norton, 1929.

BLOCH

Ernest Bloch was born in Geneva, Switzerland, July 24, 1880. He studied in Geneva with Jacques Dalcroze; in Brussels with Ysaye; in Frankfurt at the Hoch Conservatory under Knorr; and in Munich under Thuille. From 1902 to 1904 he lived in Paris; in 1909 and 1910 he conducted in Neuchâtel and in Lausanne. His opera *Macbeth* was produced at the Opéra Comique in Paris in 1910. From 1911 to 1915 he lived in Geneva; in the latter year, he was appointed professor of composition in the Genevan conservatory. In 1916 he came to America as the conductor of the Maud Allan Symphony Orchestra. His quartet was performed in New York by the Flonzaleys that season, and in May, 1917, the Society of the Friends of Music devoted a concert entirely to his works. Returning to Switzerland in the summer, he once more voyaged to America, this time with the intention of settling here. He taught composition at the David Mannes School from 1917 to 1919. In September, 1919, he won the Coolidge Prize with his Suite for viola. From 1920 to 1925 he was the director of the Institute of Music in Cleveland, and from 1925 to 1928 of that in San Francisco. In 1929 he won the Victor Prize with his symphony *America*. Once more returning to Switzerland, he remained there until 1934, when his *Sacred Service* was performed in New York under his baton.

Opera: *Macbeth*. Choral: *Avodath Hakodesh* (with baritone). Symphony in C Sharp Minor; *Vivre-Aimer; Hiver-Printemps; Trois Poèmes Juifs; Trois Psaumes* (22nd for baritone, 14th and

BIOGRAPHICAL APPENDIX

137th for soprano); *Poèmes d'Automne* (for mezzo-soprano); *Schelomo; Israel* (two movements, second with voices); *Concerto Grosso; America* (with chorus); Suite for viola and piano or orchestra; String Quintet; String Quartet; two Sonatas for violin and piano; smaller pieces for string quartet and violin and piano.

Gatti, G. M., *Musicisti moderni d'Italia e di fuori,* 2d ed., Bologna, 1925; Pannain, Guido, *Modern Composers,* Dutton, 1933; Pizzetti, Ildebrando, *Musicisti contemporanei,* Milan, 1914; Rosenfeld, Paul, *Musical Portraits,* Harcourt, Brace, 1920; *Musical Chronicle (1917-1923),* Harcourt, Brace, 1923; and *By Way of Art,* Coward-McCann, 1928; Sessions, Roger, "Ernest Bloch," *Modern Music,* 1927; Tibaldi-Chiesa, Mary, *Ernest Bloch,* Turin, 1933.

STRAWINSKY

Igor Federovitch Strawinsky was born at Oranienbaum near Leningrad June 5, 1882. His father was a famous bass singer attached to the court theaters. Igor was destined for a legal career; but in 1902 after a meeting with Rimsky-Korsakoff in Heidelberg, he abandoned all idea of studying the law, and took lessons with Rimsky till 1906. His *Scherzo Fantastique,* inspired by Maeterlinck's *Life of the Bee,* was given in 1908, and attracted the attention of Sergei Diaghilew, then ambitious to be the Lorenzo the Magnificent of Russian art. Diaghilew commissioned the young composer to write a work for his ballet: the result was *The Fire Bird*. From that time till its dissolution, Strawinsky was closely connected with the Diaghilew organization: the production of his ballets was the feature of its Parisian seasons. *Petrushka,* composed in 1911, was given the following year; and in 1913, *Le Sacre du Printemps,* composed in Clarens in 1912. Strawinsky had suddenly become the most sensational composer in Europe, and during the World War his figure grew more and more eminent. In Switzerland and in Rome during the conflict, Strawinsky completed *Les Noces,* and wrote *Renard* at the order of the Princesse de Polignac, and *L'Histoire du Soldat* in collaboration with the Swiss poet Ramuz. After the war he resided in Morges; eventually

BIOGRAPHICAL APPENDIX

he became a citizen of the French Republic. He visited the United States twice, once in 1926, once in 1935. Since the disappearance of the Diaghilew ballet, he has written pieces for the Paris opera season of Mme. Ida Rubinstein, and for the Boston Symphony Orchestra.

Operas: *Le Rossignol; Mavra; Oedipus Rex.* Melodramas: *L'Histoire du Soldat, Perséphone.* Ballets with chorus, etc.: *Renard, Les Noces.* Ballets: *Petrushka; Le Sacre du Printemps; Pulcinella* (after Pergolesi); *Apollon Musagète; Le Baiser de la Fée* (after Tchaikowsky). Symphony with choruses (*Symphonie des Psaumes*); Symphonies for Wind Instruments; *Fireworks;* Piano Concerto, *Capriccio;* violin Concerto; Octuor for wind; Rag-time. Concertino for string quartet; three pieces for String Quartet. Piano: Sonata; Serenade. Numerous songs. Prose: *Chroniques de ma vie.*

Cœuroy, André, *Panorama de la musique contemporaine,* Paris, 1928; Collaer, Paul, *Strawinsky,* Brussels, 1931; Fleischer, Herbert, *Strawinsky,* Berlin, 1931; Gray, Cecil, *A Survey of Contemporary Music,* Oxford Press, 1924; Pannain, Guido, *Modern Composers,* Dutton, 1933; Rosenfeld, Paul, *Musical Portraits,* Harcourt, Brace, 1920; Schaeffner, André, *Strawinsky,* Paris, Rieder, 1931; Schloezer, Boris de, "Igor Stravinsky," *Revue musicale,* 1923.

BARTÓK

Béla Bartók was born in Nagy Szent Miklós, Hungary (now Rumania), on March 25, 1881. His father died during his extreme youth. From his twelfth to his fifteenth year he was a piano pupil of Lászlo Erkel in Preszburg. From 1899 to 1903 he studied in the Royal Academy in Budapest: piano with Stephan Thoman and composition with Hans Koezler. Since 1907 he has been professor of piano in that institution. During the Communist dictatorship in Hungary, Bartók along with Kodaly and Dohnanyi was intrusted with the general directorship of music. He toured the United States in 1928, playing his own works; and appeared on programs with Szegeti in Rome in 1929. Bartók has recorded and

BIOGRAPHICAL APPENDIX

published innumerable folk songs of Hungary and the Balkans and written extensively about this and the Arabian folk music: it is said that he has in his possession some 2,700 Hungarian, 2,500 Rumanian, and 200 Arabian unpublished songs.

Opera: *Duke Bluebeard's Castle.* Ballets: *The Wood-carved Prince; The Singular Mandarin.* Orchestra: *Two Portraits; Two Images; Dance Suite.* Concerto for pianoforte; five String Quartets; violin Sonata. Piano: Sonata; *Bagatelles; Esquisses;* Suite; Rumanian dances; *Nénies; Allegro Barbaro; Etudes; Impromptu;* collections of short pieces; many transcriptions. Prose: *The Hungarian Folk Music,* Oxford Press, 1931; *The Musical Dialect of the Roumanians; The Folk Music of the Arabians of Biskra.*

Leichtentritt, Henri, "On the Art of Béla Bartók," *Modern Music,* 1928; Nuell, Edwin van der, *Béla Bartók,* Halle, 1930; Pannain, Guido, *Modern Composers,* Dutton, 1933.

SCHOENBERG

Arnold Schoenberg was born in Vienna September 13, 1874. He was self-taught until his twentieth year, when he received his first instruction from his brother-in-law, Alexander von Zemlinsky. In 1901 he went to Berlin and became kapellmeister of the Ueberbrettl, the esthetic cabaret conducted by Birnbaum, Wedekind, and Von Wolzogen. Owing to the influence of Strauss, he secured a position as an instructor in the Stern Conservatory. In 1903 he returned to Vienna; where, thanks to the interest it aroused in Gustav Mahler, his work gained several performances. In 1910 Schoenberg, who had been teaching privately, was appointed teacher in the Imperial Academy. He was the first to benefit by the fund left by Mahler for creative musicians. In 1911 he returned to Berlin, where he taught and worked till 1916. In 1918, back in Vienna again, he founded the Society for Private Musical Performances. In 1920-21 he lectured in Amsterdam. Until 1925 he resided in Mödling near Vienna; in that year he succeeded Busoni as instructor of composition in the Normal School in Berlin. In 1932 he was in Barce-

BIOGRAPHICAL APPENDIX

lona, and in 1933 he came to America and taught in Boston. He is at present residing in California.

Music dramas: *Erwartung* (monodrama); *Die Glückliche Hand*. Melodrama: *Dreimahls Sieben Gedichte aus Albert Giraud's Pierrot Lunaire*. Cantatas: *Gurrelieder; Die Jakobsleiter*. Orchestra: *Pelléas und Mélisande; Kammersymphonie;* five Pieces; Variations. A capella choruses; Serenade for bass voice and seven instruments; Suite for seven instruments; woodwind Quintet; three String Quartets. Piano: Suite; smaller pieces; numerous songs and ballads. Prose: *Harmonielehre*.

Berg, Alban, *Guide to Gurrelieder,* Universal Verlag, 1912; Cœuroy, André, *Panorama de la musique contemporaine,* 4th ed., Paris, 1928; Gray, Cecil, *A Survey of Contemporary Music,* Oxford Press, 1924; Pannain, Guido, *Modern Composers,* Dutton, 1933; Stefan-Gruenfeldt, Paul, *Arnold Schoenberg,* Vienna, 1924; Wellesz, Egon, *Arnold Schoenberg,* London, 1925.

BERG

Alban Berg was born in Vienna February 9, 1885. His father was a merchant from Nuremberg. His musical gift was apparent at an early age, but he was self-taught until 1904, in which year he met Schoenberg. The latter has been his only teacher, and constant adviser. In 1908, Berg's Op. I, a piano Sonata, was published. He married Helène Nabowska in 1911; and in the same year he began taking pupils. With his guide to an analysis of the *Gurrelieder* he became the most articulate of the champions of his master, and has continued to defend him and comment on him in numerous articles. From 1914 to 1920 he was at work on *Wozzeck*. After the World War, Schoenberg appointed him director of the Viennese Society for Private Musical Performances. Excepting for a few brief trips, Berg was a constant resident of the Kaiserstadt; here he taught and was a leading member of many musical organizations. He was also the recipient of the Arts prize of the city of Vienna; and was at one time a member of the Prussian Academy of Fine Arts. He died suddenly, Dec. 24, 1935.

BIOGRAPHICAL APPENDIX

Music dramas: *Wozzeck; Lulu.* Concert aria: *Der Wein.* Orchestra: *Three Pieces; Chamber Concerto* for violin, piano, and thirteen winds. *Lyric Suite* for String Quartet; String Quartet; *Four Pieces* for clarinet and piano; piano Sonata. Songs, several with orchestral accompaniment.

Machabey, Arno, "Berg," *Menestral,* 1930; Reich, Willi, *A Guide to Wozzeck,* League of Composers, New York, 1931; Wiesengrund-Adorno, Theodor, "Berg and Webern—Schönberg's Heirs," *Modern Music,* 1931.

HINDEMITH

Violist and composer, Paul Hindemith was born November 16, 1895, in Hanau. At the age of ten he began the study of music, especially that of his personal instrument, the viola; composition he studied with A. Mendelssohn and Bernhard Seekles at the Hoch Conservatory in Frankfurt. From 1915 to 1923 he was first concert master in the opera orchestra in Frankfurt; after that, violist in his brother Rudolph's Amar-Quartet. He was the soul of the Donaueschingen and Baden-Baden festivals of modern music. In 1927 he became master teacher of composition in the Berlin Normal School. Owing to the interference of the Nazis, his opera *Matthis der Mahler* was forbidden the stage in Germany. Hindemith is said at present to be in Switzerland.

Operas: *Mörder, Hoffnung der Frauen; Das Nusch-Nuschi; Sancta Susanna; Cardillac; Hin und Zurück; Das Lehrstück; Neues vom Tage; Matthis der Mahler.* Radio opera: *Sabinchen.* Orchestra: Concerto. Two piano Concerti; violin Concerto; cello Concerto; viola Concerto; Concerto for wind instruments; Concerto for brass; Concerto with organ. Four String Quartets; string Trios; three Sonatas for violin and piano; Sonatas for cello and piano, viola and piano, two for viola solo. Three song cycles: *Die Junge Magd, Das Marienleben, Die Serenaden.* Songs; piano music; etc.

Adler, Guido, *Handbuch der Musikgeschichte,* 2d ed., Berlin, 1930, 2 vols.; Fraser, A. A., *Essays on Music,* Oxford Press, 1930;

BIOGRAPHICAL APPENDIX

Pannain, Guido, *Modern Composers,* J. M. Dent and Sons, Ltd., 1932; Scott, Marian, "Paul Hindemith," Musical Association, London, *Proceedings,* 1930; Strobel, Heinrich, *Paul Hindemith,* 2d ed. rev., Mainz, 1931.

MILHAUD

Darius Milhaud was born September 4, 1892, in Aix in Provence. He was a pupil of Gédalge and of Widor. In 1915 he took the first prize of the Paris Conservatory. During the World War he was in Brazil with Claudel; and when he became a member of Cocteau's Group of Six in 1919, he did so—in contrast to the other five—as a composer of some little fame. He has been in the United States on several occasions.

Operas: *La Brébis Egarée; Juarez et Maximilien; Le Pauvre Matelot; Les Malheurs d'Orphée; Christophe Colomb.* Incidental music to: *Les Choéphores* and *Protée.* Ballets: *Le Bœuf sur le Toit; L'Homme et son Désir; La Création du Monde; Le Train Bleu.* Concerto for percussion and orchestra; six Symphonies for small orchestra; five String Quartets; two Sonatas for violin and piano; Sonata for piano and two violins; piano Sonata; *Los Saudades do Brazil;* numerous songs.

Cœuroy, André, *La musique française moderne,* Paris, 1922; Copland, Aaron, "The Lyricism of Milhaud," *Modern Music,* 1928; Krenek, Ernst, "Darius Milhaud," *Anbruch,* 1930; Landormy, Paul, "Darius Milhaud," *Musikblätter des Anbruch,* 1926; Schloezer, Boris de, "Darius Milhaud," *Revue musicale,* 1925.

AURIC

Georges Auric was born February 15, 1899, in Lodic in Hérault. He was a pupil of G. Caussade's at the Paris Conservatory, and of D'Indy's at the Schola Cantorum. He came to celebrity first as a member of Cocteau's Group of Six. He has been musical critic of *Les nouvelles littéraires.* Auric resides in Paris.

BIOGRAPHICAL APPENDIX

Opera: *La Reine de Couer*. Ballets: *Les Noces de Gamache; Les Fâcheux; Les Pélicans; Les Matelots; La Pastorale; Les Enchantements d'Alcine*. Orchestra: *Adieu, New York*, foxtrot. Piano: *Trois Pastorales*. Songs: *Les Joues en Feu;* also songs to words by Cocteau and Gérard de Nerval.

Schaeffner, André, "Georges Auric," *Modern Music,* 1928; Schloezer, Boris de, *"Georges Auric,"* *Revue musicale,* 1926; Wortham, H. E., "Auric and Poulenc," *British Musician,* 1927.

SHOSTAKOVICH

Dmitri Shostakovich was born in St. Petersburg on September 25, 1906. He matriculated at the Petrograd Conservatory in 1919, and studied piano under Nikolaiev, composition under Steinberg. Advanced composition he studied under Glazounov. He left the conservatory in 1925. His opera *Lady Macbeth of Mzensk* was first performed in 1931.

Opera: *Lady Macbeth of Mzensk*. Incidental music: *The Nose*. Orchestra: *First Symphony; October Symphony; May Day*. Concerto for piano and orchestra. Ballet: *The Golden Age*. Music for various movies; two pieces for String Octet; piano Sonata; short pieces.

Sabaneyev, L. L., *Modern Russian Composers,* International Publishers, 1927; *Musical Courier,* July 14, 1934; New York *Times,* Dec. 5, 1931.

WEILL

Kurt Weill was born on March 2, 1900, in Dessau. He studied under Albert Bing; in 1918, under Humperdinck in the Berlin Hochschule. In 1919 and 1920 he conducted theater orchestras in the provinces. He was a pupil of Busoni's in 1921. In 1932 he left Germany for Vienna and Paris. At present he is in the United States.

Operas: *Royal Palace; Der Tsar Läszt Sich Photographieren;*

BIOGRAPHICAL APPENDIX

Mahagonny; The Beggar's Opera. Orchestra: *Three Nocturnes.* Radio drama: *Die Lindberghflug* (with Hindemith).

Bekker, Paul, *Briefe an Zeitgenossiche Musiker,* Berlin, 1932; Machabey, Armand, *"Kurt Weill et le drame lyrique allemand," Revue d'Allemagne,* 1933; Noth, E. E., *"Le compositeur Kurt Weill," Les cahiers du sud,* 1935; Stefan, Paul, *"Antinomie der neuen Oper," Musikblätter des Anbruch,* 1928; Thomson, Virgil, "Most Melodious Tears," *Modern Music,* 1933.

VARESE

Edgar Varèse was born in Paris November 14, 1886. He studied music at the Schola Cantorum under D'Indy and Roussel in 1903, and at the Conservatoire under Ganaye and Widor from 1903 to 1906. During his student years he organized and conducted the chorus of the Université Populaire, and the concerts of the Château du Peuple. He received the *bourse* of the City of Paris in 1907. During these years he enjoyed the friendly counsels of Debussy and of Franck; later, in Germany, where he resided from 1907 to 1913, those of Mahler, Muck, Strauss, and Busoni. While in Berlin he organized a Symphonischer Chor, for the purpose of performing the old motets; this chorus participated in several of Max Reinhardt's productions. Mobilized in the French army in 1914, he was honorably discharged from it in 1915, and came to America in 1916; here, in New York in 1917, he conducted in honor of the dead of all nations a performance of Berlioz's *Requiem.* In 1919 he founded the New Symphony Orchestra for the purpose of performing modern and unknown classical music. Two years later he founded the first American modern-music society, the International Composers Guild: he was its director during six seasons. At the same time, he taught in a private capacity. In 1928 he founded the Pan-American Association of composers. He has made extensive researches in the domain of sound in relation with the new concepts of music. He was in Paris from 1929 to 1932. At present he is residing in New York.

Orchestra: *Trois Poèmes pour Orchestre; La Chanson des Jeunes*

BIOGRAPHICAL APPENDIX

Hommes; Rapsodie Romane; Prélude à la Fin d'un Jour; Bourgoyne; Mehr Licht; Gargantua; Les Cycles du Nord; Amériques (new version, 1928); *Arcanes* (new version, 1932); *Espace* (in preparation). Orchestral Ensembles: *Offrandes* (with soprano); *Hyperprism* (wind and percussion); *Octandre* (wind and double bass); *Intégrales; Ionization* (percussion); *Equatorials* (with bass voice).

Articles on Varèse by José André in *La Nacion,* Buenos Aires, 1930; by Alejo Carpentier in *Social,* Havana, 1929, and *Le cahier,* 1929; by Carlos Chavez in *Aelos,* 1927; by Frederick Clutsam in *The Sackbut,* 1924, and Kenneth Curwen in the same, 1925; by Robert Desnos in *Le merle,* 1929; by Artur Hoéré in *Les cahiers de Belgique,* 1929; by René Julliard in *Le cahier,* 1932; by Dane Rudhyar in the *New Pearson's,* 1923; by M. Zanotti-Bianco in the *Arts,* 1925; Paul Rosenfeld, *An Hour with American Music,* Lippincott, 1929.

GERSHWIN

George Gershwin was born in Brooklyn September 28, 1898. He grew up on the lower East Side of New York; his first piano lessons cost his parents 25 cents an hour. In his seventeenth year he found his first job as a pianist in tin-pan alley. *La, La, Lucille* was the first musical comedy to which he contributed musical numbers; in the following years, he contributed largely to George White's *Scandals.* He became famous as a composer of jazz music and musical comedy hits. Later he began writing more seriously, and studied in New York. In 1923 he met Paul Whiteman, and the *Rhapsody in Blue* was performed at the end of that year. In 1931 *Of Thee I Sing* was awarded the Pulitzer Prize. *Porgy* was produced in the fall of 1935. Gershwin lives in New York and is an amateur painter.

Opera: *Porgy;* "Blue Monday": *135th Street.* Orchestra: *Rhapsody in Blue; An American in Paris; Second Rhapsody; Cuban Overture; Variations on an Original Theme.* Concerto for piano and orchestra. Musical Comedies: George White's *Scandals 1919-1921;*

BIOGRAPHICAL APPENDIX

Lady, Be Good!; Oh, Kay!; Funny Face; Girl Crazy; Of Thee I Sing; Strike Up the Band; Let 'Em Eat Cake, etc. Piano pieces.
Goldberg, Isaac, *George Gershwin,* Simon & Schuster, 1931.

COWELL

Henry Cowell was born in Menlo Park, California, March 11, 1897. He studied music at the University of California and at the Institute of Applied Arts in New York. He has composed prolifically since his twentieth year. He went to Russia in 1929. In 1931 he received a Guggenheim Fellowship. He is director of the New Music Edition, the New Music Society of California, the North Atlantic Section of the Pan-American Association of Composers, and has been director of the musical activities of the New School of Social Research. He is the author of books and articles on modern musical subjects, and has lectured extensively. Works of his have been performed by the Berlin Philharmonic, the Orchestra Symphonique de Paris, the Budapest Symphony, the Philadelphia Symphony Orchestra, and numerous modern musical organizations in America and abroad.

Orchestra: *Synchrony; Some Music; Two Appositions;* Concerto for piano and orchestra; *Rhythmicana* for rhythmicon and orchestra; *Sinfonietta* for chamber orchestra; *Polyphonica* for chamber orchestra; *Exultation* for string orchestra; *Four Continuations* for string orchestra. *Reel; Ensemble* for eight woodwinds; *Ensemble* for String Quartet and thunder stick; two String Quartets. Numerous pieces for pianoforte; numerous songs. Prose: *New Musical Resources,* Knopf, 1930; ed. and partly author, *American Composers on American Music,* Stanford University Press, 1933; numerous articles.

Slonimsky, Nicholas, "Henry Cowell," in *American Composers on American Music,* see above; Ewen, David, *Composers of Today,* Wilson, 1934.

BIOGRAPHICAL APPENDIX

IVES

Charles E. Ives was born in Danbury, Connecticut, Oct. 20, 1876. His first musical teacher was his father. Ives matriculated at Yale with the class of 1898; he studied under Horatio Parker. He also studied music with Dudley Buck and Rowe Shelley. After graduation he became an insurance man in New York, clerking for the Mutual Life Insurance Co.; simultaneously holding the position of a church organist and making time for composition. In 1906 the insurance firm of Ives and Meyrinck was formed. The first public performance of Ives' music was by Pro Musica in 1927. Since then his works have been performed by the Pan-American Association in New York, Paris, Berlin, and Budapest, by the New Music Society in San Francisco, by the Havana Philharmonic Orchestra, and by various other smaller organizations and soloists. He has resided chiefly in Connecticut and in New York City.

Orchestra: Four Symphonies; *Lincoln, the Great Commoner,* for chorus and orchestra; *Three Places in New England;* three *Sets* for chamber orchestra; *Holidays.* Violin and piano sonata: *Concord Sonata;* one hundred and fourteen songs. Prose: *Essays before a Sonata.*

Bellamann, Henry, "The Music of Charles Ives," *Pro Musica,* 1927; Cowell, Henry, "Charles E. Ives," in his *American Composers on American Music,* Stanford University Press, 1933; Copland, Aaron, *Modern Music,* 1934.

HARRIS

Roy Harris was born February 12, 1898, in Lincoln County, Oklahoma. At five he moved to California. Except for a few lessons on the piano and the clarinet, he received no musical training before his twenty-fifth year. He served in the army during the World War in the capacity of a private, and after the war at the University of California studied composition with Arthur Farwell. In 1927 he received a Guggenheim Fellowship, and went abroad to study with Nadia Boulanger. He remained with Mlle. Boulanger for two years. During these years he had composed with the aid of a piano; in 1929, as the result of a fractured spine, he was unable to use the instrument, and learned to compose away from it. Until 1933 Harris resided in California. At present, he is a member of the teaching staff of the Westminster Choir, and resides in Princeton.

Orchestra: *First Symphony; Symphony 1933; Toccata,* Andante for strings with clarinet and flute. Concerto for strings, piano and clarinet; string Sextet; two string Quartets; Trio. Piano Sonata. *A Song for Occupations* for a capella chorus.

Bauer, Marion, *Twentieth Century Music,* Putnam, 1934; Howard, J. T., *Our American Music,* Crowell, 1931; Farwell, Arthur, *Musical Quarterly,* 1932; Rosenfeld, Paul, *An Hour with American Music,* Lippincott, 1934; Slonimsky, Nicholas, Boston *Evening Transcript,* January 5, 1934.

COPLAND

Aaron Copland was born in Russian Poland November 14, 1900, and came to this country at the age of two. He began studying piano at the age of thirteen; his teachers were Victor Wittgenstein and Clarence Adler. He studied composition with Rubin Goldmark from 1917 to 1921, and continued for three years in Paris with Nadia Boulanger. He was awarded Guggenheim Fellowships in 1925 and 1926; and won a $5,000 RCA-Victor Prize with his *Dance Symphony* in 1929. During 1927-29 he lectured on modern music at the New School for Social Research, and he has lectured in numerous cities throughout the country. During the spring term of 1935 he was lecturer on music at Harvard. Copland is one of the founders of the Copland-Sessions Concerts; a member of the executive board of the League of Composers; director of the International Society for Contemporary Music (United States section), and chairman of the Second Yaddo Festival for Contemporary American Music.

BIOGRAPHICAL APPENDIX

Ballets: *Dance Symphony;* "*Hear Ye, Hear Ye.*" Chorus: *An Immorality.* Orchestra: *First Symphony: Music for the Theater; Symphonic Ode; Short Symphony; El Salon Mexico; Statements.* Two pieces for String Quartet; Trio, *Vitebsk;* pieces for violin and piano. For Piano: Concerto; *Variations.* "As It Fell upon a Day" for voice and woodwind; songs.

Chanler, Theodore, "Aaron Copland," in Cowell, Henry, ed., *American Composers on American Music,* Stanford University Press, 1933; Goldberg, Isaac, "Aaron Copland and Jazz," *American Mercury;* Rosenfeld, Paul, *By Way of Art,* Coward-McCann, 1928, and *An Hour with American Music,* Lippincott, 1934; Thomson, Virgil, "Aaron Copland up to Now," *Modern Music,* Vol. IX, No. 2; references in Howard, J. T., *Our American Music,* Lippincott, 1934; Bauer, Marion, *Twentieth Century Music,* Putnam, 1934; Pannain, Guido, *Modern Composers,* Dutton, 1933.

CHAVEZ

Carlos Chavez was born in the City of Mexico in 1899. He took piano lessons from his sister in his tenth year; for the rest, he is practically self-taught. After the World War he traveled in Germany and France. He has been in the United States at various times; in 1932 his ballet *Horse Power* was mounted by the Philadelphia Opera under Stokowski. Chavez is the director of the National Conservatory in the City of Mexico, and the conductor of the Orquesta Sinfonico.

Orchestra: *Sinfonia di Antigona.* Ballets: *The New Fire; Four Suns; Horse Power. Energia* for chamber ensemble; Sonata for four horns; String Quartet; Three Sonatinas for piano, cello, and violin; *Tres Exagonos* for chamber ensemble; piano Sonata; Mexican pieces; songs. Prose: "The Music of Mexico," in Herring, H. C., and Terrill, Katharine, eds., *The Genius of Mexico.*

Copland, Aaron, "Carlos Chavez," in Cowell, Henry, ed., *American Composers on American Music,* Stanford University Press, 1933; Rosenfeld, Paul, "Chavez," in *By Way of Art,* Coward-McCann, 1928, and *An Hour with American Music,* Lippincott, 1934.

BIOGRAPHICAL APPENDIX

RIEGGER

Wallingford Riegger was born in Albany, Georgia, April 29, 1885. At eight years he began the study of the violin. He graduated with the first graduating class of the Institute of Musical Art in New York, in 1907: and later had cello lessons with Alvin Schroeder and lessons in compositions with Percy Goetschius. From 1908 to 1910 he studied in the Berlin Hochschule and had cello lessons from Robert Hauptmann; in Berlin he also had lessons from Edgar Stillman Kelley. In Germany from 1914 to 1917 he conducted in several German opera houses, and was conductor of the Blütner Orchestra in Berlin for more than one season. From 1918 to 1922 he taught theory and cello in Drake University; from 1922 to 1924 he taught in the Institute of Musical Art; and from 1924 to 1925 in Cornell. He won the Paderewski prize with his Trio in 1921. Works of his have been performed by Stokowski with the Philadelphia Orchestra; by Kleiber with the New York Philharmonic; by the Pan-American Association in Europe; and by the Barrère, Britt and Salzedo Trio.

Orchestra: *Rhapsody; Prelude and Fugue: Dichotomy* for chamber orchestra, *Study in Sonority* for ten violins; Dances. *Canons* for three woodwinds; Trio; *Divertimento* for flute, cello, and harp. Piano, four hands: *Bacchanale; Frenetic Rhythms; Evocation.* Piano, two hands: *Blue Voyage.* Suite for flute solo.

Weiss, Adolph, "Wallingford Riegger," in Cowell, Henry, ed., *American Composers on American Music,* Stanford University Press, 1933; Ewen, David, *Composers of Today,* Wilson, 1934; Bauer, Marion, *Twentieth Century Music,* Putnam, 1934.

NABOKOV

Nicholas Nabokov was born in Poland on April 7, 1903. He studied in the Imperial Lyceum in St. Petersburg. He left Russia in 1919, and for several years was a sailor. Later, he studied com-

BIOGRAPHICAL APPENDIX

position in the Berlin Hochschule under Ferrari-Busoni; he also studied in Stuttgart. About 1927 he went to Paris. Diaghilew produced his *Ode* in ballet form in 1928. He came to America in 1932.

Oratorio: *Job. Symphonic Ode; Symphonie Lyrique,* Concerto for piano and orchestra. Overture: *Le Fiancé.* Ballets: *Union Pacifique; Aphrodite.* Piano: *Le Cœur de Don Quixote.* Smaller pieces; songs.

Index

Ablaufsform, 224
Achilles, 306
Adagio (Goldberg Variations), 33-34
Adam and Eve (Negro), 231
Adams, Henry, 55, 56
Adler, Guido, 49
Advertising, 270, 271
Aegisthus, 131, 140
Aeschylus, 171
Agamemnon, 131, 132, 139
Alceste, 27
Alcotts, 320, 321
Alexander II and III, 94
Allegro Barbaro of Bartók, 199, 203
Also Sprach Zarathustra of Strauss, 199
Althouse, Paul, 170
America, 319, 350; artists and, 98, 99
America of Bloch, 165, 167
American art, 270
American chamber music festival, April, 1932, 349, 352
American composers, 19
American Composers on American Music (Cowell), 279-280
American in Paris, An, of Gershwin, 268-269
American journalist, 123
American life, frontier, 327-329
American moderns, 278
American music, 353, 354
American operas, 281-314; conclusions about, 310-314; greatest, 307, 310
American tradition, 315
Americanism, 269, 322
Amerindian music, 337, 339, 340, 342
Anarchist commune, 97
Anger Dance of Cowell, 274
Anne of Denmark, 14
Antheil, George, 306-308, 313, 314, 358
Antimasque, 14, 16
Anti-Semitism, 116, 117
Apollo, 135
Apollon Musagetes of Strawinsky, 183
Archaism, 179, 180, 219
Aria with Thirty Variations of Bach, 32
Ariadne, 21, 27
Ariosto, 25, 83

Armide of Gluck, 53
Artists, American, 98, 99; American artist awaited, 359-360; as anarchists, 97
Artusi, Canon, of Bologna, 25
Ashton, Frederick, 297
Atonalism, 199, 317, 323, 344, 345
Auric, Georges, 234-237; Les Matelots, 234-236; works, 236
Avila, Theresa of, 298, 301
Avodath Hakodesh, 164, 166
Aztec ballets, 340, 341, 342

B Minor Mass of Bach, 38
Bach, J. S., 92, 159, 222, 247; as colorist, 28-31; as physician, 32-36; D Minor organ Toccata and Fugue, 6, 7, 10; development, 43; Die Kunst der Fuge, 36-44; Kirkpatrick's playing of his music, 28-30; last work, 39, 40; music, 35; three glimpses, 28-44; transcriptions, 31
Bach, P. E., 39, 70
Bagatelles of Bartók, 198, 199, 202
Bahr, Hermann, 141-143
Bakunin, 95
Balakirew, 85, 87, 88
Ballet de cour, 14
Ballet opera, 18
Banshee, The, of Cowell, 274
Barbarism, 199, 259
Barn Dance of Ives, 316, 321
Baroque religion and art, 299-300
Barrère, 345
Barrès, Maurice, 93
Bartók, Bela, 197-204
Battery, 258-260
Bayreuth, Cosima Wagner and, 113-115; first Festival, 112; influence, 116, 119, 122; royal visitors, 112
Bayreuther Blätter, 116
Beaumont and Fletcher, 14
Beethoven, 40, 67-82, 92, 99; adopted forms, 69; deafness explained, 67, 74-76; earlier critics, 74; evolution of his genius, 42; fugues, 74; Man in his

391

INDEX

music, 11; music of, 8; music's debt to, 79; quartets, 6, 7, 11; revolutionary music, 247; scherzo and allegretto, 70; Seventh Symphony, 246; sonata and symphonic forms, 68, 70; symphonies, 68, 70, 71, 73; third style, 71; three styles, 67, 69; value to music, 79; work, three sections, 67
Beggar music, 251
Belaiev, Victor, 238
Bellaman, Henry, 324
Benn, Gottfried, 291
Bennett, R. R., 308-310
Berezowsky's Quartet at Yaddo, 357
Berg, Alban, 99; works, 215; *Wozzeck*, 211-217
Berger, of the *Mirror*, 352
Berlin, 251
Berlin Opera, *Matthis der Mahler* of Hindemith, 227; Nazis and, 90
Berlioz, 51, 87, 169
Bethmann, Fräulein, 106
Bewegungsvorgang, 224
Beyle-Stendhal, Henri, 61; epitaph, 62; in Dresden, 65; in Italy, 64
Biebrich, 95, 105
Binchois, 219
Birds, 44, 48, 123
Bismarck, 95
Bitonalism, 199, 201
Bizet, 51
Blitzstein, Mark, Serenade at Yaddo, 357
Bloch, Ernest, 164-170; loss of freshness, 167-169; *Sacred Service*, 164-170; works, 164-165
Blues, 230, 231, 251, 267, 268, 271, 338
Boris Goudonow of Moussorgsky, 27, 91, 124-129, 292
Borodin, 84, 87, 88
Boston Symphony, *Capriccio* and *Symphonie des Psaulmes* of Strawinsky, 184; *Perséphone* of Strawinsky in 1935, 188, 191
Boston Transcript, 352
Boucke, Maurice, 69
Boulanger, Nadia, 331
Bourgeoisie, 241, 243
Bowles, P. F., 357
Brahma-scholar, 78, 79
Brahmins, ancient, 77, 78
Brahms, 205; piano quintet, 6, 7, 11
Brandes, Georg, 111
Brangäne, 5, 10
Brant, Henry, Suite at Yaddo, 357
Brazil, 231

Brecht, Bert, 251, 252
British Grenadiers, 315
Brünhilde, 50, 95
Büchner, Georg, 212, 213
Buhlig, Richard, 41
Bülow, Hans von, 100; Cosima and, 104, 105, 107
Busoni, Ferrucio, 32, 40, 218, 219

C Major Symphony of Mozart, 59
C Minor Organ Passacaglia of Bach, 42
Calvocoressi, 84
Camerata, 14
Campion, Thomas, masques, 14
Capriccio of Strawinsky, 184
Carmen of Bizet, 51
Carnegie Hall, New York, Bloch's *Sacred Service*, 164-168
Caroline and Paolino, 65
Casella, 220
Catholicism, Roman, 151, 186, 297-301
Catholicity, 151, 227
Catskills, 349, 350
Caturla, A. G., 337
Cavalier spirit, 303, 304, 305
Cavalleria Rusticana, 19
Celestial Railroad of Ives, 320
Cénacle, 211
Cendrars, Blaise, 231
Cevenole Symphony of D'Indy, 147, 148, 149
Cézanne, 29
Chabrier, 264, 265
Chamber music festival, April, 1932, 349, 352
Chamberlain, H. S., 119-122
Charlie Rutlage (Ives), 316, 322; at Yaddo, 359
Charon, 24
Chavez, Carlos, 337-343; *Unidad* at Yaddo, 356; works, 338-343
Cherubino, 50, 58
Chopin, 53, 94; Scriabin and, 160
Choral Fantasy of Beethoven, 68
Chromatic Fantasy and Fugue of Bach, 29, 32, 43
Chrysothemis, 131, 140
Cimarosa, 61-66; Mozart and, 62, 63; music of, 63
Cipriano de Rore, 25
Circumstances, man versus, 71
Citkowitz, Israel, 355
Civilization, deadly energy, 133
Clair, René, 236
Clandestine Marriage, The, 61

INDEX

Claudel, 231
Clavichord, 29, 30
Cleveland, Ohio, *Lady Macbeth of Mzensk*, production in 1934-35, 238
Cleveland Orchestra, 238
Clorinda, 27
Clytemnestra, 131, 139
Cocteau, 123, 175, 181, 231; *Oedipus Rex* (with Strawinsky), 170, 172, 181-183
Color, 257; in J. S. Bach, 28-31
Commune, anarchist, 97
Communism, 246-249, 252, 254
Composers, American, 19, 312, 313, 326, 353, 359; chief contemporary composer, 228; Communistic faith, 247; great, 194, 248; Latin-American, 337; young, 176
Concentration of energy, 76-78, 81, 88
Concerto of Bartók, 202, 204
Concerto of Harris, 325, 326, 330, 331
Concerto of Strawinsky, 187; New York presentation in 1932, 187
Concord, Mass., 320
Concord Sonata of Ives, 312, 315, 316, 320, 321, 323
Conductors, 234
Contrapuntal principal, 218, 226
Control, 134-135
Converse, Frederick, 312
Coolidge Festival in Washington, Bach music, 41
Cooper, Fenimore, Jr., 320
Copland, Aaron, 271, 313, 314, 324, 332-337; unperformed and latest pieces, 336; Variations at Yaddo, 358; works, 332-337; Yaddo festival, 353-359
Correntos, 16
Corsair overture of Berlioz, 87
Cosí Fan Tutte, 44
Cosima, 95
Counterpoints of Bach, 39, 40
Couperin, 154
Court masque, 13-20; revivals, 17
Cowbells, 257
Cowell, Henry, 273-281, 324, 331, 332, 354; activities, 277-280; education, 275
Cowell, O. T., 277
Crane, Hart, 351
Creative energy, 133, 134
Creator, creating the, 79, 80
Creon, 171, 181
Crime, responsibility, 240, 243

Cui, 160
Czerny, Karl, 40, 41

Damrosch, Walter, 312
Danbury, Conn., 315
Dance and song literature, Elizabethan and Jacobean, 18
Dance music, 19
Dannreuther, 80
D'Annunzio, 113
Dante, 55, 290
Dante Symphony of Liszt, 51
Dantons Tod, 212
Da Ponte, 50
Das Marienleben of Hindemith, 220, 221; style, 222, 223
Das Musikalische Opfer of Bach, 43
Das Rheingold, 56
Deane, Mrs., 283, 284
Death, 10
Debussy, 21, 23, 24, 25, 26, 27, 28, 53, 84, 99, 177, 215; music of, 52; Ravel and, 152-156; school of, 152
Decadents, 209
DeFalla, 94, 95
Delibes, 183
Demeter, 188, 190
Democratic revolution, music and, 246
Demophoön, 188, 190
Der Freischütz of Weber, 91, 94
Der Jasager of Weill, 253-254; at Henry Street Settlement in 1933, 253
De Schloezer, 86
Diabelli Variations of Beethoven, 40, 72, 73, 92
Diaghilev ballet, 173
Diatonism, 201
Die Kunst der Fuge of Bach, 36-44; Buhlig version, 41; Gräser version, 41; new editions, 40; New York performance of Buhlig and Kuhnle version, 42; performances, 40, 41; title, 39; trial at Leipzig, 40
Die Meistersinger, 92, 100, 102; action, 96; idea, 95; Nazis and, 89-100; social order, 97-98
Die Walküre, 27
D'Indy, 21, 23, 79, 143-152; creative energy, 145; form and work, 147; music of, 149-152; works, 146-148
Dionysiac forces, 130-135
Dionysiac symphony, 71
Discipline, 80, 81
Divine Comedy, 55
Divinity, 73, 79; names for, 81

INDEX

Don Giovanni of Mozart, 45, 50
Don Juan of Strauss, 204
Donovan, of Yale, 352
Dramatic music, 19
Dresden, 95, 141, 142; Beyle-Stendhal at, 65
Drum, 296, 297
Dufay, 219
Du Maurier, George, 282
Duo Concertante of Strawinsky, 192
Dushkin, Samuel, 187

E Flat Minor Fugue of Bach, 33
Eddas, 11
Eden, 230, 231
Eisler, Kurt, 247
Electra, 131, 132, 134, 139
Electricity, 263
Elektra of Strauss, 130-143; Dresden performance, January, 1909, 141-143; music, 130-132; reception, 141; score, 138-140
Eleusinian mysteries, 188
Eliot, 226
Ellis, Havelock, on Beethoven, 11
Elsas Traum, 115
Emerson, R. W., 166, 320, 321
Emperor Jones, The, 19, 293-297; at Metropolitan Opera, January 8, 1933, 293-297
Empire Theater, New York, *The Threepenny Opera*, 251
Energia of Chavez, 339, 340, 341
Engel, A. L., 253
England, 92
Epilogue, 349-360
Erda, 10, 57
Eroica of Beethoven, 68, 71, 74
Erskine, John, 286; *Helen Retires*, libretto, 306-308; *Jack and the Beanstalk*, libretto, 286, 287, 288, 289-293
Essays before a Sonata of Ives, 321, 322
Eternal, 167, 168
Eumolpus, 190, 191
European society, 138
Euryanthe, 86, 289, 292
Evening (Ives), 322
Evolution, Beethoven's contribution to, 79
Ewig-Weibliche, 51, 55-56

Fairy tales, 286
Faith, 38, 149, 152; Mozart, 46
Family life, 133
Fantasia Contrapuntistica of Busoni, 40

Farlav, 85
Fascism, 90, 98
Fatalism, 196
Fauré, 153
Faust of Goethe, 55
Faust of Gounod, 51
Faust Symphony of Liszt, 51
Feminine principle, 48-56; Mozart, 48, 50
Ferrabosco, Alfonso, 15
Fidelio of Beethoven, 50, 68, 289, 292
Finck, Henry T., 152
Fine, Vivian, 356
Firebird, The, of Strawinsky, 197, 204
Fitzgerald, Zelda, 270
Flames, orthophonic music and, 4
Flavigny, Comte de, 106
Florian Geyer of Hauptmann, 228
Flower Maidens, 111
Flying Dutchman, The, 114, 116, 204
Folk music, Hungarian, 202; Latin-American, 337; Magyar, 198
Folk music dramas, 124-129
Folk songs, Russian, 174
Folklorism, Bartók, 198
Forces of the world, 130-135
Four Saints in Three Acts, at Hartford, February 8, 1934, 297-302
Four Suns of Chavez, 339, 341, 342
France, 65
Franck, César, 79, 145, 146, 149, 150, 151
Franco-Russian melodrama, 189
Frau Minne, 57
Frau Venus, 10, 57
Frederick the Great, 43
Freidank, 98
French cathedrals, 55
French life, 143, 151
French music, 235
French symphonic school, 145
Freud, Dr., 136, 137
Frobenius, Leo, 196
Fugues, 36, 39; Bach's, 37; Beethoven's, 74
Furtwängler, conductor, 227
Futurists, 262

G Minor Quintet of Mozart, 44, 46
G Minor Symphony of Mozart, 44, 49
Galliards, 16
Gautier, Judith, 111
Gay's *The Beggar's Opera*, 251
Gebrauchsmusik, 36, 225, 250-256
Geisterseher, 8

INDEX

General Booth Enters Heaven of Ives, 316, 321
George, Stefan, 209
German Communist songs, 247
German democracy, 228
German Republic, 228
Germanic race, 119-122
Germany, 91; music, 90, 92; republicanism, 94
Gershwin, George, 264-272; *American in Paris, An,* 268-269; compositions, character, 265-267; F Major piano concerto, 267-268; *Porgy and Bess,* 271-272
Gervinus' *History of German Literature,* 95
Gesualdo, 25
Geyer, Ludwig, 117
Gide, André, 188, 291
Giles, Thomas, 15, 18
Glinka, 82-89; genius, 84, 89; music of, 85, 86, 89; physicality, 87
Gluck, 27, 53
Gobineau, Arthur de, 120
God, 120, 121, 149, 162, 168, 194, 195; Jewish, 166
God of music, 32
God of storm, 11
Godhead, 10
Goethe, 55, 120, 121; on Bach, 37
Gogol, 258
Goldberg, J. G., 32
Goldberg Variations of Bach, 29, 32, 43
Good Night, Ladies, 316
Götterdämmerung, 100, 103
Gounod, 51
Gozzi, 286
Grand Fugue of Beethoven, 40, 74
Grand opera, 14
Gräser, 41
Great Mother, 10
Greek drama, 136, 171
Greek liturgical scale, 84
Greek religion, 188
Green Hill, 102, 105, 110
Gregorian chants, Orthophonic and, 3, 4, 9
Grosses Klavierbüchlein, 33
Gruenberg, Louis, 286, 313, 314; *Emperor Jones* music, 293-297; *Four Diversions* at Yaddo, 357; *Jack and the Beanstalk,* 286, 288-289
Guarini, 25
Gurre, songs of, 204

Gurrelieder, 204-210; American performance in 1932, 210

Hades, 26
Hadley, President, 320
Hammerklavier Sonata of Beethoven, 40, 72, 73, 74, 75
Händel, 26, 92; music of, 50
Händelian oratorio form, 181, 183
Handy, W. C., 230
Hanson, Howard, 302, 305, 313
Happiness, 108
Harlem, 231
Harmati, Sandor, 16
Harpsichord, 29, 30
Harris, C. R., 40, 41, 313, 324-332, 354; Sonata at Yaddo, 357; works, 325-332
Hartford, Conn., production of *Four Saints in Three Acts,* February 8, 1934, 297-302
Harvard University Glee Club, 170
Hauptmann, 228
Hawthorne, 320
Haydn, 47, 62, 70
Heaven, 163; Mozart and, 12
Heine, 116
Helen of Troy, 306, 308
Helen Retires, production at Juilliard School, February 28, 1934, 306-308
Hemingway, 176
Henry VIII, 13
Henry Street Settlement, production of *Der Jasager* in 1933, 253
Herder, 94
Hermann, Bernard, 230
Herne, Jerome, 15
Heroism, 71, 78, 79
Heyman, K. R., interpretation of Scriabin at Town Hall, New York, in April, 1934, 159-162
Hindemith, Paul, 41, 217, 239, 291; features of his music, 222-227; neoclassicism and, 217-229; new music, 220; rank, 229; recognition, 228; withdrawal from Germany, 227; works, 221, 229
Hitler, Adolf, 90, 122, 255
Hoffmann, E. T. A., 8
Hofmannsthal, 130, 136, 137, 138, 140
Holst, 257
Holy Grail, 302
Honegger, 225, 271
Hooker, Brian, 310
Horse Power music of Chavez, 343; Philadelphia production in 1932, 338

395

INDEX

Housatonic at Stockbridge, The, of Ives, 317, 320, 321
Hudson Valley, 349-350
Hugo, Victor, 55, 194
Huneker, James, 50
Hungary, 197
Hyperion Theater, New Haven, 317
Hyperprism of Varèse, 256, 258, 264

Ibbetson, Peter, 283, 284
Ideas in music, 246
Ignatius of Loyola, 299-302
Il Combattimento di Tancredi e Clorinda, 23, 24, 27
Impressionism, 152, 154, 156, 176
In Flanders Fields, 316
In the Inn of Ives, 316, 321
In the Night of Ives, 317, 321
Indian girls, 303
Individuals, 97, 255
Insomniac, 32, 34
International Composers' Guild, 276
Intuition, 135
Ionization of Varèse, 256-264
Ions, 263
Ismailova, Katerina, 240, 241
Isolde, 50
Istar Variations of D'Indy, 146, 147
Italian opera, 201, 292
Italy, 64, 65, 95; art, 65
Ives, Charles E., 79, 199, 312, 315-324, 354; Americanism, 319-324; experiments, 316-318; lyrics, 322; prose writings, 321; songs at Yaddo, 358-359; works, 315
Ivrea, 65

Jack and the Beanstalk, 286-293
Jacob, Max, 356
Jacobsen, J. P., 204, 207
James I, 14, 16
Jammes, Francis, 233
Jazz, 184, 202, 227, 230, 252, 258, 259, 265, 270, 338
Jewish Cycle of Bloch, 164, 166, 169
Jewish works: Bloch and his *Sacred Service*, 164-170
Jews, Wagner and, 116
Jocasta, 136, 137, 171, 181, 182
Johnson, Albert, 346
Jones, Emperor, 293-297
Jones, Inigo, 14, 15, 16
Jones, R. E., 170
Jonson, Ben, masques, 14-15
Joseph II, 46

Juilliard School, Bach music, 41; *Helen Retires*, February 28, 1934, 306-308; *Jack and the Beanstalk*, November 19, 1931, 286-293; *L'Incoronazione di Poppea* of Monteverde, 21-23; *Maria Malibrand*, April 8, 1935, 308-310; *Matrimonio Segreto*, in 1933, 61-64, 66
Jung, 136
Jung's *Psychological Types*, 77
Jupiter Symphony of Mozart, 45, 46, 58, 59

Kamarinskaia of Glinka, 82
Kant, 120, 121
Kapp, Julius, 118
Katerina, 240, 241
Kayserling, Count (Saxon ambassador), 32
Kazoo orchestra, 315
Keats, 322
Khovanskys, 127, 128
Khovantschina, 124-129; world's tragedy and, 6, 7
Kiesler, F. J., 308
Kings, 93
Kirkpatrick, John, 316
Kirkpatrick, R. L., playing of Bach's music, 28-30
Klaus the fool, 205, 207, 209
Kleiber, 344
Klemperer, 228
Klindworth, 100
Koshetz, Nina, 82
Koussevitzky, 184, 328
Krenek, 307
Kuhnle, Wesley, 42
Kundalini Sakti, 75
Kundry, 5, 57, 112
Kunstmusik, 254
Kussuth of Bartók, 197

La Création du Monde of Milhaud, 230-234; production in Paris in 1923, 231
Lady Macbeth of Mzensk of Shostakovich, 238-245, 249-250; production in Cleveland and New York in 1934-35, 238
Land awaits, 349-360
Landowska, Mme., 30
Landscape, Orthophonic's revelations, 3, 7
Latin-American composers, 337
Laurent, Georges, 356
Leaders, 255
League of Composers, 238

396

INDEX

Le Baiser de la Fée of Strawinsky, 183
Le Coq d'Or of Rimsky-Korsakoff, 52
Leipzig, *Die Kunst der Fuge,* in 1927, 40
LeJeune, Claude, 157
Lenz, Wilhelm von, 67
Leonore Overture No. 3 of Beethoven, 70
Le Sacre du Printemps of Strawinsky, 172, 173, 175, 180, 194, 196
Les Matelots, New York production, 234
Les Noces of Strawinsky, 176, 177, 178, 180
Lesskov, Nikolai, 239, 240; Tolstoy on, 241
Lethe, 190
Levant, Oscar, jazz Sonatina at Yaddo, 357
Levi, Hermann, 116
Lewis, Wyndham, 93
L'Histoire du Soldat of Strawinsky, 176, 177, 178, 180, 220
Libido, 77-78, 81, 135, 136, 282
Libretto, Erskine's theory of the ideal, 289-293
Lido, 113
Life, 217
Life for the Czar, A, of Glinka, 83, 84
Life-givers, 80
Like a Sick Eagle (Ives), 322
Lincoln cantata of Ives, 320
L'Incoronazione di Poppea, 21-23, 24, 26
Lindsay, Vachel, 316
Linear principle, 218, 219, 226
Lir, 273
Liszt, 51, 104; *Faust* and *Dante* symphonies, 51; music of, 110
Liszt, Cosima, 100, 103, 106. *See also* Wagner, Cosima.
Loeffler, C. M., 153
Love, 66; "climate of," 207, 209. *See also* Feminine principle; Women
"Love music," 54. *See also* Romantic music
Loyola, 299, 302
Ludwig II of Bavaria, 95, 102, 106
Luigi, Pier, 21
Lulli, 18, 26, 183
Luther, Martin, 96
Lyrical music, 88
Lyudmila, 85

MacDowell Club, *Oberon* masque, 16-17
MacLeish, Mrs. Ada, 356
MacLeish, Archibald, 346, 347, 348
Madrigals, 25, 27
Magic Flute, The, 292

Magyar folk music, 198
Mahler, Gustav, 52, 79, 204, 219, 257, 317
Malibran, Maria F. G., 308, 309
Man, 128; Beethoven's music and, 11; circumstances and, 71; "little" man, 212, 217
Mann, Thomas, 193
Maria Malibran, production at Juilliard School, April 8, 1935, 308-310
Maritain, Jacques, 186
Markevitch, 347
Markham, Edwin, 320
Marriage of Figaro of Mozart, 50
Mary Duchess of Towers, 283, 284
Masques, 13-20; present-day, 16-20
Massine cakewalk, 348
Materialism, 270
Mather, Cotton, 304, 305
Matrimonio Segreto, 61; Juilliard School performance in 1933, 61-64, 66; performances, 65
Matthieson, 39
Matthis der Mahler of Hindemith, 227, 228, 229; Excerpts presented by New York Philharmonic in 1934, 228
Matzenauer, Mme., 170
Mavra of Strawinsky, 181
May Day of Shostakovich, 237, 244
Mayence, 95
Maypole, 303, 305
Meissner, Alfred, 105
Melodrama, 189
Mendès, Catulle, 111
Mercury, 190
Merry Mount, 303, 304
Merry Mount, production at Metropolitan Opera, February 10, 1934, 302-306
Metastasio, 291
Metropolitan Opera, 83; court masque revival in order, 17-20; *Merry Mount,* February 10, 1934, 302-306; *Mona* in 1912, 310; *Oedipus Rex* performance, 170, 181-183; *Peter Ibbetson,* Feb. 7, 1831, and its success, 282-286
Mexican composers, 337
Mexican Pieces of Chavez, 341
Meyerbeer, 116
Milhaud, Darius, 230-234, 258, 271; compositions, 233; *La Création du Monde* at Town Hall, 230
Milton, 322; masques, 14
Mimsy, 283, 284, 286
Missa Solemnis of Beethoven, 68, 72, 74
Mlada of Rimsky-Korsakoff, 94

INDEX

Molière, 236
Mona of Parker, 19, 307, 310-312, 313, 314
Monarchy, 93
Monotonal system, 211
Monte Carlo troupe, New York production of *Les Matelots*, 234; *Union Pacific* performances, 346
Monteverde, 20-28; *L'Incoronazione de Poppea*, 21-23, 24, 26; music and style, 23
Moody and Sankey hymnody, 326
Moore, George, 104
Morality, music and, 254
Morton, Thomas, 303, 304
Mossolov, 249
Motorik, 224
Moulin-Eckart, Richard Graf du, 101, 103, 108, 116
Mountains, 144
Moussorgsky, 5, 10, 21, 24, 25, 27, 28, 84, 85, 87, 88, 91, 129, 173, 196, 199; *Khovanstchina*, New York performance by Russian Opera Foundation, 124-129
Mozart, 61, 62; E Flat Symphony, 6, 7, 12; frivolity, 46, 47; heartlessness, 44, 46, 47; heaven in earth, 12; music of, 8, 44, 56, 59, 60; personal life, 46, 47; romantic music, 44-61; Sonata No. 17, 47; Strawinsky on, 187, 188; tenderness, 48, 49
Music, Communism and, 246-249; contemporary evolution, 228; dance music, 19; dramatic, 19; forces of the world and, 8; love and, 66; medicinal use, 32-36; new, 220, 224, 225; ritual and useful, 250, 254-255; vulgar, 235, 236, 237, 264, 265, 270
Music drama, 21, 27
Music for the Theater of Copland, 333, 334, 336
Musical culture, 38, 46, 159; western, 227
Musical reporters, 352
Musicians, sterility, 169-170
Musicologist, 250

Nabokov, Nicholas, 346, 347, 348
Napoleon, 94
Napoleon III, 95
Narcissus, 189, 190
Nationalism, 92; Bartók, 197, 198; Ives, 318-320
Nationalistic art, 91, 92, 94, 97, 99

Nature, 28, 54, 144, 149; Monteverde and, 25; phonograph and, 3-13
Nazis, 90, 96, 98; *Die Meistersinger* and, 89-100; *Matthis der Mahler* and, 227
Negroes, 293, 299, 302; jazz, 230; singers and dancers, 272
Nenia, 202, 203
Neoclassicism, 217, 226; Hindemith and, 217-229; Strawinsky, 178, 179
Neoclassicists, 218
Neoplatonism, 162
Nero, 21
New Chamber Orchestra, Milhaud's music for *La Création du Monde*, 230
New England, 304, 305, 315
New Fire of Chavez, 340
New Haven Symphony, excerpts from *Mona*, 310
New Music School, New York, Bach's preludes and fugues by Kirkpatrick, 28
New School for Social Research, Buhlig and Kuhnle version of *Die Kunst der Fuge*, 42; Cowell and, 278
New River, The (Ives), 322
New Woman, 95
New York, *Lady Macbeth of Mzensk*, production in 1934-35, 238
New York Philharmonic, performance of *Matthis der Mahler* excerpts in 1934, 228; performance of *Rhapsody* of Riegger in winter of 1932, 344
Newman, Ernest, 101
Nietzsche, 8, 62, 107, 109, 111, 116, 117, 118, 121, 135, 141, 193; music and, 218
Norton, M. D. Herter, 40, 41
Nostalgia, 230, 231
Nuremberg, 91, 96
Nutcracker Suite of Tschaikowsky, 85

Oberon masque, 16-17, 18
Oberon of Weber, 86
Octavia, 21, 23, 27
Ode to Joy of Beethoven, 75
Oedipus, 170, 171, 181
Oedipus complex, 136
Oedipus Rex of Cocteau and Strawinsky, 291; Metropolitan performance in winter of 1930, 170-172, 181-183
Oklahoma, 327
Old Hundred, 316, 347
Ollivier, Emile, 106
Olympian afternoons, 3, 12
O'Neill, Eugene, *The Emperor Jones*, 293-297

INDEX

Opera, 14, 22, 245; American and British, 312; ancestors, 18; Italian, 292; nationalistic, 94; recent American operas, 281-314
Opéra bouffe, 61, 64
Opéra comique, 14
Oratorio, 181, 183
Orazio Vecchio, 25
Orestes, 131, 134, 139
Orfeo, 23, 24, 26, 27
Ornstein, 354
Orpheus, 24
Orthophonic, revelations of, 3; tones and unique power, 13
Otway, 138

Pagliacci, 19
Palestrina, 247
Pan-Americans, 324
Pantiliev, Max, 82
Paolino and Caroline, 65
Paolo and Francesca, 51
Paris Opéra, *Perséphone* at, 189
Parisian music, 232
Parisian *Six*, 231, 236, 265, 341
Parker, Horatio, 307, 310, 311, 312, 314, 323; *Mona*, 307, 310-312, 313, 314
Parsifal, 100, 102, 113, 116, 117, 123; second act, 5
Partita of Bach, 29
Passacaglia, Berg, 215, 216; C Minor Organ, 42
Passionate music, Cimarosa, 64
Passionateness, 53
Passy, 283
Pavannes, 16
Peace, 73, 74
Pelléas et Mélisande, 23, 27, 52, 292
Percussion instruments, 256-260, 262, 339
Pergolesi, 179
Persephone, 188, 189, 192
Perséphone of Strawinsky, 86, 188, 189, 195; presentation by Boston Symphony in 1935, 188, 191
Persian dances, 125, 127, 129
Pessimism in Strawinsky, 172, 176, 182, 194, 195
Peter Ibbetson, 19, 282-286
Petrarch, 25
Petrushka of Strawinsky, 172, 173, 174, 180, 258
Philadelphia, Chavez music for *Horse Power*, 338
Philadelphia Orchestra, *Concerto* of Strawinsky, 187

Phonograph, 3-13; unique power, 12, 13
Piano, 30, 258, 262; Bartók, 202; Cowell's use, 273, 274; Scriabin's music, 159, 160
Piano Sonata of Harris, 325, 329, 330, 331
Pierrot Lunaire of Schönberg, 205, 208, 209, 210
Pietragrua, Angela, 65
Pilgrim Fathers, 305
Pindar, 188
Pioneer music, 326-330
Piston's Sonata at Yaddo, 357
Plymouth, Mass., 303, 304
Pocahontas, 351
Poland, 94
Polovtsian Dances, 85
Poppea, 21
Porgy and Bess of Gershwin, 271-272
Post-war generation, 225
Potsdam, 121, 122
Power, higher, 9
Pratella, 258
Prayer, music as, 74
Preis, 239
Primitivism, Bartók and Strawinsky, 199, 200
Prince Igor of Borodin, 84, 85
Prokofieff, 342, 347
Pro-Musica, 324
Protestantism, 151
Proto-jazz, 316
Puccini, 169, 215
Pulcinella of Strawinsky, 179
Purcell, 26
Puritan and Cavalier, 303, 305
Pushkin, 83, 127
Putnam Camp of Ives, 316, 317
Pythian Temple, Glinka's fairy opera, excerpts in 1932, 82-89

Ramakrishna, 75
Rameau, 18, 154, 159, 170, 183
Rasoumowsky Quartets of Beethoven, 68, 71
Ratmir, 85
Ravel, 152-158; craftsmanship, 157; impressionism and symbolism, 152, 154, 156; later work, 157; music of, 153, 155, 157; style, 153
Reaction, 194; Strawinsky, 193
Recording, science of, 13
Records, phonographic, natural phenomena as related to, 3-13
Reger, Max, 41, 146, 218, 219

399

INDEX

Reich, Willi, 212
Religion, music and, 248; Strawinsky, 193
Renaissance, 23
Renard of Strawinsky, 176, 177, 178
Repin, 241
Revolutionary songs, 247
Revueltas, Silvestre, 337
Rhapsody, Op. 1, of Bartók, 197
Rhapsody in Blue of Gershwin, 231
Rhapsody of Riegger, 344, 345; performance by Philharmonic in winter of 1932, 344
Rhythmicon, 277
Riegger, Wallingford, 344-345, 355
Rilke, 48, 220
Rimsky-Korsakoff, 52, 83, 87, 94; version of *Khovantschina,* 124-129
Ring, 112
Ritual music, 250, 254-255
Rivera, Diego, 338
Rivière, Jacques, 126
Rodzinski, Conductor, 238
Roldan, Amadeo, 337
Rolland, Romain, on Beethoven, 67, 75
Romantic music, 44-61
Romantic school, Germany in 1800, 193
Romantic wit, 286, 292
Romantics, 8
Rore, Cipriano de, 25
Rossetti, 52
Roth Quartet, 41
Rubinstein, Ida, 189
Rugby, 225
Ruggles, 354
Ruslan, 86
Ruslan and *Lyudmila,* concert version of excerpts, 82-89; earthiness, 87; form, 85
Russia, 94; women in, 239, 241
Russian Artists' Mutual Aid Society, 82
Russian fatalism, 196
Russian Five, 84, 85, 87, 94, 200
Russian gods, 89
Russian nationalists, 84, 85, 86, 87, 89, 173
Russian Opera Foundation, performance of *Khovantschina,* at New York, 124-129

Sachs, Hans, 92, 96, 326
Sacred Service of Bloch, 164-170; Carnegie Hall performance, 164-168
Sadko of Rimsky-Korsakoff, 83
Sailors, The, 234

Saint Gaudens, 320
St. Louis Blues, 230
Saint-Saëns, 157
Salem, Mass., 304
Salomé of Strauss, 141
Sandys, Lady Marigold, 305
Sannazaro, 25
Sanroma, Jesus, 356
Saratoga, 349, 351, 352-353
Satie, 231, 236, 265
Sayn-Wittgenstein, Princess, 106, 117
Scheherazade of Rimsky-Korsakoff, 52
Schiller, 93
Schnitzler, 136
Schola Cantorum, Bloch's *Sacred Service* in Carnegie Hall, 164-168
Schönberg, 31, 52, 99, 179, 211, 317; atonalism, 199; career, 210, 211; *Gurrelieder,* 204-210; works, 204-211
Schopenhauer, Arthur, 8, 10, 176
Schumann, Clara, 12
Schumann, Robert, 12, 53, 170; A Minor Concerto, 53; song cycles, 51
Schweitzer, 30
Science, music and, 261
Scott, Cyril, 153
Scriabin, 87, 158-163; condemnation, 158; Heyman recital of works in Town Hall, New York, in April, 1934, 159-162; music of, 159-163
Seilliérs, E., 121
Self-responsibility, 243
Self-sacrifice, 254
Seneca, 21, 22
Serenade of Strawinsky, 179, 180
Sessions, 313, 314, 354; Sonata at Yaddo, 357
Sex, 63; sexual act, 242, 243. *See also* Women
Sextet of Harris, 325, 327, 328, 329, 330
Shakespeare, 14, 18, 62, 92, 93, 109, 290
Shaw Monument in Boston Common, The, of Ives, 320, 321
Shostakovich, Dmitri, 237-250, 258; Russian composer's characterization, 248-249
Shwetz, Michael, 82
Sibelius, Jan, 234
Siberia, 240, 242, 244
Siegfried, 95
Siegfried, 100, 104, 109, 120
Simon, R. A., 308-310
Sinfonia de Antigona of Chavez, 339, 342

400

INDEX

Sinfonia de H.P. of Chavez, 339; performance in New York, 342
Sinfonia Domestica of Strauss, performance in the Wanamaker Auditorium, New York, 141
Singspiel, 286, 287
Sirens, 256
Skyscraper mysticism, 260, 263
Slonimsky, Nicholas, 201, 324
Smith, Professor, 310
Social order, *Die Meistersinger* and, 97-98
Society of the Friends and Enemies of Modern Music, production of *Four Saints in Three Acts,* February 8, 1934, 297-302
Solesmes, Abbey of, 3
Songs, Elizabethan and Jacobean, 18
Sophocles, 171, 188
Sorrows of the world, 33, 34, 60, 73
Soviets, 237
Spengler, 92, 196
Spinoza, 168
Stabat Mater of Thomson, at Yaddo, 356
Standish, Miles, 303
Stassov, 127
Stein, Gertrude, 297, 298, 300, 302
Stein, Heinrich von, 119
Stendhal. *See* Beyle-Stendhal
Stettheimer, Florine, 299, 302
Stilo concitato, 23
Stoessel, Albert, 62, 307
Stokes, R. L., 302, 304, 305
Stokowski, 6, 41, 210, 345
Storm god, 11
Strauss, 41, 107, 115, 142-143, 215, 218, 257; contrapuntal music, 219; *Elektra,* 130-143; music of, 52; works, 139, 140, 141
Strawinsky, 26, 86, 87, 124, 125, 156, 159, 170-196, 220, 258; archaism, 179, 180; Baroque composites, 179, 180; Bartók compared with, 197-204; contemporaneity, 193; earlier works, 172-178; irony, 253; later works, 176-178; neoclassicism, 178, 179; on Mozart, 187, 188; on music, 291; *Oedipus Rex* (with Cocteau), 170, 172, 181-183; pessimism, 172, 176, 182, 194, 195; primitivism, 199, 200; productions, 172-196; rank, 228; reaction, 193; war and, 195
Suarès, André, 21
Suicide, 10

Suite for a Theater Orchestra of Ives, 315, 317
Sullivan, J. E. D., on Beethoven, 75
Swedish Ballet, *La Création du Monde,* 231
Symbolism, 152, 154, 156
Symphonic jazz, 230
Symphonie des Psaumes of Strawinsky, 86, 184, 185, 186, 187, 195, 196
Symphonies for Wind Instruments of Strawinsky, 176, 177, 178, 179, 180
Symphonies of D'Indy, 143-152
Symphony 1933 of Harris, 327, 328, 329, 331
Symphony on the Song of a French Mountaineer, 143-145

Tancred, 27
Tasso, 23, 25
Taylor, Deems, 282, 312
Teresias, 171, 181, 182
Theosophic idea, 161-162
Theremin, 279
Theresa of Avila, 298-301
Thomas, Theodore, 112
Thomson, Virgil, 297, 298, 299, 301, 356
Thoreau, 320, 321
Three Places in New England of Ives, 315, 317, 320
Threepenny Opera, The, of Weill, 251-252; production at Empire Theater in New York in 1932-33, 251
Thunderstick, 276, 278
Tibbett, Lawrence, 294
Tieck, 286
Tintoretto, 29
Tolstoy, Leo, on Lesskov, 241
Tone clusters, 273
Tove, 204, 205, 206, 208
Tovey, 40
Town Hall, New York, Heyman recital of Scriabin's works in April, 1934, 159-162; Milhaud's music for *La Création du Monde* in the season of 1933-1934, 230
Transcendentalism, 320
Triebschen, 100, 101, 104, 107, 109
Triptolemus, 188, 190
Tristan und Isolde, 27, 50, 56, 92, 95, 104, 110; second act on the Orthophonic, 4, 5, 7
Truthfulness, 27-28
Tschaikowsky, 85, 88
Turner, W. J., on Mozart, 45-46

401

INDEX

Underdog, 212, 213, 217
Underworld, 190, 192, 195
Unidad of Chavez, 341, 342; at Yaddo, 356
Union Pacific of MacLeish and Nabokov, 346-349; Monte Carlo troupe performances in April, 1934, 346
Union Pacific R. R., completion, 346-347, 348
Untermeyer, Louis, 320

Values, 81, 150, 321
Van der Null, 199
Varèse, Edgar, 261; *Ionization,* 256-264; works, 256, 260, 263-264
Variations of Copland, at Yaddo, 358
Venice, 113
Venice Preserved of Otway, 138
Venosa, Prince of, 25
Vienna, Mozart and, 46, 47
Viennese group, 211, 217
Viking chorus, 85
Villa-Lobos, Hector, 337
Villiers de l'Isle-Adam, 111
Virgin worship, 55
Vitebsk of Copland, 333, 334
Vivekananda, 75
Voice of Lir, The, of Cowell, 273
Vor deinem Thron of Bach, 42
Voyage du Condottiere, 21
Vulgarity, 235, 236, 237, 264, 265, 270, 338

Wagner, Cosima, 100-124; attacks on, 117; Bülow and, 104, 105, 107; children, 106; diary, 108, 113, 116, 122; old age, 123; personality, 115; Richard and, 101, 103-104, 107-111, 113; Richard's influence on, 112-113; rôle at Bayreuth, 112
Wagner, Eva, 119
Wagner, Richard, 8, 21, 24, 25, 27, 53, 90, 91, 92, 95, 204, 215; autobiography, 117-118; Bayreuth Festival, 112; Cosima and, relations, 101, 103-104, 107-111, 113; early works, 95; independence, 102; music dramas, 50, 56; music of, 56, 57; naïveté, 99; on Beethoven, 9; state and, 98; triumphant conclusion of his work, 100

Wagner, Siegfried, 113, 119
Wagnerism, 200, 201
Wahnfried, 110, 112, 114, 123
Waldemar I, 204, 205, 206
Waldstein Sonata of Beethoven, 69
Walther, 96
War, Strawinsky and, 195
Washington's Birthday of Ives, 316
Weber, 86, 91, 94
Weill, Kurt, 239, 307; *Gebrauchsmusik,* 250-256
Weiss, Adolph, 31, 354
Well-Tempered Clavichord, 29, 31, 32, 33, 37, 42, 43
Wellecz, Egon, 223
Wesendonck, Mathilde, 95, 111
Wesendonck, Otto, 110
Wesendoncks, 102, 105, 110, 117, 118
Whips, 257
Whitman, Walt, 38, 320, 322
Wilhelm II, 121
Wilhelm Tell of Schiller, 93
Will, 10, 81; Beethoven's, 76, 77; heroic, 71, 78, 79
Willaert, 25
Williams, W. C., 303, 304, 305
Witchcraft hysteria, 304, 305
Wittgenstein, 157
Wolzogen, Ernst von, 116
Womb of life, Orthophonic and, 5, 10
Women, 52, 306; Mozart's music and, 49, 50, 58; position in Russia, 239, 241; Wagner and, 95; Wagner's music and, 56, 57
Wood dove, 205
World, forces, 130-135; revealed through phonograph, 12; sorrows, 33, 34, 60, 73; tragedy, 6; welfare, 188
World of the phonograph, 3-13
World War, 130, 133
Wozzeck, 211-217
Wozzeck, Franz, 212

Yaddo, 349, 351, 354
Yea-Sayer, The of Weill, 253-254
Yoga, 75
Youmans, Vincent, 270

Zeitgeist, 197
Zeus, children of, 12

402

DATE DUE

nume	31		
OCT 8 1980			
FEB 27 '82			
APR 1 3 1984			
JAN 29 1996			
MAR 2 2 1996			

GAYLORD — PRINTED IN U.S.A.